THE NORDIC MODELS IN POLITICAL SCIENCE

Oddbjørn Knutsen (ed.)

THE NORDIC MODELS IN POLITICAL SCIENCE

Challenged, but still viable?

FAGBOKFORLAGET

1st Edition 2017 / 3rd printing 2020

Graphic production: John Grieg, Bergen

ISBN: 978-82-450-2175-2

Cover design by Fagbokforlaget
Typeset by Bøk Oslo AS

Inquiries about this text can be directed to:
Fagbokforlaget
Kanalveien 51
5068 Bergen
Tel.: 55 38 88 00
e-mail: fagbokforlaget@fagbokforlaget.no
www.fagbokforlaget.no

CONTENT

INTRODUCTION: THE NORDIC MODELS

Oddbjørn Knutsen

THE NORDIC COUNTRIES

The primary aim of this book is to serve as a general text for bachelor's degree students[1] and to provide an introduction for academic readers interested in Nordic politics in general and Nordic models in particular.

The five states of Denmark, Finland, Iceland, Norway and Sweden are nations at the north-western corner of Europe. The region also contains three Home Rule territories: the Faroe Islands, Greenland and the Åland Islands (see Chapter 1).

The Nordic countries are small, pluralist democracies with an advanced, typical post-industrial structure which is service dominant and information based. The populations have a high level of education and the number of people in paid work is high compared with other European countries (Gabriel and Keil 2013).

The concepts "Scandinavian" and "Nordic" countries are often used interchangeably. In strict geographical terms, "Scandinavia" refers to the three Scandinavian countries: Norway, Sweden and Denmark. Two of these, Norway and Sweden, constitute the Scandinavian Peninsula. Denmark is also one of the Scandinavian countries. In this book Scandinavia comprises Denmark, Norway and Sweden, while "Nordic" will be used for all five countries. The book aims to cover all the five countries and therefore the concept "Nordic models" is meant to characterise all five countries. If a trait is specific for only Denmark, Norway and Sweden, the term "Scandinavian model" is used.

The Nordic countries are frequently considered to be a distinct group of countries in political science studies. The designation "the Nordic model(s)" is frequently used. Most well known is the social model or the welfare state

1 This book is intended as a successor to *Nordic Politics – Comparative Perspectives*, published in 2004, edited by Knut Heidar. The editor would like to thank the Department of Political Science at the University of Oslo and the Department of Comparative Politics at the University of Bergen for financial support for this book project.

model, but the Nordic countries also have other distinctive traits that can be regarded as representing other Nordic "models" (see below).

The fact that the Nordic countries have distinct traits in several political variables is found in many comparative studies. One example from the scholarly literature is Delhey and Newton's (2005) study of generalised social trust in 60 countries, a topic that unfortunately is not included in this book. They first find that generalised social trust is comparatively larger in the Nordic countries than in other countries. When they then try to explain the cross-national variation in social trust, they show that the Nordic countries score differently on important explanatory variables such as good government, GDP per capita (high on both) and the Gini index of inequality (low), and conclude that the Nordic countries are outliers (univariate for generalisted social trust and bivariate and multivariate because they also score differently to other countries on central independent variables), which might influence their findings significantly. "[The] Nordic nations have extreme scores on the most powerful explanatory variables, as well as trust itself. Could it be that the Nordic outliers distort the results?" (Delhey and Newton 2005: 320–321). The authors therefore decided to perform a second analysis excluding the Nordic countries.

This introduction is organised as follows: First, the concept of model is discussed and illustrated by examples from the various chapters. Several aspects of the model concept as used in the book are then focussed upon, and finally the topics and research problems of the various chapters are outlined.

WHAT IS A MODEL?

The models outlined in this book are different in several ways, but an attempt is made to find traits common for all the Nordic countries that are not shared by other countries or regional groups of countries.

The term "model" has been given a variety of different meanings within the social sciences. For some scholars, the concept has been used as a synonym for "theory", while for others it is a reference to a system of abstract concepts at a more general level than a theory. A model is also seen as a more systematised version of a theory. Equally, it is used to refer to a statistical model as in causal modelling. Basically, models seek to simplify phenomena as an aid to conceptualisation and explanation. They are a framework of concepts, descriptive claims, and causal hypotheses through which the analysis seeks to abstract understanding and knowledge from the complexities of the real world. A main point is that models engage with theory and thus avoid pure empiricism.

In accordance with this quite general conceptualisation of models, we can differentiate between different types of models that are applied in various chapters of this book. Below, these model types are outlined in general and with examples from the various chapters.

A model can, for example, be associated with one or several *single* variables. These variables can be categorical or continuous.

First, a model that is based on *categorical variable(s)* is characterised by the existence of mutually exclusive and exhaustive categories that cannot be ranked. An example in this book is the Nordic five-party system model, which is based on the existence of parties from five-party families and (ideally) the non-existence of parties from other party families (Chapter 2).

Second, a model can also be based on *continuous* (or at least *ordinal*) *variables*. Such continuous variables can have extreme types at the lowest and highest values, and units (here countries) can be located according to specific values on the scale. An example from this book is Rommetvedt's conceptualisation of corporatism and pluralism in Chapter 7 as opposite extremes on a continuous variable, where corporatism – which is studied in particular – is considered a variable that can gradually change over time.

Frequently, such continuous variables have a somewhat different character than the corporatist-pluralist example in the sense that countries score high or low on features that might be considered desirable according to most scholars. This type of model evaluation is found in several chapters based, for example, on the explanatory power of central variables on party choice (Chapter 3), the Gender Equality Index (Chapter 5), net replacement rates in the chapter on the welfare state model (Chapter 9) and the World Bank's Knowledge Economy Index (Chapter 10). In all these examples, the high-score side is considered the most relevant for comparison of the Nordic countries with other (regional groups of) countries.

Cross-national studies based on such continuous variables can be based on comparisons of individual countries or average scores for groups or regional groups of countries where the average scores for the Nordic countries are compared with those of other regions.

Third, a model can also be based on *a combination of factors that are mutually exclusive and exhaustive*. That means that every case can fit into only one type, and the types are frequently designed to minimise the within-type variation and maximise the variation between the types. Such a model that includes two or more variables combined is normally labelled a *typology* (George and Bennett 2005: 237–238). An example from this book is the types of governments that Heidar and Rasch use in Chapter 4, which are based on whether the governments a) comprise one or more than one party and b) whether it is a majority or minority government.

A fourth version of a model is that it is *a conceptual framework*. A conceptual framework is used to make conceptual distinctions and organise ideas, and is an analytical tool with several variations and contexts. An example of this type of model in this book is Chapter 8 by Baldersheim, Rose and Sandberg, which uses the notion of *co-operative decentralisation* as a framework for discussing the local and regional governments of the Nordic countries in a comparative perspective. Other regional groups of countries are characterised by different concepts but along the same dimensions as those emphasised by the authors for the Nordic countries.

In this book we examine central areas where, according to scholarly research, the Nordic countries can be said to have constituted a distinct group of countries and perhaps still do. It should, however, be underscored that there are several other areas where the Nordic countries have distinct traits according to research in political science; there are many other areas where the Nordic countries are less distinct, if distinct at all. This is typically when there are large variations between the Nordic countries and they are grouped very differently in comparative research involving other Western countries or located fairly similarly, but not different to other (regional groups of) countries.

ASPECTS OF THE USE OF THE MODEL CONCEPT IN THIS BOOK

One or several models

As a point of departure the author(s) of each chapter present their own topic and how the Nordic countries represent a model with traits that deviate from other countries. The degree to which the models are interconnected or are even part of an overall model is not always clear. It has not been the aim of this book to explore this in detail. It is, however, evident from some of the chapters that the model discussed is associated with the social model or the welfare state model. This model is discussed in detail in Chapter 9. However, it is also evident that several of the other models cannot easily be linked to this model. It can then be argued that the Nordic countries have politically relevant traits that are different from other Western countries so that there are several "Nordic models". This is – at least as a point of departure -- the approach taken in this book.

Wider cross-national comparison

The notion of a Nordic model implies that some aspects of Nordic politics or policy are different from politics and policies in other regions. The most natural comparison is, of course, with other groups of countries in Western Europe such as the Central West European countries, Southern Europe and Great Britain (or the Anglo-Saxon countries if we enlarge the scope of the comparison somewhat). The chapters differ with regard to how detailed the comparisons with other countries are. Some present quantitative data which perform such a comparison in some detail. Others utilise previous research which has established the existence of a Nordic model. Using this as a point of departure, the focus is then first and foremost on describing trends and cross-national variations within the Nordic region.

Changes over time

The subtitle of this book is *Challenged, but still viable*? "Challenged" indicates that there can be forces (see the next paragraph) that have caused the distinctiveness of the Nordic countries to become less pronounced or even to disappear over time, while "still viable" with a question mark indicates that the distinctiveness can still be found despite the challenges that the Nordic countries have faced during the last few decades.

The issue of convergence between Western countries, including the Nordic countries, is of course relevant in this respect. The rising economic globalisation and the adjustment to the EU single market are two major explanations for possible convergence between the Nordic countries and other European countries. To the extent that the Nordic models have become less pronounced, it should nevertheless be underscored that such convergence can imply different things: a) that the other countries have approached the traits or level of the Nordic countries; b) the opposite, meaning that changes have taken place in the Nordic countries which have approached the other countries' level, which have been more or less stable over time; and c) finally – most relevant if the relevant variables are continuous – that the countries have converged at an intermediate level.

The roots of the Nordic models: When and why did the models emerge?

Why do the Nordic countries differ from other Western countries with regard to politics and policies? This topic is not discussed in detail in all chapters but is focussed upon in most chapters. It is evident that the explanations are found in the political history of the region, but given that there can be different models, the origins will vary in time and be caused by different factors.

THE TOPICS AND MODELS PRESENTED IN THE VARIOUS CHAPTERS[2]

In Chapter 1, *State- and nation-building*, Einar Berntzen provides an overview of state- and nation-building in the Nordic region from a comparative perspective. He investigates whether particular characteristics of the state- and nation-building trajectories of the respective Nordic countries make them stand out and thus constitute a "Nordic Model" of state- and nation-building.

The chapter commences with a presentation of the Nordic countries and then focusses on the origins of the Nordic states and early state-building. The dominant role of Denmark and Sweden in the region is underscored. For centuries, these were the only independent powers in the Nordic region. Denmark

2 This section and the reviews of the findings in the concluding chapter are written in close cooperation with the authors of the various chapters.

was the dominant Nordic power in medieval times, with Sweden emerging as an imperial rival during the 16th and 17th centuries. The two particular hybrids of absolutism in Denmark and Sweden, respectively, are compared with the two general types of European absolutism. In the subsequent analysis of the development from a situation of domestic sovereignty to full independence in Norway, Finland and Iceland, the importance of language conflicts in the cultural nation-building processes of Norway and Finland are focussed on in particular. Finally, the democratisation process is then analysed in a comparative Nordic perspective using Stein Rokkan's well-known four thresholds for mass incorporation into democratic politics as a framework.

The Nordic party system model was conceptualised as a *five-party system model* by Berglund and Lindström (1978). The major parties belong to the same five-party families: Conservative, Liberal, Agrarian, Social Democrat and Communist/Left Socialist families. These parties have varied in importance and electoral support but altogether they account for most of the votes of the Nordic electorate. In Chapter 2, *Political parties and party systems*, Oddbjørn Knutsen examines how the five-party system model emerged and the comparative strength of the parties in each of the party families, and how has this changed over time. Newer parties which were not part of the five-party system model, and which can be grouped into Religious, Radical Right and Green party families, are also examined.

How does the five-party system model deviate from party systems in other regions within Western Europe? In this chapter, this is approached in two ways. First, by examining which party families are peculiar to the Nordic countries and which parties are missing or less significant compared to other Western European countries. The second approach for examining the distinctiveness of the Nordic parties is undertaken by examining the location of the parties in the various party families in the policy space. Do the Nordic party families deviate from their sister parties in other countries?

Special traits within the party systems of each of the Nordic countries are briefly examined followed by data on trends in central party system dimensions such as the overall support for the parties in the five-party system model, party system fragmentation and polarisation, and electoral volatility. These dimensions of party systems are examined empirically by studying trends from the 1940s to the 2010s.

In Chapter 3, *Social cleavages and political value conflicts*, Oddbjørn Knutsen takes previous comparative research on the impact of socio-structural variables and value orientations as a point of departure for examining the relevance of a Nordic model. This research has shown that there are some determinants of party choice in the Nordic countries that place them in a special position and that could be referred to as a Nordic model, or several Nordic models. These variables are economically interest-based and include social class, economic values and issues. Traditional class voting has been much more pronounced in the Nordic countries than elsewhere in Europe. Due to the existence of Agrarian parties, urban–rural contrasts in voting behaviour have also been documented to be large in a comparative setting.

The chapter first analyses trends in the impact of the structural variables in the well-known Lipset-Rokkan model (regions, religion, social class and urban–rural residence), then new structural cleavages (gender and sector employment) and finally Old Politics values (religious-secular and economic left-right values), and New Politics values (environmental values, libertarian/authoritarian values and immigration orientations). Finally, the total impact of social structure and value orientations is examined.

In both Chapters 2 and 3 the approach is to examine possible Nordic models through comparisons with main patterns in Central and Southern European countries and the Island countries (Britain and Ireland).

In Chapter 4, Knut Heidar and Bjørn Erik Rasch examine a number of aspects of *political representation and parliamentarism*. They start by outlining election systems and preference voting in the Nordic countries. They then analyse the role of political parties at various stages in the process from election campaigns to governments and policy outcomes. Further, the organisation of the Nordic parliaments is outlined with a specific emphasis on the role of standing committees. The possibility of the opposition parties to influence policy is discussed, as are the types of government and parliamentarism that characterise the Nordic countries. The existence of minority governments and one-party governments in the Scandinavian countries is focussed upon in particular.

There is no clear Nordic model that is the point of departure, although Nordic political representation and parliamentarism have several similarities. Two obvious differences between the Scandinavian countries and Finland and Iceland are that the Scandinavian countries are constitutional monarchies, while Finland and Iceland are republics. More important is the dominance of minority governments in the Scandinavian countries while majority coalition governments have been dominant in Finland and Iceland. The authors outline these differences in some detail and discuss possible explanations.

In Chapter 5, Mari Teigen and Hege Skjeie examine the Nordic model of *gender equality*. The Nordic countries have been envisioned as "truly woman-friendly societies" and gender equality is regularly included in Nordic welfare state modelling.

The authors focus on the equality dimensions that form the baseline in comparative welfare state research and research on political participation. These dimensions are outlined as norms for economic equity and democratic parity. Equality norms for economic equity include equal educational opportunities, equal pay for work of equal value, gender balance in family life, and gender-balanced participation in labour markets. Equality norms for democratic parity include first and foremost inclusive opportunity structures for civil society and gender balance in political and economic decision making.

In their empirical analysis the authors examine whether and how descriptive statistics that measure these two dimensions currently rank Nordic countries compared with other European countries among EU member states. For this purpose the EU's Gender Equality Index is used. Comparable statistics on outcome and performance that include the Nordic non-EU members (Norway and Iceland) are then used to explore similarities and differences within the Nordic region. Finally, the issue of policy models is examined, discussing whether it is possible to identify a distinctive policy profile common to the Nordic countries regarding how economic equity and democratic parity can be promoted.

The Nordic countries appear to have many similarities in their political-administrative system, often referred to as a distinctive Nordic Model. But there are also important differences. In Chapter 6, *Governmental institutions and state reforms*, Karl Hagen Bjurstrøm and Tom Christensen ask what the main structural features of the central political-administrative systems in the Nordic countries were in the past and what the main structural characteristics are today. To answer this, the chapter outlines the historical background and the main structural features of the civil service in the Nordic countries today.

Over the past three decades, there have been two major public sector reform waves throughout the world: New Public Management (NPM) and post-NPM. The chapter asks what the main public sector reforms in the Nordic countries have been over the past three decades. How is the balance between NPM and post-NPM reforms typically achieved? Which perspectives can explain the similarity and diversity in the formal structures and reforms of the Nordic countries? The chapter studies these reforms from three perspectives of organisational theory – the environmental perspective, the cultural perspective and the structural perspective.

Is there a Nordic model based on structural features and reform trajectories that stands out from other models? The last part of the chapter compares the different reform processes in the Nordic countries and discusses whether there is a distinct Nordic reform profile.

The Nordic countries have been recognised as possessing a very high degree of *corporatist interest mediation* and *interest group representation*, together with countries such as Austria, the Netherlands and Germany. In Chapter 7, Hilmar Rommetvedt examines the degree of corporatism over time, focusing primarily on the three Scandinavian countries. He differentiates between an economic school and an interest-group school of corporatism. His approach is basically within the latter where he argues that corporatism is (potentially) relevant for a variety of public sectors, not only for economic policy. Corporatism is defined as the institutionalized and privileged integration of organised interests in the preparation and/or implementation of public policies. The opposite of corporatism is pluralism, and these two should be regarded as a matter of degree. In a more open pluralist system, interest groups may exert influence through lobbying which is a less institutionalized, more informal and ad hoc-based way of influencing public policy.

Rommetvedt makes a distinction between the prerequisites or causes of corporatism, corporatism as such, and the effects of corporatism, and shows how the prerequisites of corporatism have been weakened. In order to examine variations across countries and changes over time, corporatism is measured by the number of policy preparation and policy implementation committees with interest group representation, while lobbying is measured by contacts with public authorities such as members of parliament and the bureaucracy. The chapter includes assessments of policy impacts and consequences for democracy.

In Chapter 8, Harald Baldersheim, Lawrence Rose and Siv Sandberg outline various aspects of *local and regional government* in the Nordic countries and discuss this in a broader European context. A common and distinct feature of the Nordic countries is the high degree of decentralisation of public tasks (to local "welfare states") within the framework of a unitary state in which the relationship between state and municipality is characterised by "co-operative decentralisation". Co-operative governance refers not only to the volume of tasks delegated to local and regional decision-makers but above all to the close and trustful relations that typically exist between central and local levels of government. This provides a backdrop for understanding the special character of the Nordic system of *decentralised co-operative governance*.

The historical development of local self-government is outlined. The current institutional framework of local and regional government is then described. In subsequent sections the functions and finances of sub-national government are briefly summarised, and citizen involvement in local self-government is discussed. Finally, important aspects relating to various efforts to reform local and regional government in the last few decades are highlighted.

Chapter 9 deals with *the Nordic welfare state model*, and Axel West Pedersen and Stein Kuhnle commence by discussing the concept of a Nordic model. The chapter reviews commonly perceived contents of the concept and its "when, how and why". The historical roots and early paths of Nordic welfare state development are traced, and emphasis is placed on the influence of the crucial and internationally unique, formative political developments of the 1930s on the later construction of the concept of a Nordic (welfare) model. This historical account is followed by a review of the post-WWII expansion towards comprehensive, egalitarian-oriented welfare states based on the dominant principles of public responsibility and universal population coverage of social and welfare policies.

The major part of the chapter is devoted to describing and analysing the core features of the Nordic welfare states. The authors point to both intra-Nordic similarities and differences, and to how the Nordic countries compare with (other) OECD countries on indicators of generosity of various social entitlements, measures of income inequality and poverty, and patterns of expenditures for services and cash benefits. Some divergent intra-Nordic trends of development in recent decades are sketched. The chapter concludes with an outlook to the future and briefly spells out challenges for the Nordic welfare states such as ageing of the population, economic globalisation and immigration.

In Chapter 10, Johan Christensen, Åse Gornitzka and Cathrine Holst examine the *knowledge regimes'* of the Nordic countries, which they argue can be seen as the backbone of the post-war Nordic economic, political and social models. They define a knowledge regime as the range of organisations and institutions that produce and disseminate policy-relevant knowledge and how these organisations and institutions are governed. A knowledge regime encompasses such elements as how universities operate and are governed, what kind of expertise government bureaucracies possess, and what channels exist for disseminating research to policy-makers.

The authors examine the main characteristics of knowledge regimes in the Nordic countries and how these have changed over time. They discuss the Nordic countries as knowledge economies and knowledge societies by looking at the funding of schools and universities, access to higher education and the level of education in the population. They also look at the organisation and governance of universities and research institutions. Moreover, they discuss the place of professional expertise in government bureaucracies in the Nordic countries. Finally, they examine the particular institutional mechanisms that bridge science and government such as ad hoc advisory commissions.

In this review, the authors also highlight how the organisation of knowledge in the Nordic countries differs from the knowledge regimes in other Western European countries and in the United States. In particular, differences in the role of public versus private institutions in the knowledge regime and in the government control of policy advice are examined.

In the concluding chapter , the editor briefly examines the status of the Nordic models on the basis of the findings in the previous chapters and sums up the main findings.

CHAPTER 1

STATE- AND NATION-BUILDING IN THE NORDIC REGION: PARTICULAR CHARACTERISTICS

Einar Berntzen

INTRODUCTION

The main purpose of this book is to discuss whether the "Nordic models" are still viable. Hence, this chapter will seek to provide an overview of state- and nation-building in the Nordic region in a comparative perspective and to investigate whether particular characteristics of the state- and nation-building trajectories of the respective Nordic countries make them stand out and thus constitute a "Nordic model" of state- and nation-building.

We shall argue that during the classical historical period of state-building before the French Revolution, Nordic state-building was equally violent and war-ridden as elsewhere and thus did not differ very much from that of other European countries. For most of the early modern period, the Danish and Swedish kings had fought for supremacy in the Nordic region through countless bloody wars. Before 1814, the Nordic region was plagued for centuries by the same militarism as any other part of the warlike Europe.

The year 1814 represented a sea change in this respect. The last war between two Nordic countries was the one between Sweden and Norway in 1814. Relations between the Nordic countries have been exceptionally peaceful for the last two centuries. As the two Nordic imperial monarchies finally gave up their dreams of gaining hegemonic status in the Baltic region, they gradually adapted their legitimacy to principles of nationalism. Out of two medieval imperial states (Denmark and Sweden) emerged five nation-states (Denmark, Sweden, Norway, Finland and Iceland) and three home rule territories (Åland under Finland, and Greenland and the Faeroes under Denmark). Despite some sabre-rattling, the Norwegian secession from the union with Sweden in 1905 happened through peaceful means. The Icelandic secession also exemplified the new peaceful trends in inter-Nordic relations. The same can be said of the referendum redefining the Danish-German borders in the aftermath of WWI.

We shall further argue that defeat in wars often proved a blessing in disguise in the sense that "big-time" losses played a beneficial role for ushering in democratic progress. For example, Sweden's loss of Finland to Russia in 1809 triggered a revolution that turned the absolutist monarchy into a constitutional one. Denmark's territorial loss in 1864 unblocked the realization of Denmark's potential to become a peaceful, homogeneous nation-state.

Thematically, the chapter will focus on nation-building broadly, i.e. state-building, nation-building, democratization and welfare-state building. The emphasis will be on state, nation and regime development but the crucial class alliances that laid the basis for the welfare state will also be briefly touched upon (at the end) before the conclusion.

We start with a short presentation of the Nordic countries.

In terms of population size, Sweden tops the list as the most populated Nordic country with a population of roughly 9.9 million inhabitants, followed by Denmark with approximately 5.7 million and Finland taking third place with about 5.5 million inhabitants. If we look at area size, Sweden is the largest country, followed by Finland and Norway. Because of its small geographical size, Denmark is the most densely populated country. The largest unit by far is the Danish home rule territory of Greenland, which with an area of close to 2.2 million square kilometres is the world's largest island. The Scandinavian languages (Norwegian, Swedish and Danish) go back to the Old Norse of the Vikings, but strong German influences in medieval times changed them substantially in the process. Icelandic stems directly from Old Norse. Finland is bilingual. The majority language is Finnish, which belongs to the Fenno-Ugric language

TABLE 1.1 POPULATION AND LANGUAGE IN THE NORDIC COUNTRIES

	Population	Area in square kilometres	Inhabitants per square kilometre	Capital	Language
Denmark	5,707,251	43,561	131	Copenhagen	Danish
Faeroe Islands	49,188	1,396	35	Tórshavn	Faeroese
Greenland	56,483	2,166,086	0.02	Nuuk	Inuit (90 %)
Iceland	332,529	103,440	3	Reykjavik	Icelandic
Norway	5,214,900	323,787	16	Oslo	Norwegian (bokmål/nynorsk)
Sweden	9,920,881	447,420	22	Stockholm	Swedish
Finland	5,488,543	338,534	16	Helsinki	Finnish (95 %) Swedish (5 %)
Åland	29,013	1,580	18	Mariehamn	Swedish

Source: Population figures are from September 2016, taken from http://www.worldatlas.com/articles/nordic-countries.html (viewed 15 November 2016).

family,[1] whereas Swedish is the minority language (about 5 %). Swedish is spoken on the west coast and in the home rule archipelago of Åland. In the Danish home rule territory of Greenland 90 % of the inhabitants are Eskimo-speaking Inuit, whereas in the Danish home rule territory of the Faeroese Islands the language is Faeroese.

ORIGINS OF THE NORDIC STATES: EARLY STATE-BUILDING

The origins of the Nordic states lie far back in history. During the age of the Vikings (893–1066)[2] three kingdoms emerged roughly corresponding to the present territories of Denmark, Norway and Sweden (Bagge 2015: 97).

The kingdom of Norway was founded by Harald I Fairhair (c. 872–930). Early state-building was marked by a period of civil war (1130–1240) between rival kings and pretenders to the throne since no clear law of succession existed. The main criterion was to be a descendant of Harald Fairhair through the male line; legitimate or illegitimate birth was not an issue. Backed by the Church[3] a new rule of succession only allowed the oldest legitimate son to inherit the throne.

The support of the Church in favour of the ruling king strengthened the ideological legitimation of the monarchy. Norway became a hereditary monarchy as early as 1260 (not until 1544 in Sweden and 1660 in Denmark). When the death of Haakon V (1299–1319) extinguished the Norwegian male royal line, the Norwegian crown was inherited by the king of Sweden, Magnus VII Eriksson (reigned 1319–43). The development of dynasties and primogeniture increased the chances that royal marriages would become an important means for states to expand and unions between the countries to be formed.

The Old Commonwealth of Iceland (930–1262) was settled between c. 874 and 930, mainly by Norwegians. In 930 the ruling chiefs established an assembly called *Althing*, one of the world's oldest parliaments. The parliament convened each summer at Thingvellir, where the chieftains (*godar*) amended laws, settled disputes and appointed juries to judge lawsuits. Weakened by conflict between clans, the Icelandic chieftains agreed to accept the sovereignty of Norway. Iceland remained under Norwegian and Danish kings from 1262 until 1944. Greenland accepted the sovereignty of Norway in 1261. Early Norwegian state-building proceeded along the East-West axis, through westward expansion. Thus, the Old Norse sea empire also included the Faeroe Islands (from c. 1035), and the Hebrides and the Isle of Man (c. 1152–1266), which were ceded

1 In addition to Finnish, the two Fenno-Ugric languages with the most speakers are Estonian and Hungarian.

2 The last Norwegian Viking king, Harald III Hardrada (reigned 1047-66), died in the battle of Stamford Bridge on 25 September 1066.

3 A separate Norwegian archdiocese was established in Nidaros in 1152.

to Scotland in the Treaty of Perth in 1266. Orkney and Shetland (c. 875–1469) were given by the Danish king, Christian I (reigned 1448–81), as a dowry for his sister Margareta, who married the Scottish king.

The kingdom of Denmark was founded in the 9th century. What is today southern Sweden (Skåne, Halland and Blekinge) became an integral part of the Danish kingdom. Thus, early Danish state-building focused on the West-East axis, and sought Baltic eastward expansion, e.g. crusades in Estonia. Denmark also expanded southwards. The Duchy of Schleswig and the Duchy of Holstein came under Denmark in 1460.[4] Baltic expansion led to conflict with the Hanseatic League. Denmark remained an elective monarchy until 1660. The election of the monarch was held to be conditional, and the monarchs were forced to sign coronation charters, known as *håndfæstninger*, which imposed certain restrictions on their freedom of action. The peasants did not form a separate estate in the Danish Diet, which consisted of the estates of the nobility, the clergy and the burghers.

In Sweden, early state-building was marked by civil wars (1130–1230) between the House of Sverker (Östergötland) and the House of Erik (Västergötland). Swedish state-building entailed conquering areas on both sides of the Gulf of Bothnia. The first of successive Swedish crusades[5] to Finland was undertaken in the mid-12th century. When the Finnish representatives participated for the first time in the election of the Swedish king in 1362, it marked the incorporation of Finland into the kingdom of Sweden. A formal Swedish council was established by the Letter of Privilege of 1319, when Magnus VII Eriksson (reigned 1319–64) was elected king, as an agreement among the Swedish nobility to constrain the power of the king. Sweden remained an elective monarchy until 1544. In Sweden (including Finland) the farmers constituted a separate estate in the Diet (in addition to the nobility, clergy and burghers) starting in the 15th century.

THE KALMAR UNION (1397–1523)

Customs duties on traffic to and from the Baltic through the Øresund (the Sound Dues) contributed significantly to the relatively large revenues of the Danish state.[6] In general, the monarchy owed its strong position to its location at the entrance to the Baltic. For more than 400 years, until the mid-1600s, the Danish monarchy, due to its geopolitical position, ruled a dominion in Northern Europe that was formalized in the Kalmar Union from 1397 to 1523 (Østergård 2004: 26).

---

4 In the Treaty of Vibe of 1460, the knights of the two duchies had compelled the Danish king Christian I to promise to keep the two duchies forever undivided ("up ewig tosamende ungedeelt").

5 A Swedish archdiocese was established in Uppsala in 1164.

6 The Sound Dues were introduced by the Danish Crown in 1426 and remained in effect until 1857.

The Treaty of Kalmar in 1397 joined under a single monarch the three kingdoms of Denmark, Sweden (including Finland) and Norway (including Iceland, Greenland and the Faeroe Islands).

The composite state known as the Kalmar Union ruled mainly by Denmark was the largest country in Europe at the time (Jensen 2014: 4), and can be compared to the similar and contemporary personal union between Poland and Lithuania from 1386 (Østergård 2008a: 445). One main impetus for its formation was the wish to counter the influence of the Hanseatic League and block German expansion northward into the Baltic. The main reason for its failure to survive was the perpetual struggle between the monarch, who wanted a strong state, and the Swedish and Danish nobilities, who did not. Diverging interests (especially the Swedish nobility's dissatisfaction with the dominant role played by Denmark and Holstein) gave rise to a conflict that would hamper the union in several intervals from the 1430s until its definitive breakup in 1523 when Gustav I Vasa (1523–60) was elected king of Sweden.

At the same time as political unity was lost with the dissolution of the Kalmar Union, religious unity was achieved by the introduction of Lutheran state churches in both states. State Lutheranism strengthened royal power both economically and ideologically and reduced the external power of the international Catholic Church. With the establishment of homogeneous Lutheran state churches religion became nationalized in the Nordic countries. Anti-Catholicism became a central aspect of identity building and later also became important for nation-building.

In Denmark-Norway, the Norwegian Council of the Realm was abolished in 1536, and Norway was ruled as a province by the Danish king and the Danish Council of the Realm (*Rigsråd*). The Lutheran state church was introduced in Denmark in 1536 and in Norway in 1537. In Sweden, Gustav I Vasa (reigned 1523–60) laid the foundation for the Swedish nation-state by introducing the Lutheran state church in 1527–60.

In his "conceptual map" of state-building in Western Europe (Tilly 1975), Stein Rokkan placed the five Nordic countries in separate categories. Denmark and Sweden were both strong empire states but they differed with regard to their distance to the city network and in their seaward versus landward orientations,

TABLE 1.2 THE NORDIC COUNTRIES IN ROKKAN'S CONCEPTUAL MAP OF EUROPE

Territorial centres	Weak	Strong	Weak	Strong	Weak
City networks	Weak	Strong	Strong	Weak	Weak
	Seaward peripheries	Seaward empire-nations	City-state Europe	Landward empire-nations	Landward buffers
Protestant	Iceland Norway	Denmark	(The Hanseatic League)	Sweden	Finland

respectively. As for the new states, Norway and Iceland were both categorized as seaward peripheries, whereas Finland constituted a landward buffer against the Orthodox Russian Empire.

SWEDEN VS. DENMARK-NORWAY: STATES MAKE WARS AND WARS MAKE STATES (1523–1814)

For the next three centuries (1523–1814) Denmark and Sweden were the only independent powers in the Nordic region. Denmark was the dominant Nordic power in medieval times, with Sweden emerging as an imperial rival during the 16th and 17th centuries.

The Swedish empire (1560–1720)

Starting in 1560 Sweden established a vast Baltic empire in Northern Europe that lasted until 1720. It began with territorial expansion across the Baltic: Estonia (1595), Ingria and Karelia (1617) and Livonia (1621). Then Gustav Adolph II (1611–32) entered the Thirty Years' War (1618–48) in 1630, and the Treaty of Westphalia in 1648 gave Sweden territories in northern Germany: Bremen-Verden (1648–1718), Wismar (1648–1803) and Swedish Pomerania with the island of Rügen (1648–1814). In the Great Northern War (1700–1720) Sweden and Russia fought for control of the Baltic. The Swedish defeat in the battle of Poltava in 1709 and the death of Charles XII (1697–1718) marked the end of Sweden as a great power. In the treaty of Nystad in 1721 Sweden lost Ingria, Karelia, Estonia, Livonia and the islands of Dagö and Ösel to Russia, which thus replaced Sweden as the leading Baltic sea power.

TABLE 1.3 STATE-BUILDING AND WARS

	Early state formation	Converted to Christianity	Lutheran Reformation	Domestic sovereignty	Wars since 1800	Full independence
Denmark	9th & 10th centuries	10th–11th centuries	1536		Napoleonic 1803–15; 1st Schleswig (1848–51); 2nd Schleswig (1864); Germany 1940–45	
Norway	872–1380	11th century	1537	1814–1905	Sweden 1814; Germany 1940–45	(1814); 1905
Iceland	930–1262	11th century	1538	1904–1944	Allied occupation 1940–45	1944
Sweden	11th & 12th centuries	11th century	1527–60		Napoleonic 1803–15; Norway 1814	
Finland	Part of Sweden	12th century	1527–60	1809–1917	Civil war 1918; USSR 1939–40; USSR 1941–44	1917

Military defeat and absolutism in Denmark (1660–1849)

After the dissolution of the Kalmar Union, Sweden and Denmark fought ten bloody wars between 1520 and 1720 in their ambition to dominate the Baltic region (Knudsen & Rothstein 1994: 205).

The balance began to shift in favour of Sweden. With Denmark's involvement in the Thirty Years' War ending in severe defeat and a humiliating peace agreement in 1629, Danish hegemony in the Baltic was over. The wars with Sweden in 1643–45 and 1657–60 were catastrophic for Denmark, and only the heroic defence of Copenhagen and the death of the Swedish king, Charles X Gustav (reigned 1654–60), saved Denmark from being completely swallowed up by Sweden (Johansen 2006: 158). Consequently, Denmark's very survival as a state was in jeopardy (Kaspersen 2004: 77). By 1660 Denmark had lost the following territories to Sweden: the Norwegian provinces of Jämtland & Herjedalen and Bohuslän, the Danish provinces of Halland, Skåne (Scania) and Blekinge, and the island of Gotland. Denmark was only saved by its geographic position. The Netherlands intervened in favour of Denmark because they feared total Swedish dominance of the Sound at the entrance to the Baltic Sea (Kaspersen 2004: 79).

During this crisis, the assembly of the three estates – nobility, clergy and burghers – (but not the peasants) was summoned to Copenhagen in 1660.[7] The burghers, especially, felt that the privileged nobility had not lived up to their responsibilities and had failed to defend the country. As a result of this alliance between king and burghers absolutism was introduced and the monarchy became hereditary in Denmark in 1660. The Danish king, Frederik III (reigned 1648–70), and his army (introduced in 1614 as a permanent institution), compelled the nobility to accept a new constitution, the *Kongeloven* (Act of Royalty) of 14 November 1665, the only written absolutist constitution in Europe. His coronation charter (*håndfæstning*) was annulled and he no longer depended on the *Rigsråd* (Council of the Realm). Absolutism lasted until Denmark became a constitutional monarchy with the Constitution of 5 June 1849.

As Denmark lost its provinces in Sweden a transformation of Denmark's geopolitical orientation took place: from a West-East axis to a North-South axis towards Schleswig and Holstein.

---

7 The Diet was only summoned four times between 1536 and 1660 (Johansen 2006: 157).

Absolutism in Sweden (1680–1718; 1772–1809)

In Sweden the period of absolute monarchy was comparatively short: between 1680 and 1718. The Diet (*Riksdag*) of four estates (nobility (*riddarhus*),[8] clergy, burghers and farmers) had existed since the 15th century. Royal absolutism in Sweden was (as in Denmark) aimed at the power of the nobility. In Sweden the monarch and the farmers often found themselves in a coalition against the nobles. The Diet of 1680 ruled that the Council of the Realm (*Riksråd*) was to give its advice to the king "only when asked" (Upton 1987: 306).

Sweden lost the Great Nordic War (1700–20). In this case, the effect of losing the war proved beneficial to democratic regime development. In the vacuum created by the death of Charles XII in 1718, the estates grasped the initiative. In the Instrument of Government of 1720 the Diet laid down the constitutional foundations of rule by the estates during the Age of Liberty (1720–72). Although the monarchy and the Council (Senate) were retained, the Diet became the dominant organ of government in legislative and financial matters. The Age of Liberty was characterized by a weak monarchy and strong estate rule largely dominated by the high nobility. During the Age of Liberty Sweden would, like Poland, greatly resemble an aristocratic republic or a "constitutional monarchy" (Wolff 2007: 363–364). The Senate (the Council chosen by the estates to assist the king) was dependent on the Diet of the estates, and since the parliament (Diet) had the power to force individual members of the Senate out of office, the regime might be seen as a primitive form of parliamentarism.[9]

As a reaction to the rule of the estates during the Age of Liberty, Gustav III (1771–92) reintroduced absolutism with a *coup d'état* in 1772. According to the Instrument of Government of 1772, the Council (Senate) was to be appointed by the king and be responsible to him alone. The Diet of the estates could only assemble when summoned by the king (Winton 2012: 433). In a second *coup d'état* in 1789, Gustav III issued the Act of Union and Security, which gave him an absolutely free hand in foreign affairs and command of the army. In 1788, the king had decided to start a war against Russia without asking for the Diet's approval.

Nordic absolutisms compared

In *The Lineages of the Absolutist State*, Perry Anderson (1974) draws a distinction between Western and Eastern Europe: Absolutism in Western Europe was founded on a comparatively free class of peasants together with a network

8 The so-called *riddarhusordning* of 1626 divided noble families into three classes. Class I was the *herreståndet*, the counts and barons who constituted the titled nobility. Class II was the *riddareståndet*, untitled families who had had members in the Council of the Realm (*Riksråd*). Class III, the great majority, was the *svenneståndet*, the esquires (Upton 1987: 285).

9 A form of party structure developed as groups of like-thinking members joined together in various clubs: the "Hats" (*Hattarna*), who wanted to reconquer the lost Baltic territories vs. the "Caps" (*Mössorna*), who wanted peace with Russia.

of powerful and independent towns and cities. In Eastern Europe, absolutism held sway over a peasantry, who were little more than serfs, and ruled over subjugated cities. The economic bases of state-building diverged. In the west, state-building was based on capitalist and monetized economies, whereas in the east it was based on the exploitation of peasants. The divergent economic bases created variations in the character of absolutism, which in turn led to the development of democratic or autocratic institutions. Sweden and Denmark represent two different hybrids between the two general types of European absolutism.

Sweden was a "hybrid" of coexisting "eastern" and "western" patterns: the weak towns represented the "eastern" anti-liberal element, while the free peasantry constituted the "western" element. Denmark constituted another hybrid case, with characteristics exactly opposite to those of Sweden: strong towns representing the "western" element and peasants in serfdom representing the "eastern" element.[10] Absolutism in Sweden was based on a coalition of king and peasants against the noble aristocracy. Absolutism in Denmark was based on a coalition of king and burghers against the noble aristocracy (Knudsen & Rothstein 1994).

THE FRENCH REVOLUTION AND THE NAPOLEONIC WARS (1789–1815)

In Denmark and Sweden the Napoleonic Wars resulted in crises with consequences for state- and nation-building: Sweden lost Finland to Russia, and Denmark lost Norway to Sweden. The French Revolution was both a national and a democratic revolution. In Norway, Finland and Iceland the process of democratization coincided with the struggle for national independence, and in Denmark the national and democratic revolutions coincided.

In 1800 there were two Nordic states, the Danish and Swedish monarchies. In 1814 there were four. As a consequence of shifting alliances on opposite sides in the Napoleonic Wars, both Finland and Norway acquired new and separate status as states (Barton 2006: 221).

TABLE 1.4 TOWNS AND PEASANTS IN EARLY MODERN EUROPE

	Strong free towns	**Weak dependent towns**
Free peasants	Western Europe	**Sweden**
Peasants in serfdom	**Denmark**	Eastern Europe

Source: Knudsen & Rothstein 1994: 208.

10 Serfdom was abolished in Denmark in 1788.

Sweden loses Finland to Russia and becomes a constitutional monarchy in 1809

Finland was conquered by Russia in the Finnish War (1808–1809). The Grand Duchy of Finland was established as a separate entity and became an autonomous part of the Russian empire ruled by the Russian Tsar as Grand Duke, represented by a governor-general. The superior executive organ, the Senate, whose members were all Finns, was appointed by the Tsar. The capital was moved from Turku (Åbo) to Helsinki in 1812. In 1812, Tsar Alexander I also reincorporated the so-called "Old Finland", the territories in the southeast that Sweden had been compelled to cede to Russia in 1721 and 1743, into his new grand-duchy.

During the war the four estates of occupied Finland (nobility, clergy, burghers and landowning peasants) were assembled by Tsar Alexander I of Russia at the Diet of Porvoo (Borgå) in 1809. Each of the estates swore an oath of allegiance to the Tsar, who in return guaranteed that the constitution and the form of government (the Swedish Instrument of Government from 1772, which had applied equally to Finland) would be left unchanged. The constitution of 1772 stipulated that summoning the estates was the monarch's prerogative (Barton 2006: 222).

When half the territory of the Swedish state was lost to its large eastern neighbour the survival of Sweden as a state was at stake. The effect of losing a war might act as a trigger for reform. The main mechanism through which reform could thus be triggered would be a revolution (Teorell & Rothstein 2015: 221). The loss of Finland in the war against Russia triggered the "Revolution of 1809".

King Gustav IV (reigned 1792–1809) was dethroned in a *coup d'état* by a number of disgruntled officers in March 1809.[11] His childless uncle became the new king, Charles XIII, after accepting the new liberal constitution of 1809. In 1810 the Diet elected the French marshal Jean Baptiste Bernadotte as crown prince (he was adopted by Charles XIII under the name of "Charles John" and became king as Charles John XIV in 1818). The Diet created a new constitution which bore the stamp of both domestic traditions (the Diet of the four estates) and ideas from abroad (Montesquieu's doctrine of the separation of powers). The executive (State Council) was appointed and dismissed by the king. The legislative (Diet of the four estates) was given some freedom to oversee the workings of the State Council, but the status of the estates depended on their control over taxation and the state purse. Finally, the estate of the peasants allied itself with the liberal politicians in the burgher's estate in demanding the abolition of the old estate Diet and its replacement with a more representative

11 The officers who took the initiative for the revolution of 1809 were convinced that Napoleon and the Tsar had decided to divide the country, incorporating the southern half into Denmark and giving the northern part to Russia (Teorell & Rothstein 2015: 231).

parliament. In 1866, a new constitution replaced the Diet of the four estates with a bicameral parliament (*Riksdag*).

Denmark loses Norway to Sweden: the Treaty of Kiel 1814

In the early 19th century Denmark ended up an adversary of Britain in the Napoleonic Wars. The battle of Copenhagen in 1801, the British bombardment of the capital in 1807, the subsequent loss of the navy and the final defeat at the hands of the anti-Napoleon coalition led to the so-called *statsbankerot* (bankruptcy of the state) in 1813 and the loss of Norway to Sweden in 1814 (Østergård 2004: 29).

The chief objective of elected Crown Prince Charles John of Sweden (the former French Field-Marshall Jean-Baptiste Bernadotte) was the acquisition of Norway as compensation for the loss of Finland. Great Britain, Russia[12] and Prussia promised Norway to Sweden in return for joining the final battle against Napoleon. In late 1813, Crown Prince Charles John of Sweden attacked Napoleon's ally Denmark, and quickly forced Frederik VI to surrender and accept his terms of peace.

According to the Danish-Swedish Treaty of Kiel of 14 January 1814, as punishment for the alliance with France, the Danish king was compelled to cede Norway to King Charles XIII of Sweden in return for Swedish Pomerania.[13] The treaty specifically excluded Iceland, the Faeroe Islands and Greenland from the transfer from Danish to Swedish rule. The Duchies of Schleswig and Holstein[14] were returned to the king of Denmark.

However, the Danish Governor-General in Norway, Danish hereditary prince Christian Frederik, decided to oppose the Treaty of Kiel, arguing that Frederik VI had no legal right to relinquish his inheritance, asserting that he was the rightful king of Norway, and that Norway had a right to self-determination.

Norway becomes an independent constitutional monarchy in 1814

On 16 February Christian Frederik assembled a meeting of prominent Norwegian men at Eidsvoll (north of Christiania) to discuss the situation. The participants at the meeting advised Christian Frederik to let the people elect a constituent assembly, which in turn would adopt a constitution and elect a king. On 19 February Christian Frederik proclaimed himself regent of Norway and ordered all con-

12 At the meeting between Crown Prince Charles John of Sweden and Emperor Alexander I of Russia in Åbo (Turku) in Finland in September 1812, Charles John formally renounced any future Swedish claim to Finland in return for Russian help, which he received in 1813–1814, in acquiring Norway for Sweden in compensation (Barton 2006: 223).

13 At the Congress of Vienna in 1815 Swedish Pomerania was given to Prussia instead. In return, the Danish king received the tiny Duchy of Lauenburg.

14 However, Holstein, annexed to the Danish monarchy after the Holy Roman Empire was dissolved in 1806, became one of the member states in the new German Confederation after the Congress of Vienna in 1815 (Berg 2014: 268).

gregations to meet on 25 February to swear loyalty to the cause of Norwegian independence and to elect delegates to a constituent assembly to convene at Eidsvoll on 10 April. On 10 April 112 delegates of the constituent assembly convened at Eidsvoll. On 17 May the constituent assembly in one single document signed the Norwegian Constitution and unanimously elected Christian Frederik as king of the independent kingdom of Norway. Emissaries from Russia, Prussia, Austria and Great Britain tried in vain to persuade Christian Frederik to back down and comply with the provisions of the Treaty of Kiel. On 29 July 1814 Charles John invaded Norway, quickly demonstrating Sweden's military superiority. The brief war, which rather amounted to a series of skirmishes, was the last war between two Nordic countries, and ended with peace negotiations at Moss.

Through the Convention of Moss of 14 August 1814, Charles John Bernadotte accepted Norway's new constitution and recognized the Norwegian parliament as a negotiating partner in setting up the dynastic union with Sweden.[15] On 7 October the newly elected *Storting* (in reality a new constituent assembly) convened in Christiania and Christian Frederik abdicated according to the conditions agreed on at Moss and embarked for Denmark. On 4 November the *Storting* adopted the constitutional amendments required to allow for union and on the same day elected Charles XIII of Sweden as king of Norway (he never set foot in Norway). On 18 November Charles XIII's adopted heir Charles John Bernadotte arrived in Christiania, and appearing before the *Storting*, accepted the election and swore to uphold the Constitution of 4 November on behalf of the king. On 15 August 1815 the Act of Union, a bilateral treaty, formalized the personal union between the two kingdoms. Thus, the union was established as a two-state confederacy, in which the king and the king's prerogatives were the only joint institutions, and otherwise Norway had home rule[16] (Berg 2014: 277).

NATION-BUILDING IN THE 19TH CENTURY AND BEYOND

The most explicit and conscious efforts at (re-)creating a national identity were naturally most vigorous in the dependent countries of Norway, Finland and Iceland. Denmark and Sweden[17] could fall back on long traditions of historical

15 Although the Swedish king recognized Norway as a sovereign state and had accepted the Moss Convention as the basis for negotiations, the stronger party did not hesitate to use threats towards the weaker party. Russian troops occupied Holstein while the *Storting* negotiated its place in the inevitable union. Swedish troops occupied the border area east of Christiania, and none of them were demobilized before the *Storting* voted on 20 October that Norway agreed to join the union (Berg 2014: 276).

16 Hence, the Danish-Swedish Kiel Treaty was never implemented the way it had been formulated in January 1814. Norway was not transferred from the Danish to the Swedish king and Swedish Pomerania was not bartered in the other direction.

17 The Swedish success in integrating Scania and the other territories wrested from Denmark in 1658 was helped by the fact that the conquest occurred before the introduction of compulsory mass education.

continuity in their construction projects. In Norway and Finland the task was to construct a new nation.

Norway (1814–1905): From domestic sovereignty to full independence

As demonstrated above, Norway's status as a separate kingdom under the Swedish monarch was a negotiated agreement, beginning with the Convention of Moss, finally accepted by the *Storting* in November 1814, and confirmed by the joint Act of Union in 1815. With the 4 November 1814 Constitution Norway became a constitutional monarchy: the Swedish king ruled Norway as a constitutional monarch. Norway's constitution of 1814 was the most democratic of its time in Europe, far more so than Sweden's.[18] Charles XIV John, who ascended to the Swedish-Norwegian throne in 1818, made determined efforts between 1821 and 1836 to amend the Norwegian constitution to strengthen the crown's authority, but these were effectively blocked by the *Storting*,[19] which convened every three years (Barton2006: 222).

Since Norway legally had the status of a separate state, the only institutions common to both countries were the king and foreign affairs. All other ministries and government institutions were separate to each state, even armies, navies and treasuries. As a state, Norway kept most of the symbolic apparatus of sovereign states, such as her state borders, even along the Kjølen mountain range, with its own border defence, a government, a parliament and its own judicial institutions (Berg 2014: 274). Early nation-building focused on national symbols: the flag, the national anthem, and celebration of the national day (17 May). The national mobilization had two dimensions.

The first centred on the struggle for cultural independence from Denmark through cultural mobilization against the Danish linguistic standard. Language therefore played a central role in cultural nation-building in Norway. The distance between the Danish metropolitan language and the local languages and dialects in Norway was much less pronounced than in Finland.

Upon independence in 1814 the written and printed standard was Danish, but the language was pronounced differently throughout the country. The history of the liberation of Norwegian from the Danish inheritance is largely the history of the reduction of this distance between the written and the oral language. The language question produced protracted conflicts, first over the urban standard to replace Danish as the written norm, and then between this standard and an indigenous counter-standard developed out of rural dialects. The latter represented a radical solution to the creation of a Norwegian linguistic distinctiveness. This linguistic counter-standard was invented by Ivar

---

18 For example, while the king could exercise an absolute veto over legislation in Sweden, he possessed only a suspensive veto over two consecutive *Storting* sessions in Norway.

19 The *Storting* abolished the nobility by law in 1821 (Neumann 2000: 240).

Aasen, a self-educated scholar who during the 1840s synthesized a distinctive, new Norwegian language, *landsmaal* (later called *nynorsk*), from several existing, mainly West Norwegian, dialects.

The *nynorsk* counter-standard not only caught on within the rural areas of the south and west, but it became an expression of identity for the rising peasant intelligentsia after 1870. The broad left alliance (*Venstre*) took up its cause and forced through legislation to recognize *nynorsk* as an official norm, both of administrative communication and in the schools. The staunchly nationalist *Venstre*, or party of the Left, then dominating the *Storting*, made *landsmaal* coequal with Dano-Norwegian in 1885 (see chapters 2 and 3 for some details regarding Venstre and the language conflict).

It was the advocates of *landsmaal* who most strongly supported the liberal party (*Venstre*) in its constant efforts to widen Norway's autonomy and eventually to dissolve the union with Sweden. The second dimension of national mobilization concerned the struggle for political independence from Sweden through political mobilization against Swedish supremacy in foreign affairs. The demand for separate Norwegian consuls became the issue that finally led to the end of the Union.

Norway achieved its full independence under peaceful conditions. In June 1905, the Norwegian *Storting* cut short a protracted conflict with Sweden over the management of foreign affairs by provoking a ministerial crisis and thereafter declaring the union dissolved when King Oscar II proved unable to appoint a new government. A face-saving formula was found for dissolving the union through negotiation (Barton 2006: 225).

This resulted in a peaceful divorce.[20] A plebiscite on the union was held on 13 August 1905. A total of 368,392 Norwegians voted in favour of the dissolution of the union, whereas only 184 voted against. Negotiations took place in Karlstad, and on 26 October the Swedish king, Oscar II, recognized Norway as an independent country, and abdicated the Norwegian crown. A second plebiscite on monarchy vs. republic was held on 12 and 13 November: 259,563 (78.9 %) voted in favour of monarchy and 69,264 (21.1 %) voted in favour of republic. On 18 November 1905 the *Storting* elected Prince Charles of Denmark as king of Norway. Prince Charles was married to Princess Maud (daughter of King Edward VII of Great Britain) and had a son, Olav. The new royal family arrived in Norway on 25 November 1905 and Prince Charles became King Haakon VII of Norway (reigned 1905–57).

20 It was a "velvet divorce" of the type that took place with the peaceful dissolution of Czechoslovakia into the Czech Republic and Slovakia in 1992.

Finland (1809–1917): From domestic sovereignty to full independence

In stark contrast to the kingdom of Norway, the Grand Duchy of Finland was governed according to Gustav III's Swedish absolutist constitution of 1772. The executive (*Senatet*) and its members (all Finnish) were appointed by the Tsar. The Tsar's representative in Finland, the Governor-General, was always a Russian.

The dominant political line in Finland, in contrast to Norway, was unwavering loyalty to the Tsar in the hope of preserving its special preferred status within the Russian empire. In recognition of the Finns' loyalty during the Crimean War and especially the second Polish Rebellion, Alexander II in 1863 at last convened their Diet, the *Lantdag* or *Valtiopäivät*, for the first time since 1809. After that the Diet convened in practice every three years.

As in the case of Norway, nation-building had two dimensions. The first dimension was the cultural battle against the dominant Swedish-speaking elites. In Finland, Swedish had for centuries been the language of administration and higher culture. As in Norway, language also played a central role in cultural nation-building in Finland, but the distance between the peripheral and the colonial elite language was much greater in Finland than in Norway. The Fenno-Ugric Finnish language was very different from Swedish.

In what came to be known as "Fennomania", the cultivation of the indigenous Finnish language called upon the educated classes (in Swedish) to abandon Swedish entirely and to make Finnish the sole official and cultural language of Finland.

The Russian government favoured the Fennoman movement and Finnish cultural nationalism as a welcome means to weaken the country's Swedish attachments and increase loyalty to Russia. The Fennomans were thus steadfastly loyal to the empire, whereas Swedish-speaking liberals, the Swecomans, took the lead in resisting any encroachments upon Finland's autonomy, especially during the "Russification" crisis from 1899 to 1906. Thus a certain conflict of priorities emerged among the respective elites: the Fennomans were split between the Old Finns who prioritized the fight against Swedish cultural dominance and saw cooperation with Russia as the best way to improve the position of the Finnish language, whereas the so-called Young Finns joined with the Swecomans in their opposition to Russian autocracy.

The loyal Fennomans received their reward in 1863, when Alexander II elevated Finnish to the status of national language. The Swedish-speaking elite had a direct interest in the development of a broad-based Finnish movement as an essential element in a strategy to protect the inherited structure of government against tsarist Russia. Nationalism served as a safeguard of the Finnish state, and for this reason it proved possible to reach agreement on measures of accommodation between the two linguistic communities. The Finnish language became coequal with Swedish in 1883, and after independence in 1917, Finland was made an officially bilingual country in the 1919 Constitution. The highest proportion of Swedish speakers is found on the west coast, in Ostrobotnia.

The second dimension of nation-building was the political battle against the Russians. After the Diet started to convene regularly starting in 1863, many important state- and nation-building measures were implemented. In 1865 Finland got its own national bank, currency (*markka*) and stamps. The law on military service of 1878 gave Finland its own army (5000–6000 men).

A setback in domestic sovereignty came with the policy of "Russification" which led to a period of repression (1899–1905). Governor-General Bobrikov (served 1898–1904) started to roll back Finnish autonomy after the publication of the so-called February Manifesto of 1899, and Russian was declared the language of administration. In 1903 Bobrikov was given dictatorial powers, and he was shot in the Senate in 1904 by the Finnish activist Eugen Schauman. Russian defeat in the war with Japan (1904–05) led to a general strike in Russia, which extended to Finland. The Tsar ended the Russification policies in Finland in his October Manifesto of 1905.

The Russian Revolution of 1905 triggered the democratization of the power to elect the parliament. The Finnish Diet used this window of opportunity to transform itself from the most archaic to the world's most modern and democratic parliament, by replacing the medieval four estates with a unicameral parliament (*Eduskunta*) elected by universal suffrage for both men and women in 1906 (Barton 2006: 224). However, the power to appoint the government (*Senatet*) remained in the hands of the Tsar until 1917.

In contrast to Norway, Finland achieved its full independence under conditions of turmoil in the wake of the breakdown of the Romanov Empire during the Russian Revolution of 1917. Finland declared its independence unilaterally on 6 December 1917, which was accepted by the Bolsheviks on 4 January 1918. This triggered a civil war in January 1918 by an uprising of the radical socialist "Reds", many of whom aspired to a Finnish socialist republic within the new Soviet federation. Thus the Civil War of 1918 in Finland was a full-blown ideological class war. The social revolution in Russia led to a conflict between class ("Reds") and nation ("Whites"). The "Reds" were defeated in May 1918 after bitter fighting by the Finnish "Whites", who with German support defended Finland's newly won, complete independence (Barton 2006: 225).

After the Civil War there was a conflict between monarchists and republicans. A German prince, Friedrich Karl, was elected king of Finland, but abdicated when Germany lost WWI. A compromise between monarchists and republicans was reached in the Finnish constitution of 1919: Finland became a republic with a strong president in a semi-presidential regime. The motive for creating a dual executive with a strong president was related to the struggle for the control of executive power. The right, the victors of the civil war, had little confidence in a pure parliamentary democracy. After all, in 1916 the social democrats had won an absolute majority in the Finnish parliament. A strong president was viewed as a check on a parliament controlled by the left.[21]

Finland experienced several border changes between 1920 and 1944. In the treaty of Tartu (Dorpat) in 1920 between Finland and Soviet Russia, Finland acquired Petsamo. In the treaty of Moscow in 1940 after the Winter War (1939–40) between Finland and the USSR, Finland lost Karelia, Salla and the western part of the Rybachi peninsula north of Petsamo. In the armistice of Moscow in 1944 after the Continuation War (1941–44) between Finland (allied with Nazi Germany) and the USSR, in addition to the territories lost in 1940, Finland also lost Petsamo, its only ice-free winter harbour.

Denmark (1814–64): synchronized simultaneous nation-building and democratization

The loss of Norway in 1814 completely changed the balance between the German and Nordic elements in the Danish composite state.

In France, the July Revolution of 1830 triggered a reform that modified absolutism by the introduction of estate representation in four regional Diets: Holstein, Schleswig, the Islands and Jutland in 1834. The influence of the February Revolution in 1848 finally led to the abolition of absolutism and the founding of Denmark proper ("the Kingdom") as a constitutional monarchy with the Constitution of 5 June 1849.[22] The war with Prussia concerning the status of Schleswig-Holstein had already begun when the constituent assembly started its work. Thus the questions regarding universal military conscription (the duty to defend the nation) and suffrage rights (democracy) were linked. The Danish so-called *Helstat* (unified state) was a multi-national state that, in addition to Denmark proper, contained the Duchy of Schleswig and controlled the duchies of Holstein and Lauenburg in the German Confederation. Germans thus made up a third of Denmark's population. Danish nationalists believed that Schleswig (their slogan was "Denmark to Ejderen!", a river in the border area between Schleswig and Holstein), but not Holstein and Lauenburg, should be part of Denmark. German nationalists (the Schleswig-Holstein movement) believed that Schleswig, Holstein and Lauenburg should remain united.

Ignited by the wave of European revolutions of 1848, a civil war broke out in the Danish monarchy in March 1848. Supporters of a united state of Schleswig-

21 After 1918 semi-presidential systems had mostly been a compromise between democrats and monarchists, leading to a republican variation of constitutional monarchy (Finland 1919; Germany 1919, Spain 1931).

22 As for the duchies of Schleswig, Holstein and Lauenburg, not covered by the Danish constitution, the formal power of the king was still close to absolute.

Holstein as part of a greater Germany were pitted against those who wanted to tie Schleswig more closely to Denmark proper.

Inspired by the vision of a unified Germany and spurred on by its intra-German competition with Austria, the Prussians intervened in the military conflict on the side of the Schleswig-Holstein forces. However, the advantage caused by this strong military reinforcement was nullified later in the war, as Prussia and other intervening German states were forced to pull out due to diplomatic pressure, primarily from Russia. The other European powers were united in opposing any dismemberment of Denmark, so what became known as the Three Years' War or First Schleswig War (1848–51) ended in the *status quo ante bellum* with the international treaty that became known as the "London Protocol" of 1852. Thus, the Danish-German monarchy was re-established on its pre-war basis, with the exception that Denmark proper changed during the war from being an absolutist state to being a constitutional monarchy (Clausen 2014: 713–14).

Many Danes wanted the new democratic Constitution of Denmark of 5 June 1849 to apply to all Danes, including those in Schleswig. The issue concerning the status of the Duchy of Schleswig within the national framework ended with the abortive Danish attempt to annex Schleswig in November 1863. The Constitution of November 1863 integrated the Duchy of Schleswig into the Danish kingdom by establishing a common parliament for both Schleswig and Denmark in violation of the London Protocol. Prussian and Austrian troops crossed into Schleswig on 1 February 1864 and war became inevitable. The Second Schleswig War ended with the treaty of Vienna of 30 October 1864, according to which the coalition of Prussia and Austria took Holstein, Lauenburg and all of Schleswig, with a large Danish population in Northern Schleswig (Østergård 2004: 32).

The war ended with the dismemberment of the Danish monarchy after the self-inflicted debacle of 1864. Denmark survived as a sovereign homogeneous small nation-state only with help from outside. Again it was the interests of the great powers, this time first and foremost Russia and Great Britain, in maintaining a neutral power at the entrance to the Baltic that saved Denmark as a sovereign state. Had this not been the case, the country would have become either German or Swedish, the latter eventuality being termed Scandinavianism[23] (Østergård 2004: 31).

23 Parts of the national liberal intelligentsia favoured a union between Denmark and Sweden, which had already formed a union with Norway. This programme went by the name of Scandinavianism and would have implied a de facto Swedish hegemony. The political aspirations of the Swedish and Danish Scandinavianists came to naught in the Danish-German wars in 1848–51 and 1864. There was no Scandinavian state because none of the established states was strong enough to play the role that Prussia played in the German and Piemonte in the Italian national unification processes.

Only the defeat of the German Reich in WWI provided an opportunity for Denmark to retrieve the Danish speakers in North Schleswig. The Versailles conference granted a request from the Danish government for a plebiscite in the disputed North Schleswig region to determine the border between Denmark and Germany. The plebiscites were held in two zones that had been defined according to the wishes of the Danish government. In the plebiscite in Zone I (North Schleswig), on 10 February 1920, 74.9 % voted to come under Danish rule, and 25.1 % voted to stay German. In the plebiscite in Zone II (Central Schleswig) on 14 March 1920, 80.2 % voted for Germany, and 19.8 % for Denmark. The border therefore became almost identical to the border between the two zones.

Iceland (1874–1944): stepwise extension of political rights until full independence

Iceland had not succumbed to the linguistic standards of its Danish masters, but retained a strong cultural identity. Thus the process of mass mobilization focused directly on political independence, which was achieved in three steps. The process started with the foundation of the new Althing as a consultative assembly in 1843. The independence movement was led by Jon Sigurdsson (Hálfdanarson 2000: 94). In 1874 Denmark granted Iceland a constitution. The Althing gained legislative powers, but executive power remained in Denmark.

In the first step, in 1904 Iceland was granted home rule. After the triumph of the principle of parliamentarism in Denmark in 1901, a minister for Icelandic affairs, residing in Reykjavik, was made responsible to the Althing. The first of these was Hannes Hafstein (Hálfdanarson 2006: 246).

The second step was the Act of Union of 1 December 1918, by which Denmark recognized Iceland as a fully sovereign state, joined with Denmark in a personal union with the Danish king. The Act of Union was approved by 93 % of the voters in a prior referendum held on 19 October 1918. The German occupation of Denmark on 9 April 1940 cut communications between Iceland and Denmark. As a result, on 10 April, the Icelandic parliament took temporary control of foreign affairs electing a provisional governor, Sveinn Bjørnsson, who later became the first president of the republic. On 10 May 1940, British military forces invaded Iceland to prevent German occupation. In July 1940 responsibility for Iceland's occupation and defence passed to the USA.

The third, and final, step on Iceland's road to full independence came through the two constitutional referendums on 20–23 May 1944. A total of 99.5 % voted in favour of abolishing the Act of Union with Denmark, and 98.5 % voted in favour of adopting a new republican constitution. Iceland became an independent republic on 17 June 1944, when the parliament chose Sveinn Bjørnsson as the first president of the republic, the only one not elected directly by the people of Iceland.

HOME RULE FOR ÅLAND (1921), THE FAEROE ISLANDS (1948) AND GREENLAND (1979)

The Swedish-speaking Åland Islands were part of the Russian Grand Duchy of Finland starting in 1809 and became a demilitarized zone in 1856. After Finland became independent in 1917, the Ålanders wanted to become part of Sweden. An unofficial referendum on integration into Sweden in June 1919 was approved by 95 % of the voters. The League of Nations, however, ruled in 1921 that Åland should be subject to Finland and simultaneously awarded the archipelago a considerable measure of autonomy. Swedish is the sole official language in Åland. Åland is entitled to elect one member to the Finnish parliament. Åland has its own parliament (*Lagting*). Only inhabitants with the right of abode (having been born in Åland or having continuously resided there for at least five years) may vote.[24]

The Faeroe Islands became an integral part of the Danish Realm starting with the first Danish constitution of 1849. The Faeroese parliament (*Løgting*) was re-established in 1852 as an advisory body. The Faeroese language was standardized as a written language in 1890, and was used in public schools from 1938 onwards and in churches from 1939 onwards. As in the case of Iceland, the British pre-emptively occupied the Faeroes in 1940 to prevent a German invasion. The experience of wartime self-government was crucial in paving the way for formal autonomy in 1948. On 14 September 1946 a referendum on full independence was held. A total of 50.7 % voted in favour of independence and 49.3 % voted against. The unilateral declaration of independence was annulled by the Danish government, which dissolved the *Løgting*. The new *Løgting* election on 8 November 1946 was won by the parties which were against full independence (Østergård 2008b: 68). Denmark granted the Faeroes home rule on 30 March 1948 (*Hjemmestyreloven*). Faeroese was recognized as the official language and the Faeroese flag was officially recognized.[25] A planned referendum in 2001 on independence was cancelled when the Danish prime minister warned that money grants would be phased out if there were a yes vote.

In 1953 Greenland became an integral part of the Danish Realm and was granted two seats in the Danish parliament (*Folketing*).[26] The Danish *Folketing* approved devolution in the Home Rule Act (*Hjemmestyre*), endorsed in a referendum held in Greenland in 1979. The capital Godthåb was renamed Nuuk, and a local flag was adopted in 1985. The Home Rule Act applied to all

---

24 Åland voted in favour of the EU in 1994 and has thus been a member of the EU together with Finland since 1995.

25 The Faeroese refused to join the EEC in 1973 and are thus not members of the EU.

26 In 1973 Greenland, alongside Denmark proper, became a member of the EEC even though a majority of 70 % of the Greenlanders had voted against membership in the 1972 Danish EEC referendum. On 23 February 1982, a bare majority (53 %) of the Greenlanders voted to leave the ECC. Brexit *avant la lettre*!

inhabitants of Greenland, Inuit and Danish alike, a classic example of territorial autonomy. All inhabitants of Greenland have the right to vote in elections for the Greenland parliament (*Landsting*) provided they are Danish citizens. In practice the government (*Landsstyre*) is Inuit-run since almost 90 % of the inhabitants are Inuit or of mixed Danish-Inuit descent.

On 25 November 2008 a referendum was held on whether to substitute the old home rule arrangement by a new form of self-government (*Selvstyre*). A total of 75.5 % of the voters supported such an increase of autonomy, and 23.6 % voted against. The *Selvstyre* regime took effect on 21 June 2009, the 30th anniversary of the establishment of home rule in 1979.

THE SÁMI: A NORDIC INDIGENOUS PEOPLE

The Sámi are an indigenous people (about 84,000) in the northern regions of Norway, Sweden, Finland and the Kola Peninsula in Russia, and they are a nation divided by four states. The area populated by the Sámi people, Sápmi/Sámi Ædnan/Samiland, was first divided by the border treaty between Sweden and Denmark-Norway of 1751. The ownership rights to land and water and free passage across the borders were codified in a codicil to the border treaty. The international border between Sweden and Finland of 1809 and between Norway and Russia of 1826 completed the division of Sápmi. The various Sámi language groups belong to the Fenno-Ugric linguistic family. A policy of cultural assimilation and discrimination towards the Sámi was practised from approximately 1860 to 1970. These policies were reversed from the 1970s onwards, when the Sámi people were recognized as an indigenous people in the areas they traditionally inhabited. Sámi Acts were passed in Norway (1987), Sweden (1992) and Finland (1996), which allowed for political empowerment through the establishment of advisory Sámi parliaments, inaugurated in 1989 in Karasjok (Norway), 1993 in Kiruna (Sweden) and 1996 in Enare (Finland). The Sámi parliaments are not territorially based institutions of home rule, but are meant to represent an ethnic category of people in their respective countries: only the Sámi enrolled in the Sámi census in their regions of residence can vote in elections for the Sámi parliaments.

DEMOCRATIZATION: NORDIC ROADS TO DEMOCRACY

Building national identities was one part of the nation building process; building citizenship was another. The political sociologist Stein Rokkan enumerates four thresholds for mass incorporation in democratic politics (Rokkan 1987). His argument is that nation-building is only completed when the whole adult population becomes part of the polity and a democratic system is established. Normally this process of integration takes the form of political opposition to an established elite, an opposition that needs to surmount several thresholds on its way to inclusion and, finally, to power. To pass the first threshold the opposition requires legitimacy; in other words, there must be freedom of assembly, expression and organization. Second, the population must be granted the political right to participate in free elections, meaning universal suffrage. Third, the voters must be fairly represented in the political institutions. The institutional mechanism to secure fair representation is the electoral system of proportional representation (PR). Finally, the chain of citizen influence must extend to the executive. Incorporating the citizens ought to have consequences for political power, so elected parliaments should select the executive and decide the fate of governments.

The power to appoint the government or the democratization of executive power ranges from constitutional monarchy (dualism between king and parliament with independent royal power based on the principle of the separation of powers) to parliamentary government (unity between government and parliament based on the principle of the sovereignty of the people), or from constitutional monarchy to democratic parliamentary monarchy (Stepan et al. 2014: 36–37).

A "constitutional monarchy" is a regime that has a basic law that binds the monarch (thereby making the regime "constitutional") but still remains undemocratic. Thus the full democratization of monarchies implies the transformation of constitutional monarchies into democratic parliamentary monarchies, the defining characteristic of which is that only the freely elected parliament forms and terminates the government (Stepan et al. 2014: 36).

Concerning the democratization of the power to appoint the government, constitutional monarchy was introduced in Sweden (1809), Norway (1814), Denmark (1849) and Iceland (1874). Parliamentary government was introduced in Norway (1884), Denmark (1901), Iceland (1904), Sweden (1917) and Finland (1917).

The power to elect the parliament or the democratization of legislative power ranges from restricted to universal suffrage. The Norwegian 1814 constitution has been regarded as the most democratic of its time. It has been calculated that 45.5 % of the male population above 25 years of age was formally enfranchised according to the 1814 constitution. Thus Norway was the first of the five Nordic countries to come close to mass democracy, but universal male suffrage was not introduced until 1898. In Denmark, with the introduction of suffrage for men above 30 years in the constitution of 5 June 1849, the percentage of the population with the right to vote increased from 2.8 % to 15 % (Kaspersen 2004: 86). However, the democratization of the suffrage was reversed in 1866, when conservative forces pushed through a revision of the constitution which restricted the franchise for the Upper Chamber of the bicameral parliament (*Rigsdag*), the *Landsting*, giving large landowners a permanent majority in that chamber. However, liberal forces in the popularly elected Lower Chamber, the *Folketing*, finally managed to achieve the approval of universal and equal suffrage for men and women as well as the introduction of the proportional (PR) electoral system in 1915.

In Sweden, the reform of 1866 brought a first set of extensions of male suffrage, with 22 % of men above 21 years of age obtaining suffrage. But the decisive change did not come until 1907, when suffrage was extended to all men in elections to the Second Chamber of the bicameral *Riksdag*, although the marked inequalities produced by the tax-weighing of votes were not abolished until 1920. The conservative First Chamber blocked female suffrage until 1921. In Finland the transition to universal suffrage for both men and women happened abruptly in 1906. Finland became the first European country to introduce universal suffrage, followed by Norway in 1913.

Table 1.5 lists when each of the Nordic states passed the four thresholds. Some of the dates, particularly those concerning freedom of the press and parliamentarism,[27] must be considered approximate. E.g. it is not totally "correct" to say that 1884 is the year when parliamentarism came into effect in Norway. The year 1884 was when a belligerent parliamentary majority for the first time forced the king to appoint a new government acceptable to them. This does not mean that a new constitutional principle was enacted in Norwegian history. In the period from 1884 to 1905, the principle was not always followed in practice. For example, the government of Prime Minister Emil Stang did not resign after the votes of no confidence in the Storting in 1893 and 1894, because he enjoyed the support of King Oscar II. As an uncontested constitutional procedure, parliamentarism was not in place until well after 1905 (Rasch 2004: 37–38).

TABLE 1.5 ROKKAN'S THRESHOLDS FOR POPULAR POLITICAL PARTICIPATION

	Legitimacy: Freedom of the press	**Incorporation: Universal suffrage**	**Representation: PR electoral system**	**Executive: Parliamentarism**
Denmark	1849	1915	1915	1901
Finland	1917	1906	1906	1917
Iceland	1849	1915 (1920)	1959 (1942)	1904
Norway	1814	1913	1919	1884
Sweden	1809 (1766)	1921	1909	1917

Source: Heidar 2004b: 18.

27 The principles of parliamentarism were introduced and practiced *de facto* for a very long time before they were incorporated *de jure* into the constitution. In Denmark, the parliamentary principles were not explicitly spelled out in the constitution until the Constitution of 1953, in Sweden in the Constitution of 1974, and in Norway with a constitutional amendment to the Constitution of 1814 as late as 2007.

Denmark became a constitutional monarchy with the constitution of 1849, but not until 1901 did King Christian IX agree to form a government that would have the confidence of the elected national legislature's lower house. In 1919, his grandson Christian X formally declared that he would not form any government without a lower-house majority. But just a year later, he violated the spirit of this pledge. The Treaty of Versailles called for Germany and Denmark to hold plebiscites in North and Central Schleswig, respectively. North Schleswig voted overwhelmingly to rejoin Denmark, while in Central Schleswig the result was the reverse. Christian X sided with Danish nationalists and ordered the premier to ignore the Central Schleswig vote and claim the area for Denmark. When the premier said no, the king sacked him and his cabinet. This last clash between a Danish monarch and the parliament ended only when the king, worried by protesting crowds in Copenhagen and the example of the Bolshevik takeover in Russia, accepted the parliament's right to be the final authority on public policy. No Danish monarch has since dared to challenge a prime minister heading a parliamentary majority. Denmark had finally become a democratic parliamentary monarchy (Stepan et al. 2014: 40).

Sweden did not become a democratic parliamentary monarchy until after WWI. It was only in the threatening context of 1918, when the German and Russian monarchies had fallen and Swedes were protesting on behalf of republicanism and even revolution, that King Gustav V acceded to universal manhood suffrage in both houses and thus at last accepted parliamentary government.

With regard to suffrage extensions, it is common to date the introduction of universal suffrage in Iceland as 1915, when suffrage was extended to women and servants, since the general principle was adopted that year. But in 1915 the age limit for women and servants was set to 40 years, instead of the general age requirement of 25 years that applied at the time, with the proviso that the age limit of 40 would be lowered step by step over the next 15 years. Therefore, it is perhaps more correct to say that universal suffrage was not introduced in Iceland until 1920. In 1918 Iceland became a separate state under the Danish crown, in which the inhabitants of both states were to enjoy dual citizenship. Because Denmark could not accept the prospect of Danish women as second-rate citizens in Iceland, the Icelandic parliament was therefore obliged to give men and women equal rights in 1920 (Raaum 2005: 894).

The introduction of PR electoral systems was a step-by-step process in Iceland. Starting in 1942, some of the seats in the Althing were elected by PR. In 1959 PR was expanded to every seat in the parliament (Heidar 2004b: 18)

Table 1.5 conveys how the Nordic countries followed each other chronologically, in particular with regard to the passing of the final three thresholds to democracy; these obstacles were more or less all overcome during a relatively short time span of two decades, from 1900 to 1920 (Heidar 2004b: 18). See chapter 4 for details regarding political representation and parliamentarism in particular.

Successful state- and nation-building and democratization obviously did not preclude political divisions. Industrialization spawned class divisions and conflict over socioeconomic redistribution also in the Nordic countries. The bloody civil war in Finland (1918) constituted an extreme manifestation of this type of class conflict, stoked in large part by the successful Bolshevik Revolution in Russia. Norway's labour movement also went through a radical period, with the Norwegian Labour Party becoming a member of the Communist Third International (1919–23). Class tensions fell in the interwar years, bringing social democratic governments to each of the Nordic countries: Denmark in 1929–40, Sweden in 1932 and Norway in 1935. In Iceland the Social democratic party formed a coalition government in 1934, and likewise in Finland in 1937. The interwar fascist parties of the radical right were very weak in the Nordic countries. Finland's fascist movement (*Lapporörelsen-Lapuan like*) was short-lived and ended in a failed coup attempt in 1932.[28] In all the Nordic countries, the social democratic parties reached red-green class compromises with the agrarian parties through crisis settlements,[29] which helped lower the political temperature and defuse tensions in the wake of the political threats the radical right was issuing during the turbulent 1930s. Mainly due to the interwar crisis settlements, the fascist movements remained a small and marginal phenomenon in the Nordic countries (Heidar 2004b: 20–21).

The "historical compromise" between capital and labour in the 1930s that brought social democratic governments to power in the Nordic countries, particularly in Scandinavia, laid the basis for the subsequent development of corporatist bargaining arrangements and universal welfare state regimes.

CONCLUSION

For most of the early modern period, Denmark and Sweden fought for domination in the Nordic region. The end of the Napoleonic Wars represented a sea change in inter-Nordic relations. The sense of the region as a cultural community gradually grew, eventually becoming an important basis for the termination of the pre-Napoleonic image of Scandinavia as a natural area of strife. The last war between a Nordic country and another Nordic country was the brief war between Sweden and Norway in July-August 1814. There have been no wars between the traditional enemies in the Scandinavian region since 1814. The

28 The so-called Mäntsälä rebellion between 27 February and 6 March 1932.

29 Red-green political deals between the social democrats and the agrarians took place in Denmark (*Kandslergadeforliget* of 30 January 1933), Sweden (*Kohandeln* [literally "the cow trade", but the English translation of "kohandel" is "horse trade"] of 27 may 1933), Norway (*Kriseforliket* ["the crisis settlement"] of 20 March 1935) and Finland (*Rödmyllan* in 1937).

new geopolitical balance that was established after the Kiel Treaty may have laid the foundation not only for the elimination of the idea of war as a natural feature of the region, but also for the absence of violence in conflict resolution that Karl Deutsch claimed to be a Nordic peculiarity after 1905 (Berg 2014: 279).

The two Scandinavian conglomerate states were dismantled, and they were split from each other. Sweden slid out of the continent; Denmark was forced away from the Scandinavian Peninsula. While Sweden left continental Europe after the loss of Pomerania, Denmark was pushed closer to the powerful German states. The latter in 1864 forced Denmark to retreat into a position of a south-Scandinavian peninsular nation state. The long-term effects of war loss for both countries appear to have been largely beneficial. Instead of leading to revanchism against the former enemy (Russia for Sweden, Prussia for Denmark), in both cases the result was an acceptance of military defeat and territorial loss and of being reduced to "small states" (Teorell & Rothstein 2015: 231–32).

The Norwegian secession from the union with Sweden in 1905 and the Icelandic secession from Denmark in 1944 happened through peaceful and democratic means. Likewise, the border between Denmark and Germany was settled by plebiscite in 1920.

The Nordic roads to liberal democracy were equally smooth and uniquely peaceful. The respective democratization processes were completed relatively early, roughly by 1920. With regard to the democratization of executive power, constitutional monarchies were transformed into democratic parliamentary monarchies in the three Scandinavian countries by 1917 and into semi-presidential regimes with democratically elected presidents in Finland and Iceland, in 1919 and 1944, respectively. With regard to the democratization of legislative power, all five Nordic countries had introduced universal suffrage for both men and women by 1921.

In conclusion, the "Nordic model" of state- and nation-building is still valid and viable. The state- and nation-building trajectories of the Nordic countries stand out as exceptionally peaceful with the notable partial exception of Finland.

CHAPTER 2
POLITICAL PARTIES AND PARTY SYSTEMS

Oddbjørn Knutsen

INTRODUCTION

The Nordic party system model was conceptualised as a five-party system model by Berglund and Lindström (1978). The major parties belong to the same five-party families:[1] Conservative, Liberal, Agrarian, Social Democrat and Communist families. These parties varied in importance and electoral support but altogether they account for most of the votes of the Nordic electorate. In order to be considered as having a lasting impact on the party system, the Communist party family should be extended to include Left Socialist partieswhich, from the late 1950s, started to take over as the dominant force which could be referred to as the radical left, or simply a Left Socialist force.

How does the five-party system model deviate from party systems in other regions within Western Europe? There are two ways of approaching this research question: first, by examining the existence of party families, and second, by examining the location of the party families in the policy space. Do the Nordic party families deviate from their sister parties in other countries?

Concerning the first question: the Agrarian parties are distinctive of the Nordic countries. They do not exist or gain significant support in other West European countries. Christian parties emerged later and are small today in comparison with the support they have had, and still have, in many Western continental countries.

Conservative parties do not exist in many of the central continental countries. The United Kingdom, Ireland and some Southern European countries are exceptions. The Nordic Conservative parties will be compared with these parties below.

1 Party families are similar or equivalent parties in different countries. They can be identified by historical origin, policy or ideology, affiliation to the same transnational party organisations, and by their names.

This chapter is organised as follows. In the first part, the focus is on the party families commencing with families in the five-party system model. This is followed by an account of new parties which can be grouped into the Religious, Green and Radical Rightist parties and which represent a challenge to the five-party system. The parties within each party family are briefly described. In order to compare the location of the parties and party families on central policy dimensions, data from an expert survey are used. This is a survey where specialists on party politics within the various European countries were asked to locate the parties on 20-point scales for central policy dimensions (Beloit and Laver 2006). The policy dimensions covered here are central dimensions related to Old Politics (economic left–right and moral issues) and New Political (environmental and immigration policy).[2] The survey was conducted in 2003–4 for 47 countries. Here, the survey is used to locate the party families and individual parties within these families on central policy scales. This survey is also used to compare the Nordic party families with equivalent parties in Western Europe.[3] Finally, electoral support in the post-war period is examined by presenting figures showing trends in average support during each decade commencing in the 1940s. Systematic analyses of change in support focus mainly on the 1950s and 2000s (2000–09). Electoral results for 2010–16[4] are also commented upon, but for two countries (Iceland and Norway) the results are based on only one election where the database is too small for reliable comparisons. For the newer party families, more detailed electoral results are presented for shorter relevant time intervals.

In the second part, special traits within the party systems of each of the Nordic countries are briefly examined followed by data on trends in central party system dimensions such as the overall support for the parties in the five-party system model, party system fragmentation and polarisation, and electoral volatility.

---

2 Economic left–right orientations are measured by locating the parties on a scale on 'raising taxes to increase public services' versus 'cutting public services to reduce taxes'.

The moral dimension is measured by locating the parties on a scale of liberal or opposing liberal policy on matters such as 'abortion, homosexuality and euthanasia'.

Location of environmental policy is measured by supporting protection of the environment 'even at the cost of economic growth' versus the precise opposite priorities.

The parties' location on the immigration scale is measured by special policies designed to help asylum seekers and immigrants integrate into the country versus helping them return to their country of origin.

3 Most comparisons (when others are not indicated) are undertaken with the Central countries (Austria, Belgium, Germany, Luxembourg, the Netherlands and Switzerland), while the Southern European countries (France, Greece, Italy, Portugal and Spain) will also be used. Britain will be another point of comparison.

4 The late October election 2016 in Iceland is not covered in the figures for 2010–2016.

THE ORIGIN OF THE FIVE-PARTY SYSTEM MODEL

The formative era of party systems in the Nordic countries comprises three distinct stages (Arter 2008b: chapter 3; Elder, Thomas and Arter 1982: chapter 2). First, there was an initial bipartisan stage when the power-seekers based mainly in the rural areas (the Left) challenged the holders of power in the towns and capital cities (the Right). The power-seekers were broad and partly unstable alliances between farmers and other enfranchised groups, and non-incorporated groups such as tenants and workers in the rural areas along with radical intellectuals, while the power holders were high-status and mainly town-based groups of aristocrats, bureaucrats and merchants.

The main divisive issues were related to the extension of suffrage to include peasants and the lower classes, the democratisation of the political system by the introduction of parliamentarianism to replace a system where the monarch chose his government, and the question of independence in Iceland, Finland and Norway.

The second phase took place after 1900 when predominantly rural communities were transformed into increasingly urban-industrial societies. The industrial cleavages (based on economic interests and social classes, see chapter 3) created new parties. Mass-based parties emerged. The Social Democratic and Labour parties, and the Agrarian parties articulated the economic interests of the workers and farmers, respectively. The Social Democratic parties had their electoral breakthrough during this period and became some of the largest parties in the respective party systems.

In the 1920s, ideological divisions in the socialist camp produced a radical left in the wake of the Russian Revolution. Revolutionary Communist parties split from the reformist Social Democratic parties. Communist parties were established in all the Nordic countries, but their significance differed greatly different in the separate countries (see below).

Originally, the Right or Conservative parties defended the power-holders' interests in opposition to demands from the lower classes and the Left for mass democracy and parliamentarianism. Support came first and foremost from the civil servants ('embetsmenn'), landowners, landlords and upper classes in the cities. The Right parties gradually transformed themselves from being parties which opposed democratisation, anchored among the elites in the Old Regimes, to become 'modern' parties which fully accepted democracy and supported laissez-faire economic liberalism. The Old Left parties gradually lost electoral support and became centrist parties positioned between the Conservatives and the Social Democrats.

THE SOCIAL DEMOCRATIC PARTIES

The Social Democratic parties have been dominant in the party systems of Norway and Sweden, and partly also of Denmark. Apart from those in Iceland, the parties in all the Nordic countries were established before 1900 and gained increasing support during the industrialisation process. During the 1930s, all Nordic Social Democratic parties formed Red–Green alliances with the Agrarian parties in order to overcome the economic crisis. The Social Democratic parties pursued reformist policies through Keynesian-style reflationary measures, attacking unemployment through programmes of social policy and public investment. This laid the basis for the Nordic welfare states (Elder, Thomas and Arter 1982: 51–57). It could be argued that basic political realignment took place during the 1930s, at least in Denmark, Norway and Sweden, strengthening the Social Democrats. These parties maintained their predominant positions in the decades after the Second World War.

The long period of Social Democratic rule is associated first and foremost with the universal or institutional welfare states (see chapter 9). These were comprehensive welfare states with income-maintenance schemes and social services. Further features included consensual democracy, incorporation of various interests in the political decision-making process, in particular labour and employers' organisations (corporatism) (see chapter 7), and a compromise between labour and capital, occasionally referred to as democratic socialism.

Reasons for the strength of the Social Democrats are manifold:

1. Party support was anchored in a strong and unified working-class trade union movement.
2. Reforms of the 1930s are considered as a major explanation. The parties presented themselves as people's parties, more so than class-based parties; they pursued reformist Keynesian policy and formed 'green' alliances with the Agrarian parties.
3. The ability of the Social Democrats to form intra-class alliances regarding policies and coalitions as in the 1930s, and to appeal to classes other than urban workers. The parties gained support from agricultural workers, smallholders, small tenants, fishermen and lumberjacks. Later, these parties adopted more moderate economic policies in order to appeal to the new middle class.
4. Opponents on the non-socialist side became fragmented.
5. The religious segments in the populations were small. Comparative research has shown that a large religious segment contributes to considerable support for Christian parties, also among working-class voters.

The Finnish Social Democratic party has been one of the four larger parties in the Finnish party system (three from the 1980s), but has not played a dominant role. The party has participated in several coalition governments and its ideological profile has been an emphasis on the welfare state and full employment.

The Icelandic Social Democratic party was formed in 1916 and represented reformist leftist policies. For a long time, the party was the smallest of the four largest parties. In the late 1990s, negotiations took place between the Social Democrats, the Left Alliance and the Women's Alliance[5] with the aim of unifying the leftist forces in Icelandic politics. The results were a Social Democratic Alliance Party (and the formation of a new Green left, see below) which in subsequent elections gained considerably stronger support than the Old Social Democratic Party (Hardarson and Kristinsson 2001: 325–327).

Location in the policy space

The Social Democratic parties are located at a moderate leftist position on the economic left–right dimension. They have a moderate liberal position on moral issues and a fairly centrist position regarding immigration policy. They are also fairly centrist regarding environmental policy but are generally closer to the anti-environmental pole than all other party families apart from the Conservatives and the Radical Right.

Compared with Social Democratic parties in the Central region, there are small differences. The Nordic parties seem, however, to focus relatively more on growth than the environment compared with the Social Democratic sister parties, and to be more restrictive regarding immigration policy.

Trends in electoral support

Figure 2.1 shows the average support for the Social Democratic parties throughout each decade. Apart from the 1950s and 2010–16, the Swedish party has received the largest support followed by the Norwegian and then the Danish parties. Support has been considerably smaller for the Finnish and, in particular, the Icelandic Social Democrats. Support for the Social Democratic Alliance increased greatly after the merger of the leftist parties in Iceland, but declined dramatically after 2010. The latter period is, however, only based on one election.

If we focus on the changes from the 1950s to 2000–09, the decline is only 5 percentage points on average, but if we exclude the quite deviant Icelandic development with the exceptionally high support in 2000–09, the average decline is 10 percentage points. The decline is largest in Norway (17 percentage points), followed by Denmark (13) and Sweden (8), and considerably smaller in Finland (3). The figure shows that there has been a considerable decline in

5 The Women's Alliance emerged in the early 1980s to promote women's interests and representation in Iceland. The party received between 5 % and 10 % of the vote in the elections from 1983 to 1995. It defined itself as situated to the left of the political spectrum and – before the emergence of the Left–Green Movement – was regarded as the party that was closest to being a 'green party' in Iceland (Hardarson and Kristinsson 1987: 222–223). The party disappeared with the merging of the leftist parties in the late 1990s.

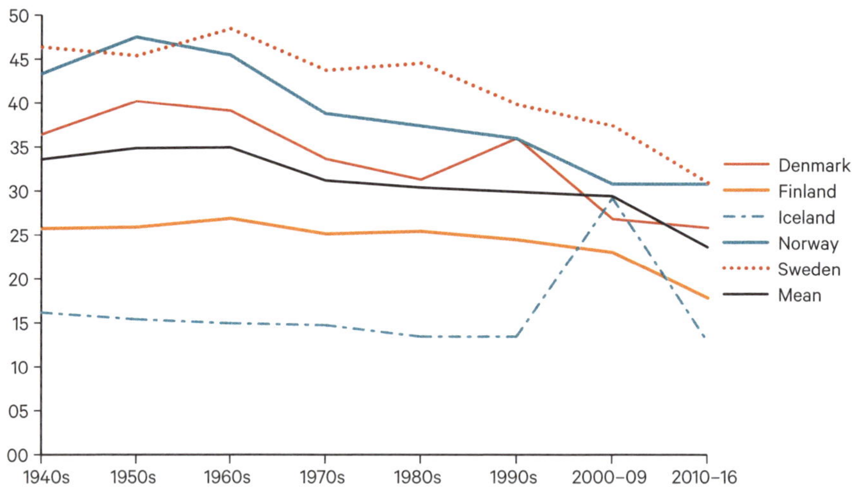

Figure 2.1 Trends in support for Social Democratic Parties

support after 2000 in Finland, Sweden and Iceland while support has remained stable in Norway. Support for the Social Democrats declined commencing in the 1970s.

THE COMMUNIST AND THE RADICAL LEFT PARTIES

The left-most parties in the five-party system model are represented by two, not one, party families. Originally, these were the Communist parties, but they gradually declined and have – in somewhat different trajectories – been replaced by non-communist radical left or socialist left forces. This is due to the gradual transformation of existing parties and as a result of the emergence of new parties.

The Communist parties became major political forces in Finland and Iceland, especially in the 1950s, but less so in Denmark, Norway and Sweden, although the Norwegian Labour Party was split and the majority group was also radicalised (1918–27). In a larger model for explaining deep splits in contrast to unified labour movements, Rokkan explains national differences with reference to the nation-building process during which the working class was formed and gained the right to vote. 'The less settled the issue of national identity and the deeper the conflicts over cultural standardisation, the greater the chances of radicalisation and fragmentation within the working class' (Rokkan 1970: 137).

The Finnish Communist party was founded as the Finnish Socialist Workers party in 1920 and participated in elections in the 1920s, but the party was outlawed in 1930. After the Second World War, the party participated in elections under the umbrella 'the Finnish People's Democratic League' (SKDL). The aim was originally to build a broad alliance of 'democratic forces' based on a popular front strategy. This strategy was successful and SKDL received considerable support, although this declined in the 1980s (see below). There was lengthy internal strife within the Communist Party concerning its relationship with the Communist movement. In 1986, there was a formal organisational split as the Stalinist minority was expelled from the party and went on to form a party of its own. By 1990, following the changes in Eastern Europe, a new party was formed on a left socialist platform – the Left Alliance (Arter 2002; Karvonen 2014: 37–38).

The Communist Party in Iceland was founded in 1930 and had moderate success in the first decade, joining the left-wing Social Democrats in 1938 to form the United Socialist Party. This party was to achieve considerably stronger support in subsequent elections. In 1956, the Social Democrats split again and formed an alliance with the United Socialist Party. This Alliance – called the People's Alliance – formally became a party in 1968, and was then a left socialist party, not a communist party (Hardarson 1995: 30). In the late 1990s negotiations took place between the Social Democrats, the Left Alliance and the Women's Alliance with a view to unifying the leftist forces in Icelandic politics. The results of these negotiations were two new parties: a Social Democratic Alliance (see above) and a Left-Green Movement. The latter was based on the core of the People's Alliance support and also attempted to appeal to the post-material concerns of the Icelandic voters (Hardarson and Kristinsson 2001: 325–327).

Like the Finnish Left Alliance, the Swedish Left Party is a successor to the Communist party rather than a new party. The party first changed its name from the Swedish Communist Party to the Left Party Communists in 1967, and then dropped the suffix 'Communists' in 1990 in an attempt to build a left-socialist platform following the collapse of communism.

In Denmark and Norway, the change from communist to left socialist forces took place via splinter parties from the Communists and Social Democrats, respectively. In Denmark, a Socialist People's Party split from the Communists in 1959 and in the subsequent election became the largest party to the left of the Social Democrats. During the 1970s, new parties emerged and there was considerable fragmentation among the Left Socialist and Communist forces, but the Socialist People's Party was the largest and survived this turbulent period. The other force that survived and became significant was the Unity List, formed as an electoral alliance between Communists and Left Socialist parties. The Unity List developed into an independent party and gained considerable support in the elections after 2010.

The Norwegian Socialist People's Party was established in 1961 and was a splinter party from the Social Democrats based on disagreement with foreign policy and economic policy. In 1975, the Socialist Left Party was formed on the basis of mergers of various groupings to the left of the Labour Party. This party has successfully opposed Norwegian membership of the European Union. Most of the party's members and voters came from the Socialist People's Party.

Location in the policy space

The Left Socialist parties are clearly to the left of the Social Democrats on the economic left–right dimension and have the most leftist position in the Nordic party systems. On moral and religious issues they are liberal and secular. Together with the Green parties in their respective party systems, they represent the environmental pole. They also support a liberal immigration policy. However, regarding the two New Politics dimensions, the Finnish, and to some degree the Swedish, parties (the Left Socialist parties with a communist past) do not have the same significant New Politics profiles as the other Left Socialist parties.

There are small differences between the Nordic Left Socialist parties and their sister parties elsewhere in Western Europe except in matters of environmental policy, where the Nordic parties are considerably more environment-oriented.

Trends in electoral support

Figure 2.2 shows the trends in support for the Radical Left in the Nordic countries. The figure includes Communists, various Left Socialist splinter parties and the main Left Socialist parties. The larger support for the Communists in Denmark, Norway and Sweden in the 1940s reflects sympathy for the Communists and the Soviet Union in the first election after the Second World War. Until the 1980s, there was a clear division between Finland and Iceland compared with the other three Nordic countries. The Radical Left was much stronger in the former countries and generally stronger in Finland than in Iceland. Commencing in the 1970s, there was a strong decline in support for the Finnish Communists, and a similar decline occurred in Iceland from the 1980s. Support for the Icelandic Left Socialists seems to be much more stable and at a considerably higher level than in Finland in recent decades. On the other hand, there was an increase in support for the Left Socialists from the 1950s in Denmark, Norway and Sweden. This increase was most pronounced in Denmark and then Norway, but much more moderate in Sweden. Support for the Danish radical left peaked in the 1980s but is nearly at the same level in 2010–16, while there is a peak 2000–09 in Norway. The support for the Left Socialists is generally lowest in Sweden.

The mean for the five countries reflects the general trend, and is very stable around 10–12 % throughout the post-war period. There were nevertheless wide comparative changes in electoral support. There was a strong decline in Finland (13 percentage points), a small decline in Iceland (2), a small increase in Sweden (3) and some larger increases in Denmark and Norway (6–7).

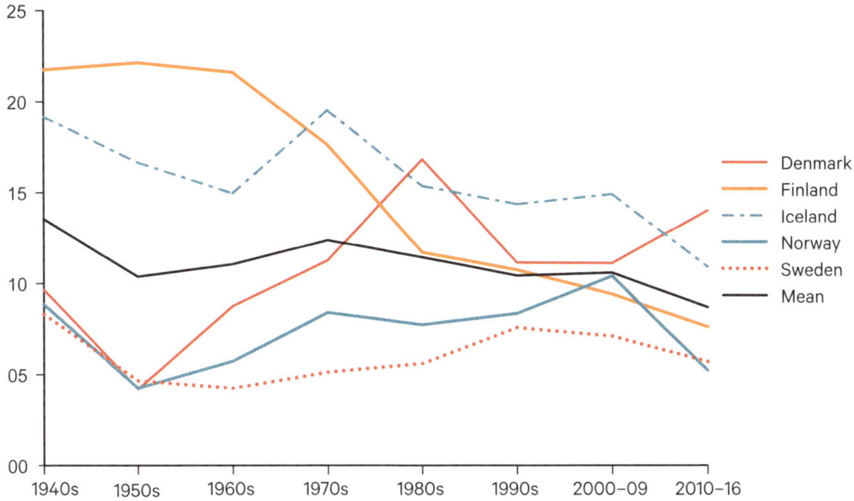

Figure 2.2 Trends in support for Left Socialist Parties (incl. Communists)

CONSERVATIVE PARTIES

In the Nordic countries, the Conservative parties became the standard-bearers for the rightist location on the economic left–right dimension, defending the economic interests of employers and the higher new middle class. These parties generally became the largest non-socialist party in each country with a distinct profile, and have become the main opponents to the Social Democrats with the Danish party as an exception from the 1990s.

Unlike the Conservative Party in Britain, the Nordic Conservatives have not been able to bring about an alliance of urban and rural elites (Lipset and Rokkan 1967: 41–42). The parties have been denied significant support from the rural population, first by the Old Left parties and then by the emerging Agrarian parties.

The Conservative parties focus first and foremost on economic issues, positioning themselves to the right and with strong opposition to aspects of the economic regulation and the high-tax policy of the Social Democrats. On the other hand, they have come to accept the basic principles of the established welfare state in the region. They nevertheless resist comprehensive economic reforms and increases in collective influences over production and investment. The right to own private property provides the basis for a market economy and for freedom and prosperity according to the Nordic Conservatives.

The Finnish Conservatives, the National Coalition Party, received considerably less support than the Social Democrats, Agrarians and Communists in the 1950s and 1960s. From 1966 to 1987 the party was not permitted to participate in government. However, since the 1980s this party has emerged as the one of the largest parties together with the Social Democrats and Agrarians.

The Danish Conservatives both cooperate and compete with the Agrarian Liberals. The two parties have been located fairly similarly to the right on the economic left–right dimension. The party had some of its most successful elections during the 1980s, but thereafter support has declined dramatically.

The Norwegian Conservative Party has been the dominant non-leftist party in nearly all elections after World War II. The exceptions are a few elections in the 1990s and the 2000s where the radical rightist Progress Party has received higher support.

The Swedish Conservatives competed for several decades with the Liberal and Agrarian parties to be the largest non-leftist party. Only since the 1980s has the Conservative Party established itself as the largest non-leftist party with considerably higher support than in previous decades.

In Iceland, the parties on the right joined forces in 1929 when the Independence Party (IP) was formed following a merger of the Conservative and Liberal parties. IP was a combination of elements of liberalism and conservatism, with an emphasis on nationalism and opposition to class conflicts in contrast to the Social Democratic Party and the agrarian Progressive Party. The party's policy orientations have developed from economic liberalism in the 1930s to an acceptance of the welfare state and favouring state intervention and protectionism. It has been characterised as a 'catch-all' party, also with considerable support among the working class (Arter 2008b: 90–92). It was also the largest party in Icelandic politics in all elections except the 2009 election, and had in many ways the same dominant role in the party system as the Social Democrats in Norway and Sweden and partly also Denmark.

Location in the policy space

The Conservative parties are clearly the most rightist parties on economic left–right issues in all five Nordic countries. They are clearly more to the right of even the Radical Rightist parties. With regard to moral and religious issues, they are not 'conservative' in a traditional sense. In addition to the Christian parties, the Radical Rightist and Agrarian parties have more restrictive positions on moral issues. Regarding environmental policy, the Conservatives are clearly located close to the anti-environmental pole together with the Radical Right. The Conservatives are also in favour of a restrictive immigration policy. Only the Radical Rightist parties have a more restrictive position, but the distance between the Conservative and the Radical Right is fairly large. This is strongly confirmed also in a comparative context. There are no Conservative parties in Central Europe. Consequently, we compare parties in Southern Europe and Britain. There are generally small distances between the Conservative parties in the Nordic countries and in these regions although the Nordic parties are somewhat more rightist on the economic left-right scale and somewhat less restrictive regarding immigration. On the moral dimension, however, there are large differences. The Nordic Conservatives are considerably less restrictive than the British Conservatives and the Conservative parties in Southern Europe.

Trends in electoral support

Figure 2.3 shows the outstanding position of the Icelandic Independence Party regarding support. Support has, however, declined since the 1990s. For the Danish, Finnish and Norwegian parties there is a peak in support in the 1980s. The Swedish party also increased its support in the 1980s but this high level of support continued after the 1980s in contrast to support in the other parties. The Norwegian and Swedish parties also received greater support in 2010–16 than in previous decades. The strong decline in support for the Danish Conservatives from the 1980s onwards is remarkable.

When we compare the 1950s with 2000–09, the trends in support for the Conservatives are quite different: the Finnish and Swedish parties have increased their support with 6 and 5 percentage points respectively, while support for the Norwegian party has remained fairly stable (-1). The Icelandic (-9) and the Danish (-7) parties have clearly received less support over time. Concerning the Norwegian party, it should be emphasised that average support has been higher than in the 1950s in all other decades until the period 2000–09.

On average, support for the Conservative parties has been remarkably stable. The change from the 1950s to the 2000s is small, from 21 % to 20 %, with support peaking at 25 % in the 1980s. Even when the strong decline in support

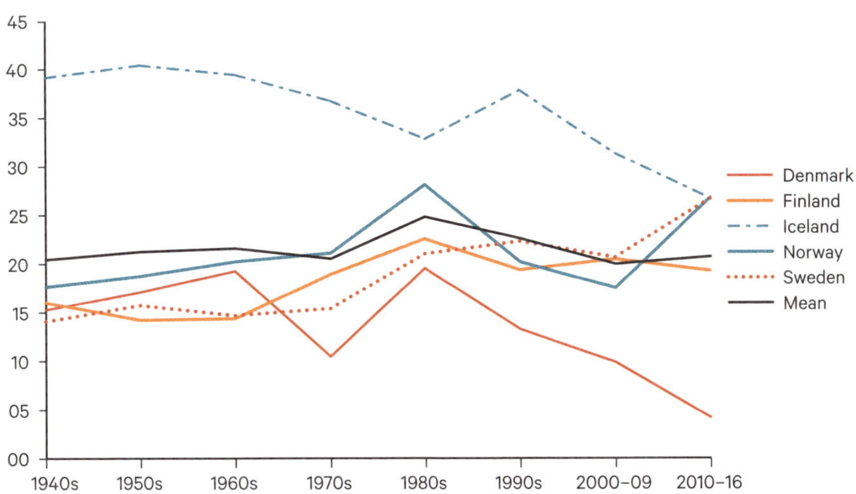

Figure 2.3 Trends in support for Conservative parties

for the Icelandic Independence Party is excluded, average support throughout the post-war period was between 17 % and 19 %.

LIBERAL PARTIES

Twentieth-century Scandinavian liberalism was a descendant of the parties of the 'old' non-socialist Left. From a position as leading parliamentary force prior to 1915, these parties lost significant ground. In several countries, the Agrarian and Christian parties have emerged from splits and have taken many of their voters.

Historically, the Liberal parties in the Nordic countries have been anchored in the religious segment of the population, and following the emergence of the Labour parties have been located towards the centre on the economic left–right axis. The Liberal parties are then more social-liberal than economic-liberal, and also identity themselves as such. They have a strong ideological commitment to a mixed economy, with support for comprehensive but market-based welfare state programmes. This can be contrasted with the Liberal parties in Continental European countries, which have been secular and economically right-wing (Steed and Humphreys 1988: 412–417). Today the Liberal parties are more secular and liberal in moral issues.

The Liberal parties have had difficulties in finding a distinct political identity in the post-war period. They have been located in the centre between the Conservatives and the Social Democrats, and have not been anchored in distinct organisations such as is the case with the Christian and Agrarian parties.

The Swedish Liberal Party had a revival period after the Second World War and was in several elections the largest opposition party to the Social Democratic governments. Support was to decline considerably later (see below).

In Norway, the Liberal Party was split on the issue of EU membership in the early 1970s and support declined considerably. Since the 1970s, the party has focused on environmental issues and attempted to be identified as an environmental party.

The Finnish Liberal Party has retained only minor support in the post-war period and has ceased to be part of the political scene. In a historical perspective, the demise of the Finnish Liberal party is considered to be the most significant long-term change in the Finnish party system (Karvonen 2014: 24).

In Iceland, a new Liberal party emerged prior to the 1999 election, attaching importance to reforms in fishery management. A fishing-quota system had been established and many considered the system of selling and buying quotas unfair (Hardarson and Kristinsson 2001: 327). The Liberal Party emerged as a protest to this system and received between 4 % and 7 % of the votes in the subsequent elections, but failed to be represented in the Althing in the 2009 election. However, before the 2013 election, another party was founded – Bright Future – which defined itself as liberal and gained representation in the Icelandic parliament.

Liberalism and Agrarianism in Denmark

In Denmark, two parties refer to themselves as 'liberal': the (Agrarian) Liberal and the Radical (or Social) Liberals.[6]

The Agrarian Liberals (Venstre) is a deviant case among Nordic Agrarian parties. The party adopted its present name in 1910, but its forerunner was formed in 1870. The party has not changed its name to a Centre Party, and although the name of the party means 'Left', it is more to the right than the other Agrarian parties. In 1970 the party added 'Denmark's Liberal party' to its name in an attempt to broaden its appeal. The party has, however, been a genuine farmer's party from the time of the forerunner's foundation and remained essentially an agrarian party until the 1980s. The reason for its more rightist orientation in economic issues is that the Danish rural class structure was dominated by medium-sized farmers rather than smallholders, and that agriculture in Denmark was export-oriented. From the late 1980s, the party used neo-liberal rhetoric, emphasised rightist economic issues, and located itself even to the right of the Conservatives. Since the mid-1990s, the party has been indisputably the largest non-socialist party with the exception of the 2015 election.

The Radical Liberals (also called Social Liberals) broke away from Venstre in 1905, partly due to economic conflicts between the larger farmers and the smallholders, and partly because of defence spending. The Radical Liberals party is located towards the centre on the economic left–right dimension and for a long period (1929–1964) was closely aligned with the Social Democrats. The Agrarian Liberals, on the other hand, has clearly located itself as a rightist liberal party, close to the Conservative Party on the economic left–right dimension.

In the following, the Radical Liberals will be considered as the Liberal Party in Denmark, and the Agrarian Liberals as an Agrarian party, but calculations for the Agrarian party family will be undertaken without the Danish party when it deviates from the other parties.

Location in the policy space

The Liberal parties as well as the Christian and Agrarian parties are centrist parties, located between the Social Democrats and the Conservatives on the economic left–right dimension. The Liberal parties are generally somewhat more rightist than the Christian and Agrarian parties.

The Liberal parties are today liberal and secular on moral and religious issues. In Denmark and Sweden they are clearly more liberal than the Social Democrats. With regard to environmental orientations there are large differences: the Danish and Norwegian parties are among the most pro-environmental parties in their respective party systems while the Swedish party is much closer

6 This section is based on the more detailed analyses in Andersen and Jensen (2001) and Thomas (1988).

to the anti-environmental pole. With regard to immigration issues, all Liberal parties have a liberal immigration profile. Only the Greens and the Left Socialists have a more liberal profile.

As indicated above, the Nordic Liberal parties are quite distinct in a comparative perspective, but not exactly in the same way as indicated by more historical material. In the 2000s, there are small differences regarding moral issues, but on the other policy dimensions there are considerable differences: the Nordic parties are much more pro-environment and liberal in immigration policy, and to the left of the fairly rightist orientations of the Liberal parties on the economic left–right dimension.

Trends in electoral support

Figure 2.4 shows trends in support for the Liberal parties.[7] The figure shows that support for the Liberal Party in Sweden is outstanding, but has declined significantly. Support for the Norwegian party has also declined considerably while the Danish party has had fairly stable support and has partly recovered from low support in the 1980s and 1990s.

The average decline for the Liberal parties in the four relevant countries indicates the declining importance of the Liberal parties in Nordic politics, from 12 % in the 1950s to 5 % in 2000–09. It should be emphasised that the conclusion would be somewhat different if the Danish Agrarian Liberal party had been included in the Liberal party family for Denmark.

AGRARIAN PARTIES

According to Lipset and Rokkan (1967: 45), strong Agrarian parties appear to have emerged in countries or provinces where:

- cities and industrial centres were still small at the time when suffrage was extended,
- the bulk of the agrarian populations were active in family-size farming and either owned their farms themselves or were legally protected lease-holders largely independent of socially superior landowners,
- there were important cultural barriers between the countryside and the cities and much resistance to the incorporation of farm production in the capitalist economy of the cities,
- the Catholic Church had no influence.

The first condition is related to the level of urbanisation and industrialisation; the second concerns the social structure of the farm population; the third con-

7 The mean is based on four parties, excluding the Icelandic Liberal Party which was only significant in a few elections.

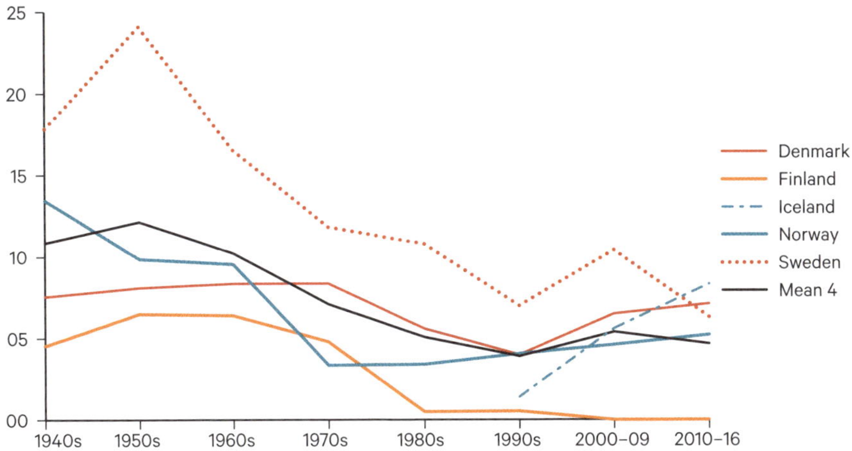

Figure 2.4 Trends in support for Liberal parties

cerns the cultural differences along an urban–rural conflict line; and the fourth is associated with the fact that Catholicism has been an important force for mobilising the support of the agrarian population for Christian or Catholic parties, a competing party family.

The Agrarian parties are a particular feature of the Nordic five-party system model in a comparative perspective. Agrarian parties also emerged in other European countries both before and after the First World War. The notable characteristic of the Nordic parties was their durability and survival in predominantly industrialised and also post-industrial societies.

The Agrarian parties were essentially interest groups or farmers' parties which promoted the class interests of the agricultural producers and workers at varying stages of integration into the capitalist economy. Major concerns were to maintain the level of prices for agricultural products, to ensure protection for the home market against the import of cheap foreign grains, to promote land reform, and to secure the provision of credit facilities.[8]

Between 1957 and 1965 the Agrarian parties in Finland, Norway and Sweden changed their names to Centre parties with the aim of gaining electoral support from new social groups.[9]

The Finnish party is the most significant Agrarian party in size and influence. It has been described as a genuine pivot party or hinge group since it was the dominant governing party for a long time. Until the 1960s, it was the

8 This does not apply to the Danish party which has been dealt with under the review of Liberal parties above.

9 The review of the parties below is partly based on a detailed analysis of the various contributions in Arter (2001a).

Agrarians party, not the Social Democrats, which was the natural governing party in Finland. The party played a significant role in the completion of Finnish state building in a comprehensive land reform in the 1920s, and in the resettlement of the displaced Karelian population after the wars with the Soviet Union (Arter 2001b: 169).

The Swedish Agrarian Party had considerable electoral success in the late 1960s and 1970s. The party broadened its profile to include regional and environmental interests, and became the main party opposing nuclear energy. The strategy was successful and in four elections between 1968 and 1976, the party was the largest non-leftist party, a position it took over from the Liberals. The nuclear policy was not successful and the party was not able to persuade the other non-leftist parties to endorse its stance. Consequently, support declined considerably from the early 1980s onwards.

The Norwegian agrarian party has been a leading opponent of EU integration and enjoyed increased support in connection with elections close to the EU referendums in 1972 and 1994. But the party has not been able to integrate anti-EU interests into a broad permanent coalition after the referendums and subsequent general elections. The Norwegian party has relocated to a centre-left position since the early 2000s and moved closer to the leftist parties.

Location in the policy space

The Agrarian parties are centrist parties as is evident on the economic left–right dimension. The exception is the Danish Agrarian Liberal Party, which is located close to the Conservative Party towards the rightist pole. The parties in Finland, Iceland and Norway are clearly closer to the Social Democrats than to the Conservative parties on economic left–right policy, while the Swedish Party seems to be located mid-way between the Conservatives and the Social Democrats. The Norwegian and the Finnish parties are those closest to the Social Democrats.

On moral issues, the Agrarian parties are located moderately towards the restrictive pole, and are generally somewhat more restrictive than the Conservatives, but much less so than the Christian parties. On environmental issues, the Agrarian parties are located close to the centre: they do not occupy a 'green' position. The Norwegian and Swedish parties have a much more green policy than the Danish and Icelandic parties, placing the Finnish party in a median position among the Agrarian parties. Regarding immigration policy, the Agrarians are moderately restrictive, far from the Radical Right, but nevertheless somewhat more restrictive than the Christian and Social Democratic parties.

Trends in electoral support

Figure 2.5, which depicts the trends in support for the Agrarian parties, shows considerable fluctuation over time as well as differences between the countries.

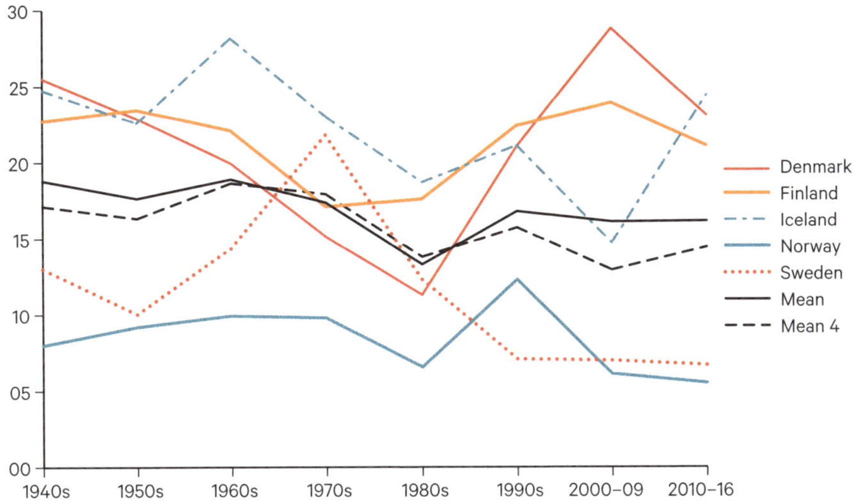

Figure 2.5 Trends in support for Agrarian Parties

The patterns in the figure can be decomposed as follows:

Support for the Agrarian parties is generally larger in Denmark, Finland and Iceland than in Norway and Sweden.

Support for the Agrarian Liberals declined strongly to the 1980s, increasing in 2000–09, thereafter declining again.

Support for Finnish and Icelandic parties has been more stable, although support for the Icelandic party declined considerably in the elections during 2000–09, but increased in 2010–16.

When support in the 1950s is compared with that of 2000–09, national variations are clearly manifest. Support increased by 6 percentage points in Denmark over the period and remained stable in Finland. In Norway and Sweden, support declined by 3 percentage points and as much as 8 in Iceland.

Mean support with and without the Danish party has been calculated. Based on the average for all five parties support has been fairly stable and the decline is small, from 18 % in the 1950s to 16 % in the 2000s (two percentage points). When the Danish party is excluded the decline is marginally larger, from 16 % to 13 % (three percentage points).

DEVIATIONS FROM THE FIVE-PARTY SYSTEM MODEL UNTIL THE 1970S

If we consider the party systems of the 1960s,[10] prior to the major changes that took place in these systems, there are three main deviations from the five-party system model.

The first concerns the Swedish People's Party, which was established in 1906 to defend the Swedish-speaking minority's cultural and language interests. This is an ethnic-regional party which is not part of the five-party system model. The party has been highly successful in mobilising the Swedish-speaking population. The Social Democrats also tried to appeal to the Swedish-speaking vote and established a bilingual organisational structure. It subsequently received a significant part of the votes of the Swedish-speaking working class. The two main bourgeois parties, the Conservatives and the Agrarians, were opposed to special language rights for minorities (Arter 2008b: 63–66; Karvonen 2014: 21).

The Swedish People's Party is fairly rightist on economic policy, located midway between the Conservatives and the Agrarian and Christian parties in Finland. The party is liberal regarding moral and immigration policy, and fairly centrist concerning environmental policy.

The second deviation from the five-party system model is the existence of a Christian party with significant electoral support in Norway (see below). The third deviation is the absence of a Liberal party in Iceland as described above.

THE NEW PARTIES AND PARTY FAMILIES

The new parties can be grouped into the Religious, Radical Right and Green party families. The Left Socialists can also be considered as a new party family, but here we have considered these parties as a party family within the five-party model as part of the radical left force which has gradually replaced the Communists as the main force within the radical left. Other parties and formations have emerged but most have been short-lived; these are not discussed here.

THE RELIGIOUS PARTIES[11]

The Nordic countries are religiously homogeneous. The starting point for understanding the relationship between religion and politics in the Nordic countries is the fact that the dominant religion since the Reformation has been Lutheran Protestantism. The classic form of church–state relations in Scandinavia dates back to the Reformation when the influence of the Catholic

---

10 Support for the parties in the five-party system model was on average 95 % in the 1960s, varying from 98 % in Iceland and Sweden, to 95 % in Denmark and 91 % in Finland and Norway (see Figure 2.8).

11 The discussion of the religious parties is based on Karvonen (1994), Madeley (1982, 2000, 2004) and Elder, Thomas and Arter (1982).

Church was markedly reduced. This implied that the churches were no longer independent of the state and were not able to form a basis for a mobilisation against the state in its attempts to take over the functions and activities which the Church had performed in other countries, such as religious education. Conflicts associated with the national revolution consequently failed to produce a sharp religious cleavage or conflict, and religious parties generally did not emerge. Religious voters were, however, a central component in the 'Left' coalitions in opposition to the established power holders who – in the words of Lipset and Rokkan – 'recruited decisive support among orthodox Protestants in a variety of sectarian movements outside and inside the national churches' (Lipset and Rokkan 1967: 38).

The Norwegian Christian Party constitutes a special case among the Nordic Christian parties due to its longer history and relatively stronger electoral position. This party was established in 1933 in Western Norway and prior to World War II was mainly a regional party. It rose to national significance in the post-war period – a position it has been able to retain even though support has declined. In the other Nordic countries, Religious parties were established in 1958 (Finland), 1964 (Sweden) and 1970 (Denmark).[12] There is no significant Religious party in Iceland.

The Religious parties emerged as protest parties against secularisation trends and perceived threats to religious values and interests. The Norwegian party became the model, which largely set the standard for the programmatic orientations of the other parties.

The Religious parties did not represent official standpoints of the Lutheran state churches or the general opinion of church members. The centre of gravity lay among nonconformists and revivalist groups and also with lay activists within the Lutheran state churches. The leadership of the Christian parties drew heavily on the various Low Church revivalist organisations within the Evangelical Lutheran Church as well as non-conformist groups such as the Baptists and the Pentecostalists outside it (Elder, Thomas and Arter 1982: 67–69).

The parties were not 'Christian Democratic' in the sense that they tried to gain support among Christians with a variety of interests and values. Their policy along the religious–secular dimension has been more deviant in relation to the other parties in their respective party systems than the Christian Democratic parties in the Continental European countries.

12 The names of the parties were the Christian People's Party in Denmark and Norway and Christian League in Finland. The Swedish party was originally called the Christian Democratic Rally, but changed its name to Christian Democratic Social Party in 1991. From 1996 to 2003 the parties in Denmark, Finland and Sweden changed party names to Christian Democrats. Only the Norwegian Party has kept its original name.

Location in the policy space

The Christian parties are considered centrist parties due to their location between the Conservatives and the Social Democrats on the important economic left–right dimension. According to the expert surveys, they are closer to the Social Democrats in Denmark, Finland and Norway, but more right-oriented towards the Conservatives in Sweden. On the moral dimension, they clearly have the most restrictive position compared with all other parties in the respective countries. The policy distance, both to the Radical Right and the Conservatives, is large. The Christian parties have developed fairly green policies and are located closer to the green pole than the Social Democrats with the Swedish party as a clear exception. They have a centrist policy regarding immigration orientations.

Compared with the larger Christian parties in Central Europe, the Nordic parties are quite distinct: they have a more leftist and green policy and a less restrictive policy towards immigration. On the other hand, they are considerably more restrictive regarding moral policy compared with their continental sister parties.

Trends in electoral support

Figure 2.6 shows the level of support for the Christian parties in the various general elections. It reflects that the support for the Christian parties is very low with the exception of the Norwegian party. The support for this party was largest in the 1970s and in 1997 and 2001, but subsequently declined sharply. Support for the Swedish and Finnish parties increased considerably in the 1990s and 2000s, but subsequently declined. Electoral support for the Swedish party approached the level experienced by the Norwegian party from around 2000 such that the latter is no longer exceptional with regard to electoral strength. Electoral support for the Danish party has declined from a low level to insignificance in Danish politics.

THE RADICAL RIGHTIST PARTIES

The Radical Rightist parties in Denmark, Finland and Norway have emerged with different issues dominating their agenda. They have gradually been transformed into Radical Rightist parties with an anti-immigration profile; all have changed their name. The history of the parties is briefly reviewed in the following.

The Danish and Norwegian parties emerged in the early 1970s as anti-tax and anti-bureaucracy parties, protesting against the post-war consensus on the welfare state, regulations and high levels of taxation.[13] The Danish party was called the Progress Party, a name which was also adopted by the Norwegian party in 1977, which had previously had a longer name within which the

13 For a thorough analysis of the Danish and Norwegian Radical Right, see Andersen and Bjørklund (2000).

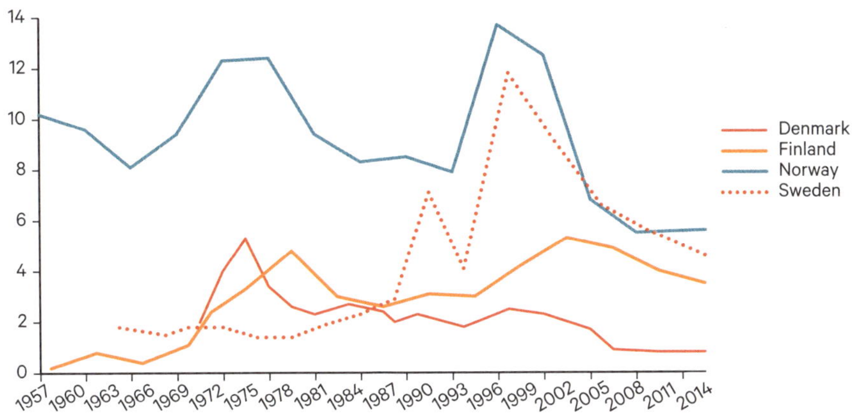

Figure 2.6 Electoral support for the Christian parties, 1955–2015

name of the founder was incorporated.[14] The parties adopted anti-immigration issues as a main theme in the late 1980s. For the Norwegian party, the focus on immigration issues contributed to electoral success almost immediately. The Danish party split in 1995, and the Danish People's Party was founded as a breakaway faction of the Progress Party. The new party had almost immediate electoral success and the Progress Party disappeared from the political landscape. According to Rydgren (2004), the Danish People's Party is a pure Radical Rightist party in contrast to its predecessor.

In Finland, the background for the present True Finns party was an agrarian protest which resulted in a splinter party from the Agrarian Party in in 1959 (Smallholders' Party). The party took on a new name in 1966 – the Finnish Rural Party. The main issue of the party's policy was the interests of poor smaller farmers in the peripheral areas who had been heavily hit by the programme of rationalisation. The party made an electoral breakthrough in 1970 in the Finnish 'earthquake election' which preceded the more well-known 'earthquake elections' in Denmark and Norway in 1973. The party challenged the Agrarian party, which had participated in the governments and was responsible for the rationalisation programmes. The party retrieved its electoral success in 1983 and participated in governments during the 1980s. Cabinet responsibilities weakened its anti-establishment profile and the Finnish Rural Party disappeared from the political scene in 1995. The True Finns party was established the same year and can best be viewed as a successor party to the Rural Party; nearly all founding members came from the Rural Party (Arter 2010: 485). The party also used some of the same anti-establishment rhetoric as its predecessor.

---

14 The name was 'Anders Lange's Party for a Strong Reduction in Taxes, Duties and Public Intervention'.

The party focuses on anti-immigration issues, and a weaker and less ubiquitous European Union, but at the same time is centre-leftist regarding economic issues (Arter 2010: 494–496; Karvonen 2014: 22).

In Sweden, a populist and Radical Rightist party, New Democracy, emerged and gained parliamentary representation in the 1991 election, but this was a flash party and failed to survive the next election in 1994. Another party, Sweden Democrats, was founded in the late 1980s. This party was deeply embedded in far right networks and did not receive significant electoral support during the 1990s. During the period 2000–2009, the party gained some support in local and national elections, but the breakthrough came in the 2010 election when it passed the 4 % hurdle and achieved parliamentary representation.

Location in the policy space

The expert data do not contain information on the Swedish party, which was insignificant at the time when the data were collected. As for the economic left-right dimension, the Radical Right in Denmark and Finland have a centrist position close to the Radical Liberals in Denmark and the Agrarian Party in Finland. The Norwegian party has a more rightist position, but to the left of the Conservative Party. On moral issues, the Finnish party is nearly as restrictive as the Christian Party, while there is a larger distance between these parties in Denmark. In Norway, there is a large distance between the Christian Party and the Radical Right. The Norwegian party is considerably less restrictive than its sister parties in Denmark and Finland. Concerning position on environmental issues, the Radical Rightist parties clearly belong to parties that take anti-environmental standpoints. The Norwegian party is the most anti-environmental party in Norway while the Danish People's Party has a similar position to the Conservatives and Agrarian Liberals. The Finnish party is less anti-environmental than the Conservatives, with a location similar to the Social Democrats. All Radical Rightist parties have positions that are most restrictive regarding immigration policy. In Finland and Norway there is a large distance between the Radical Right and all other parties, while in Denmark the distance is smaller to the Conservatives and the Agrarian Liberals due to the more restrictive positions of these parties.

Compared with the Radical Rightist parties in Central Europe, the Nordic parties are more centrist on the economic left–right dimension and considerably less restrictive on moral issues. However, the Nordic parties share the anti-environment and restrictive immigration policies with parties in the same party family in Central Europe.

Trends in electoral support

Figure 2.7 shows electoral support for the Radical Rightist parties. Support for the predecessors of the True Finns is also included because there are clearly some of the same populist and anti-establishment traits there as in the Radical

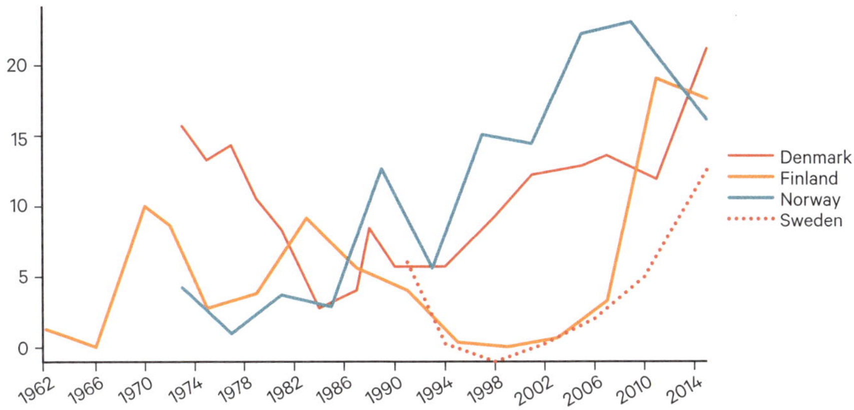

Figure 2.7 Support for the Radical Right, 1962–2015

Right. The figure shows the significance of the 'earthquake elections' in Finland (1970), Norway (1973) and especially Denmark (1973).

The Danish Radical Right declined significantly from 1977 to 1984 and remained small (apart from the 1988 election) until the Danish People's Party became the dominant Radical Rightist party in the late 1990s.

Some of the same decline applies to the Norwegian party, but since the support was comparatively low in the first election, the decline is less significant. The decisive breakthrough for the party was in the 1989 election and support has remained at a high level since, apart from the 1993 election.

The Finnish party had a new peak in support in 1983 following the strong support seen in the early 1970s. It subsequently declined. The breakthrough in the 2011 election is clearly manifest. The breakthrough for the Sweden Democrats is clearly seen in the 2010 and 2014 elections.

THE GREEN PARTIES

For a long time, Green parties only were significant in Finland and Sweden.[15] Green candidates were already standing for election in these countries in the 1970s. The Swedish Green Party was established in 1981, while the Finnish party was established as late as 1988.

The background for the establishment of the Swedish party was the failure of the Centre Party to live up to its promise to withhold approval for the operation of new nuclear power reactors. The referendum on the future of nuclear power energy in 1980, with the alternative of the anti-nuclear policy, was defeated by a small margin. There was a demand for a Green party given these events. The

15 The discussion of Finnish and Swedish Green parties is to a large extent based on Bolin (2016).

party had its electoral breakthrough in 1988 when it was represented in the Swedish Riksdag for the first time.

The Green movement in Finland was fragmented and there was also scepticism concerning the formation of a political party. Instead, a voters' association was established which participated in the 1983 election, gaining two representatives in parliament. Resistance to the party form became weaker and the Green League was founded. This party was to have considerable electoral success.

In Norway and Denmark, Green parties have not had electoral success. One important reason for this has been that the Left Socialist parties in these countries, which are not successor parties of Communist parties, have focused on green and alternative issues. The Norwegian Green Party was established in the late 1980s, but received less than 0.5 % support in general elections until 2013 when it finally won representation in the national parliament.

In Denmark, a Green party was established in 1983. The party only participated in the general elections in 1987, 1988 and 1990 and received little support (between 0.9 % and 1.4 %), and has been insignificant for a long time. However, in 2013 a new party – the Alternative – was formed by two members of the parliamentary group of the Radical Liberal party. The party defines itself as a green alternative and received considerable electoral success in the 2015 election.

Location in the policy space

The data set contains locations of only the Finnish and Swedish Green parties. On the economic left–right dimension, these two parties are located clearly to the left. The Swedish party is at about the same position as the Social Democrats while the Finnish Green Party is to the left of the Social Democrats. The parties are, however, clearly to the right of the Left Socialist parties.

Concerning moral issues, the Finnish party is clearly the least restrictive of all the Finnish parties while the Swedish party is the next least restrictive, surpassed only by the Left Socialists. The two parties are decisively closest to the Green pole compared with all other parties in their respective party systems; they are also the most liberal regarding immigration policy together with the Left Socialists. The Finnish party is clearly more liberal than the Left Socialists, while the Swedish Left Socialists are somewhat more liberal than the Greens.

There are interesting differences between these parties and the Greens in Central Europe. The parties share the position close to the Green pole on the environmental dimension; on the other dimensions there are some significant differences. On economic policy, the Nordic Greens are located in a somewhat more moderate leftist position. They are generally less liberal in moral issues and also regarding immigration policy.

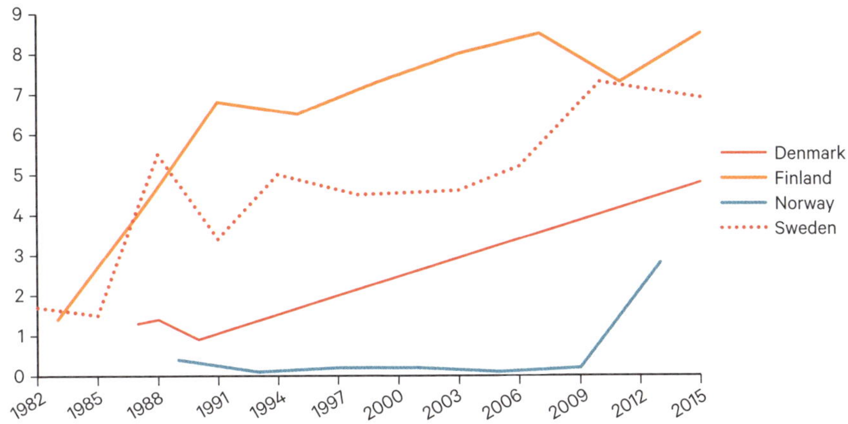

Figure 2.8 Electoral support for Green parties, 1982–2015

Trends in electoral support

Figure 2.8 shows that the Green parties have generally increased their electoral support. Finnish Greens tend to have received larger support than the Swedish party, particularly in the 1990s and up to the late 2000s.

SPECIAL TRAITS FOR THE PARTY SYSTEMS IN EACH COUNTRY

This section characterises the special traits of the party system in each of the Nordic countries and is to a large extent based on the characteristics of the party families above.

Denmark

- Less support for the Social Democrats than in Sweden and Norway
- Strong and politically fragmented left socialist force in the 1970s and 1980s
- 'Strange' Agrarian Party (the Agrarian Liberal Party) which is anchored in both Liberalism and Agrarianism
- Many new parties in the Folketing after the 'earthquake' election in 1973
- Small but influential centre upon which many governments have been dependent
- Strong Radical Rightist force, the Progress Party (1973 – ca. 1995); from 1995, the Danish People's Party
- A basic deviation from previous patterns from 2001 to 2011: minority governments comprising Agrarian Liberals and Conservatives, with support from the Danish People's Party, not the centre parties.

Finland

- Agrarian/Centre party's strength and central position. The party has been considered as a nation-building party

- Strong support for the Communist party (and alliances) until the 1970s
- Small and since the 1990s insignificant Liberal party
- Ethnic/language party for the Swedish-speaking minority: the Swedish People's Party.

Iceland

- Partly dominant Conservative party, the Independence Party
- Only one party in the centre, the Agrarian Progress Party
- Comparatively weak and fragmented left-wing parties, Social Democrats and the People's Alliance; the People's Alliance has regularly been the larger of the two until 1999
- The Women's Alliance 1983–99
- Change in the party system before the 1999 election
- Merging of the three parties on the left (Social Democrats, People's Alliance and Women's Alliance) to the (Social Democratic) Alliance (considered a Social Democratic party)
- Another green-left socialist party was formed from the leftist forces within these parties: the Left Movement – a Green Alternative
- New Liberal party was also formed with opposition to the quota system in the fisheries as the main issue, significant 1999–2007.

Norway

- Early establishment of a Christian party which normally has been stronger than the Christian parties in the other countries
- Significant 'pure' Left Socialist force (Socialist People's Party/Socialist Left Party)
- Significant and fairly stable Radical Rightist force, the Progress Party
- Early weakening (and split) of the Liberal party during the 1970s
- Fairly weak Agrarian Party, comparatively speaking
- Great instability of the party system 1989- 2005.

Sweden

- High degree of stability in the party system
- Dominant position of the Social Democrats
- Left Socialist party important for the formation of governments although electoral support has been modest
- Large change in support for the non-socialist parties. The Conservative party has been the largest non-socialist party from 1979. The Liberals and/or the Agrarians were larger before 1979
- No significant Radical Rightist force apart from 1991–94 and since 2010
- Major political change 2006–14 with stronger support for the Conservatives and the non-socialist parties.

TRENDS IN THE DEVELOPMENT OF THE PARTY SYSTEMS[16]

It has been seen that new parties have emerged and gained significant electoral support. In this way, the five-party system model has been challenged, but how serious is this challenge? One way of examining this is to study the overall support for the parties in the five-party model.

Figure 2.9 shows support for the five-party system model for the various decades. The main trend is that the five-party system model is challenged, meaning that overall support for the five-party families has declined. On the other hand, most voters still support the parties in the model. From the 1950s to the 2000s, support for the five-party families has declined from an average of 94 % to 81 %. There is, however, a further decline to 71 % based on the data from 2000–16.

In the 1950s, support for the five-party model was 100 % in Sweden, 92–95 % in Denmark, Iceland and Finland and 90 % in Norway. In the 2000s, support was highest in Iceland (96 %), followed by Sweden (83 %), Denmark (81 %), Finland (77 %) and Norway (68 %). The decline in the overall support for the five-party system model is largest in Norway (22 percentage points), then Sweden (17), Finland (16) and Denmark (12), while support for the five-party system model has increased by 1 percentage point in Iceland.[17]

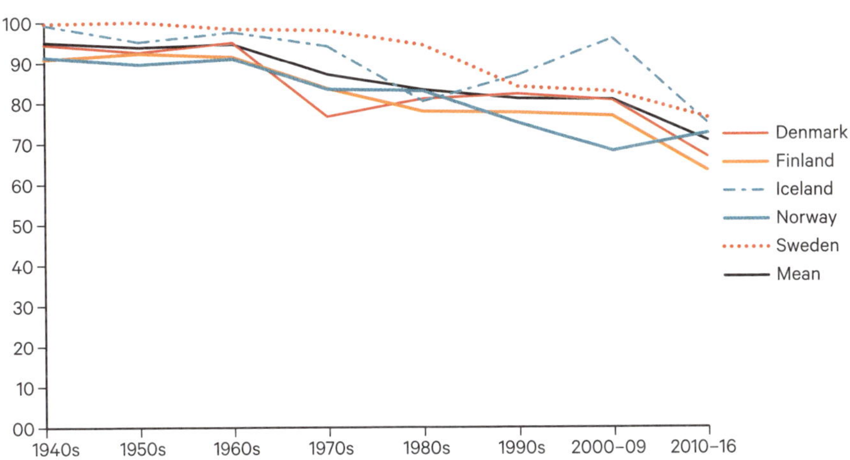

Figure 2.9 Trends in combined support for the parties in the five party model, 1940s–2010s

16 Important analyses of the development of the Nordic party systems are found in Arter (2012), Heidar (2004a) and Sundberg (1999).

17 The comparative figures become very different if we examine changes from the 1950s to the 2010s so far: the decline is smallest in Norway (17) and Iceland (20), but 24–29 in Denmark, Finland and Sweden.

Fragmentation in the party systems refers to the number of significant parties and also takes into account their electoral support. This is frequently measured by the *effective number of parties*. The higher the effective number of parties, the more fragmented the system. Given that we have seen that new parties have gained significant support, we might expect that the Nordic party systems have become more fragmented.

Figure 2.10 shows the trends in the number of effective parties. If we first calculate the average for the various decades in order to obtain an impression of the comparative fragmentation of the party systems, Finland has the most fragmented party system (5.7), followed by Denmark (4.9), Iceland and Norway (4.2–4.3) and Sweden (3.9). It is evident that the party systems have become more fragmented. The average number of effective parties has increased from 3.9 to 5.0 from the 1950s to the 2000s, and to 5.5 in 2010s. The increase in fragmentation in the same period (1950s – 2000s) is largest in Norway (1.8), then Sweden (1.3) and Denmark (1.2), while it is smaller in Finland (0.7) and Iceland (0.5).

Based on average figures, the largest increase in fragmentation took place from the 1960s to the 1970s when the so-called 'earthquake' elections took place in Finland (1970), and in Denmark and Norway (1973). These saw the emergence of the Radical Rightist parties. From the 1970s to the 2000s, fragmentation increased on average from 4.7 to 5.0, significantly in Sweden (1.0) and Norway (0.9), weakly in Iceland (0.3), but declining in Denmark (0.4) and Finland (0.2). We note however, that fragmentation has increased significantly in all countries apart from Norway from the 2000s to the 2010s.

Net electoral volatility is the sum of the changes in support for the various parties from one election to the next. One way of calculating this measure is to

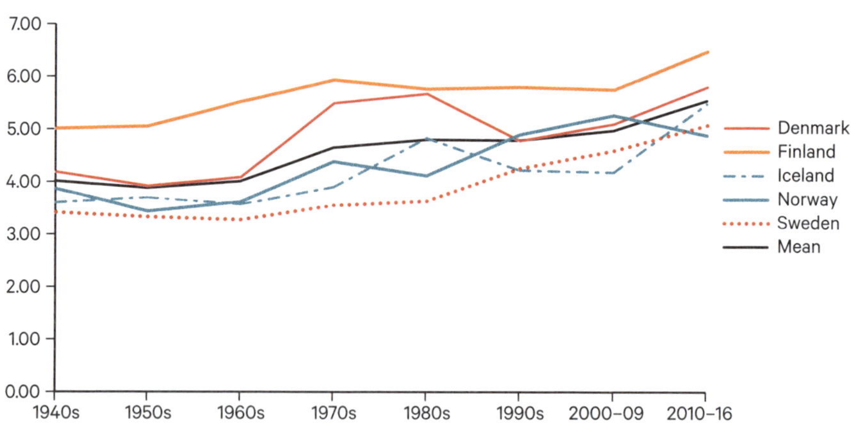

Figure 2.10 Trends in number of effective electoral parties in the Nordic countries, 1940s–2010s

sum up the percentage increase in support for those parties that have received increased support in successive elections, or to sum up the declining support of all parties that experienced a decrease in support.

Electoral volatility indicates instability in the party system and a lack of close identification with a political party on the part of the voters. Given the emergence of new parties that have gained considerably electoral support in the Nordic countries, we can expect increased electoral volatility.

Figure 2.11 shows the trends in electoral volatility. We note first the decline in electoral volatility from the 1940s to the 1950s. This is discussed above. According to the averages for the five countries, there is a small increase from the 1950s to the 1960s, and then a strong increase up to the 1970s. After this, volatility is fairly stable until the 2010s when volatility increases again. The increase in volatility from the 1960s to the 1970s is largest in Denmark and Norway, and then in Iceland. The main explanation is again the earthquake elections, which increased the support for several parties, notable the Radical Right in Denmark and Norway. The average volatility for Denmark and Norway in the 1970s is the highest volatility level for all countries in any decade apart from the extreme volatility in Iceland in the 2010s. From the 1970s to 2000s volatility has declined significantly in Denmark (6.6 percentage points) and somewhat less in Norway (3.7), while the main increase in Sweden took place in this period (8.5 percentage points). The overall trends in volatility from the 1950s to the 2000s are increases in all countries, from just 2 percentage points in Finland, to 5 in Denmark and Iceland and 11 percentage points in Norway and Sweden.

Polarisation in a party system is the distance between the political parties for selected policies. Equivalent scales are not available for all five countries

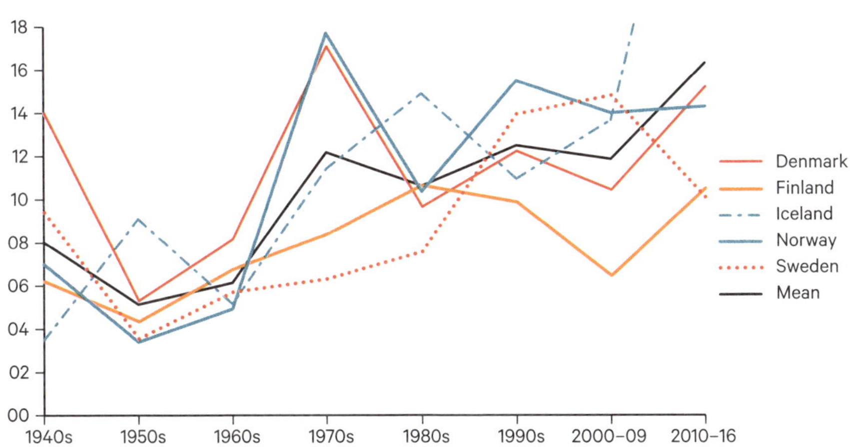

Figure 2.11 Net electoral volatility in the Nordic countries, 1940s–2010s

for the post-war elections. We have instead focused on support for the party families which are considered as representing the poles in the party system, and which have challenged the quite consensual policies of the other party families – the Communists, Left Socialists and Radical Right. It should be emphasised that the Radical Right (at least in recent decades) does not represent the party family that is closest to the rightist pole on the economic left–right dimension, but on other dimensions. Stable policy orientations over time, as assumed by the present polarisation measure, are not very likely. On the other hand, it can be argued that the party families in themselves represent polarising forces with their anti-establishment orientations.

Figure 2.12 shows the trends in polarisation measured in this way. If we first calculate the average level of polarisation for the various decades, polarisation is strongest in Finland (20) followed by Denmark (18), Iceland and Norway (15–16), and finally Sweden (8). Polarisation has increased first and foremost due to increased support for the Radical Right. From the 1950s to the 2000s the average increase is 8 percentage points, from 10 to 18. The increase is 26 in Norway, 20 in Denmark and 5 in Sweden, while there has been a decline in Finland (10) and Iceland (2) due to the declining support for the Left Socialists. We note, however, that polarisation has increased greatly in Finland, Denmark and Sweden from the 2000s to the 2010s. The increased level of polarisation in this period is the result of the large increase in support for the Radical Right in Finland and Sweden, and of the increase in support for both the Radical Right and the Left Socialists (radical left) in Denmark.

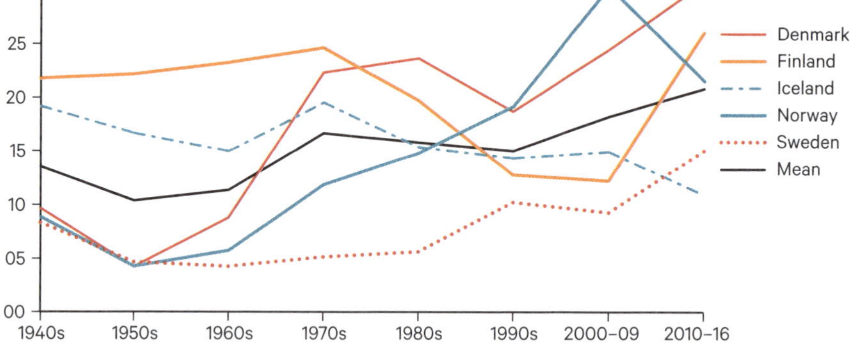

Figure 2.12 Polarisation index for the Nordic countries, 1940s–2010s: Support for the Communists, Left Socialists and Radical Rightist parties.

CONCLUSIONS

The Nordic five-party system model comprises Agrarian parties that are unique compared with the party system elsewhere in Western Europe.

The policy location of the other party families has shown the following main differences between parties in the same party families elsewhere in Western Europe:

The Liberal parties are centre parties between the Conservatives and the Social Democrats. They are not the main rightist party on economic policy as in many Central countries.

The Conservative parties in the Nordic countries are first and foremost located firmly to the right on the economic left–right dimension. On moral and religious issues, they are considerably less restrictive than elsewhere in Western Europe.

Compared with the larger Christian parties in Central Europe, the Nordic parties are quite distinct: they are considerably more restrictive regarding moral policy compared with their continental sister parties. They also have a more leftist and green policy, and a less restrictive policy towards immigration.

Compared with the Radical Rightist parties in Central Europe, the Nordic parties are more centrist on the economic left–right dimension, and considerably less restrictive on moral issues.

The two party families in the five-party model that has declined the most are the Social Democrats and the Liberals by 5 and 7 percentage points respectively, from the 1950s to the 2000s. The decline for the Social Democrats is 10 percentage points when the deviant Icelandic pattern is excluded. For the other party families, long-term support is fairly stable although there are compensating tendencies within the party family. For example, for the Left Socialist parties there is a strong decline for the Finnish party and increases for the Danish and Norwegian parties.

Support for the new party families has increased considerably as might be expected. It is difficult to obtain average data because neither of the party families has made inroads among the Icelandic electorate, and for some of the other countries parties have emerged fairly late. However, the new party families have gained considerable support among the electorate in the last decade. The development of the Radical Right is most pronounced. Based on average scores (for the four relevant countries), they received 6 % support in the 1990s, 9 % in 2000 and as much as 15 % in 2010–16. Altogether, the three new party families increased their support from 15 % in the 1990s, to 19 % in the 2000s, and further to 24 % in 2010–16.

The five-party system model is thus challenged, but it is far from dead. Whereas 94 % of voters supported parties in the model in the 1950s, an average of more than 81 % of voters still supported parties in this model in the 2000s. So far in the 2010s it is evident that there has been a sharp decline from the 2000s.

The party systems in the Nordic countries have become considerably more fragmented over time. The main increase in fragmentation took place from the 1960s til the 1970s, but it continued also after the 1970s.

Net electoral volatility increased significantly from the 1960s to the 1970s and has remained at the same level since.

Polarisation in the party systems is measured by the aggregated support for the right-wing parties, Radical Right, Left Socialists and Communists. First and foremost, due to the increase in support for the Radical Right, polarisation has increased, notably after 2000.

CHAPTER 3
SOCIAL CLEAVAGES AND POLITICAL VALUE CONFLICTS

Oddbjørn Knutsen

INTRODUCTION

This chapter examines important determinants of voting patterns in the Nordic countries, and whether there are particular variables that are significantly more or less important determinants than elsewhere in Western Europe. Two types of variables are focused upon: sociostructural variables and central political value or issue orientations.

Previous comparative research on the impact of sociostructural variables and value orientations has shown that there are some determinants of party choice in the Nordic countries that place them in a special position and could be referred to as a Nordic model, or several Nordic models. These variables are economic interest-based and include social class and economic values and issues. However, some research documenting this is fairly old. Due to the existence of Agrarian parties, urban–rural contrasts in voting behaviour have also been documented to be large in a comparative setting.

This chapter is organised as follows:

First, the impact of the structural variables incorporated in the Lipset-Rokkan model for party choice in industrial societies is examined. Other structural variables such as gender and sector employment are analysed. Focus is then placed on value orientations. Finally, the total impact of social structure and value orientations is reviewed. The main objective is to examine the strength of the relationship between the various variables and party choice, and where voters for the various party families are located on the various conflict variables.[1] Regarding the strength aspect, the variation between the Nordic countries is examined and compared with the other regions in Western Europe. The grouping of the Nordic political parties into party families is based on Chapter

1 This means the average for the party voters on a scale or the percentage of a specific social class that is supported by voters for a party.

2. The same applies to the grouping of countries into regions.[2] The comparisons with the other regions of countries are mainly done by examining average correlations and measures of impact for the various regions.

The empirical data in this chapter are based on many sources. Most important are data from the Nordic election studies and comparative survey data such as the European Social Survey (ESS) and European Values Study (EVS). Cumulative files of the three first rounds of ESS (2002–06) are frequently used because these data have large numbers of respondents. The results are published in Knutsen (2013). A cumulative file based on the first four rounds is also used (2002–08). Generally, EVS (fourth round, 2008–10) is prioritised since all five Nordic countries are included and the author has worked extensively with this data set (Knutsen forthcoming). Iceland is not included in the ESS surveys which are used.

The election studies are valuable sources for examining trends over time, but they commence at very different time points. The oldest are those from Norway and Sweden, originating in the 1950s, while the Danish studies started in 1971, and the Finnish and Icelandic somewhat later. Sometimes only trends from Norway and Sweden are used to illustrate long-term patterns without including the other countries.

THEORIES AND CONCEPTUAL FRAMEWORK

What are social cleavages and political values?

A traditional notion of social cleavage is to consider a cleavage as reflecting broadly-based and long-standing social and economic divisions within society. The political cleavage structure is thought of in terms of social groups, the loyalties of individuals to their social group and how these loyalties influence party choice and political action (Franklin, Mackie, Valen et al.1992: 5).

Political values and basic attitudes are central beliefs held by individuals regarding central policies. These beliefs are frequently discussed according to dimensions or orientations based on theoretical criteria and empirical analyses. These orientations are outlined below under the section on the impact of value orientations.

Stability and change in the impact of social cleavages and value orientations: Stable alignment, dealignment and realignment

One important perspective in Lipset and Rokkan's work (see below) was the persistent impact of social structure on party choice, which they called the 'freezing of party alignments'. With few but significant exceptions, the party

2 The regions of countries are: the Central countries (Austria, Belgium, Germany, Luxembourg, the Netherlands and Switzerland), the Southern European countries (France, Greece, Italy, Portugal and Spain) and the Island countries (Britain and Ireland).

systems of the 1960s reflected the cleavage structure of the 1920s, and the party alternatives had mainly tended to survive (Lipset and Rokkan 1967: 50–54). The 'freezing hypothesis' is basically explained by a strong relationship between the sociostructural variables that Lipset and Rokkan emphasised and party choice. Lipset and Rokkan's 'freezing' perspective is one of stable alignment. This contributes to stability in the party system and fairly stable support for the various parties over time.

Starting in the 1970s considerable change took place in the electoral behaviour of voters in the Nordic countries. Rather than stable alignment, researchers began talking about dealignment and realignment.

Dealignment means that the impact of the structural cleavages has become smaller. Increased instability in the party system is caused by the fact that voters do not vote according to their position in the social structure to the same degree as previously.

Realignment implies the eclipse of old cleavages and the rise of new ones. *Sectoral realignment* implies that there is first a dealignment from the old cleavages followed by an alignment related to the new cleavage structure. While Lipset and Rokkan focused on the national and the industrial revolutions, Dalton et al. (1984: 455–456) referred, for example, to a third post-industrial revolution which could lead to the creation of a new basis for social cleavage.

Two kinds of new conflict have been focused on in this research. These are new structural cleavages and value-based conflicts which, to a larger degree than in industrial societies, have become important. Gender and sector employment are examples of new structural cleavages, while various New Politics value orientations are examples of values that have increasingly come to influence party choice.

Another type of realignment is that which follows directly from changes in social structure. *Ecological or demographic realignment* implies that changes in party support follow directly from the changes in social structure. Ecological realignment contributes to change in support for the various parties, but also to changing the political agenda and party strategies. Parties attempt to appeal to some of the new expanding social groups.

The Lipset-Rokkan model

In their seminal essay on the development of the conflict structure in Western democracies, Lipset and Rokkan (1967) focused on the historical origins of structural party conflicts. They saw the main political cleavages as direct products of two revolutions: national and industrial.

Two cleavages originated from the National Revolution, the first being the centre–periphery cleavage which was anchored in geographical regions and related to different ethnic and linguistic groups as well as religious minorities (confessions). The second was the conflict between the Church and the State which pitted the secular state against the historical privileges of the churches, also over control of the important educational institutions. This cleavage has more specifically polarised the religious section against the secular section of the population.

The conflicts which became prominent in connection with the Industrial Revolution were labour market cleavages involving owners and employers versus tenants, labourers and workers. Finally, the conflict in the commodity market was between buyers and sellers of agricultural products or, more generally, between the urban and the rural population (Lipset and Rokkan 1967: 15–23).

THE LIPSET-ROKKAN STRUCTURAL CLEAVAGES

Centre–periphery: The regional cleavage

Lipset and Rokkan identified the regional division as a centre–periphery cleavage associated with the National Revolution. It was a 'conflict between *the central nation-building culture* and the increasing resistance of the ethnically, linguistically and religious *subject population* in the provinces and peripheries' (Lipset and Rokkan 1967: 14 [emphasis in the original]). The origin of regional conflicts is thus associated with the nation-building process, and the regional conflict is essentially equivalent to the degree to which linguistic, religious and ethnic groups are opposed along territorial lines.

Based on the existing literature on regional differences, the main perspectives and findings from Finland, Norway and Sweden are outlined below.

In Finland the differences in voting according to region have had several components. The dividing line in Finnish politics has been between the South and West versus the North and East. The northern and eastern parts, which have been less economically developed, have been the basis for radicalism. The Communists gained strong support on these regions as has the agrarian Centre Party (Allardt and Pesonen 1967: 350--358). In the North of the country, the Centre and the Communists for a long time comprised nearly a two-party system. Support for the Conservatives, the Social Democrats and previously also the Liberal Party has been most prevalent in the south and western parts of the country (Pesonen 1974: 295–298). Based on more recent data, Arter (2001a: 88–90) shows, however, that support for the agrarian Centre Party has had its stronghold in a central belt *between* Northern and Southern Finland.

The Communist Party had its strongholds partly in the industrialised southern and western Finland, and partly in the North. In northern Finland, support for the Communists has been labelled 'backwood and forest Communism' because the industrial life of these sparsely settled regions was dominated by smallholder farming. Moreover, it is the geographic isolation which has influenced the attitudes of the inhabitants (Rintala 1967). The Swedish People's Party received its vote where the Swedish speaking population was located, partly in the western part of the country, partly around the capital, and on the island of Åland.[3]

In Norway three 'countercultures', which were mainly located in the western and southern regions, have been considered as the main reasons for regional differences in voting behaviour (Rokkan 1967: 415–425; Valen and Rokkan 1974):

- The rural language movement ('nynorsk') (see chapter 1)
- The temperance and prohibition movements
- Lutheran orthodoxy and pietistic fundamentalism.

These countercultures explain why the southern and western regions (peripheries) have voted for the Liberals (Venstre), and later for the Christian People's Party, and why class polarisation/class voting has been low in these regions. The countercultures have, however, been severely weakened, and regional differences have declined.

In Sweden, the leftist parties (the Social Democrats and the Left Party) have gained considerably stronger support in the northern part of Sweden (Oscarsson and Holmberg 2008: 247–258).

EMPIRICAL ANALYSIS

Territorial penetration and cultural integration are more likely in old nation states such as Denmark and Sweden compared with relatively 'new' states such as Finland, Iceland and Norway. We therefore expect regional variation in voting choice to be larger in the latter countries.

In the most extensive study of the regional cleavages in Western Europe, Caramani (2004) examined the impact of the territorial cleavage from the time of the first democratic elections in 17 countries up until 1999 using data on electoral results in general elections from territorial units.

Caramanie's study showed that the strength of the regional cleavage varied greatly between the Nordic countries. Of the Nordic countries, the regional differences in voting choice are largest in Finland. Only in Switzerland and Belgium are the regional differences larger. In Iceland and Norway, the regional differences are somewhat below the average for Western European countries while regional differences are among the three smallest for Denmark and Sweden. Regional differences in voting behaviour have declined in the post-war period in all of the Nordic countries apart from Finland.

The Swedish People's Party in Finland is outstanding regarding regional variation in electoral support. Apart from this party, which is the only signi-

3 See chapter 1 for some details regarding the Swedish speaking population in Finland and the language conflict in Finnish history.

ficant ethnic-regional party in the region, regional variations in support are on average largest for the Agrarian parties, and then the Left Socialists, Social Democrats, Radical Right and Christian parties. Support is smallest for the Liberals, Conservatives and Greens. These relative patterns are fairly similar across the various countries, but the regional variations in electoral support for the Social Democrats are larger in Iceland and Finland than elsewhere. The Liberal Party in Norway also shows larger regional variations than its sister parties in the other Nordic countries.

The religious cleavage

The religious structure in the Nordic countries has been related to the established Lutheran State Church. The religious cleavage has had a specific character, between the secular and tolerant urban population, and the orthodox and fundamental Lutheranism of large sections of the rural population (see Chapter 2). This was not only a secular/religious cleavage, but a conflict between the religious fundamentalists organised in various lay organisations within (and partly outside) the state church, on the one hand, and the more tolerant government-appointed clergymen (civil servants) together with the more passive religious population, on the other. These fundamentalists were active in various revival movements, missionary organisations, and also in 'Free Churches'.

In their comparative discussion of the character of the religious cleavage, Lipset and Rokkan emphasised that the established churches in the Scandinavian countries (and in Britain) did not stand in opposition to the nation-builders as did the Roman Catholic Church. 'The "Left" movements opposed to the religious establishment found most of their support among newly enfranchised dissenters, nonconformists, and fundamentalists in the peripheries' (Lipset and Rokkan 1967: 38). Christian parties did not emerge in the early stages in the formation of the party systems (for details see Chapter 2).

Support for the pre-industrial left movements and, later, the Christian People's Parties in the Scandinavian countries has not been highest among active members of the dominant state churches. The strongest support has been found, and still is found, among active members of more fundamentalist sects, found partly within and partly outside the Lutheran Church. The Nordic Christian parties have been far more deviant than their continental counterparts in their national settings (see Chapter 2). To be a Christian party voter in the Nordic countries has also meant taking a stand which goes beyond conformist church membership or identification with general Christian values. The threshold created by the active stands taken by the Scandinavian parties on moral questions continues to be too high for the average voter (Karvonen 1994: 137–38).

EMPIRICAL ANALYSIS

The strong fundamentalist or non-conformist support is strongly supported by data from the ESS.[4] In Norway and Sweden support for the Christian parties is 3 % among those who are not members of any religious denominations, 12–13 % among those who are members of the Lutheran Protestant Church, and around 55 % of those who are members of 'other Christian denominations' (Catholics are not included). Corresponding percentages for Finland are 1 %, 4 % and 47 %, respectively. This group of nonconformists is, however, small (1 %–2 % of the voters according to the data), such that most of the Christian Party voters come from the Lutheran Church.

When the religious cleavage is measured according to religious denomination, the strength of the cleavage is not particularly strong in the Nordic countries, being clearly smaller than in the Central region and at the same level as the Islands and in the South. The strength is considerably greater in the three countries with significant Christian parties (Finland, Norway and Sweden) than in the two others.

The difference in voting patterns between those who are members of a denomination and those who are not is decisively largest for the Christian parties. The Agrarian and Conservative parties also receive strongest support from those who are church members, while the Left Socialists and the Greens decisively get strongest support from those who are unaffiliated. The Liberals, Social Democrats and Radical Right receive equally strong support among members and the unaffiliated.

The religious cleavage is also sometimes measured by frequency of church attendance. However, church attendance can also be considered as an indirect measure of religious values, and the pattern for the various parties and party families is very similar for church attendance and religious values. Therefore we focus upon religious denomination (as a structural variable) and religious values (see below).

Conflicts in the labour market: class voting

The two economic cleavages which sprang out of the Industrial Revolution are very important for understanding Scandinavian party systems. Comparative analyses of voting according to social class have documented that class voting has been more prevalent in the Scandinavian countries than in other democracies (Nieuwbeerta 1995, chap. 3).

4 ESS Cumulative file, Rounds 1–4.

ROKKAN'S TRIANGULAR MODEL OF ELECTORAL FRONTS

In the 1960s, Stein Rokkan (1966) formulated a model for these cleavages based on the Norwegian situation, but this model has been used in the other Nordic countries for understanding the major cleavages and economic divisions in the Nordic societies (Oskarson 1994, chap. 2; Elklit 1984).

Rokkan's model considered the economic conflicts as comprising three poles of electoral attraction. At each pole we find economic interests, issues, interest organisations and a major social class. These poles also comprise the major political parties strongly associated with the economic interests and interest organisations. Between the three poles we find voters with 'contradictory' economic and social positions, and – according to Rokkan – the decisive electoral struggles took place at the halfway stages between these poles, and involved different political parties.

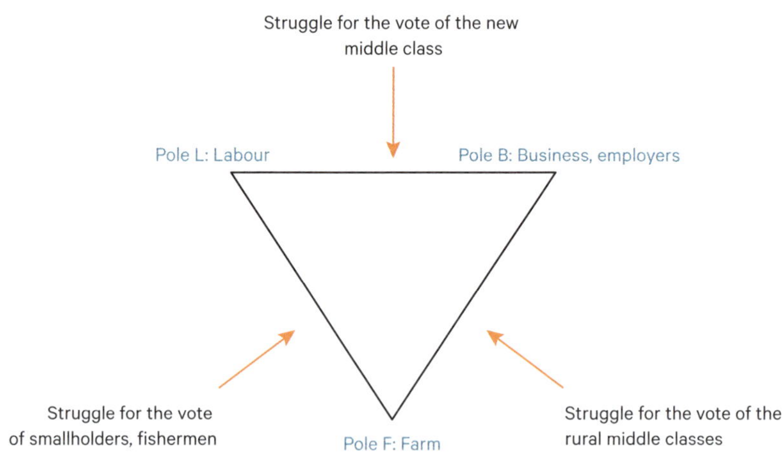

Pole L: The workers and their unions
Issues/concerns: Wages, pensions, social security, welfare
Organisations: Trade unions and their union confederations
Parties: Labour/Social Democratic P.

Pole F: Farmers (and self-employed in other primary industries) and their organisations
Issues/concerns: Prices, subsidies, toll protection and restrictions on import of provisions/food
Organisation: Farmers' League
Parties: Agrarian/Centre parties in Finland, Norway and Sweden, Agrarian Liberals in Denmark, Progress Party in Iceland.

Pole B: Trade and industry/employers
Issues/concerns: Prices, taxes and fees, economic regulations
Organisations: Trade/employer associations and their confederations.
Parties: Conservative P., Independence P. in Iceland

Figure 3.1 Rokkan's model of electoral fronts: The triangular model

Source: Rokkan (1966: 92–94, Figure 3–3).

The 'poles of electorate attraction' are shown in Figure 3.1. In the text below the figure, the various issues, peak interest organisations and parties located at the poles are indicated. The three interests are the labour unions and their peak organisation, the farmers' organisations, and the business community together with their peak organisations. The three party families which are located at the poles are the Social Democratic, the Agrarian and the Conservative parties.

This model is partly an institutional model because it is based on the organisational linkages between the interest organisations and the three class parties which have developed historically. It is, however, also based on the assumption that most voters belonging to the various classes located at the three poles vote for 'their' parties. The most important types of class voting are the degrees to which the workers support the Labour parties, the share of farmers (and other self-employed in the primary industries) supporting the Agrarian parties, and the share of employers supporting the Conservative parties.

Table 3.1 shows the class variable used in the analyses below.

The Erikson/Goldthorpe (hereafter EG) class schema is frequently used in studies of social class and originally developed in connection with social mobility studies (Erikson and Goldthorpe 1992; Goldthorpe 1980). An important division exists between the predominantly salaried professional – higher technical, administrative and managerial – positions and the predominantly wage-earning manual occupations. The service class comprises administrators and managers, employed professionals, higher-grade technicians and supervisors of non-manual workers. This class is divided into a higher and a lower level according to administrative responsibility and education.

Routine non-manual employees in the EG schema do not belong to the service class. This includes routine non-manual positions, usually involving

TABLE 3.1 THE ERIKSON/GOLDTHORPE CLASS SCHEMA

Higher-level service class	Higher-grade professionals, administrators and officials, managers in large industrial establishments, large proprietors
Lower-level service class	Lower-grade professionals, administrators and officials, higher-grade technicians, managers in small industrial establishments, supervisors of non-manual employees
Routine non-manual employees	Routine non-manual employees in administration and commerce, sales personnel, other rank-and-file employees
Petite bourgeoisie	Small proprietors with and without employees
Farmers	Farmers and small-holders and other self-employed in primary production
Skilled workers	Lower grade technicians, supervisors of manual workers, skilled manual workers
Unskilled workers	Semi- and unskilled manual workers, agricultural workers and other workers in primary production

clerical, sales or personal-service tasks which exist on the fringes of professional, administrative and managerial bureaucracies (Goldthorpe 1980: 40).

The working class group comprises skilled and unskilled manual wage-earners in all branches of industry as well as supervisors of manual workers (foremen) and lower-grade technicians.

The petite bourgeoisie comprises small proprietors. Farmers and other self-employed persons in the primary sector could also be grouped under the petite bourgeoisie, but due to their special economic interests they are grouped separately.

EMPIRICAL ANALYSIS

Changes in the class structure: First, the large changes in class structure should be emphasised. The main changes involve those which have taken place for the workers and the service class. According to the survey data the workers comprised about half of the working population in the 1960s. This has declined to 20–25 % in the 2010s. The service class has increased from around 20 % to nearly 50 %. The size of the farmer class has declined markedly.

It is evident, then, that the competition for voters has increasingly taken place between the L and B poles, but New Politics concerns (see below) have made the triangular model more irrelevant for both worker class and service class voters.

Changes in voting at the poles: In Sweden, where class voting has been resistent to change in a comparative Nordic perspective (see below), the share of the working class which has supported the Social Democrats has declined from 73 % in the 1950s to 66 % in the 1970s and to 45 % in the 2010s. For the other pole parties data are only available from the 1970s: the Conservative Party has increased its support from employers somewhat from 33 % to 39 % from the 1970s to the 2010s, while support for the Agrarian Centre Party by farmers has decreased dramatically, from 67 % to 29 %.[5]

Studies of class voting have undergone changes over time and have become more detailed and sophisticated in their use of statistical measures (Knutsen 2006, chapters 2 and 4).

Different types of class voting: Below, 'generations' of class voting and how class voting has been measured according to the various generations are briefly reviewed. The main features are as follows.

1) 'Traditional (left–right) class voting' examines the left–right division of parties and incorporates only two social classes (the manual/non-manual division). Traditional class voting has been measured by the Alford index,

5 Source: Swedish Election Surveys.

which is based on the percentage difference between workers and other social classes which vote for the leftist parties.[6]

2) Overall or total left–right class voting' examines the left–right voting of all social classes.
3) 'Total class voting' considers class differences (based on a detailed class schema) in voting for all the parties in the party system.

Here, the class voting in the Nordic countries is examined for all three generations of class voting. However, trends over time are only outlined for traditional class voting.

Traditional class voting can be examined for the longest time period. Such class voting was considerably more prevalent in the Nordic countries than elsewhere in Western Europe. Survey data 1945–1960 showed that class voting was largest in all four Nordic countries that were included, with a somewhat greater prevalence in Finland, Norway and Sweden (48–53) than in Denmark (40). The average level for the Nordic countries was 48 percentage points, while it was 26 for Continental European countries and 19 for Anglo-American countries (Nieuwbeerta 1995, chap. 3). The decline in traditional class voting in the Nordic countries has been largest in Denmark and Norway where traditional class voting has been just above zero in the 2000, while still remaining significant in Finland and Sweden (around 20). Traditional class voting in Iceland has been considerably lower but available data are for a shorter time period (Bengtsson et al. 2014: 150–152).

Based on the EVS data (round 4), class voting is still highest in Sweden and Finland (27 and 23, respectively), and considerably lower in Norway (7), Denmark (4) and even negative in Iceland (-4). Several other Western European countries have higher traditional class voting than the three latter countries, and on average the level of class voting is the same in the Central region and on the Islands as in the Nordic countries (11–12). Only in the Southern region is class voting lower according to the average for these countries (4 percentage points). There is, then, no longer a Nordic model for traditional class voting.

Overall left–right class voting is studied by examining support for the leftist parties within the various classes in the EG class schema. Average support for the leftist parties in the Nordic countries in the various EG classes is shown in the last row of Table 3.2. The leftist parties still receive strongest support from the working class categories and also the routine non-manual workers. They

6 The Leftist parties are parties that belong to the Social Democratic, Left Socialist and Communist parties when left–right class voting is examined. This is conventional in the class voting literature. For an examination of the other structural variables, the Greens are also included among the Leftist parties.

TABLE 3.2 PARTY CHOICE AND SOCIAL CLASSES

	Means for the various countries							
	Higher-level service class	**Lower-level service class**	**Routine Non-manuals**	**Petite bourgeoisie**	**Skilled workers**	**Unskilled workers**	**Farmers**	**Total**
Communists	1,0	2,7	3,2	0,0	2,1	1,4	0,0	2,0
Left Socialists	8,6	13,5	15,8	7,3	10,0	13,4	6,2	12,2
Social Democrats	21,1	22,0	28,6	11,5	35,6	33,4	6,0	25,1
Greens	12,3	16,3	15,3	5,3	3,4	11,3	4,5	12,9
Ethnic-regional	3,2	1,0	0,0	5,0	1,8	1,4	0,0	1,6
Agrarian	11,4	12,3	11,8	23,2	11,3	14,1	52,4	13,6
Liberals	12,1	9,5	6,1	3,3	3,7	2,1	0,0	7,1
Christian	3,8	4,7	5,8	0,9	1,3	3,1	1,3	4,1
Conservatives	34,2	25,4	17,5	31,1	13,0	11,1	20,4	22,6
Radical Right	9,1	9,6	13,2	28,8	25,3	21,0	7,0	14,1
Agrarian 4[1)]	5,4	8,7	8,8	16,5	7,3	11,6	47,7	9,6
Agrarian Liberals	35,4	27,0	24,1	50,0	27,2	24,1	71,0	29,6
Leftist parties	30,1	36,6	45,7	18,8	46,4	47,4	12,2	38,0

The figures do not sum up to 100 because they are based on different number of countries.
Only countries where parties in a given party family exist, are included in the calculations of the means.
1) The Agrarian parties without the Danish party.

receive somewhat smaller support from the service class and much less support from the petite bourgeoisie and the farmers.

Overall left–right class voting is, again, largest in Sweden (0.300)[7] and Finland (0.287) than in Denmark (0.193), Norway (0.172) and Iceland (0.070), and due to the high level of this type of class voting in the two former countries, the average level is higher in the Nordic region (0.220) than in the other regions (0.133–0.183).

For total class voting, it is of interest to examine the following:

a) Variation in support for the various party families according to social classes: from which of the classes do the various parties receive highest and lowest support?

7 Standardised coefficients are used in this chapter. They vary from 0.00 (no correlation) to 1.00 (perfect correlation).

b) The extent to which the various party families are class-based: which party families are most distinct with regard to class support and which are less distinct?
c) The strength of the correlations between the overall party choice variable with all significant parties as separate categories and the EG class schema in a broader comparative perspective. Based on total social class voting, is class voting in the Nordic countries comparatively high or low?

The Conservatives, Social Democrats and Agrarian parties are referred to as the pole parties in some of the literature (Arter 2011; Sundberg 1999) because their electoral support has been anchored in the three social classes in Rokkan's three poles. Here, we commence by examining support for these parties from different social classes and then proceed to the other party families. The mean support in the various classes for the various party families is shown in Table 3.2. Variations between the Nordic countries are outlined in the text.

The Social Democrats receive strongest support from the working class categories, but also considerable support from the routine non-manual workers and the service class while support is considerably smaller from the petite bourgeoisie and the farmers. Differences between the main classes are considerably larger in Sweden and Finland than in Denmark and Norway, and very small in Iceland. The Icelandic Social Democrats receive about the same support from the service class as from the working class.

The Conservatives receive strongest support from the higher-level service class and the petite bourgeoisie, and clearly least support from the workers. The main deviation within the party family is the Icelandic Party which has much more cross-class support than the other Conservative Party, receiving only 9 percentage points higher support from the service class than from workers, and receiving 37 % support from the farmers – greater support than the Agrarian Progress Party. Differences in class support from the major classes are larger in Finland than in the other countries.

The Agrarian parties have a clear class profile with, on average, support from more than half of the farmers, considerable support from the petite bourgeoisie, and much smaller support from the other social classes. The exception to this is the Icelandic Party, which gains most support from the farmers (26 %), but this is considerably less support than the other agrarian parties, and even less than the Conservative Independence Party.

Data for the Danish Agrarian Liberals are shown separately. Class support is fairly similar to that of the other Agrarian parties but is much higher among all social classes and in particular the service class and the workers. These differences contribute to making the party a much less distinct class party than the other parties within the party family, although support from the farmers is even higher than for the other Agrarian parties.

The Nordic Liberals are clearly class parties with considerably greater support from the service class than from workers. The Christian parties receive strongest support from the service class and the routine non-manuals. The low support of the farmers is very different from in the Central region, where the farmers constitute the class which is clearly most likely to support these parties.

The Left Socialists seem to receive very similar support from the various classes although somewhat less support from the farmers, higher service class and petite bourgeoisie. Indeed, the parties have a very different class base: the Finnish party receives decisively strongest support from the workers, while the Norwegian party receives strongest support from the service class. Differences are smaller for the parties in the other countries.

The Greens receive strongest support from the service class and the routine non-manuals, while the Radical Right receives strongest support from workers and the petite bourgeoisie in accordance with findings from elsewhere in Western Europe.

The examination of which party families are the most pronounced class parties yields somewhat surprising results. The Agrarian parties are decisively the most pronounced class parties, even when the deviant Danish party is included. The next two party families are the Liberals and the Greens, and then – with a considerably smaller level of class differences – the Radical Right and the Conservatives. Finally, the Christian, Left Socialists and Social Democrats are to the least extent class parties.

Total class voting is largest in Finland (0.495), Norway and Sweden (0.440), followed by Belgium and the Netherlands with about the same level of such class voting as Denmark (0.400–0.420), which follows with the highest level after the first three countries mentioned. Iceland has, however, a total class voting level below the average for the 18 countries, in fact the third smallest (0.313). The Nordic countries have on average a higher level of class voting (0.418) than the other regions (0.336–0.365). For total class voting we find, then, what is close to a new Nordic model for class voting.

Urban–rural residence

According to Lipset and Rokkan, another cleavage is the conflict in the commodity market between peasants and others employed in the primary sector and those who wanted to buy the products of the primary sector, particularly the urban population. The peasants wanted to sell their wares at the best possible prices and to purchase what they needed from the industrial and urban producers at low cost while the urban population often had opposite economic interests (Lipset and Rokkan 1967: 20–21).

This is, then, essentially an urban–rural conflict. Such conflicts did not invariably prove party-forming. They could be dealt with within broad party fronts or could be channelled through interest organisations into more narrow arenas of functional representation and bargaining. In many countries the religious interests of the rural population were more influential than the strictly economic interests, and the economic interest articulation took place within the Christian parties. Distinct Agrarian parties emerged only in some countries where strong cultural opposition had deepened and embittered the strictly economic conflicts (Lipset and Rokkan 1967: 44–46, see chap. 2).

There are generally two aspects of the commodity market conflict: a) how the class of farmers (and other self-employed in the primary sector) vote compared to other social classes, and b) the differences in voting behaviour between the urban and the rural population. Both of these factors can be a continuing source of division in contemporary party systems.

We should expect the urban–rural cleavage to be particularly strong in the Nordic countries because of the existence of Agrarian parties only in the Nordic countries, which articulate the economic interests of the farmers. However, in the Central region the Christian Democrats also receive strong support from the rural population, so this hypothesis can be challenged.

EMPIRICAL ANALYSIS

Election and other surveys have shown that voting according to an urban–rural territorial dimension has declined in Denmark, Norway and Sweden. The data (EVS Round 4) show, however, that the urban–rural cleavage is stronger in the Nordic countries than in other regions, but the difference to the Central region is not large (0,232 versus 0.204). The urban–rural cleavage is strongest in Finland and Norway than in all other Western European countries, but considerably smaller in Denmark and in particular Sweden. Several Central European countries have correlations between party choice and urban–rural residence that are stronger than in the latter countries (Iceland lacking data).

The Agrarian parties receive much stronger support from the rural population than from the urban population, followed by the Christian and Radical Rightist parties. The Liberal, Conservative, Green and Left Socialist parties, on the other hand, receive stronger support from the urban population, while differences are small for the Social Democrats.

NEW STRUCTURAL CLEAVAGES

Gender

Until the end of the 1960s, women tended to have more conservative and traditional political orientations than men. Thus, women were more inclined to vote for religious and conservative parties and less inclined to vote for socialist parties. According to the *traditional gender gap*, women were expected to be more conservative or centre–right than men. Traditional women's values emphasising 'private' orientations associated with religion and family responsibilities were identified as the basis for these differences. The most important explanation was their higher degree of religiosity since major differences were found with regard to support for the Christian parties (Rose 1974).

In the course of the past two or three decades, women in many Western countries have changed from being more conservative than men to being more radical. The term *modern gender gap* has been used to characterise these new gender-based value differences and differences in voting patterns between women and men in many Western democracies (Norris 1999: 150).

Researchers have advanced various explanations for how and why gender differences occur and what they imply. We distinguish between two main explanations: those emphasising structural accounts or *economic interests*, and those emphasising *cultural and value differences* between women and men.

Explanations that emphasise structural factors and interests see changes in the gender-based division of work associated with the labour market and the family as the most important reasons for changes in women's and men's interests. The transition from an economy based on one breadwinner to one based on the two-income family has meant that women have increasingly become independent economic actors. Paid employment directly exposes women to gender inequalities that they are less likely to experience as homemakers, while also providing them with a means of economic independence that may shape their political behaviour. Women are also more dependent on the public sector and the welfare state for employment than men, and they tend to depend more on social welfare to support and subsidise their families.

Cultural or value-based explanations have also been applied to observed differences in political attitudes. This approach emphasises that there are extensive and deep-rooted value differences, or differences with regard to central political issues between women and men. This applies both to traditional economic left–right issues and moral and political questions such as peace, welfare, the environment and social care.

Another explanation focuses on generational changes among women. The traditional gender gap is expected to be found among the older cohort, while the post-war cohorts who gained their formative experiences in the 1960s and 1970s have been more strongly influenced by the transformation of gender roles, the women's movement and changes in political attitudes and values (Norris 1999: 154).

Given that the religious parties have been small, we can expect to find that the traditional gender gap has been small in the Nordic countries. On the other hand, given that the Nordic countries have advanced social structures in a comparative setting, with a high level of female employment, we can expect the modern gender gap to be comparatively large.[8]

8 See chapter 5 for various aspects of politics and gender in the Nordic countries.

EMPIRICAL ANALYSIS

For Norway and Sweden, and partly also Denmark, it is possible to examine voting patterns according to gender from the 1960s on the basis of the election surveys.

In Norway, which is the only country with a significant Christian party before the 1980s, the major gender gap relates to voting for this party. In the 1950s, 1960s and 1970s, between 5 and 8 percentage points more women than men voted for this party. In the elections in the 1970s the average support among women and men for the two elections was 16 % and 8 % respectively. This traditional gender gap still exists, although of a somewhat smaller magnitude in the last decades (between 3 and 6 percentage points). However, a modern gender gap developed from the late 1970s: men started to support the Conservative Party to a larger extent than women, and this also applied to the Radical Rightist Progress Party. Gender differences in support for the rightist parties increased gradually from 5 to 11 percentage points from 1977 to the 2000s. An opposite gender gap developed for the leftist parties. From the mid-1980s women supported these parties to a larger extent than men. The size of this gender gap has increased from 4–5 percentage points in the late 1980s to 11 percentage points in the 2000s, and is more significant for the Left Socialists than for the Social Democrats.

Somewhat similar gender gaps have developed in Sweden. In the 1950s and 1960s there were weak tendencies for the leftist parties to gain stronger support from men than from women, and the opposite for the Conservatives, and first and foremost for the Liberal party. From the late 1970s, the Conservative Party gained strongest support from men. The size of this gap has been modest (3–7 percentage points in the various decades), but if we include the gender differences for the Sweden Democrats the size of this gender gap for the right is 11 percentage points in 2010s. An opposite gender gap emerged in the 1980s for the leftist parties, which gained stronger support from women. This gender gap has been modest (3–6 percentage points), and most significant for the Environmental Party.

In Denmark, a gender gap developed from the 1980s of fairly similar size to Norway and Sweden.

In Iceland, the emergence of the Women's Alliance in the 1980s created a large gender gap in voting choice. The average support for the party was 4 % and 17 % for the elections in 1983, 1987 and 1991 among men and women, respectively (Hardarson 1995: 286; Oskarson 1995: 68). In Finland there is evidence of much stronger support among *men* for the Left Alliance as late as 1991 (Oskarson 1995: 68).

The EVS data (round 4) show the following comparative voting pattern for the Nordic countries according to gender. A modern gender gap where women support the leftist parties and men support the rightist parties (Conservatives and Radical Right) is evident in all five countries. The size of the former component varies in the following way: Denmark and Sweden (12–13), Finland and Norway (8–9) and Iceland (6). If this modern gender gap is decomposed into the various relevant party families (Left Socialists, Greens and Social Democrats) the following interesting comparative differences emerge. In Denmark, Iceland and Norway, the main gender difference is found for the Left Socialists. In Finland and Sweden the main difference is found for the Greens, while there is no significant gender difference for the Left Socialists. These parties are successor parties of Communist parties in contrast to the other Left Socialist parties.

As for the other aspect of the modern gender gap in the Nordic countries, the tendency for men to support the Conservative and Radical Rightist parties, the strengths are as follows: 17 percentage points in Norway, 12 in Denmark,[9] 7–8 in Finland, Iceland and Sweden. A similar decomposition as for the leftist parties shows that men support the Conservatives and the Radical Right equally more than women in Finland and Sweden, while the Norwegian Progress Party had the largest gender gap in Norway and the Agrarian Liberals in Denmark. In Iceland there is only one relevant party, the Conservative Independence Party.

The modern gender gap, indicating that women are more inclined to support the parties on the left, is largest in the Nordic countries (10 percentage points) versus 7 in the Central region, 3 in Southern Europe and zero on the Islands. Similar comparative differences in absolute magnitude are found for the rightist parties, where men are most inclined to support these parties.

Which of the various explanations for the modern gender gap receives most support from empirical analysis? It is evident that the modern gender gap is most significant among the younger generations (Oskarson 1995: 71–74). In a comparative study of Denmark, Norway and Sweden, gender differences seemed to be strongly explained by sector employment. The fact that a larger portion of working women is employed in the public sector could explain why they support parties on the left. The hypothesis regarding low hierarchical position in the class structure did not receive support (Knutsen 2001: 338–344).

Generally, when taking into account the size of the various parties, women are more likely than men to support the Greens, Left Socialists and Christian parties, while men are more inclined to support the Radical Right and Conservatives in the Nordic countries.

Sector employment

Another potential new cleavage is the contrast between the public versus the private sector. This cleavage can be explained on the basis of the different economic interests of employees in the two sectors as well as the cognitive conditions associated with different educational backgrounds and occupational experiences.

The extent to which personal economic interests are directly linked to political decisions is perhaps the most noticeable difference between working in

9 The Agrarian Liberal Party is included among the rightist parties in Denmark.

the public or the private sector. The public employee has clear self-interests connected with ample public budgets, a well-developed welfare state and market restrictions. A large public sector means more jobs and greater possibilities for a better career and higher economic rewards. In contrast, the interests of many private sector employees are connected with the market and with capturing parts of it for the organisations or firms in which they are employed (Knutsen 2005: 594).

Many public sector employees are confronted with social problems in their work, something which can be expected to create attitudes which favour social reform and greater public initiative. These aspects of work can also be expected to create an awareness of the weaknesses of market-oriented solutions. Furthermore, the ethics of welfare occupations, coupled with professional norms about what is best for the clients, often leads to a focus on the lack of resources and to demands for more vigorous public initiatives, resulting in a stronger public sector ideology (Knutsen 2005: 594–95).

Large numbers of service class public employees are recruited from educational institutions and persons with an educational background characterised by the values of public sector ideology (education for the professions, social science education (Knutsen 2005: 595; Tepe 2012).

A macro-approach to political conflicts in advanced industrial democracies is put forward by Iversen and Wren's (1998) model of 'trilemma of the service economy'. The neoliberal model emphasises budgetary restraint and high private sector employment, accepting large wage inequality wherein wages are low in the (expanding) private service sector. The second model also emphasises budgetary restraint, but places greater weight on equality. The model has its origins in corporatist and Christian Democratic thought. High employment levels are given relatively low priority in this model because 'women are viewed as the guardian of the traditional family and hence are encouraged to stay at home and care for children and spouse'. The third model gives priority to earning equality and high employment performance at the expense of budgetary restraint. This is the Social Democratic model, which combines a strong egalitarian ethos with a work ethic that emphasises employment as the root of collective identity and pride.[10]

Each model involves its own costs and political conflicts according to Iversen and Wren. Suffice it to mention here that the Liberal model creates additional income inequality and perpetuates class division. The Christian Democratic model creates high unemployment and breeds labour market exclusion and resentment among outsider classes. The Social Democratic model generates its own political conflicts about the size of the public budgets, and structu-

10 See chapter 9 for the Nordic welfare state model.

ral conflicts between public and private employees (Iversen and Wren 1998: 517–518, 539–540, 544–545).

EMPIRICAL ANALYSIS

For Denmark, Norway and Sweden it is possible to examine the development of the impact of sector employment from the 1960s and early 1970s on the basis of election surveys. Differences in voting behaviour according to sector employment were small in the 1960s. From the 1970s, public employees have voted for the leftist parties to a larger degree than private employees, who increasingly have been inclined to support the Conservatives and also the Radical Right when these parties emerged. In the 1990s, these differences were considerable. Based on average support from the elections surveys in this decade, sector differences were 16–18 percentage points in Denmark, 12–15 in Norway and 6–7 in Sweden. The figures cover both patterns indicated above and must then be considered as absolute values.

Questions about sector employment are not frequently asked in comparative surveys, but in ESS 4 (Iceland is not included) from 2008, which also covers countries from the other regions that we use for comparison, these questions were included.

The impact of sector employment is generally larger in the Nordic countries than elsewhere, but significantly lower in Finland than in the other Nordic countries. The correlation is largest in Norway (0.262) and Denmark (0.212) followed by Switzerland and Sweden (0.18–0.19), while the correlation in Finland is below average (0.11). The average correlation for the Nordic countries is 0.190, while it is 0.138 in the Central region and 0.10–0.11 on the Islands and in the Southern region. The two central components of voting according to sector employment are still the most important. Public sector employees support the leftist parties to a larger extent than private employees, while the private employees support Conservative parties, rightist Liberal parties in the Central region and Radical Rightist parties. Both patterns are strongest in Denmark and Norway (around 20 percentage points), and then Switzerland and Sweden, and considerably smaller in Finland.[11] The averages for both patterns are largest in the Nordic countries (13 and 16 percentage points, respectively), and in the Central region (10 and 9 percentage points). In the two other regions where we have seen that sector employment has a smaller impact, the only pattern

11 Sector employment is also an important determinant of party choice in Iceland. Hardarson (1995: 322–324) reports that the parties on the left receive 14 percentage points higher support from the public sector employees than from the private employees. Bengtsson et al. (2014: 155–159) report that private employees are 16 percentage points more likely to support the non-leftist parties than public employees according to the Icelandic election survey from 2007. Only in Denmark is the percentage difference higher in a comparison of all five Nordic countries.

that conforms to those outlined above is that the Conservative parties on the Islands receive stronger support from the private employees than the public employees. In Greece, Portugal and Spain there are weak tendencies in the opposite direction: public employees are inclined to support the Conservative and Liberal parties to a larger extent than private employees.

As for the party families in the Nordic countries, sector differences in voting are largest (ranked according to the relative difference) for the Left Socialists, Conservatives, Radical Right and Social Democrats when the sizes of the parties are taken into account.

Two other aspects of sector employment voting should be mentioned:

The impact of sector employment is largest within the service class. It is within the service class that the argument about the awareness of social problems is most clearly coupled with the work in the public sector, and the arguments about professional ethics and educational background are also most relevant for more highly educated personnel, i.e. the service class (Knutsen 2005).

Those who work in the health, social and educational sectors vote to the largest degree for leftist parties compared with those who work within other parts of the public sector. This difference is greatest in the Nordic countries. It is, then, not those working in the public administration who are the most left-wing (Tepe 2012).

THE IMPACT OF VALUE ORIENTATIONS

The central political value orientations are first outlined. Christian values focus on the importance of Christian morals and principles in society and politics, and on traditional moral guidelines in schools and society in general. Secularisation is often understood as a process whereby mundane reality is interpreted less from a supernatural perspective, and secular values are based on more modern norms of morality where the individual wants to make decisions for him- or herself without the guidelines of the church (Halman and Moor 1994; Norris and Inglehart 2004).

The most important political value orientations that emerged from the Industrial Revolution were economic left–right values. These values include workers' control and state regulation of the economy versus private enterprise, private property and a market economy. They also encompass the size of the welfare state and economic and social equality versus the need for differentiated rewards for stimulating effort (Knutsen 1995).

The moral value dimension and economic left–right values are often referred to as 'Old Politics' because they capture the essence of the traditional lines of conflict in industrial society. In contrast, 'New Politics' refers to value conflicts emerging from post-industrial society. The most well-known political value dimension is that of the materialist/post-materialist value orientations. These value orientations were originally formulated by Inglehart (1977, 1990), who argued that new post-materialist values are deeply rooted and stand in opposition to more traditional materialist values. Materialist values emphasise economic and physical security such as economic stability and growth, law and order, and a strong defence. Post-materialist values emphasise self-expression, subjective well-being and the quality of life. New Politics values can, however, be conceptualised along three different dimensions: The value conflict between *environmental versus economic growth values* is firmly rooted in the public mind, and in many Western European countries conflicts over environmental values seem to be the most manifest expression of the 'New Politics' conflict (Dalton 2009).

In a series of articles, Scott Flanagan emphasised that *a libertarian/authoritarian* dimension is the central New Politics dimension (Flanagan 1987; Flanagan and Lee 2003). The libertarian/authoritarian value orientations are also central components of Herbert Kitschelt's (1994, 1995) works.

The third set of New Politics orientations is related to *immigration and immigrants*. This has become a major policy area in Europe with different views among the mass publics. Comparative research has shown that these orientations are closely related to, and reflect basic values and beliefs about, different conceptions of national identity, ethnicity and multiculturalism (Hainmueller and Hiscox 2007: 429–434).

EMPIRICAL ANALYSIS[12]

Table 3.3 shows the mean scores for voters for the various party families on scales for each of the value orientations in the Nordic countries. The data are also based on the means for parties within the various party families in the five countries on scales from 0–10 based on indices with 5–8 items for each value orientation.[13] The strength of the correlations is compared with the mean correlation from other regions in the Nordic countries.

The high correlations between party choice and *economic left–right orientation* are outstanding in a comparative perspective, and the correlations are higher in all the five Nordic countries than in any of the other Western European countries, varying from 0.608 in Sweden to 0.502 in Iceland. The party families are located fairly similarly to those in chapter 2 based on the policies of the party families. We note that the Radical Rightist parties are located close to the centre parties, Agrarians, Liberals and Christians.

The correlations between *religious–secular values* and party choice are generally higher in the Central countries with larger Christian parties. The average correlation in the Nordic countries is fairly similar to that of Southern

12 This section is based on EVS data from round 4.

13 Economic leftist, religious, green, libertarian and liberal immigration orientations are assigned high values in the indices. Details about the items and the index constructions can be obtained from the author.

TABLE 3.3 PARTY CHOICE AND VALUE ORIENTATIONS IN THE NORDIC COUNTRIES

Means on scales from 0 to 10									
A. Economic left-right orientations		**B. Religious-secular orientations**		**C. Environmental orientations**		**D. Libertarian-authoritarian orientations**		**E. Immigration orientations**	
Communists	6,45	Christian	8,63	Communists	7,42	Communists	7,02	Communists	6,52
Left socialists	5,55	Agrarian	4,43	Greens	7,23	Greens	6,72	Greens	6,38
Greens	4,91	Ethnic-regional	3,96	Ethnic-regional	7,08	Liberal	6,44	Left socialists	6,05
Social Democrats	4,83	Social Democrats	3,68	Left socialists	6,69	Left socialists	6,16	Liberal	5,55
Christian	4,18	Radical right	3,58	Liberal	6,31	Ethnic-regional	5,54	Social Democrats	5,08
Ethnic-regional	4,14	Conservative	3,54	Radical right	6,28	Social Democrats	5,38	Christian	4,92
Radical right	3,90	Left socialists	3,13	Social Democrats	6,05	Conservative	5,37	Conservative	4,68
Liberal	3,83	Liberal	3,01	Christian	5,86	Agrarian	5,27	Agrarian	4,56
Agrarian	3,79	Greens	2,71	Agrarian	5,81	Radical right	5,16	Ethnic-regional	4,43
Conservative	2,87	Communists	1,76	Conservative	5,75	Christian	5,09	Radical right	3,11
Other p.	4,45	Other p.	3,11	Other p.	6,02	Other p.	5,60	Other p.	4,38
Mean all	4,12	Mean all	3,74	Mean all	6,07	Mean all	5,53	Mean all	4,90
Mean correlations for countries in various regions									
Nordic	0,555	Central	0,364	Nordic	0,274	Central	0,295	Central	0,372
Central	0,347	Nordic	0,285	Central	0,243	Nordic	0,258	Central West	0,367
South	0,290	South	0,272	Islands	0,208	South	0,237	South	0,265
Islands	0,216	Islands	0,210	South	0,175	Islands	0,172	Islands	0,251
All countries	0,375	All countries	0,299	All countries	0,229	All countries	0,255	All countries	0,327

Europe. There are, however, large differences within the Nordic countries. Only in the Netherlands and Germany are the correlations higher than in Norway and Finland (0.40–0.42). In Sweden the correlation is also among the highest (0.37), while the correlations in Denmark and Iceland are the lowest among all 18 countries (0.11–0.12).

The locations of the parties indicate how much the Christian party voters deviate from the other party voters. The centrist orientations of the Conservative and Radical Rightist voters are remarkable, even more pronounced than for the party policy location in chapter 2. These party voters are also more secular than the Social Democratic voters.

The average correlations between *environmental values* and party choice are somewhat higher in the Nordic countries than in the Central region and generally higher than in the other regions. The correlations are fairly similar among the Nordic countries, from 0.31 in Finland to 0.23 in Denmark. In only a few of the central countries (Belgium, Switzerland and Luxembourg) are correlations at the same level.

The Greens and the Left Socialists (and in addition the very small Communist and ethnic-regional parties) have the voters with the most green orientation while the Conservatives, Agrarians and Christians are located closest to the anti-green pole, placing the Liberals, Radical Right and Social Democrats in a 'centrist' position.

As for *libertarian-authoritarian values,* the average correlations with party choice are largest in the Central region, followed by the Nordic countries. The correlation in Denmark (0.30) is larger than in the other Nordic countries (0.23–0.26).

The Greens, Liberals and Left Socialists have the most libertarian voters, and the Christian, Radical Right and Agrarian parties the most authoritarian, placing the Conservatives and Social Democrats in a centrist position.

Finally, the average correlations between party choice and *immigration orientations* are largest in the Nordic countries and in the Central regions. Among the Nordic countries the correlations are largest in Denmark and Norway (0.40–0.43), then Finland and Sweden (0.36–0.37), and finally Iceland (0.29). Only in Austria and Switzerland are there higher correlations than in Norway, as well as in Italy compared with Denmark.

Only on this scale do we find that the Radical Right comprises an extreme position at the voter level with the most restrictive orientations to immigrants and immigration policy. The party families closest to the Radical Right are the Agrarians and Conservatives, and then the Christians and the Social Democrats. The two latter party families can be considered as centrist along these orientations, while the Greens, Left Socialists and Liberals comprise the party voters with a liberal immigration policy orientation.

By comparing the average correlations for the five value orientations in the Nordic countries, it is evident that economic left–right values are dominant (0.555). Immigration orientations are the second most important (0.372), followed by the three other orientations which are of fairly similar importance (0.258–0.285). In the other regions, economic left–right values are far from being as pronounced. In the Central region immigration and religious–secular values have the highest average correlations, but in the Southern region economic left–right and religious–secular values are most significant and of similar importance, but with much lower correlations. There are two countries outside the Nordic region where economic left–right values are the most important of the five value orientations, viz. Britain and France.

THE TOTAL IMPACT OF SOCIAL STRUCTURE AND POLITICAL VALUE ORIENTATIONS ON PARTY CHOICE

Finally, the total impact of the sociostructural variables and the value orientations are examined in a comparative perspective on the basis of EVS data, Round 4, which is based on 18 Western European countries. Do the sociostructural variables and the value orientations explain a larger portion of voting choice in the Nordic countries compared with elsewhere in Western Europe?[14] Table 3.4 shows the total explanatory power of the sociostructural variables and the value orientations. In Table 3.4C the value orientations are entered into the analyses after the sociostructural variables because the sociostructural variables can be considered as prior variables in a causal sense.

The sociostructural variables have largest explanatory power in the Central region, placing the Nordic countries somewhat below, but clearly ahead of, the Islands and Southern Europe. Of the Nordic countries, the sociostructural variables have the strongest impact in Finland (0.444), then Norway (0.373), Sweden (0.345), Denmark (0.274) and finally Iceland (0.235). The five Nordic countries vary, having the second highest explanatory power in Finland (only after the Netherlands) and the fourth lowest in Iceland.

Value orientations clearly have the greatest impact on party choice in the Nordic region according to Table 3.4B. In four of the Nordic countries value orientations have the greatest explanatory power (0.473–0.567), as they also do in the Netherlands. In Iceland the explanatory power (0.378) is close to average, placing the country as number 9.

When value orientations are included after the sociostructural variables in the analyses (Table 3.4C), the impact of value orientations is decisively greatest in the Nordic countries, and in this case the impact in the five countries is greater than in any other country.

14 The sociostructural variables are those discussed in this chapter but do not include sector employment. The value orientations are the five outlined in the previous section.

TABLE 3.4 THE EXPLANATORY POWER OF SOCIAL STRUCTURE AND VALUE ORIENTATIONS IN THE NORDIC COUNTRIES IN A COMPARATIVE PERSPECTIVE

Nagelkerke's R-squared. Means for the countries in the various regions			
A. The impact of social structural variables		**B. The impact of value orientations**	
Central	0,380	Nordic	0,502
Nordic	0,334	Central	0,412
Islands	0,270	South	0,265
South	0,243	Islands	0,211
All	0,317	All	0,374
C. The impact of value orientations in addition to social structure		**D. The total impact of social structure and value orientations**	
Nordic	0,275	Nordic	0,610
Central	0,185	Central	0,565
South	0,152	South	0,395
Islands	0,120	Islands	0,391
All	0,194	All	0,511

Finally, Table 3.4D shows the impact of both social structural variables and value orientations. Again, the impact is greatest in the Nordic countries, somewhat ahead of the Central region, and far ahead of the averages for the other regions. The total impact of social structure and values is greatest in Finland and the Netherlands (0.704), followed by Sweden (0.666) and Norway (0.629), while Denmark (0.562) and Iceland (0.493) rank seventh and tenth. Several of the other countries in the Central region have a higher explanatory power than these latter Nordic countries.

CONCLUSION

This chapter has examined the impact of social structural variables and political value orientations in the Nordic countries. The focus has been on trends over time, differences and similarities between the five Nordic countries and whether there are significant differences between the Nordic countries and other regions within Western Europe such that a Nordic model regarding determinants of party choice can be distinguished.

Two conclusions are formulated here. The first is related to changes over time, which is discussed in relation to the concepts of stable conflict lines (stable alignment), dealignment and realignment. The second is related to possible Nordic models of determinants of party choice.

Regarding changes over time, it has not been possible to examine this aspect for the religious cleavage and the value orientations.

Regional differences in voting behaviour have declined in all Nordic countries apart from Finland in accordance with the dealignment model. Traditional class voting has declined in all Nordic countries, particularly in Denmark and Norway where the decline has been large. Urban–rural differences in voting behaviour have also declined as have class differences in voting for the Social Democrats, which has been considerable.

Sectoral realignment is first and foremost taking place with the change from a traditional to a modern gender gap, and with the increased importance of voting according to sector employment. The changing pattern of class voting is also an example of such realignment: working class support for the Radical Right has increased greatly and the service class has developed fairly large electoral support for the Greens and the Left Socialists although the latter varies between the Nordic countries.

Demographic or ecological realignment is related to changes in the social structure. Some parties enjoy increased support because the social groups where they have the greatest support have increased as a share of the population. Although not all changes in social structure have been documented above, it is evident that parties with the greatest support from secular citizens, the service class, urban residents and the public sector receive increased support as a result of changes in social structure. The Christian, Social Democratic and Agrarian parties have serious problems with their electoral support because of these factors.

As for the Nordic models, we started by indicating that class voting and the impact of economic values had been established as determinants of party choice, which had an impact not found elsewhere.

The empirical analyses in this chapter have documented that a significant number of determinants of party choice are higher in the Nordic countries than elsewhere in Western Europe, while this is not the case for several other aspects that have been focused upon. As a basis for classifying the various elements that have been analysed in this chapter, the findings are classified into four categories.

1. Elements where the determinants of party choice are highest for all five Nordic countries.
2. Some of the analyses have shown that Iceland is a deviant case with lower explanatory power than the other countries. This category is, then, based on the four other countries and these have the strongest impact on party choice in a comparative perspective.
3. In this category the average impact of the determinants of party choice is highest in the Nordic countries, but not all of these countries have the strongest impact (even when Iceland is not included).
4. The impact is not particularly high in the Nordic countries and/or is fairly diverse in a comparative perspective in this last category.

The impact of economic left–right orientations and the impact of all value orientations when social structure is included first in the analyses are the two elements which are grouped in the first category.

There are formally no elements that can be grouped in the second category, but for total class voting, the impact of values (without controls) and for both aspects of the modern gender gap, there is only one country that splits the four Nordic countries. These elements are then marginal elements to be grouped in this category.

For all of the elements mentioned in the last paragraphs, the average is highest in the Nordic countries. This also applies to the overall left–right class voting, the impact of urban–rural residence, sector employment, environmental orientations and immigration orientations,[15] and the overall impact of both social structure and value orientations.

The following elements can be grouped in the fourth group where there is no Nordic model: the impact of region, religion (both religious denomination and religious–secular values), traditional class voting, libertarian–authoritarian values and finally the total impact of social structural variables.

15 The impact of immigration orientations is fairly similar in the Central region.

CHAPTER 4
POLITICAL REPRESENTATION AND PARLIAMENTARISM

Knut Heidar & Bjørn Erik Rasch

Constitutions regulate representative processes in democracies. Elections, parliaments and governments are constitutional instruments designed to reflect and channel electoral preferences. They translate the will of the people from votes into seats, government portfolios and policy decisions. Within the democratic family, however, there are an almost infinite variety of institutional designs to accomplish this. This variety reflects differences in how democracy itself is understood. It also reflects different views on what kind of system is needed in a particular country, given its history and political setting. Some constitutions are deliberately designed to create strong, efficient government (de Gaulle's Fifth Republic of 1958), while others aim to reflect the peoples' voice as closely as possible at all levels (the German Weimar Republic of 1919). In the comparative literature this is basically the distinction between "majoritarian" and "consensual" democracies (Lijphart 2012). Some constitution-makers feared the strong "leviathan" state and put in place numerous "checks and balances" on state power (USA). Others created a centralized state structure to introduce more unity into the government of fragmented societies (Turkey). The Nordic democracies are generally seen as consensual. This means that parliamentary elections translate the party votes fairly proportionally into parliamentary seats, creating a multi-party system (Ch. 2).

In this chapter we study how electoral preferences are channeled into the political institutions, how parliaments are organized and how governments are selected or deselected. First, we describe the electoral systems organizing selection processes to parliament. Second, we discuss how the political parties develop programs, select candidates and run electoral campaigns. Third, we ask who the parliamentarians are: are they representative of the voters? What about women in parliament? Fourth, we discuss how parliaments are organized: are the Nordic parliaments "working" or "debating" parliaments? Fifth, we focus on the type of governments we observe in the Nordic countries, and we use some of the insights from previous parts of the chapter – most notably factors related to elections, the organization of parliaments and the party system – to get a better understanding of why minority governments are so common in the Scandinavian part of the Nordics. The chapter ends with a brief conclusion.

ELECTIONS AND ELECTORAL SYSTEMS

There are basically two types of electoral systems: majoritarian systems, on the one hand, and proportional systems, on the other. In recent years, systems that mix elements from both have become quite popular. Majoritarian systems come in two main forms. In the proper majority systems, a majority of votes is required to win a seat. Normally there is a run-off second ballot between the (two) top candidates if nobody gets a majority in the first round (as in French parliamentary elections). In what are labeled plurality systems, more votes than any other candidate (or list) are required in the first (and only) round in order to be elected. This is the "first-past-the-post" system practiced in Great Britain and the US. Both systems normally operate with single-member constituencies and they produce less proportional results and a low number of major parties (but not necessarily a two-party system). This means that the discrepancy between the parties' share of votes and share of seats is larger than in proportional systems.

In systems with proportional representation (PR) the seats are distributed to party candidate lists according to their share of votes in multi-member constituencies. At the election the voters select a party list or tick off for a candidate on one of these lists. All Nordic parliaments are elected on the basis of a PR system, but they differ in terms of electoral formula, district size, number of adjustment seats and preferential voting. These are all elements that impact degrees of proportionality and which party representatives are elected. Preferential voting (voting for a particular candidate) also affects the balance between parties and candidates in the elections. In Table 4.1 we see that in the recent elections the electoral systems have produced higher proportionality in Denmark than in Norway and Finland. Still, all countries have fairly proportional systems with scores of less than four percentage points of deviation from complete proportionality in all recent elections. Majority/plurality systems usually have disproportionality scores of more than ten percentage points (Lijphart 2012: 150; Lundell 2008).

Only Finland practices the D'Hondt formula alone for the overall seat distribution. This gives less proportional results than Saint-Laguë.[1] And the Finns have no adjustment seats to improve proportionality at the national level. On the other hand, a high number of seats per constituency improves proportionality. With a high number of seats in one constituency the parties

1 Both are so-called divisor methods of proportional allocation. With the D'Hont formula one divides the votes of each party by 1-2-3-4 etc. before the available seats are distributed according to the quotient. The Sainte-Laguë system works similarly, but the divisors are 1-3-5-7 etc. instead. Norway and Sweden use a modified version of Sainte-Laguë, with 1.4 as the first divisor.

TABLE 4.1 NORDIC PARLIAMENTS AND ELECTORAL SYSTEMS.

	Cameral structure and size (seats, seats per 100 000)	Electoral formulae (percent adjustment seats)	District magnitude[1]	National threshold for winning adjustment seats	Deviation from proportionality[2]	Average deviation from proportionality 1945–2010[4]
Stortinget (Norway)	Unicameral (since 2009) 169 seats 3.3 per	Modified Sainte-Laguë (11 % adj. seats)	M = 7.9	4 % of the national vote	2001: 3.3 2005: 2.7 2009: 3.0 2013: 2.6	4.53
Folketinget (Denmark)	Unicameral (since 1953) 179 seats 3.1 per	D'Hondt and LR-Hare (23 % adj. seats)	M = 13.5[3]	2 % of the national vote	2001: 1.6 2005: 1.8 2007: 0.7 2011: 0.7 2015: 0.53	1.7
Riksdagen (Sweden)	Unicameral (since 1971) 349 seats 3.6 per	Modified Sainte-Laguë (11 % adj. seats)	M = 10.7	4 % of the national vote	2002: 1.5 2006: 3.0 2010: 1.3 2014: 2.6	2.4
Eduskunta (Finland)	Unicameral 200 seats 3.6 per	D'Hondt (No adj. seats)	M = 13.2	-	2003: 3.2 2007: 3.2 2011:2.9 2015:3.0	2.96
Althingi (Iceland)	Unicameral (since 1991) 63 seats 19.0 per	D'Hondt and LR Hare (14 % adj. seats)	M = 9.0	5 % of the national vote	2003: 1.9 2007: 3.5 2009: 2.6 2013: 6.2	3.85

1) Source: Inter-parliamentary Union (www.ipu.org). M is calculated by taking total number of seats minus adjustment seats, divided by the number of districts or constituencies.
2) Least Square Index for most recent elections. The scale runs from 0 to 100, with 0 representing full proportionality. Note that the figures are dependent on how the category "others" (parties or lists without any seats) are treated before calculations are made. Source: Michael Gallagher's electoral systems web page http://www.tcd.ie/Political_Science/staff/michael_gallagher/ElSystems/index.php.
3) Refers to Denmark proper (135 district seats). In addition, there are two constituencies (Faroe Islands and Greenland) with four seats.
4) Source: Lijphart 2012: 150

have fewer "wasted votes" at the district level, i.e. votes that do not produce any seats. The adjustments seats, found in all countries but Finland, are distributed on the national level to create a better overall fit after districts seats have been awarded. The Danish electoral system is the most proportional of all the Nordic systems, and only slightly less so than that of the Netherlands, which has the most proportional system of all democracies (Lijphart 2012: 150). In the Netherlands the whole country is one district, which results in very few wasted votes. The high proportionality in the Danish system is due to a high number of adjustment seats and a low threshold for parties to be eligible for these seats (2 %). Although they use the D'Hondt method for selecting constituency winners, the method for distributing the national adjustment seats produces a much more proportional distribution of party seats in the Folketinget.

One important difference between the Nordics is on preference voting. Can voters vote for particular candidates in order to influence candidate selection, or do they have to vote for the party list as given by the parties? This reflects on the degree to which the selection of MPs is an internal party affair which the voters cannot influence. The degrees of candidate influence vary, and among the Nordic countries Finland and Norway are at opposite poles in terms of preferential voting. In Norway voters do formally have the option of supporting a particular candidate, but this has never had any effect in practice; thus, for all practical purposes Norway operates with closed lists. The voters decide how many are elected from the different parties; the party lists determine which candidates are elected. This is decided during their internal nomination process. The Finnish voters, on the other hand, have substantial influence on which candidates are elected to parliament. At the election they have to vote for a particular candidate who is listed on one of the party lists. This vote is then counted as a party vote, and the allocation of seats to each party is based on the number of votes the candidates on a particular party list get. Which candidates are selected to parliament from each party is dependent on the number of personal votes for the different candidates on the party lists. Such an open list system is quite rare.

In Denmark, the voters can vote either for a candidate or for a party, and it is the candidate votes that decide which of the party candidates are elected. The Swedes also have the option of expressing a preference for a particular candidate, but the changes produced, compared to the party nominations, are fairly limited. Iceland has in practice a closed list system, but about half the constituency parties operate open primaries for the party candidates. Roughly 30 per cent of all voters participate in such party primaries (Bengtsson et al. 2014: 88). The primaries decide which place the candidate gets on the party lists and therefore also who is elected to the parliament. In general, preferential voting has been invoked to give the voters influence on the particular candidates elected. This also – to some extent – gives the elected candidates a personal mandate that may strengthen their position vis-à-vis the party in case of conflicts.

PARTIES AT ELECTIONS

The parties present a list of candidates, develop a political program and organize electoral campaigns. The party nominations are important in all the Nordic countries as they pick the able and the willing for the party list. The certified and nominated candidates basically emerge from discussions within the constituency parties. Particularly in the three Scandinavian countries few parties allow outsiders, without a proven party record, to enter the list. In Finland, well-known sports stars and media figures may be selected. The point then is to boost the party vote with the help of popular candidates. The national leadership is usually not much involved in putting together the party lists (Aylott 2011: 322); in fact, nominations are decentralized to the constituency parties. They guard their local power and – by implication – their influence over their constituency representative(s). The lists are usually composed to balance gender, age, district and intra-party political tendencies. The national parties present a political program at elections, stating their goals and priorities for the next election period. All candidates must support the party manifesto unless they have explicitly declared a different policy stand on a particular issue before receiving the nomination. This is rare, but may happen on moral or religious issues such as abortion. All parties have internal processes and debates to decide on their new electoral programs. These are finalized at a party congress with representatives from the local party branches.

How strong is the parties' link to civil society? In most West European countries the party organizations have experienced a decline in membership numbers. Norway, Sweden, Finland and Denmark actually lost from 40 to 60 per cent of their registered members between 1980 and 2009 (van Biezen et al. 2012: 34). In four Nordic countries roughly between four and eight per cent of the electorate were, in 2006, party members (ibid. p. 28). In Iceland there was an extraordinarily high level with 25–30 per cent of all voters being party members. This was most likely due to the mobilization triggered by the parties' primary elections (Bengtsson et al. 2014: 106). Even though Nordic parties by and large still formally have membership-based decision-making processes, there are arguments that parties in general have become both more leadership centered and more professionalized in terms of organizational processes (Poguntke and Webb 2005; Katz and Mair 2009). There is no systematic comparative discussion on this for the Nordic arena. However, the scattered information available shows that parties have substantially increased their professional staff.[2]

Election campaigns were professionalized early on in Finland. There were fewer restrictions on media campaigns (advertisements) and such campaigns required more professional assistance. The Finnish parties have used large sums on TV advertisements. Today this is legal in commercial television in Finland, and in all media in Iceland and in Sweden (since 2009). This is not legal in Denmark and Norway. All the Nordics, however, have since 2000 expe-

2 The number of party professionals in Norway has increased substantially both in the national party organizations and in the parliamentary groups (Heidar 2014a: 164). In Denmark, too, the growth of central party secretariats is well documented (Togeby et al. 2003: 184). Poguntke et al. 2016: 666 show that the party staff in Scandinavian parties is slightly below the European average.

rienced an increased centralization and professionalization of campaigns. The parties have organized professional media training for candidates, they have hired internal and external campaign specialists, commissioned polls, conducted focus groups and made increasing use of the social media (Bengtsson et al. 2014, ch. 7). Among the Nordic countries these developments came latest to Denmark. Increased public funding of parties has played an important part in the increased professionalization of campaigns and of party work in general. There has also been a stronger focus on the party leader – in the parties' own campaigns, but also in symbiosis with the media.

WHO ARE THE PARLIAMENTARIANS? DO THEY MIRROR THE ELECTORATE?

Parliamentarians in every democracy are predominantly men, middle-aged, with higher education and with an income above the average. A comparative study of Nordic parliamentarians in the 1990s basically confirms these tendencies (Narud and Valen 2000: 89). Men are better represented than women, traditionally more so among Icelandic parliamentarians than in the other Nordic parliaments. The age group between 45 and 55 is more prominent among parliamentarians, again mostly so on Iceland. The same patterns are also found in terms of education, white-collar occupations and public sector employment. The congruence between voters and MPs is highest in Sweden and Norway. The Icelandic deviations are explained by the primary election system, which puts a stronger focus on the candidates at the expense of the effort evident from internal party nomination processes which try to balance the party list with candidates appealing to a broad group of voters.

More recent national studies of MPs indicate two trends. First, there is a clear tendency in all countries for increased female presence in the Nordic parliaments. Today all parliaments have around 40 per cent female MPs, highest in Sweden with 44 and lowest in Denmark with 37 (see chapter 5 for details regarding female political representation).[3]

A second trend is the increase in levels of political professionalization, making parliaments even more exclusive. In Norway there is a marked increase in MPs' level of education and in MPs with a background from "higher professional" types of occupation. Most notably, the MPs with an occupational background from the voluntary organizations increased from about 10 per cent in the 1980s to close to 30 per cent in the 2010s (Allern et al. 2014: 306). This figure included a strong increase from the party secretariats at national and county levels, including political advisors, media advisers, etc. The number of full-time salaried party workers increased because the parties ran more media-focused

3 Statistics can be found on the web pages of the Inter-Parliamentary Union, see http://www.ipu.org/wmn-e/classif.htm. See also Wägnerud 2000 and Raaum 2004.

campaigns and because they could afford it. The public funding of the political parties has increased substantially and has made it possible to hire more political professionals – both in the party organization and in the parliamentary party groups. We do not have precise figures for the other Nordic countries on this, but the trend appears to be the same (e.g. Aylott 2011: 319).

According to democratic theories, representative assemblies should mirror the people they represent (Pitkin 1967). Democracies are about citizens being governed by their equals. This also introduces legitimacy and thrust into the system. Parliamentarians should therefore mirror the electorate both in terms of social background and in political attitudes. Without fair representation of women one cannot expect to get a fair hearing for female interests (Phillips 1995). In a comparative study from the 1990s it was found that the social background of Nordic MPs was related to political preferences. Male MPs represented male voters' preferences better than they represented those of female MPs – and vice versa (Narud and Valen 2000: 103). In this study it was also found that the level of issue congruence in the Nordic countries varied substantially from one issue to the other, but there was still generally a high level of congruence in all countries. This indicated that representative processes, like the elections, worked well and generated representative MPs (Holmberg 2000: 170). Holmberg also added, though, that this was by and large the case in most electoral democracies (ibid. 170). In other words, the Nordic democracies are not special. This view, however, is challenged for example by Lijphart, who argues that constitutional designs make a difference: the "consensual democracies" (such as the Nordic systems) outperform the "majoritarian democracies" (such as those in the UK and the US) in terms of democratic qualities (Lijphart 2012: 295).

THE ORGANIZATION OF PARLIAMENTS

We see in Table 4.1 that the size of Nordic parliaments varies and to some extent reflects the size of the populations – from 349 MPs in Sweden with 9.7 million inhabitants to 63 in Iceland with 0.33 million. The Icelanders are by far the best represented in terms of voters per MP with 19 MPs per 100,000 inhabitants. The other countries have between 3 and 4 MPs in comparison. All Nordic parliaments are organized to make laws, to decide on the budgets and to control the executive. Here we shall look at the role of the Speaker, the committees and the party groups.

The Speaker does not hold significant political power in any of the Nordic parliaments. He or she heads a speaker's collegium recruited proportionally from the party groups. Their task is to organize the constant flow of government proposals, the parliamentary initiatives and the regular business at a large workplace. They are supported by the administrative staff in parliament. In the three Scandinavian monarchies the Speaker is also often consulted by the king or the queen when a new government is to be formed, but without any impact on the outcome. The house debates are in practice organized to let parties present their positions according to their parliamentary relevance. The sequence of speakers and the time they are accorded in debates are in practice decided by the parliamentary groups and their secretariats. The MP responsible for the committee majority is generally first to speak in debates on the committee recommendation, followed by the spokesperson for the opposition. Other MPs are given time according to the priorities of the party group leadership, basically according to committee position. In any case, by the time an issue reaches the house floor, it is generally decided. The debates are meant for the public, although the media are not particularly interested unless there is some kind of crisis emerging. The media prefer to follow the processes in the committees and in the party groups. These are in principle arenas that are closed to journalists. Still, they usually find out what is going on. The house is also the arena for parliamentary interpellations and questions to the ministers. These are parliamentarian tools to raise issues and to criticize the government.

The number of standing committees varies between 26 (Denmark) and 8 (Iceland), while the other countries have between 12 and 15 such committees. Danish and Norwegian MPs are all members of a committee, the Norwegian MPs only of one each. Committees mirror by and large the structure of ministries, and all government proposals are discussed in the relevant committee before coming up for debate and decision on the floor. They scrutinize laws and budget proposals closely and invite interested groups (lobbyists) to present their views and their criticisms. Committee members are selected for a particular committee by their party groups. Seniority is a basis for committee assignments, most strongly followed in the Swedish Riksdag, less so in the Icelandic Althingi (Hagevi 2000).

The committee proposals usually display a broad common ground between the parties. The Nordic parliaments are not very polarized. But on the controversial points they split between the government and opposition parties. Sometimes the committee members produce cross-partisan changes in the government proposal – mostly with the consent of the relevant minister. In a 1996 study all parliamentarians rated the policy influence of committees as high: highest in Norway and Sweden, lowest in Denmark (Heidar 2000: 201). At the same time, they all rated the parliamentary power of ministers and parliamentary party groups even higher. These are, of course, old figures. However, a more updated study from 2013 for Norwegian parliamentarians shows that the average rating of committees, although still important, had declined (Rasch 2014).

The party groups and the group leaderships are the centers of power in the Nordic parliaments. These are composed by all MPs that are elected on the party list. The basis for their political work is the party's election program. The party programs have to be translated into day-to-day policies in the committees and on the floor. In parliamentary votes the party MPs almost always vote the same way. The Nordic parliaments are close to a "world record" in party cohesion (Jensen 2000: 218–19, 233). Sometimes the odd "free rider" speaks and votes differently from the group, but in those cases he or she has usually gotten permission from the party whip, and these votes will not change the voting outcome substantially. Sometimes the MPs have a "free vote", particularly on matters affecting moral issues or constituency interests. The uniformity of voting is based on political and ideological coherence more than on disciplinary mechanisms (ibid. 234). This coherence is anchored in the internal party processes, thousands of members and party officials working out a program decided at the party congress. Likewise, the candidates are selected and vetted through the party nomination process.

The work of all MPs is coordinated and monitored by the party group leadership/secretariat, and important issues are debated and decided at the group meetings (Jensen 2000). Clearly there may be the occasional "free rider", attracting a lot of media attention, but overall the party groups are the centers of power in all Nordic parliaments.

PARLIAMENTARY GOVERNMENT

The Nordic countries have a long parliamentary history. Iceland's Althingi operated as a consultative assembly from the year 930 until 1800, when it was abolished. All of the Nordic countries were fully democratized during the first quarter of the twentieth century, as universal suffrage (men and women) for parliamentary elections was introduced in this period. All of these countries have for many decades operated a parliamentary form of government: Denmark from 1901 and Finland and Sweden from 1917. The other two countries had such systems prior to their independence. Norway's first parliamentary cabinet was formed in 1884, and Iceland's first in 1904. Parliamentarism can be understood as a system where the government is responsible to the legislature. As a minimum, responsible government means that the government has to be tolerated by the legislature. If it is not tolerated, the government can be voted out of office and replaced with a new one. The move to parliamentarism around a century ago can be seen as a form of gradual democratization of executive power, as control over the cabinet shifted from an unelected monarch to the elected parliament.[4] Parliamentarism became constitutionalized well after the practice of responsible government was firmly established.

4 It may be argued that one of the first instances of parliamentary government in Europe was to be found in Sweden during the "Age of Liberty" (1718–1772), well before democracy emerged. Changes in what we today would call the government took place as a consequence of alterations in the composition of the four-chamber Estates Riksdag (von Sydow 1997). Thus, the Estates dominated the Crown.

The upper part of Table 4.2 shows governments by type and country since parliamentarism was introduced, or since independence in the case of Iceland. To ensure a unique parliamentary basis for each government, we consider it a change of government if (i) the partisan composition of the cabinet changes; (ii) a new prime minister takes office; or (iii) general elections are held (whether or not the same government remains in power). A few short-lived national crisis coalitions in Norway and Denmark are excluded as well as some caretaker administrations in Finland. The table is based on two dimensions. First, we distinguish between majority and minority governments. Second, governments are coalitions of two or more parliamentary parties or they are

TABLE 4.2 GOVERNMENTS IN NORDIC COUNTRIES[1)] IN PERCENTAGES (ABSOLUTE NUMBERS).

Type of Government	Norway 1884–2016	Denmark 1901–2016	Sweden 1917–2016	Finland 1917–2016	Iceland 1944–2016
Majority One-Party	20 (14)	5 (3)	5 (2)	0 (0)	0 (0)
Majority Coalition	18 (13)	17 (10)	18 (8)	68 (46)	88 (28)
Minority One-Party	46 (32)	44 (26)	66 (29)	12 (8)	9 (3)
Minority Coalition	16 (11)	34 (20)	11 (5)	20 (14)	3 (1)
Total Number of Governments (Number of elections)	N=70 (36)	N=59 (45)	N=44 (30)	N=68 (30)	N=32 (21)
Average Government Durability (in Years)	1.88	1.94	2.25	1.46	2.25
Share of Time Governed by Minority Cabinets 1945–99[2)]	56	83	73	22	3
Average Duration of Government Formation Process (in Days)[3)]	4.2	8.3	5.4	26.9	32.8
Percent Discretionary Termination of Governments 1945–99[4)]	32	77	20	60	48

1) The latest governments included in the table are Solberg 2013 in Norway, Løkke Rasmussen 2015 in Denmark, Löfven 2014 in Sweden, Sipilä 2015 in Finland and Jóhannsson 2016 in Iceland.
2) Source for the percentages: Rasch (2004: 118).
3) Source: See Golder (2010).
4) Source: Calculations based on Damgaard (2008: 306). Examples of discretionary termination are early elections, cabinet defeat, voluntary cabinet enlargement and (cabinet) party conflicts.

one-party cabinets. These dimensions yield four types of governments. Danish and Swedish governments during the time period before legislatures became unicameral were accountable to the popularly elected lower chamber only. Norwegian (and Icelandic) governments have always been accountable to the entire legislative assembly.

If we look at the time during which parliamentary systems have been in operation, Denmark, Sweden and Norway have had more minority cabinets than majority cabinets (78, 77 and 62 per cent of total governments, respectively). Most of the minority governments in all three countries have been single-party cabinets rather than coalitions. Denmark, however, has also had a substantial number of minority coalitions (34 per cent). Iceland, in contrast to the Scandinavian countries, has a history of majority coalitions (88 per cent); minority governments have been few and short-lived. The pattern in Finland is more varied. Finland frequently had minority governments before World War II, but majority coalitions have been the norm since the 1940s. The table also shows the proportion of time each country has been governed by minority cabinets after 1945, and again, Scandinavia differs from Finland and Iceland. Some variation in government stability between the countries is also indicated in the table. On average, cabinets have been more durable in Iceland and Sweden.[5] Stability in Finland is lower on average, but since the early 1980s, the country has moved towards more stable majority cabinets (Raunio 2004).

The process of government formation may be complex and time-consuming. There are, however, marked differences in this respect between countries with a large number of minority governments (and many one-party cabinets) and those countries where majority cabinets are the norm. It takes time to negotiate platforms for majority coalitions.

Compared with most other parliamentary countries in Europe, Scandinavian governments have two distinctive features. The first is the prevalence of minority governments, measured both as their share of the total number of governments (74 per cent in Scandinavia combined) and as their share of time in office. Actually, no other country in Europe has had more minority administrations than Denmark (with Sweden in second place). The second feature is the frequent occurrence of one-party governments (61 per cent in Scandinavia combined), indicating that political parties may be reluctant to enter formal coalitions (Strøm 1986; Sannerstedt 1996). Also, it indicates that there have been parties both able and willing to govern alone with shifting majority constellations in parliament on different policy matters. It should be emphasized that the prevalence of minority governments is not associated with political malaise, instability or poor performance, which used to be the conventional wisdom associated with governments without majority backing in parliament (Strøm 1990b; Field 2016).

The distinctiveness of Scandinavian governments, compared both to the two other Nordic countries and to a selection of other European systems, becomes even more apparent in Figure 4.1. The British-style countries are domina-

5 Note that even if the same government continues after an election, it is counted as a new government here because its support in parliament has changed as a consequence of the election.

ted by single-party majority governments. In these cases, majoritarian electoral systems tend to "fabricate" majority parties in parliament (or its lower house). Thus, minority governments are not an option. If there is no majority party after the election, which is typical if the electoral system belongs to the PR family, any majority government obviously has to involve two or more parties. Iceland and Finland have the same governmental experience as many of the countries on the European continent. Typically, majority coalitions are formed. The situation in France, Ireland and Southern European countries is more mixed (not shown), with a substantial share of minority governments. The same is true for some of the new democracies in Eastern Europe (such as Romania and the Czech Republic).

NEGATIVE PARLIAMENTARISM

There is no general agreement on why minority governments form, and why they are clearly viable and stable cabinet solutions in some political systems (see Strøm 1984, 1986 and 1990b; Field 2016). It is no easy task to explain why minority governments have been dominant in Scandinavia, while majority governments prevail in Finland and Iceland. In many respects, the polities of the Nordic countries are similar, and some of the differences clearly have no influence on government formation. It is challenging to locate potential causal factors that are shared by the Scandinavian countries but not by Finland and Iceland. As mentioned earlier, it is also worth noting that some of the countries

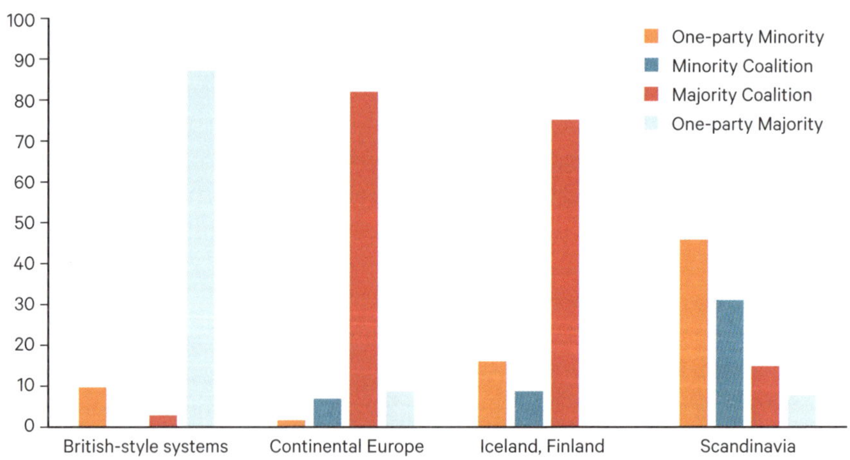

Figure 4.1 Type of governments in selected countries 1945–2015. Source: Data from the UiO-project "The Evolution of Parliamentarism and Its Political Consequences." British-style systems are the UK and Malta. Continental Europe includes Belgium, Germany, the Netherlands, Luxembourg and Austria. Scandinavia consists of Denmark, Norway and Sweden.

have, for no obvious reason, moved from minority to majority governments or vice versa over time.

In countries with a majoritarian electoral system, the process of government formation is relatively simple, at least as long as one party receives a majority of the seats. In multi-party systems, the formation processes may be complicated and lengthy, involving several actors in intense negotiations dragging out over weeks or even months. Typically, a complex set of formal and informal rules regulates government formation. Finland (particularly after 2000) and Sweden have important constitutional provisions, while the other Nordic constitutions – most notably Norway's – put few specific restrictions on the formation and resignation processes. Still, clear practices and expectations have evolved over time.

Parliamentary rules, be they formal or not, may be of a *negative* or *positive* type. The negative rule implies that the government simply has to be tolerated by the parliament, but it does not need to achieve active support of any majority in the chamber when it is formed. Acceptance of a no-confidence proposal makes it apparent that a cabinet is not tolerated.

In a system of positive parliamentarism, a majority of legislators has to support a government at some stage during the formation process (Rasch et al. 2015). Investiture rules are varied. In some cases, parliament elects the (prospective) prime minister (which is the case in both Sweden and Finland), while in other cases a vote of confidence in the newly formed government is required. Similarly, the decision rule differs. It could be absolute majority (support from at least half of the members of parliament), simple majority (at least half of those voting) or negative majority. The latter rule means that the prime minister or government is supported unless an absolute majority of the parliamentarians votes against. Until recently, all of the Nordic countries had informal, negative formation practices. Finland introduced an investiture vote in the mid-1990s. Swedish prime ministers are elected by the parliamentarians, but the decision rule is a weak negative one: a proposal for a prime minister is accepted as long as an absolute majority in the *Riksdag* does not reject it.[6] Thus, majority backing is not required, which is equivalent to saying that the government only needs be tolerated by the majority.

Today, the head of state is not actively involved in the government formation process of any Nordic country. The power of the Finnish president has recently been reduced, and the country has been fully "parliamentarised." In

6 The investiture vote in Sweden in 1978 is illustrative. The candidate for prime minister, Ola Ullsten, was supported by only 39 out of the 349 members of the parliament. A majority of 66 MPs voted against Ullsten, and a total of 215 abstained. Obviously, an absolute majority had not turned Ullsten down. One year later Torbjörn Fälldin was a candidate. He was supported by 170 MPs. It did not matter that a majority of 174 voted against Fälldin, as long as this number was less than an absolute majority of at least 175 MPs (i.e. 349/2).

the former system, which was semi-presidential in nature, "the president was the incontestable executive head of Finland" (Paloheimo 2003: 222). The president often was quite free in selecting the prime minister, especially before the 1980s. Under the current constitutional framework, the parliament nominates the prime minister, and the president is only left with the task of formal appointment. Thus, the president plays a role that is not very different from that of the monarch in Denmark and Norway. In Sweden, however, the new Constitution of 1975 also robbed the king of his formal and symbolic duties related to government formation and resignation (Bergman 2004). Constitutionally, Iceland seems to have a rather strong head of state who is directly elected by the people (Kristjánsson 2004; Indridason 2005). In practice, Iceland's political system has never functioned as a truly semi-presidential system (at least not before the recent financial crisis), and Icelandic presidents have been considerably weaker than the Finnish presidents formerly were. With respect to government formation, the parliament and the parties in Iceland undoubtedly have the upper hand.

Finland and Iceland have presidents, and at least on paper they consequently have had a situation of dual executive powers. Does this explain the overwhelming predominance of majority cabinets in the two countries? The answer is mainly negative. No one has demonstrated that majority governments are primarily the result of presidential influence, although strong presidents – such as Finland's Urho Kekkonen – may have been of help in finding viable governmental solutions (or in blocking weak alternatives).[7] In fact, Finnish presidents also strongly influenced government formation during the earlier decades when minority governments were common. In a semi-presidential system, the executive branch tends to be stronger relative to the legislature than is the case in a purely parliamentary system.

OPPOSITION INFLUENCE AND MINORITY GOVERNMENTS

Processes of government formation in minority situations may be complex. Several parties interact, and each tries to attain the best possible outcome given other players' preferences and actions. Party leaders and their more-or-less fractionalized party groups may be motivated by short-term as well as long-term goals. Governmental office is sometimes an end in itself, but most politicians seek office as a means to affect policy decisions and legislation or to influence their electoral fortunes (Strøm 1990a; Laver and Schofield 1990). Naturally, entering government and obtaining government portfolios is the only way to satisfy office-seeking motivations. However, policy-seeking and vote-seeking parties under some circumstances may find that they can

7 The last case of a president strongly influencing the process of government formation was in 1987, when President Mauno Koivisto intervened (Raunio 2004: 136).

achieve as much in opposition as in government. In general, parties will be more inclined to seek office if the net benefits of governing outweigh the net benefits of being in opposition (which in turn depends heavily on the type of government). Government participation almost always increases the policy influence of a party, but the extra influence normally comes with an electoral cost. Incumbent governments tend to lose support at the polls, which makes governing less attractive than it would otherwise be. Governments in Western Europe have on average lost two and a half percentage points in post-WWII elections (Petersson et al. 2002). These losses have increased decade by decade and reached more than six percentage points during elections in recent years. Additionally, in Western Europe, members of majority coalitions tend to lose more votes than parties in minority governments. Countries differ widely in the extent to which governments maintain their strength in the election that follows their term in office. Danish governments perform comparatively well in this regard, that is, they perform better than the European average (Müller and Strøm 2000: 589). Norway is close to the average, while Finnish and Swedish governments have a slightly poorer record: three out of four governments have been punished by the voters.

A parliamentary opposition could be strong or weak. It can be assumed that the greater the potential influence of opposition groups in parliament, the fewer the benefits of governing and the less tempting governmental office becomes. Thus, we should expect minority governments to occur more frequently (see Strøm 1990b). If this is an important factor in the Nordic case, opposition groups should potentially be more influential in Scandinavian legislatures than they are in Finland and Iceland. Influence, of course, is hard to measure, and a comparative judgment based on extensive analyses of actual decision-making is not available.

Nordic parliaments can influence the formulation of policy and legislation in a variety of ways. All of them have been regarded as "working parliaments," in contrast to the less influential "debating parliaments" that are also found in Europe. All of them have well-structured committee systems, as we already have shown in a previous section. Let us elaborate a little more.

Working parliaments have a specialized system of standing committees that broadly correspond to government ministries. They have rules of enactment and deliberation that give priority to committee recommendations, proposals and participation in the final stages of parliamentary decision-making. Committees can be organized to facilitate the dispersal of policy-making influence throughout the assembly, spreading it to opposition groups as well as to members of the government parties. Influential committees have "invested" in expertise and use their specialized knowledge to control and revise, rather than just rubber-stamp, decisions from the government. In this perspective, potential influence is linked to such things as the existence of a relatively high number of (not very large) committees, restrictions on the number of committee assignments per legislator (to allow MPs to gain expertise), the ability of committees to rewrite government bills and the proportional distribution of committee chairs (which implies that the opposition gets a leadership position in parliament). The scholarly classifications of Nordic committee systems according to these factors are ambiguous. Powell (2000, 34) claims that committees in Scandinavian legislatures facilitate opposition influence to a larger degree than do Finnish committees (Iceland is not included in his data set). Mattson and Strøm (1995) distinguish between the drafting authority (e.g., authority to initiate and rewrite bills and to demand documents) and agenda control (e.g., control of timetables and the right to summon witnesses) of standing committees, but Scandinavian committees do not come out consistently ahead of their Finnish and Icelandic counterparts. For instance, Finnish standing committees are among the strongest with respect to drafting authority but are rather weak when agenda control is considered. Surprisingly, Mattson and Strøm's data indicate that Danish committees are among the weakest in Western Europe when it comes to authority to initiate legislation and rewrite governmental bills. As we have seen, Denmark is also the country with more minority governments than any other. Similarly, Döring (1995) does not consider the overall balance between the government and the standing committees with respect to setting the legislative agenda and passing legislation to vary significantly among the Nordic counties, but he notes that the institutional framework leaves Danish committees with a somewhat less central role than standing committees in the other countries.

In a broader perspective, Damgaard (1994) has noted that Scandinavian parliaments stand out as strong and influential. He observes a trend indicating a "decline of governments" or a "resurgence of parliaments," and not a "decline of parliaments" over time as some of the standard literature claims. Kristjánsson (2004: 159), however, notes that the Icelandic Althingi seems to possess the formal means of asserting itself as a principal institution but that parliament has "steadily been losing power" to the executive. The semi-presidential character of the Finnish political system until recently may have generated a different legislative-executive balance than in the other Nordic countries. A slightly stronger executive branch also implies that the policy-making influence of opposition forces might be somewhat weaker. Damgaard (1990, 2000) also observes differences between Finnish and Scandinavian parliaments with respect to levels of activity and involvement.

THE PARTY SYSTEM AND TYPE OF GOVERNMENT

Traditionally, minority governments have been explained as the result of party fragmentation and polarization. In an early discussion, Janson (1928) pointed to the gradual development of a multi-party legislature and a reluctance to enter coalitions as the main background for the formation of Swedish minority governments in the 1920s. Some authors suggest that minority cabinets tend to be formed in unstable and highly conflictual political systems, emerging when everything else has failed. In general, these claims have not been substantiated. Herman and Pope (1973) demonstrated that minority governments were more common than previously assumed (constituting 36 per cent of governments in their cross-national data set). They also suggested a variety of reasons for this phenomenon. First, a substantial proportion of the minority governments they studied were caretaker administrations. These governments typically came to power as a result of some sort of crisis and were deliberatively established for only a short period of time. Second, some minority governments took office because one or more coalition partners withdrew from majority coalitions. Third, a few minority governments came to office because elections that usually provided one party with a legislative majority surprisingly ended with no party winning a majority of seats (and, typically, a new election was held soon thereafter). Fourth, minority cabinets arose because extreme parties on either side of the political spectrum were not credible, reliable, formal coalition partners for parties closer to the center. Fifth, and probably most interesting in this context, some minority cabinets were formed in situations in which one of the parties fell only a few seats short of a legislative majority. Often in such cases, the dominant party formed a one-party minority government and usually did so with the formal support of one of the smaller parties.

All of the Nordic countries have had multi-party systems at least since the 1920s. Still, there are important differences among the countries in this respect, and marked changes in the number and relative size of the parties have occurred over time (see chapter 2). The number of seats in parliaments is the hard currency of coalition bargaining, obviously making features of the party system relevant in our context. Not surprisingly, the party system variable seems to have resurfaced in recent coalition research (e.g., Schofield 1993; Laver and Shepsle 2000; van Roozendaal 1992; Crombez 1996; Skjæveland 2009; and Laver and Benoit 2015).

As an indication of the overall party fragmentation after 1945, Figure 4.2 shows the effective number of parties in each of the Nordic parliaments since WWII.[8] The effective number of parties is a measure that captures the actual level of party fragmentation or fractionalization in the parliament. For most of

8 This index is calculated as follows: one divided by the sum of squares of the proportion of seats won by each parliamentary party (Laakso and Taagepera 1979). This index takes the relative size of parties into account, instead of just counting the number of parties (some of which might be very small and insignificant).

the time period we cover, the Finnish *Eduskunta* has had the most fragmented party system – a five-party system. From 1973 to the late 1980s, Danish elections resulted in an equally fragmented parliament. In recent years, Norway has reached almost the same level. Iceland had a fragmented legislature in the late 1980s, but it has generally had a moderate number of parties. Sweden has had, on average, the lowest level of fragmentation. Over time the Nordic countries have become more similar, with four to five effective parties. Today, the countries split in two groups, with somewhat higher fragmentation in Denmark and Finland than in the three other countries.

Mattila and Raunio (2002: 266) claim that the predominance of majority coalitions in Finland can be explained by the fragmented party system. The claim is at best only partly supported by the data in Figure 4.2. More important than the overall level of fragmentation, as measured by the effective number of parties, is the existence of one strong or dominant party in the midst of the legislature. Even in a fragmented assembly without a majority party, if one party has a far larger share of the seats than any other party, it should occupy a strong bargaining position. In many minority situations, dominant parties will be able to negotiate their way into governmental offices as minority administrations. In fact, Crombez (1996) has argued that as the largest party grows larger and more central, minority governments become more likely. A number of cross-national studies support this hypothesis (e.g., Martin and Stevenson 2001; Volden and Carrubba 2004; Laver and Benoit 2015). Almost all of the minority governments in Schofield's (1993) data set were based on large, centrist parties.

If we take a closer look at the Nordic party systems, the largest party in Finland after 1945 has, with few exceptions, been substantially smaller than the largest party in Scandinavian parliaments. The Scandinavian countries have all had a relatively centrist social-democratic party as the dominant group. Iceland has also mostly had a dominant party. Here, however, the Conservatives have been the largest group in parliament. Data from party manifestos indicate that the Icelandic Conservatives have tended to be less centrist on the left-right scale compared with the other Icelandic parties than are the Scandinavian social democrats in their respective legislatures (Budge et al. 2001) (see also chapter 2). Majority coalitions in Finland and Iceland and minority governments in Scandinavia, then, seem to be roughly in line with expectations from Crombez (1996) and others. If we look at the era of minority governments in Finland, the Social Democrats was the largest party and, after some elections, the dominant force in the legislature (over 30 per cent of the seats in most elections from 1919 to 1939).

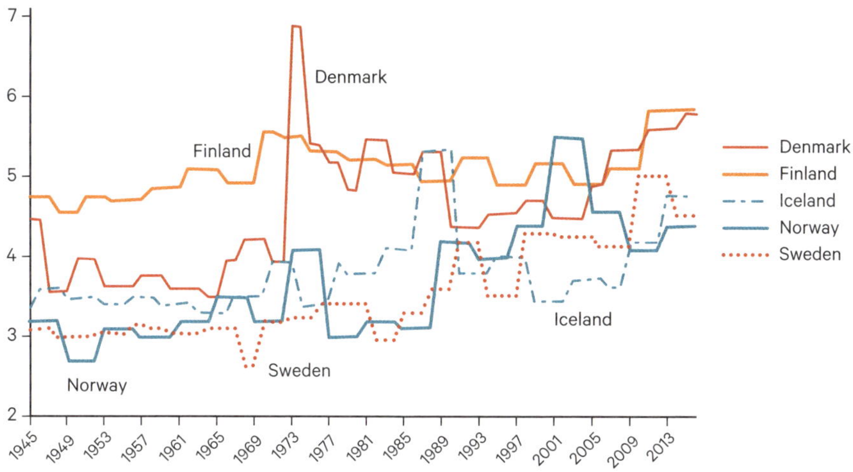

Figure 4.2 Effective number of parties (seats) in Nordic parliaments, 1945–2016.

CONCLUSION

In this chapter we have discussed how votes are transformed into seats in parliament, and how and to what extent the distribution of seats determines what kind of government is formed. The first part has to do with political representation, and is mainly regulated by the electoral system. The latter has to do with the principle of parliamentarism or the confidence relationship between elected representatives in parliament and the executive branch. At every stage of the processes from election campaigns and parliamentary elections, via parliamentary organization and politics, to governments and policy outcomes, political parties play a central – or rather *the* central – role.

With respect to political representation and parliamentarism, the similarities between the five Nordic countries are perhaps more striking than the differences (see also Bergman and Strøm 2011). All of these countries have proportional electoral systems. All of their parliaments are today unicameral, organized in a roughly similar way internally. All of the countries, except Finland after they introduced a simple majority investiture in 2000, have a negative form of parliamentarism. In Lijphart's (2012) terms, all of the Nordic democracies are of a consensual type. Still, we have highlighted some differences. First, the Scandinavian countries are constitutional monarchies, while Finland and Iceland are republics with presidents as heads of state. Politically, the monarchs are insignificant (and the Swedish king plays no political role whatsoever). The Nordic presidents are popularly elected, and have occasionally been politically significant (in Finland chiefly before 2000). Second, even if all elections are conducted by proportional systems, the countries differ significantly with respect to the candidate choice given to the voters. Finland and Norway are the Nordic extremes, with open party lists and closed party lists respectively. Third, the countries differ with respect to type of government. In Scandinavia, minority governments over time have been far more common than majority governments. Finland and Iceland are typically governed by majority cabinets. A likely source of the dissimilarity in government types is differences in the party systems of the countries.

CHAPTER 5
THE NORDIC GENDER EQUALITY MODEL

Mari Teigen & Hege Skjeie

INTRODUCTION[1]

The exploration of Nordic models in comparative welfare state research often includes gender equality as an important dimension (c.f. Kautto 2010). International indexes that map degrees of gender equality regularly rank the Nordic countries at the top of either global or regional surveys, as seen in for instance the United Nations Development Program's (UNDP) Gender Inequality Index, the World Economic Forum's Global Gender Gap and the European Union's (EU) Gender Equality Index . Feminist scholarship on gender regimes (Walby 2009) groups the Nordic countries as more equal than others. Some have claimed that the Nordic countries embody a state form that makes it possible to transform them into "truly woman-friendly societies" (Hernes 1987). In some instances, Nordic model thinking has become so value-laden as to portray Nordic countries as nearly "nirvanas" of equality (cf. Lister 2009).

As these examples show, the basis for modeling Nordic gender equality varies. Indexes mainly depict gender gaps in performance on various equality indicators. Regime theory, in contrast, ties public institutions and public policies directly to what are then seen as outcome variables, assuming and/or testing causal links between policies and performance or practice. However, as noted by Kautto (2010), views of the Nordic model often suffer from a lack of consensus on the precise specifications that define the model. Traditionally, Kautto claims, the notion of a Nordic model simply and somewhat vaguely refers to an active state, a large public sector, and a broadly conceived public responsibility for the social welfare of citizens all within the framework of a market economy (Kautto 2010: 587). In welfare state research, the treatment of gender equality as an important dimension is often related to a strong performance on various employment indicators. Economists who investigate Nordic

1 Many thanks to Marie Andersen Hulthin for her highly competent and conscientious research assistance throughout the process of writing this chapter.

model institutions establish conceptual ties between mainly increasing female labor participation since the 1960s, and welfare state expansion through public care for children and the elderly.[2] The institutional framework of Nordic welfare state policies is then seen as generally beneficial to the inclusion of women in paid work, and the specific orientation of family policies as either helpful in furthering, or partly designed to promote, such inclusion (Ellingsæter & Leira 2006, Leira 2012, Ellingsæter 2014).

International gender equality indexes commonly apply gender gap measures to employment rates and monthly earnings, but also to levels of education, forms of political participation and representation, and/or health and life expectancy. Such indexes are outcome-oriented in the sense that they address forms of social progress and the equalization of such over time among the citizens of specific countries, for instance, EU member states. However, they are often (at the same time) meant to provide general guidelines for relevant policy making in the sense that observed discrepancies in the outcomes between men and women could prompt political measures to reduce gender gaps.[3]

In this chapter, we investigate the descriptive premises involved in portrayals of a Nordic model of gender equality. Mainly, however, we focus on the equality dimensions that form the baseline in comparative welfare state research and research on political participation. We outline these dimensions as norms for *economic equity* and *democratic parity*. Broadly speaking, an equality norm for economic equity would include equal educational opportunities, equal pay for work of equal value, gender balance in family life, and gender-balanced participation in labor markets. An equality norm for democratic parity would, of course, presuppose equal rights to vote, assemble, and hold office but, more importantly in this context, stress inclusive opportunity structures for civil society and gender balance in political decision making.

First, we examine whether and how descriptive statistics that assess these two dimensions currently rank Nordic countries compared with other European countries among the member states of the European Union. For this, we utilize the EU's Gender Equality Index.[4] We then search for comparable statistics on outcome and performance that include the Nordic non-EU members Norway and Iceland to explore similarities and differences within the Nordic region, as well as see how these countries compare to the Nordic EU members: Denmark, Finland and Sweden. Finally, we approach the question of policy models, discussing whether it is possible to identify a distinctive policy profile common

2 ESOP project description http://www.sv.uio.no/esop/english/about/reports/plans-reports/The%20CoE%20Application

3 One example is the stated purpose of the EU's Gender Equality Index to "provide decision makers with support when assessing how far a given Member State is from reaching gender equality" (C.F. Holst forthcoming).

4 http://eige.europa.eu/gender-statistics/gender-equality-index

to the Nordic countries for how to promote economic equity and democratic parity. We conclude this investigation with a set of what we regard as informed speculations regarding how policy might matter to gender equality in the Nordic countries today.

ECONOMIC EQUITY AND DEMOCRATIC PARITY

Much model-oriented welfare state research departs from Esping-Andersen's (1990, 1999) influential typology of three forms of welfare state regimes. A historically distinct Northern European model of gender equality policy is depicted as embedded in the dominant welfare state arrangements of the (ideal type) social democratic regime, in contrast to the liberal and conservative corporatist regimes. Briefly outlined, the liberal model is characterized by limited state involvement and market-based services. Welfare state services are typically means-tested assistance, and modest universal transfers are directed toward those most in need. The conservative-corporatist regime model is strongly committed to traditional family values, where social insurance excludes non-working wives and family benefits are directed toward supporting motherhood. The social democratic regime type builds on a welfare system where all benefit, all are dependent, and thus the willingness to pay for the system includes the many (Esping-Andersen 1990: 27–28), see also chapter 9.

As summed up by Kautto (2010: 592), the Nordic welfare states have developed into dual-earner societies in contrast to Continental and Southern European countries where female labor market participation is significantly lower, and the male-breadwinner family is still relatively prevalent. Along the "social democratic public service route" (Walby 2004) that characterizes the Nordic countries, public services (in particular publicly financed childcare and parental leave) were developed to provide women with the capacity to increase their paid employment. Feminist scholarship on the Nordic model is often tied to a broader notion of gender-inclusive citizenship. The citizenship framework incorporates aspects of gender equality across paid work, care work, and income, as well as across areas of participation in political life and decision-making (Bergqvist 1999, Siim & Borchorst 2002, 2016, Lister 2009). More recently, aspects related to violence against women and intersectional forms of discrimination[5] have been increasingly addressed in model terms (Lister 2009, Borchorst et al. 2012, Siim & Borchorst 2016). If we apply the universal UN-based framework of the Convention to Eliminate All Forms

5 Intersectionality refers to the interaction between gender, race, and other categories of difference in individual lives, social practices, institutional arrangements, and cultural ideologies, and the outcome of these interactions in terms of power (Davis 2008: 68; Krizsan, Skjeie & Squires 2012: 18). The key issue of an intersectional analysis is how oppression, subordination, and privilege cut across systems of differentiation (Borchorst & Teigen 2010: 19).

of Discrimination Against Women (CEDAW) as a baseline for what gender equality is all about, we see that norms and policies for legal equality, bodily integrity, and democratic parity are as important as norms and policies for economic equity.

For democratic parity, Lister (2009) cites the mid-1990s work by Karvonen and Selle (1995) on women's political representation in the Nordic countries as a development that "transformed the face of politics." Central to Hernes' (1987) work on Nordic state feminism is the combination of "mobilization from below" through movement politics and "integration from above" through party politics. Comparative politics scholarship has, nevertheless, taken care to underline the incremental approach to parity in political participation that has characterized Nordic polities: a gradual increase in political representation across all parties since the early 1970s and a common unwillingness to apply legal measures, for instance, in the form of electoral quotas, to determine the composition of parliaments (Freidenvall, Dahlerup & Skjeie 2006).

In line with most Nordic model debates, research on gender equality now asks about the impact of different ties among Nordic countries to the European Union. Although Sweden and Finland joined Denmark as EU members in 1995, Norway and Iceland chose to remain outside, building new EU ties through the European Economic Area (EEA) agreement. Gender equality policies vary considerably among the EU member states. However, there has also been substantive hard law harmonization as a result of EU regulations and court decisions (Kantola 2010, cf. Skjeie, Holst & Teigen 2016, also Krizsan, Skjeie & Squires 2012). Various studies of general trends in welfare policy development through the 1990s and 2000s tend to leave a question mark. Seen from afar, the Nordic welfare states still look similar. A closer examination of reforms and institutional developments, however, suggests that Nordic distinctiveness is not as self-evident as it was two decades ago (Kautto 2010: 600, Engelstad & Hagelund 2015).

In the early 2000s, Siim and Borchorst formulated a minimalist conception of the Nordic gender equality model as one combining (policies to promote) high levels of participation in political life and in paid work (2002: 92). Based on the Nordic model research presented in this introduction, we agree with this conception. These two dimensions have been particularly relevant to the academic debate on the Nordic model of gender equality. As outlined in the introduction, we discuss these dimensions as the equality norms for economic equity and democratic parity.

EUROPEAN PATTERNS: ECONOMIC EQUITY AND DEMOCRATIC PARITY

In this section, we describe a core set of statistics that measure gender gaps on the two dimensions that are particularly relevant to the Nordic gender equality model. We apply the Gender Equality Index (GEI) monitored by the European Institute for Gender Equality (EIGE). The Gender Equality Index is constructed to map country variation within the EU in gender equality outcomes on a spectrum of variables. We first present an overview of European variations in the index as such.[6] This overview is followed by a more detailed analysis of the differences between the three Nordic EU countries limited to economic equity and democratic parity measures. Third, the average Nordic scores are compared to the EU average for these same dimensions. Finally, we compare different groupings of EU member states in line with Esping-Andersen's classic typology of welfare state models, which was limited to clusters of Western European states. The question we pose is simply whether it is possible at present, based on core gender equality statistics (from 2012), to identify a common Nordic pattern, one that at the same time distinguishes Nordic EU member countries from other EU member countries.

The Gender Equality Index is built around six core domains (work, money, knowledge, time, power, and health) and two satellite domains (violence against women and intersecting inequalities).[7] The index provides an overview of total scores, where all three Nordic member countries have an average score of about 70 points (the maximum is 100): Sweden is followed by Finland and then Denmark. No other European country scores above 70. Only the Netherlands is in proximity to the Nordic group of countries, with an overall score just below 70. Belgium and the United Kingdom (UK) follow more than 10 points below the Netherlands. A mixed group of countries from continental Europe, the UK, and Ireland score around the EU average on the Gender Equality Index. The lowest-scoring countries are Eastern and Southern European countries, such as Romania, Slovakia, Portugal, Greece, Bulgaria, and Croatia. Slovenia is the only country in the Eastern European region that scores above the EU average (see Figure 5.1).

Our analysis singles out two core dimensions in the Nordic gender equality model. In this analysis, *economic equity* includes the two domains on the GEI: work and money. *Democratic parity* includes the only relevant domain, power. The work domain measures participation,[8] segregation,[9] and quality

6 Note that the Gender Equality Index does not include Norway and Iceland, as they are not EU member countries.

7 The core domains of the EIGE index provide a common measure of gender equality, but it is possible to analyze the scores for each domain separately. The index scores vary between 1 = total inequality and 100 = full gender equality. In this overview of Nordic similarities and differences in gender equality outcomes, we focus on five of the domains measured by the index: work, economy/money, knowledge, use of time, and power, which we view as being at the core of the Nordic gender equality model.

8 Full-time equivalent employment (%)

9 Sectoral segregation (%)

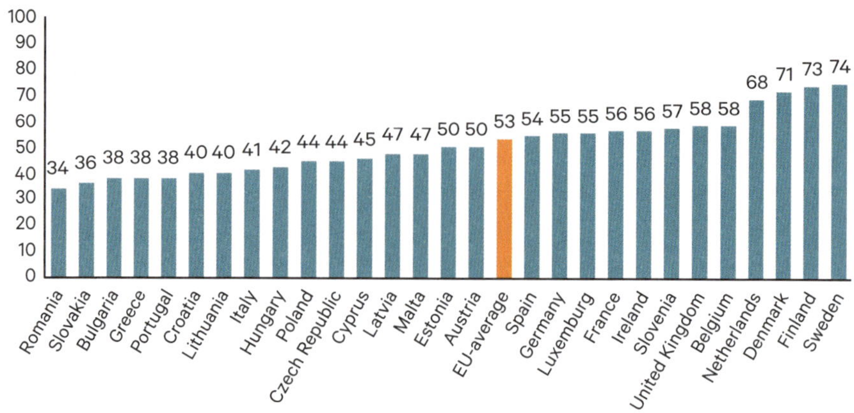

Figure 5.1 The EIGE Gender Equality Index, EU comparison 2012, average country scores.

of work.[10] The money domain measures gender gaps in the distribution of financial resources and economic situation. The power domain measures the representation of women and men in decision-making positions and includes political[11] and economic power,[12] which is in line with formalized EU gender equality strategies.[13]

Sweden scores the highest on economic equity, Finland the highest on democratic parity. Although the differences between the Nordic EU member countries are small for economic equity, and particularly small for the money domain, the differences between the Nordic countries are more pronounced for democratic parity than for economic equity (see Table 5.1). Denmark scores significantly lower than Finland and Sweden. Sweden is doing the best if we understand democratic parity in a limited sense, as gender balance in political decision-making positions. When we include economic decision making, Finland scores the highest.

Thus, internal Nordic variation is most clearly shown in the comparatively low scores of Denmark for democratic parity. However, the Danish score is still well above the EU average.[14]

10 Flexible personal/family arrangements (%)

11 Ministerial representation (%), parliamentary representation (%), regional assemblies' representation (%)

12 Members of boards (%) and members of Central Bank (%)

13 http://ec.europa.eu/justice/gender-equality/

14 In the economic equity dimension, the work domain shows more variation in the segregation measure than the participation measure. The country differences in the money domain are relatively small on the measurement of economic situation, while the variation in scores is large for financial resources, varying from Romania with the lowest score (21.1) to Luxembourg with the highest score (96.4), followed by Ireland (75.8). On this measurement, the Nordic countries do well, but several other countries do just as well.

TABLE 5.1 SCORES OF THE NORDIC EU COUNTRIES ON THE GENDER EQUALITY INDEX (THREE DOMAINS: WORK, MONEY, AND POWER).

	Economic Equity		Democratic Parity
	Work	**Money**	**Power**
Denmark	76.8	76.4	55.7
Finland	72.6	79.9	75.7
Sweden	81.0	80.6	71.7
Diff.: Lowest vs. highest	8.4	4.2	20.0

TABLE 5.2 AVERAGE SCORES OF THE NORDIC EU COUNTRIES AND AVERAGE EU SCORES ON THE GENDER EQUALITY INDEX (THREE DOMAINS: WORK, MONEY, AND POWER).

	Economic Equity		Democratic Parity
	Work	**Money**	**Power**
Nordic average	76.8	78.9	67.5
EU average	61.9	67.8	39.7
Diff.: Nordic – EU	14.9	11.1	27.8

These gender gap and gender equality measures clearly show that on the two dimensions most central to common Nordic model examination, i.e. (economic equity and democratic parity) the Nordic EU member countries fare particularly well. On the democratic parity dimension, several countries do relatively well on the political power measure, but Sweden and Finland, with exceptionally high scores, clearly belong in a group of their own. Also on the economic power measure, Sweden and Finland, with Slovenia, score the highest. Nordic exceptionalism is thus most clearly pronounced in indicators that assess democratic parity. While the indicators of economic equity cover large population strata, the indicators of democratic parity cover only small, select groups of decision makers. Information on broader aspects of democratic parity, such as voter and civil society-based participation, is not included in the EU Gender Equality Index. This simply means that when the Nordic countries stand out in EU-based comparisons, they do so primarily because women participate on more equal terms among the countries' political and economic elites.

As outlined in the introduction, Gøsta Esping-Andersen's (1990, 1999) classic typology highlights three forms of welfare state regimes. In such welfare state regime analysis, the Nordic EU member states are regularly classified as social democratic welfare states. Germany, France, and Italy are regularly grouped as conservative-corporatist welfare states, while the United Kingdom and Ireland are examples of countries that are grouped as liberal welfare states. When we apply this grouping to the Gender Equality Index scores for two specific dimensions (economic equity and democratic parity) on 2012 data, we see that the social democratic countries still score higher on gender equality than the liberal and conservative countries and that the distance is most clearly pronounced for democratic parity. In the economic equity dimension, the distance is highest between the social democratic and the conservative-corporatist countries;[15] on the democratic parity dimension, the conservative welfare states are closest to the scores of the social democratic welfare states.

However, in the money domain of the Gender Equality Index, the differences between the social democratic welfare state and the liberal and conservative welfare states are astonishingly small, given the overall picture of the variation between the regimes. Briefly, the money domain measures gender gaps in the distribution of financial resources and the economic situation, while the work domain measures labor market participation, labor market segregation, and quality of work. The index scores on money show that differences between women's and men's income and other financial resources persist in the social democratic welfare states and are almost as clearly pronounced here as within the other regime types.

NORDIC VARIATION: ECONOMIC EQUITY AND DEMOCRATIC PARITY

In the previous section, we compared Nordic EU member countries to other EU member countries. In this section, we check for broader Nordic patterns and internal Nordic variations by including the Nordic non-EU members Norway and Iceland in the analysis. The Nordic Council of Ministers has developed a set of statistical indicators that shed light on the gender equality status in the Nordic region—and within the regional variations. The indicators are intended to monitor progress, address challenges, and inform policies. The collection of

TABLE 5.3 THE AVERAGE SCORES ON THE GENDER EQUALITY INDEX (THREE DOMAINS: WORK, MONEY, AND POWER) FOR THE THREE TYPES OF WELFARE STATES.

	Economic Equity		Democratic Parity
	Work	**Money**	**Power**
Social democratic	76.8	78.9	67.5
Liberal	67.6	76.8	32.3
Conservative	59.1	74.4	38.6
Diff.: Lowest and highest	17.7	4.5	35.2

15 This is most clearly shown in the work domain. The differences between the three types of welfare states are modest in the money domain, although they follow the pattern where the social democratic welfare state tops the list followed by the liberal welfare state and then the conservative welfare state.

gender equality data has resulted in a joint statistical databank: Nordic Statistics.[16] The indicators include important issues, such as family and care, education, labor market, economy, and influence and power. Nordic Statistics was completed in 2014. The Nordic dataset also allows for comparison over time, although the statistics differ depending on the actual timeline. Some figures show developments since the early 1990s, others only the last 10-year period.

The analysis of data retrieved from Nordic Statistics is used to map variations in economic equity, including the following four indicators: men's and women's participation in the labor market, gender segregation in the labor market, the gender pay gap, and part-time work. Nordic variations in democratic parity include only two indicators: representation of women in the Nordic national assemblies and representation of men and women on listed company boards.

Economic equity

In the Nordic countries, women's labor market participation has increased rapidly since the 1960s (Chafetz & Hagen 1996, Leira 2002). Nordic Statistics shows the employment rates for women and men from 1990 to 2015. The figures reveal relative stability and small cross-country variations. Country-specific changes follow, by and large, the same pattern for men and women.

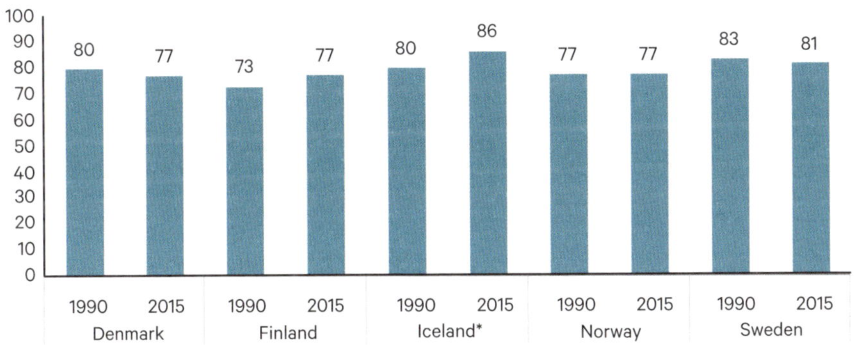

Figure 5.2 Labor market status: proportion of women (15 to 65 years) employed and unemployed for Denmark, Finland, Iceland, Norway, and Sweden, 1990 and 2015 (%).[17]
**Iceland 1990=1991. Nordic Council of Ministers (2016) http://norden.statbank.dk/work02*

16 http://www.norden.org/en/fakta-om-norden-1/numbers-and-statistics

17 The figures included the entire labor force, meaning employed and unemployed. The percentage of unemployed women per country in 1990 and 2015 is 9 % and 7 % for Denmark, 3 % and 7 % for Finland, 3 % and 4 % for Iceland, 3 % and 4 % for Norway, 2 % and 7 % for Sweden, respectively. http://norden.statbank.dk/work02

Although the main picture is stability, some differences in employment rates (including unemployment) can be noted. In 1990, the employment rates for women were highest for Sweden and lowest for Finland; in 2015, the employment rates for women were the highest for Iceland but the same for Denmark, Finland, and Norway (see Figure 5.2).

Regarding gender segregation in the labor market, a number of researchers have identified what they call a "welfare-state paradox" (Birkelund & Sandnes 2003, Mandel & Semyonov 2006), referring to the counterintuitive finding that equality-oriented welfare states, such as the Nordic countries, have more gender-segregated labor markets than more conservative welfare states, for instance in Southern Europe. Recent European comparative studies, however, now show that the Nordic countries are placed in the middle and not on the extreme of segregation statistics (Bettio & Verashchagina 2009). Researchers further claim that the main reason some countries' labor markets seem to be less gender segregated is that a large share of the female (care) work is carried out outside the labor market (Bart, Hardoy, Schøne & Østbakken 2014). Nonetheless, the gender segregation within Nordic labor markets should mainly be characterized as stable and strong. Some occupations have become more gender balanced, in particular as a consequence of more women entering these occupations, but very few women work in some of the most common occupations for men, and very few men work in some of the most common occupations for women (Reisel & Teigen 2014).

Nordic Statistics presents data on the proportion of men and women in the most female- and male-dominated occupations. Data from 2015 show variations in the proportion of men in female-dominated occupations of between 10 % and 16 %. The cross-country differences are marginally smaller for women in male-dominated occupations, varying between 13 % and 16 % (Figure 5.3).

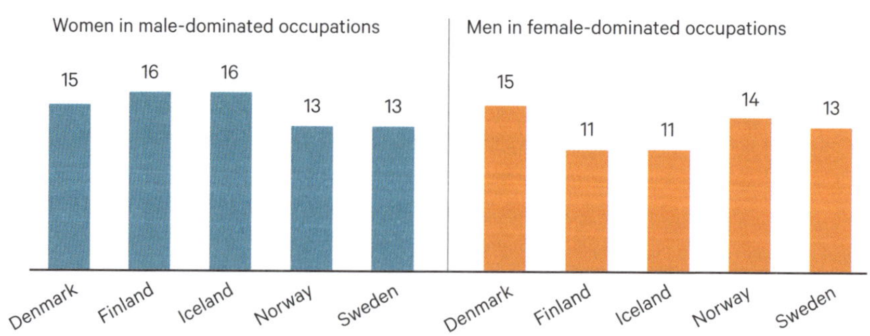

Figure 5.3 Women in male-dominated occupations and men in female-dominated occupations in the Nordic countries 2015 (%).

Nordic Council of Ministers (2016) http://norden.statbank.dk/labo06

Gender segregation in the labor market is connected to the gender pay gap as many female-dominated occupations within the public sector are placed on a lower pay scale than male-dominated occupations within the private sector (Østbakken, Barth & Schøne 2014). The gender pay gap is remarkably stable in all the Nordic countries. A persistent pay gap between men and women exists in all the Nordic countries, varies between 15 % and 20 %, and decreases only modestly between 2007 and 2013.

The Nordic labor markets are characterized by a significant number of employed women in part-time positions, with Finland the exception (see Figure 5.5). As shown in the figure, about one-third of employed women in the Nordic countries work part-time. In Finland, where the employment rates for women are somewhat lower, only one-fifth of women work part-time. Very few men in the Nordic countries work part-time (see Figure 5.5). On the one hand, access to part-time jobs may help to include women. On the other hand, a labor market that supplies and facilitates part-time jobs may be self-reinforcing and impede the supply of full-time positions.

Different indicators of economic equity thus show relatively small country differences within the Nordic region, and a main pattern of stability over time. On these indicators, the Icelandic and Norwegian scores do not differ significantly from those of the Nordic EU member states.

Democratic parity

As shown in previous sections, Nordic exceptionalism is demonstrated primarily through the country's high scores on the indicators of democratic parity, which reveal gender gaps in representation in political and economic elites. Traditionally, the Nordic countries are world-famous for their steady progress in women's political representation (Karvonen & Selle 1995). At present,

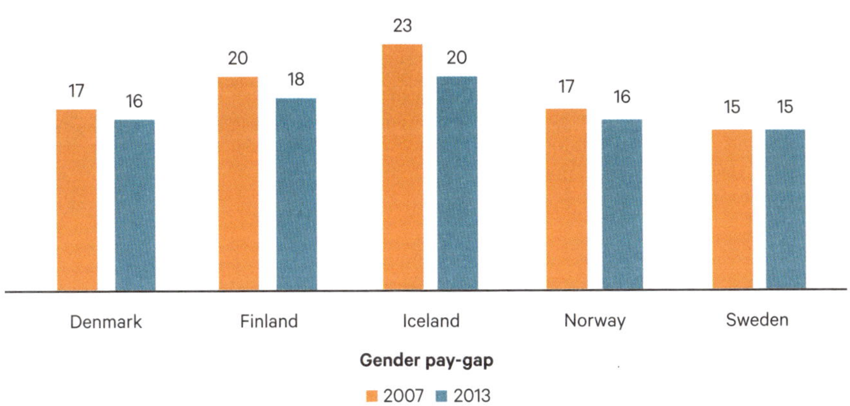

Figure 5.4 Gender pay gap in the Nordic countries in 2007 and 2013 (%).
* Norway 2007 = 2010.
Nordic Council of Ministers (2016) http://norden.statbank.dk/inco05

however, global surveys show that Rwanda, Bolivia, Cuba, and the Seychelles rank above Sweden in the representation of women in the lower and single houses of parliament. In the Inter-Parliamentary Union ranking (September 2016), Finland is 10th, Iceland 11th, Norway 14th, and Denmark 21st.[18]

None of the Nordic countries achieved full gender parity in national assemblies in 2015. Overall, women constitute about 40 % of the Nordic parliamentarians. The Swedish parliament is the most gender balanced and the Danish parliament the least. The period shown here (1997–2015) shows only small changes, with the exception of Iceland, where the proportion of women increased dramatically from one-fourth to more than 40 % (Figure 5.6). However, in Iceland's parliamentary election in late October 2016, women constituted 47 % of the national assembly.

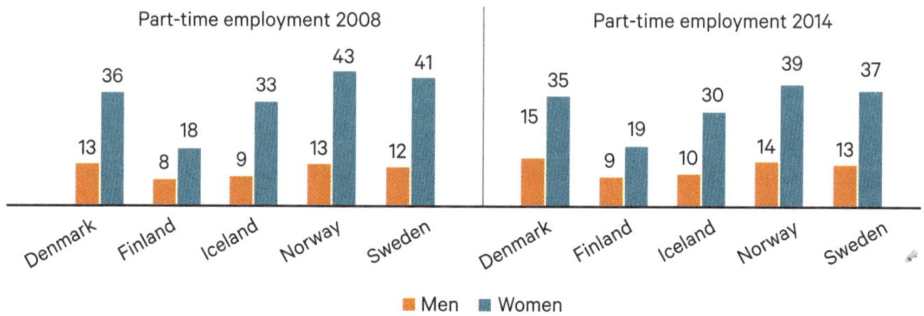

Figure 5.5 Men and women in part-time positions in the Nordic labor markets in 2008 and 2014 (%).

Nordic Council of Ministers (2016) http://norden.statbank.dk/labo03

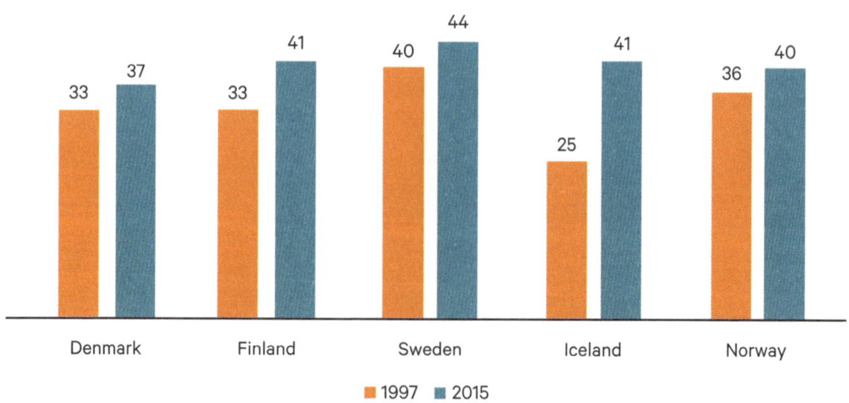

Figure 5.6 Women in national parliaments in the Nordic countries, 1997 and 2015 (%).

Inter-Parliamentary Union, IPU, (2016) Women in National Parliaments – Archived Data. *http://www.ipu.org/wmn-e/classif-arc.htm*

18 http://www.ipu.org/wmn-e/arc/classif010916.htm

TABLE 5.4 GRADUAL DEVELOPMENT OF WOMEN'S REPRESENTATION IN NATIONAL PARLIAMENTS IN THE NORDIC COUNTRIES.

	Denmark	Finland	Iceland	Norway	Sweden
1st election	1918	1907	1922	1921	1921
1st election more than 10 %	1966	1907	1983	1972	1953
1st election more than 20 %	1979	1970	1987	1977	1973
1st election more than 30 %	1988	1983	1999	1985	1986
1st election more than 40 %	Never	2007	2009	2009	1994
Highest female representation	39 %	42 %	43 %	40 %	47 %
Female representation in last election	37 %[19]	42 %[20]	40 %[21]	40 %[22]	44 %[23]
First female prime minister	2011	2003	2009	1981	Never
First female president	N/A	2003	1980	N/A	N/A

N/A 0= not applicable.

Source: Inter-Parliamentary Union (2016)

Source: Revision of Table 2 in Dahlerup (2011) Women in Nordic Politics – A Continuing Success Story?

As shown in Table 5.4, women were represented in the Finnish parliament at a historically early stage, much earlier than in the other Nordic parliaments. The differences decrease over time, and as of today, Sweden and Iceland stand out with the closest to gender-balanced national parliaments. The picture of Nordic exceptionalism is still mainly due to earlier progress in women's presence in political assemblies, particularly during the 1980s, when more than 30 % representation was achieved in Denmark, Finland, Sweden, and Norway (see Table 5.4). More generally, Finland has been the frontrunner and Iceland the latecomer (see Table 5.4). See chapter 1 for democratization in the Nordic countries and chapter 4 for political representation in general.

In contrast, no Nordic country can be depicted as a frontrunner in gender balance in economic decision-making compared with major countries in Europe or the US. The presence of women in senior executive positions in the economy has been modest, and the presence of women on corporate boards has progressed significantly only over the last decade (see Figure 5.7).[24]

---

19 June 18th 2015, IPU: http://www.ipu.org/parline-e/reports/2087_A.htm

20 April 19th 2015, IPU: http://www.ipu.org/parline-e/reports/2111_E.htm

21 April 27th 2013, IPU: http://www.ipu.org/parline-e/reports/arc/2143_13.htm

22 September 9th 2013, IPU: http://www.ipu.org/parline-e/reports/arc/2143_13.htm

23 September 14th 2014, IPU: http://www.ipu.org/parline-e/reports/2303_E.htm

24 The Norwegian Gender Balance Scorecard, monitored by the Centre for Research on Gender Equality (CORE) at the Institute for Social Research in Oslo, reported relatively small differences in the marginal presence of women in senior executive positions in the economy in Norway, Europe, and the US (Figure 4.1). http://likestillingsforskning.no/Topplederbarometer

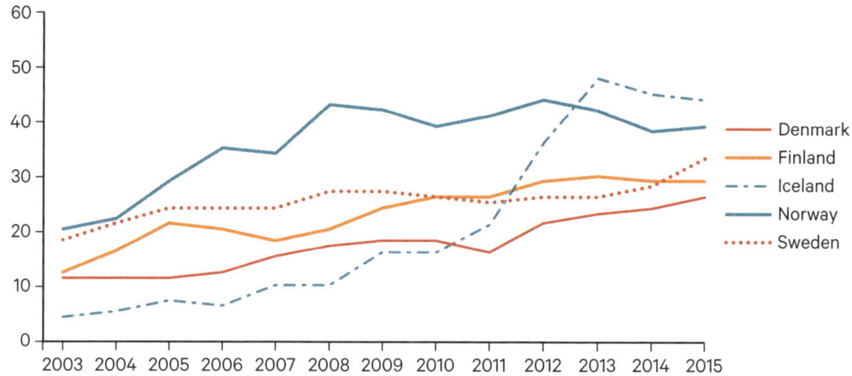

Figure 5.7 Women on corporate boards in the Nordic countries, 2003–2015 (%).[25]
Nordic Council of Ministers (2016) http://norden.statbank.dk/labo08

Indicators of democratic parity thus show some internal Nordic regional differences, although the picture is not clear. Women's political representation has been strong and stable in Finland and Sweden, and has increased sharply in Iceland in the last few years. Women's representation on corporate boards has increased particularly rapidly in Norway and Iceland, where gender balance regulations have been introduced. More generally, these gender equality statistics show that differences between the Nordic countries are modest. Inclusion of non-EU members Norway and Iceland does not contribute to a significant change in the overall portrayal of a distinct Nordic profile for gender equality, where comparatively high scores for democratic parity indicators contribute the most. In other words, the inclusion of women among the political and economic elite today most clearly marks the Nordic countries as gender equality frontrunners.

Policies to promote economic equity and democratic parity in the Nordic countries

In the previous section, we applied data from Nordic Statistics to map economic equity on the following four indicators: participation in the labor market, gender segregation in the labor market, the gender pay gap, and part-time work. To map democratic parity, we used the only available indicators: representation of women in Nordic national assemblies and representation of men and women on listed company boards. A central question in the current research on gender equality concerns whether and how gender equality policies actually lead to greater gender equality. In this section we ask, first, whether it is possible to identify a distinctive policy profile common to the Nordic countries on

25 Corporate boards are specified by Nordic Statistics for the largest listed companies.

how to promote economic equity and democratic parity, and second, whether differences in gender equality performance correspond with differences in gender equality policy profiles. However, at present, large-scale comparative implementation and effect studies on gender equality policies are few and far apart. Thus we are able to provide only a few—mainly speculative—comments about policy–performance links on gender equality issues.

Policies on economic equity

All Nordic gender equality legislation combines protection against discrimination with active duties for public authorities and employers to promote equality. All Nordic gender equality legislation includes equal pay regulations. As of today, Nordic equality legislation, furthermore, has to conform to EU directives on gender equality. Although protection against discrimination is a right at the individual level, proactive work is a duty, or obligation, of enterprises and institutions. In creating this double aim for equality legislation (individual protection and collective duties), Nordic legislators have, nevertheless, generally speaking, demonstrated strong equality ambitions. Binding regulations on proactive duties can be seen as one way to try to ensure that equality work is integrated into the everyday business of enterprises and organizations. In EU terms, this is seen as mainstreaming gender equality (cf. Kantola 2010).

Apart from this traditionally strong double aim, it is not possible to identify a common Nordic legislative profile on gender equality (Borchorst et al. 2012). No mapping of Nordic equal pay policies or of mainstreaming policies is available. Thus, on most of the indicators used to identify levels of economic equity, at present we simply do not know how policies in the Nordic countries differ from or resemble each other, nor do we know what effects these policies might have on promoting gender equality. Thus, antidiscrimination laws, equal pay regulations, and labor market desegregation policies have not been sufficiently analyzed to make conclusions about the Nordic model possible.

When we turn to work–family balance policies, however, studies abound. The work–family balance includes the central gender equality policies named by welfare state theorists. These policies commonly include two sets of related public policies: publicly subsidized or paid parental leave arrangements and publicly subsidized childcare arrangements (kindergartens). In contrast to equal pay or desegregation policies, work–family balance policies are distinctive life-phase policies aimed at assisting young parents, foremost mothers, in overcoming care-based barriers to equal participation in working life. When a father's quota is part of the parental leave scheme, it aims to assist young fathers in gaining more equal participation in family life (cf. Skjeie & Teigen 2012, Halrynjo & Kitterød 2016).

Research on the work–family balance mainly regards such policies as crucial for the high labor market integration of women in the Nordic countries. The more recent development of weeks reserved for the father in parental leave is seen as a means of strengthening fathers' relationships with their children and weakening the segmentation of gender roles in the family as a result of the long absences from employment among women in connection with childbirth (Halrynjo & Kitterød 2016). Still, it has been argued that Nordic family-friendly policies have contributed to a culture where "lagged careers" have been acceptable, although they lead to gender differences in career progress.

As Table 5.5 shows, generous parental leave schemes exist in all the Nordic countries, although there are important differences between the countries in the specification of the parental leave arrangements. Sweden has the most flexible parental leave scheme, in which parental leave may be used until the child is 12 years old. The parental leave scheme in Iceland provides the fewest weeks, however, with most weeks reserved for the father. Denmark is the only country without weeks reserved for the father; a father's quota in the parental leave scheme was introduced in 1998 and abolished in 2002.

Access to publicly financed childcare facilities as the child grows older is commonly seen as crucial to foster equitable sharing of domestic childcare between mothers and fathers and to make the work–life balance a reality (cf. Mahon 2009).[26] Denmark was an early developer of accessible childcare arrangements (Borchorst & Teigen 2015). For children between 3 and 5 years, the childcare coverage in the Nordic countries is close to 100 %; only in Finland is the coverage lower (see Figure 5.8). For children between 0 and 2 years, the coverage is about 50 %; again, Finland is the exception with less coverage (see Figure 5.7). The lower coverage for the youngest children in Sweden is probably affected by the generous parental leave arrangement. Norway and Iceland differ

TABLE 5.5 THE PARENTAL LEAVE SYSTEMS IN THE NORDIC COUNTRIES.

	Denmark	Finland	Iceland	Norway	Sweden
Year of introduction	1984	1985	1981	1978	1974
Number of weeks (year)	52 (2002)	48 (2013)	39 (2000)	49 (2014)	69 (2002)
Year of introduction of father's quota	1998–2002	2013–	2000–	1993	1995
Number of weeks reserved for fathers	0	6	13	10	8

Source: Halryno and Kitterød (2016), Fedrekvoten – norm for fedres permisjonsbruk i Norge og Norden. ISF-rapport 2016: 06.

26 Childcare coverage is used as an indicator of the development of childcare facilities.

with a strong increase in childcare coverage for all pre-school children. This means that today, Norway and Iceland have reached the level of Denmark and Sweden in childcare coverage.

Although publicly subsidized childcare services have been considered vital to support women's employment (Ellingsæter 2014), cash-for-care schemes are commonly posed as a policy challenge to work–family balance policies, and as an example of a "neofamialist" turn in childcare policies (cf. Mahon 2002). Finland was the first to institute cash-for-care benefits at the national level, in 1985. Denmark followed in 1992, then Norway in 1998—and finally Sweden in 2008. In Iceland, cash-for-care benefit schemes exist in only a small number of municipalities. The cash-for-care benefit schemes vary in terms of duration, age of the child, and the size of the benefit. The monthly allowance is highest in Norway, followed by Finland. The use of cash-for-care benefits is clearly

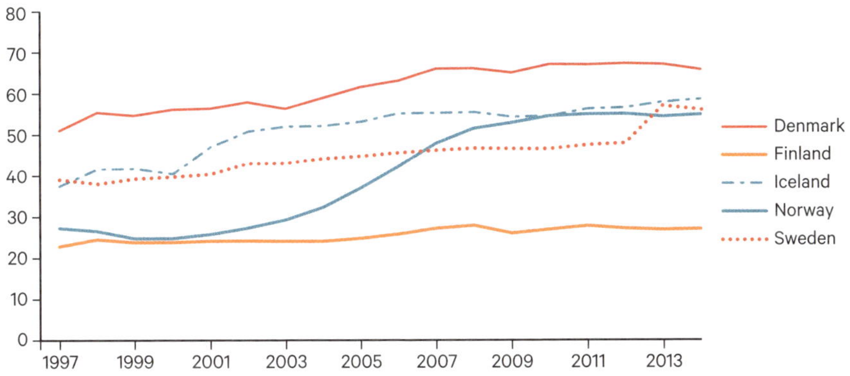

Figure 5.8 Children in daycare (age 0–2) in the Nordic countries, 1997–2014.
Nordic Council of Ministers (2016) http://norden.statbank.dk/chil03

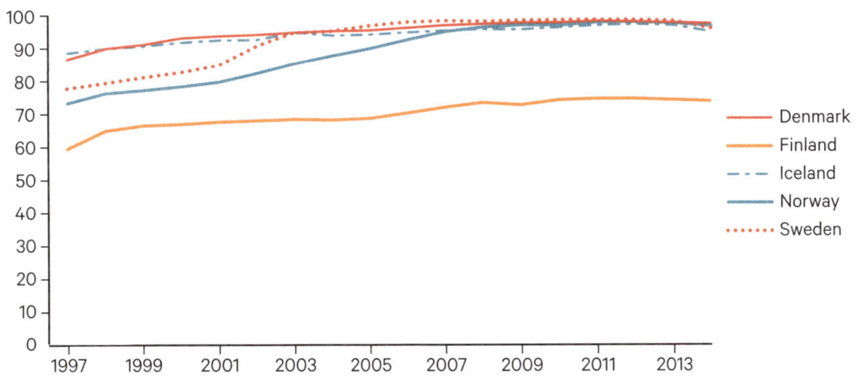

Figure 5.9 Children in daycare (age 3–5) in the Nordic countries, 1997–2014.
Nordic Council of Ministers (2016) http://norden.statbank.dk/chil03

the most popular in Finland, where 50 % of families with children between 9 months and 3 years receive cash-for-care benefits. Less than one-third use cash-for-care benefits in Norway, only 4 % in Sweden, and about 1000 children in Denmark (Østbakken 2016).

Work–family balance policies are generally considered a hallmark of Nordic model policies to promote gender equality. A recent survey does not indicate any fundamental changes in this policy model. On the contrary, we mainly see gradual increases in the public investment in such policies over time. Mahon (2002) named this policy profile "the egalitarian horizon," where childcare policies incorporate parental leave arrangements that include the father, affordable non-parental care services, and the right to early childhood education (Mahon 2002: 346–350). Only Denmark has rejected the policy of father's quotas in parental leave; only Finland relies extensively on a combination of cash-for-care and publicly subsidized kindergartens. Work–family balance policies can best be characterized as an infrastructure to promote economic equity. Such policies are neither aimed at securing equal pay nor aimed at desegregating, or actually promoting the desegregation of, gendered Nordic labor markets. Mainly, these policies contribute to facilitate women's inclusion within the Nordic labor markets.

Policies to promote democratic parity

Since the 1970s, various forms of parity policies have been established in all the Nordic countries to promote and regulate the gender composition of decision-making assemblies. Voluntary electoral quotas have been introduced by several political parties in all these countries, although most broadly in Norway (Freidenvall, Dahlerup & Skjeie 2006). Legal gender quotas for corporate boards exist in Norway, Finland, and Iceland; Denmark has a less specified gender balance law, while Sweden relies on voluntary measures (Niskanen 2011). In the Nordic context, Norway thus stands out with the strongest emphasis on the formulation and implementation of gender quota measures to promote democratic parity (Teigen 2011).

Voluntary political party quotas have been adopted in Iceland, Norway, and Sweden, combining internal gender quotas (minimum and maximum of 40 % and 60 %, respectively) and a zipper principle on election lists, where one sex alternates with the other on election lists (see Table 5.6). In Norway, voluntary gender quotas have been adopted by five of the seven main parties and have been recognized as important to further women's presence in the Norwegian electoral system. In Finland, however, there is a long tradition of gender balance in political decision-making without gender quotas. In Denmark, voluntary party quotas were first instituted in the late 1970s and early 1980s by some of the political parties but were later abolished.

TABLE 5.6 VARIATION IN NORDIC POLITICAL PARTY QUOTAS.

	Denmark	Finland	Iceland	Norway	Sweden
Type of gender quota arrangement	No quota legislation today	No quota legislation	Voluntary political party quotas	Voluntary political party quotas	Voluntary political party quotas
Scope	–	–	Social Democratic Alliance, Left-Green Movement, Center Party (Framsoknar-flokkur)	Socialist Left Party, Norwegian Labor Party, Center Party, Christian People's Party	Social Democratic Party, Left Party, Green Party, Moderate Party
Year of intro-duction (and liquidation)	1977–1996[27] 1983–1990[28] 1983–1996[29]	–	1999– 1999– 2005–	1970– 1983– 1989– 1993–	1978– 1978– 1981– 2009[30]–

Source: http://www.quotaproject.org/

Norway was the first country to propose (1999), adopt (2003), and implement (2008) gender quotas for corporate boards, and became an initiator of the later wave of corporate board quotas that has swept across Europe and other parts of the world (Fagan, Gonzalez Menendez, & Gomez Ansón 2012; Teigen 2012; Armstrong & Walby 2012; Terjesen et al. 2015). However, consensus has not characterized the Nordic region regarding the introduction of gender quotas for corporate boards to further the gender balance in economic decision-making. Iceland followed Norway's example in 2010, after being seriously hit by the economic crisis (see Table 5.7). Sweden and Norway discussed the adoption of gender quotas for corporate boards in the early 2000s in tandem. Finally, Norway ended up adopting gender quotas for corporate boards, while Sweden ended up dismissing the quota proposal (Heidenreich 2012), although a new proposal is being prepared.[31]

The proportion of women on corporate boards has increased considerably in all the Nordic countries, but is lowest in Denmark (see Figure 5.7). It seems reasonable to tie this development to the overall issue actualization of a gender balance on corporate boards, as well as a prevalent quota threat that gender

27 The Socialist People's Party (Socialistisk Folkeparti) was the first party to introduce a 40 % quota system in 1977 but abandoned it in 1996.

28 Candidate quotas for the European Parliament (40 %) were adopted in 1983 and abandoned in 1990.

29 The Social Democratic Party (Socialdemokratiet) adopted quotas of 40 % in 1983 and candidate quotas for local and regional elections in 1988, but the quotas were abandoned in 1996.

30 Moderate Party, party quotas: two women and two men shall be placed in the top four positions on the party list for election to the European Parliament.

31 http://www.regeringen.se/remisser/2016/09/remiss-av-ds-201632-jamn-konsfordelning-i-bolagsstyrelser/

TABLE 5.7 VARIATION IN GENDER QUOTAS FOR NORDIC CORPORATE BOARDS.

	Denmark	Finland	Iceland	Norway	Sweden
Arrangement	Codes for good governance that include board gender recommendations	Gender board quotas	Gender board quotas	Gender board quotas	Codes for good governance that include board gender recommendations
Quota	–	40 %	40 %	40 %	–
Publicly traded firms (PTFs)	–	No	Yes	Yes	–
State-owned enterprises (SOEs)	–	Yes	Yes	Yes	–
Adoption year	2010	2005	2010: PFTs 2007: SOEs	2003	2010; 2007

Source: Terjesen, Aguilera & Lorenz 2015.

quota regulations will be introduced if the businesses do not achieve progress in the gender balance on their own.

The introduction of a parity scheme for public limited company boards in Norway clearly had a wider aim of promoting gender parity in the economic sector (cf. Skjeie & Teigen 2012). The wider ripple effects of corporate board parity are limited, however. For instance, there are few signs of the spread of gender parity to company boards not affected by the scheme, and there exists little evidence that gender balance in corporate boards has led to gender balance in senior executive positions.[32]

While the traditional policies to promote women's inclusion among the political elite have been carried out mainly through the adoption of internal party regulations, newer policies to include women in economic elites have a more clear-cut legislative basis. Yet there is no discernable common Nordic policy model in such policy adoptions. Policy adoption is either decided by (diverging) party strategies in different Nordic countries or imposed through legislation in only some Nordic countries. However, the Nordic examples of legislative gender quotas for corporate boards have undoubtedly put male dominance in economic decision-making on the agenda globally and on the EU policy agenda, which includes the development of corporate governance codes in the Nordic countries, as well as in the EU corporate governance framework (which addresses rules and norms of gender balance).

CONCLUSION

In this chapter, we analyzed how the Nordic countries perform on two equality dimensions that are particularly relevant to the conceptualization of a Nordic

32 http://likestillingsforskning.no/Topplederbarometer/Topplederbarometeret

model of gender equality. We treated these dimensions as norms for economic equity and democratic parity. The analysis utilized data retrieved from the Gender Equality Index and from Nordic Statistics. In addition, we collected mappings of relevant gender equality policies from different sources. We caution that the descriptive statistics and policy mappings we applied present only crude measures to address such a model.

First, we examined how descriptive statistics today rank Nordic countries compared with other European countries among the member states of the European Union. Utilizing the average scores on the EU's Gender Equality Index, we conclude that Nordic EU member countries still form a distinct group of high achievers, with only the Netherlands in close proximity. The average gap between Nordic EU countries and other EU member states is, generally speaking, large enough to conclude that the Nordic scores are exceptional. When we concentrated the analysis on indicators of economic equity and democratic parity and calculated the average Nordic scores compared to the average EU scores, we found the Nordic scores for democratic parity were more exceptional than those for economic equity. In this Europe-oriented comparison, we then checked how the social democratic regime of welfare state analysis fared compared with the conservative-corporatist and liberal regimes. Again, the differences were most pronounced for the indicators of democratic parity. Differences were less pronounced for the indicators that summarize working life equality. The differences are almost negligible for the indicators that show gender gaps in income and other financial resources.

So, yes, the Nordic EU countries still form a distinct group of high achievers, but their distinctiveness is more pronounced for democratic parity than for economic equity. Keeping in mind that only crude measures were applied here, it is particularly interesting to note that on the central issue of gender gaps in income, traditional social democratic regime countries hardly perform better than traditional liberal regime countries.

However, although a Nordic cluster can be identified, we also found interesting variations within the Nordic region. On the economic equity dimension, Sweden stands out as clearly the most successful, followed by Denmark, while Finland's scores are the lowest within this Nordic club. The differences between the Nordic EU member countries are more pronounced on the democratic parity dimension than on the economic equity dimension. Here, Finland and Sweden stand out as high performers, while Denmark is clearly lagging behind.

We then utilized comparable statistics on outcome and performance that included the Nordic non-EU members of Norway and Iceland, to further explore similarities and differences within the Nordic region. For this purpose, we put together comparable data from the databank Nordic Statistics.

The main picture of the general similarities within the Nordic region is not disturbed by including Iceland and Norway. Norway is regularly placed in the middle for most parameters. To the extent that we have data showing changes over time, Iceland differs from the others in the economic equity and democratic parity dimensions, due to the rapid development in gender equality witnessed in Iceland in recent years.

Finally, we approached the question of policy models, discussing whether it is possible to identify a distinctive policy profile common to the Nordic countries on how to promote economic equity and democratic parity. In general, this discussion suffers from a lack of available broad cross-sector comparative research. This holds for central work–life policy issues, such as antidiscrimination efforts, equal pay efforts, and desegregation efforts. On the central gender equality theme of work–family balance, however, comparative studies abound. Well-developed policies to promote work–family balance characterize all the Nordic countries, in the form of extensive public subsidization of parental leave and childcare arrangements. We have characterized work–family balance policies as an infrastructure for the promotion of economic equity. Such policies are neither aimed at securing equal pay nor aimed at desegregating, or actually promoting the desegregation of, gendered Nordic labor markets. The policies mainly contribute to facilitate women's firm inclusion within the Nordic labor markets. These policies have been gradually expanded in all the Nordic countries. At present, only Denmark rejects the policy of father quotas in parental leave; only Finland relies extensively on a combination of cash-for-care and publicly subsidized kindergartens. At present, childcare coverage is much weaker in Finland, and the cash-for-care benefit scheme appears to be more strongly institutionalized here than in other Nordic countries. In policies to promote work–family balance, Finland thus seems to have chosen a somewhat different track.

Various forms of parity policies have been established in all the Nordic countries to promote and regulate the gender composition of decision-making assemblies. Voluntary gender quotas have been adopted by some political parties in most countries, and most broadly in Norway. Legal gender quotas for corporate boards exist in Norway, Finland, and Iceland; Denmark has a less specified gender balance law, while Sweden still relies on voluntary measures.

Policies to further democratic parity clearly vary. On the specific issue of applying gender quotas to achieve parity, there is no Nordic consensus. Nor is it possible to discern any clear effect of quota policies on the gender composition of parliaments. Neither Danish nor Finnish political parties have adopted such arrangements. Yet the presence of women in the Danish and Finnish parliaments differs, and the Finnish score for the gender balance in Parliament is consistently very high.

When it comes to economic decision-making, however, gender quota arrangements obviously affect gender balance in corporate boards. Iceland and Norway are the only Nordic countries with legal regulation of the gender balance.

The patterns of sharp increase in the presence of women on such boards clearly follow the development and adoption of such legal measures. Nonetheless, women are also relatively well represented on Swedish corporate boards, without a quota regulation. Presumably this can be tied to the consistent political attention paid to the issue and a continuous political threat to adopt quota measures if companies do not improve their own recruitment efforts.

Since the 1970s, Nordic governments have introduced and implemented a range of policies to implicitly and explicitly promote gender equality. Different Nordic countries have been forerunners in addressing political means to further democratic parity, such as zipper systems on party lists and quota regulations for company boards. However, there is no discernible common Nordic policy profile on such issues. In other words, policy measures to promote democratic parity show no common Nordic model. Work–family balance policies are, generally speaking, very advanced in the Nordic countries, yet here, as well, national policy profiles vary. The tendency to ignore variations and differences in equality performance and policies within the Nordic region has often been emphasized by gender equality scholars (for a comprehensive outline, see Bergquist et al. 1999). Our analysis mainly shows that in terms of gender equality performance, yes, it still makes sense to talk about a Nordic model. Its core traits have not eroded. Its existence might, however, not be as dependent on a common set of policies as is often assumed.

CHAPTER 6
GOVERNMENT INSTITUTIONS AND STATE REFORMS

Karl Hagen Bjurstrøm & Tom Christensen

INTRODUCTION

Viewed from the outside, the Nordic countries – Denmark, Finland, Iceland, Norway and Sweden – appear to have somewhat similar political-administrative systems, i.e. there exists a Nordic model. While that view is accepted inside those countries, it is also problematized because of the perceived abundant diversity (Greve, Lægreid and Rykkja 2016). For this reason, both convergence and divergence between the political-administrative systems of the five Nordic countries must be analyzed. This chapter examines two important aspects of those systems: the structure of the central executive apparatus, particularly that of the civil service; and the reforms that have taken place within that apparatus over the past two to three decades.

Gulick (1937) argued that in examining the structural trajectories of political-administrative systems, the structural design of specialization and coordination measures is important because public goals can be achieved through different structures. This does not mean that there is only one structure at any one point in time that might influence the content of policy and the societal impact; rather, it is the actors' awareness of the different effects of the various structural designs that is very important. Taking his cue from Gulick, Egeberg (2012) says that it is possible to characterize the structure of a central civil service in terms of both vertical and horizontal specialization measures, whether intra- or inter-organizational. As regards vertical specialization, we will focus on the inter- organizational aspect, i.e. how the relationships between ministries and subordinate entities, such as agencies and SOEs, have been or are organized. But those relationships are also defined by how the central civil service is horizontally specialized, which, in turn, is reflected in public sector reforms in various ways.

Over the past three decades, there have been two major public sector reform waves around the world that have affected the Nordic countries:

New Public Management (NPM), which was first introduced in Australia and New Zealand in the early 1980s; and post-NPM, which first emerged in the same countries in the late 1990s (Christensen and Lægreid 2007, Pollitt and Bouckaert 2011). On the one hand, NPM can be viewed in terms of ideology, ideas and symbols related to how political-administrative systems should be organized; on the other hand, it can be seen as constituting more specific instrumental reform measures and structural reorganization (Christensen and Lægreid 2001). The Anglo-Saxon countries have been the front runners of the reform movement (Hood 1996), while international organizations such as the OECD, the EU, the IMF and the World Bank have also served as reform entrepreneurs (Sahlin-Andersson 2001). At the national level, both public sector actors (political and administrative leaders) and private actors (such as consulting firms) have systematically sought to further NPM and, later, post-NPM.

NPM was taken on board for various reasons (Christensen and Lægreid 2007). For example, political and administrative leaders thought that NPM could solve problems in a practical and instrumental way; at the same time, they wanted to be regarded as modern and rational (Meyer and Rowan 1977). It was therefore tempting to import reforms whose benefits were taken for granted by many. Post-NPM was seen as rebalancing the system and as a counter-reform. It was argued that NPM could not deliver on the economic promises and undermined the political control of the executive branch; and it was also pointed out that NPM had emerged during a period in which society was confronted with different types of threats – i.e. there existed the "fear factor", which had led to increased centralization and coordination (Christensen and Lægreid 2007). The Nordic countries tended to be included in the group of what were called "reluctant reformers" or "laggards", having been slow to adopt NPM reforms, in particular (Olsen and Peters 1996), and sought to rebalance the two reform waves somewhat later than other countries.

Accordingly, the main questions discussed in this chapter are:

- What have been the main structural features of the central political-administrative systems in the Nordic countries in the past and what are the main structural characteristics today?
- What have been the main public sector reforms in the Nordic countries over the past three decades? How is a balance between NPM and post-NPM reforms typically achieved?
- From which perspectives can the similarity and diversity in the formal structures and reforms of the Nordic countries be explained?
- Is there a Nordic model based on structural features and reform trajectories that stands out from other models?

PERSPECTIVES THAT HELP EXPLAIN SIMILARITY AND DIVERSITY

We combine three perspectives from organization theory – the *environmental* perspective, the *cultural* perspective and the *structural* perspective – to adopt a *transformative approach* towards explaining the similarity and diversity in the formal structures and reforms of the Nordic countries (Christensen and Lægreid 2001). The *environmental* perspective sees national trajectories as driven primarily by international and/or national environmental pressure. There are two different types of environment that can influence a country's reform processes – the *technical* environment and the *institutional* environment (Meyer and Rowan 1977). The *technical* environment views public organizations as instrumental systems whose role is to provide specific services or products in an effective and efficient way. When problems related to the efficient provision of services occur, strong pressure will be brought to bear on the government to reform and restructure.

The *institutional* environment is more closely related to the development of myths (Meyer and Rowan 1977). Because of the complexity in the public sector and the need for simple guidelines, myths develop in this environment and spread fast from the private to the public sector as well as within countries and from one country to another (Christensen et al. 2015). These myths consist of ideologies, ideas and symbols based on the assumption that there are optimal ways to structure and organize government. Countries and national public organizations import these myths and imitate them to increase legitimacy. Above all, they endow an organization with a modern, rational appearance, without requiring much structural or behavioural change. This is what Brunsson (1989) calls "hypocrisy" or "double-talk". Clearly, there is a discrepancy between politicians' predilection for speaking in symbols and their actions.

The second perspective is the *cultural* one, which focuses on informal norms and values (Selznick 1957, Christensen et al. 2015). A political-administrative system evolves over time by adapting to internal and external pressures, i.e. it is institutionalized. Informal norms and values – the building blocks of a distinctive culture or "soul" – are developed and add to the formal structure. Cultural traditions in public organizations change only gradually through so-called path-dependency; this means that the context or situation in which they were established (the *roots*) will eventually have an impact on further development (the *routes* taken) (Krasner 1988). According to this perspective, different political-administrative systems develop different cultures, which are determined by both the formal structure of the civil service systems and the reforms implemented. This divergence argument differs from the isomorphic or convergence argument based on the institutional environment.

The cultural perspective suggests that reforms like NPM and post-NPM must undergo some kind of compatibility test (Christensen and Lægreid 2001).

A crucial question is whether the norms and values of the reforms are compatible with those of the cultural traditions of a country's public sector – for example, the way in which the civil service is organized. If they are incompatible, the reforms may well meet with cultural resistance; conversely, if they are compatible, they may well be implemented. And it stands to reason that if they are only partly compatible, only those elements that are compatible will be implemented.

The third, *structural* perspective focuses on how the polity is organized (Egeberg 2012). What matters here is whether the country's constitutional constraints are strong enough to withstand reorganization and reform efforts and whether the powers inherent in the political system are balanced. Moreover, the form of government plays a role, too – for example, whether the country has a presidential system, a Westminster parliamentarian system or some other type of parliamentarian system – as does whether the government is a majority or minority one (Hood 1996). Whether the public sector is structurally homogeneous or heterogeneous, or put another way, the degree to which government is fragmented, is also important.

Countries without constitutional constraints but with a dominant executive backed by a dominant party – which is often referred to as an "elective dictatorship" – and characterized by structural homogeneity may find it relatively easy to introduce radical reforms (Pollitt and Bouckaert 2011); such a system is to be found in several Anglo-Saxon countries. A fragmented presidential system or a parliamentary system with a minority coalition government – the latter of which is more common in the Nordic countries (see chapter 4) – will clearly face an uphill struggle to make decisions about and implement reforms.

The *transformative approach* combines these three perspectives and emphasizes their different features – environmental pressure, cultural factors and structural constraints – whose dynamic interaction frequently impacts on the leeway that political and administrative leaders have to make changes, undertake reorganization efforts or push through larger reforms and implement them (Christensen and Lægreid 2001). Dynamic processes often produce qualitatively new hybrid structures and cultures. Countries in which such processes occur tend to outnumber those countries in which there is either a high-pressure environment with compatible, reform-facilitating cultures and instrumental structures or a low-pressure environment with incompatible, heterogeneous, non-reform friendly structures.

FORMAL STRUCTURE OF CIVIL SERVICES IN NORDIC COUNTRIES

The Nordic countries have many similarities. They are all small homogenous states; they all have a large universal welfare system and an egalitarian culture; and they all boast a strong tradition of well-established central agencies as well as a relatively high level of mutual trust between the political and administrative executives (Balle Hansen et al. 2012). Such similarities notwithstanding, we note that there are several differences between the state administrations of the Nordic countries. For example, a distinction can be made between what can be referred to as the West Nordic model (Denmark, Iceland and Norway) and the East Nordic model (Finland and Sweden) (Greve, Lægreid and Rykkja 2016). The West Nordic model bears many Danish hallmarks, as both Iceland and Norway have historically been under Danish influence; while the East-Nordic model has many Swedish characteristics as what is now Finland was a part of Sweden for centuries. Below we outline the historical background of the Nordic state administrations.

Historical background[1]

Denmark. Autocracy was introduced in Denmark-Norway in 1660, when a new constitution was drafted naming the monarch as the absolute sovereign (Norway was subordinated to Denmark from 1380 to 1814). At the same time, a new central administrative system was introduced enshrining the principle of the full responsibility of civil servants who headed the administrative bodies. This period ushered in the doctrine of ministerial responsibility and the centralized civil service, which remains important to this day (Foss Hansen 1999). The first central administrative bodies – which were named "colleges" and whose members were required to have formal qualifications – bore similarities to those in Sweden. Denmark received its first democratic constitution in 1848–49, at which time the system of ministerial rule and hierarchical central administrative bodies was formally established (parliamentarism was not introduced in practice in Denmark until 1901). Denmark differed from Norway and Sweden concerning the agency structure. The ministries often had two or three departments, each of which was responsible for a different policy area. In reality, these departments were agencies integrated into the ministries, an arrangement that allowed the political leadership to exercise more control over them.

The period 1890–1914 was marked by the expansion of the central administrative apparatus, which included the emergence of several new ministries and agencies. Though comparable to the expansion of the civil services in Norway and Sweden, the Danish enlargement took place at a later date. It was also during this period that interest groups could secure whichever ministry they wanted – the agriculture portfolio and the trade and industry portfolio being two examples – and were included as members of the newly established public colleges or councils. These were the first corporate features of the Danish state administration. In 1920 the contours of the welfare state became evident with the establishment of the Ministry of Social Affairs; but the hard times during

1 See chapter 1 for a general historical overview.

the 1920s and 1930s prevented further administrative expansion in Denmark, as was the case in Sweden and Norway. It was not until after the end of World War II that new ministries and agencies were established. In the post-war period, particularly until the early 1970s, the central administrative apparatus grew rapidly and became more structurally differentiated. Many collegial bodies, corporatist councils, boards and public committees emerged – a trend that was also evident in Norway and Sweden during the same period.

Finland was established as an independent state in 1917, having been part of Sweden for more than 700 years and thereafter an autonomous Grand Duchy of Russia for almost 100 years (1808–1917) (Sjöblom 2011: 41). Today Finland is a republic whose political system has fluctuated between a presidential and a parliamentary one depending on the degree to which the president has used his prerogatives – something that the Finnish head of state has increasingly tended to do during the post-war period (Sjöblom 2011).

Established at the end of the 19th century, the Finnish system of state administration was adopted mainly from Sweden, not least owing to that country's long rule over Finland. Traditionally, the state administration was under collective ministerial responsibility, but over time more individual ministerial responsibility has developed (Ahlbäck Öberg and Wockelberg 2016). The early system and culture of state administration was dominated by the legalistic (legal) tradition – the majority of civil servants at that time were lawyers – but since the 1950s the share of social scientists in the state administration has gradually increased (Ylikangas 1999, Sjöblom 2011: 242, Salminen et al. 2012: 226).

Several agencification trends can be identified in Finland. When the Grand Duchy of Finland was established (in 1809), it was essential to create new central government structures to undertake public tasks. But at the same time, the creation of those new agencics was seen as a way of increasing Finnish autonomy. After the country had gained independence (in 1917), several agencies were integrated into ministries in order to eliminate any overlap between these bodies, and new agencies were established in various policy areas, especially agriculture (Savolainen, 1999, Salminen et al. 2012: 229). After World War II, the Finnish welfare state gradually emerged and new agencies came into being to accommodate the new welfare services (Salminen 2003: 57). Economic recession in the 1980s and 1990s promoted reforms that switched the focus back to ministerial, rather than agency, power. As a result, the role of the agencies as regulators was reduced and some functions were transferred either to ministries or to regional or local governments (Salminen et al. 2012, Ahlbäck Öberg and Wockelberg 2016).

Iceland, which has a population of just 330,000, is significantly smaller than the other Nordic countries. Step by step, it gained its independence from Denmark between 1874 (when Iceland passed its own constitution) and 1944 (when the union was dissolved); other major developments occurring within this timeline were the introduction of Icelandic home rule in 1904 and the country's formal sovereignty in 1918. Home rule gave Iceland its own state administration: because the Icelandic administration had previously been a part of the Danish bureaucracy, the country's new government and bureaucratic framework was to a large extent based on the Danish model; thus collegial authority in the cabinet was weak, a ministerial form of government was established and public appointments were based on formal merit. However, Iceland's state administration has been politicized more than what might have been expected among the Nordic democracies (Kristinsson 2012 and 2013). As a result of the strong tradition of ministerial responsibility, it is unclear whether responsibility for coordination and effective action lay in the ministries or agencies (Kristinsson 2013). Hence, Iceland's ministries are relatively weak vis-à-vis the parliament and the scope for inter-ministerial coordination and control over the agencies is small (Greve and Ejersbo 2016, Kristinsson, 2016). In order to deal with these issues, reforms have recently been passed strengthening the coordination role of the Prime Minister's Office (Kristinsson 2013).

With its focus on developing arm's length government and increasing agency autonomy, Iceland fitted well into the NPM era of the 1990s. However, these trends slowed in the early 2000s and especially after the financial crash in 2008, which hit Iceland far harder than the other Nordic countries. Indeed, since the financial crash there has been general scepticism towards NPM reforms and a "whole of government" approach has tended to be favoured (Kristinsson 2013).

Norway. In 1814 Norway formed a union with Sweden (which lasted until 1905) and established a centralized and hierarchical state. Over the next 190 years, this state model was fine-tuned on numerous occasions (Christensen 2003). The period 1814–84 is commonly referred to as that of the "civil servants' state" because during this period the leadership of the central administrative apparatus was dominated by a powerful group of legally trained individuals. The first challenge to their domination came in the 1840s and 1850s from professional groups demanding more autonomous administrative bodies. The government responded to that challenge by setting up several independent agencies. The second challenge came in 1884 with the introduction of parliamentarism. While the balance of power shifted away from the civil servants, the government agencies came under stricter control and there was less willingness to establish new ones. Above all, politicians did not want to see their authority or democratic control powers undermined.

The centralized state expanded further after World War II, when several national interest groups gained the right of integrated organizational participation or formal participation in public decision-making processes (Olsen 1983). This development suggests either an increase in the influence of interest groups or seeing them as a democratic addition to the existing system. This period was also characterized by fresh moves to hive off the agencies from the ministries, fronted on this occasion by the political leadership rather than professional groups in what was an official attempt to solve capacity bottlenecks (Christensen 2003). While the new administrative doctrine led to the emergence of several new independent agencies, it was applied in practice only until the early 1970s, when constraints on establishing new agencies were reimposed.

From the 1990s onwards, agencies, particularly regulatory ones, and SOEs became more autonomous through what can be termed vertical inter-organizational specialization. At the same time, there was an increasingly horizontal specialization of functions, either within or between units in the civil service. The last 10–15 years have seen yet more structural reforms inspired by post-NPM, as result of which civil-service units have been centralized and merged.

The development of Norway's administrative apparatus after World War II was characterized by a strong and increasing vertical and horizontal differentiation. New hierarchies and positions were created, and there was considerable structural devolution within the agency structure, which became endowed with numerous horizontal divisions. The number of staff grew more sharply in the agencies than in the ministries. Immediately after the war, lawyers dominated the civil service (Christensen et al. 2014). In the 1950s, national economists were in demand and from the 1970s onwards, social scientists were preferred; today it is the latter who make up the largest group of civil servants. From the 1980s onwards business economists were recruited too. Thus, over time, the background of civil servants has become much more varied.

Sweden already had a professional civil service in the early modern era (c. 1500–1800), whereas most other European states at this time were subject to the powers invested in the monarch (Premfors 1999). During Sweden's so-called Age of Greatness (1611–1718), the state was run by a particularly powerful civil service. Several independent central administrative or non-hierarchical collegial bodies were established, which, though weakened, are still in existence today. Besides their collegial form, these bodies displayed certain features of the Weberian ideal type, which was rather advanced for that time; for example, they were subject to formal rules, functions were highly differentiated, job security was high (civil servants could be liable for dismissal only after a court hearing) and hiring and promotion depended on a standardized civil-service education. During the Age of Freedom (1718–72), a dualistic form of central government emerged in Sweden: a strong monarch surrounded by a court of advisers (later a cabinet) coexisted alongside a strong and independent central administrative wing consisting of several agencies.

Sweden's modern civil service came into being around 1800. This multi-tiered structure exhibited internal organizational differentiation within ministries and spawned several new independent agencies, mainly in the communications sector – a development that also took place in Norway during the same period. Around 1910, SOEs began to emerge, enjoying somewhat more freedom than the agencies, and collegial bodies were formed as boards or councils that supervised SOEs and agencies. This was the start of what is known today as administrative corporatism. Interest groups and associations were given the opportunity to participate in public decision-making processes; and, as in the case of Norway, a civil service eventually emerged that had strong corporatist features overall, accompanied by the development of an intricate "society of interest groups". From the 1930s onwards, the Swedes started to develop their welfare state and expanded the civil service, whose functions were differentiated accordingly, particularly after World War II. Indeed, the 1960 and 1970s witnessed the biggest expansion.

Table 6.6.1 below sums up the main differences between the central political- administrative apparatuses of the Nordic countries stemming from their different historical backgrounds, as explained above.

Main Structural Features of the Nordic Countries' Civil Services Today

The main structural features of the civil services of the Nordic countries today may be explained to a large extent by path dependency and historical background. As the individual historical backgrounds of the Nordic state administrations described above show, the Nordic countries have many similarities but at the same time differ in the degree of both the agencification and autonomy of public agencies, even if there are signs of some overall convergence between the individual systems (Lindbom 1997, Bo Smith 2015).

If we compare the state administrations of the Nordic countries, Sweden stands out as having the largest number of public agencies.[2] Based on a broad

TABLE 6.1 MAIN HISTORICAL DIFFERENCES IN THE CENTRAL POLITICAL-ADMINISTRATIVE STRUCTURES OF THE NORDIC COUNTRIES

	Denmark	Finland	Iceland	Norway	Sweden
Centralization	High	High/moderate	High/moderate	High/moderate	Dual – strong cabinet and strong agencies
Responsibility base	Individual ministerial	Developed from collective ministerial (cabinet) towards individual ministerial	Individual ministerial	Individual ministerial	Collective ministerial (cabinet)
Agencies	Integrated agencies in the ministries	Strongly independent agencies	Independent agencies	Independent or semiindependent agencies	Strongly independent agencies

2 Some differences in the number of agencies in each country might be the result of different inclusion criteria.

definition of what constitutes a public agency, Sweden has 349 in all (Swedish Agency for Public Management 2015). Using a more narrow definition, the number is 255 (Greve and Ejersbo 2016), compared with Iceland's about 165 (Greve and Ejersbo 2016) and Norway's 166 (NSD 2016). Finland and Denmark stands out as the Nordic countries with the smallest number of agencies – around 100 (Greve and Ejersbo 2016, Ministry of Finance, Finland 2016). The West Nordic countries (Denmark, Iceland and Norway) have a rather similar number of agencies (Denmark has somewhat fewer than Iceland and Norway), while there is a large difference between the number of agencies in Sweden and Finland as the latter seems to deviate from the East Nordic model. Also interesting is the apparent trend towards a reduction in the number of agencies; for example, Sweden and Norway had 613 and 225 public agencies, respectively, in 2000.

An important structural feature of the civil services is the responsibility base. While Sweden still practises cabinet collective responsibility and Denmark, Iceland and Norway individual ministerial responsibility, Finland has undergone an interesting development from a semi-presidential system towards a parliamentary one. In the old semi-presidential system, the president exercised significant influence over the nomination of ministers while the ministers themselves were recruited from various sectors, not least the civil service. In the present parliamentary system, the president's role in ministerial nominations is limited while that of the prime minister has increased, and almost all ministers are professional politicians. Moreover, Finnish reforms strengthened the role of the individual ministers and introduced individual ministerial responsibility for public agencies; at the same time, the independent Swedish-type agencies were abolished (Tiihonen 2007). Through these reforms, the number of similarities between Finland and the West Nordic countries has grown. Hence, in terms of ministerial responsibility and agency independence, it seems that rather than talking about an east-west Scandinavian divide, we can say that Sweden stands out from the other Nordic countries.

Recent reforms have left the state administrations of the Nordic countries more market-oriented (for more details, see the next section) and generally with more autonomy in their day-to-day activities. Above all, this can be seen in the way that ministries exercise control over the agencies. All the Nordic countries have introduced a performance management system. A common feature is that the ministries identify their goals through letters of allocation sent to the agencies specifying what the agencies must achieve; at the same time, they intervene less in the agencies' day-to-day activities. In other words, political steering has developed in such a way that there is now a clearer divide between policymaking by the ministries and policy implementation by the agencies.

Another manifestation of the increased autonomy of the agencies is the recruitment of civil servants by these bodies. The ministries appoint only senior management, leaving the heads of agencies to recruit personnel without the intervention of political leaders. At the same time, there has been a change in the status of the agencies. In all Nordic countries, there has been a transition from public service delivery through traditional government agencies controlled directly by the ministries towards the increased use of SOEs, which are subject to less direct ministerial control.

PUBLIC SECTOR REFORMS

Main Features of the Two Reform Waves

To understand the reception and implementation of NPM and post-NPM in the Nordic countries, it is necessary to be informed about the reform waves of the past three decades. But first we need to understand what administrative policy means both in theory and in practice. There are two different types of policy related to government activities and functions (Egeberg 2012). The first is externally directed policy in various sectors, including regulation and general resource allocation, and in relation to individual decisions taken in accordance with the rules; the second is internally directed policy, which is often labelled *administrative policy*. The latter intentionally seeks to alter the government apparatus through systematic changes in its formal structure, personnel and/or demography, culture and so forth, the logic being that administrative policy is supposed to have an indirect influence on externally directed policy and therefore achieve collective public goals. NPM and post-NPM are examples of this type of policy.

The central governments of many Western countries, particularly the Nordic ones, combine a centralized state with a large public sector and structural centralization and homogeneity while espousing strong state values and norms and emphasizing collectivity, equality and non-economic values, among other things (Christensen 2003). In addition, Nordic countries incorporate elements of the corporatist state that favour the integrated participation of interest groups in government (Olsen 1983). Corporatism is, however, in decline in the Nordic countries, see chapter 7.

NPM runs counter to many of these features. It advocates a "supermarket state" or fragmented state model (Olsen 1988) and a neo-liberal ideology, often combined with anti-political or apolitical views (Christensen and Lægreid 2001), that envisions a leaner, services-oriented state (as encapsulated in the catchphrase "Roll back the state"). NPM is based on two theories: a new institutional economic theory that promotes centralization and contracts; and a management theory that favours decentralization, delegation and the increasing autonomy of managers (Boston et al. 1996). The latter theoretical approach tends to dominate in most countries.

NPM is relatively one-dimensional in that it is strongly focused on cost efficiency, to which most other essential elements of government, including political loyalty, professional competence, corporatist features and the rights of the people, are subordinated (Christensen and Lægreid 2001). This focus on efficiency leads to an emphasis on market principles, increased structural differentiation and fragmentation, and the provision of services to consumers, among other things.

There are two dimensions to the structural fragmentation of public organizations: the *vertical specialization* of government and the *horizontal specialization* (Egeberg 2012). Vertical specialization or devolution can be either *internal*, meaning that politicians grant more autonomy to (regulatory) agencies which remain in regular public administrative bodies, or *external*, whereby former government enterprises are reorganized to form independent SOEs or new independent SOEs are established. In both types of vertical specialization, the formal control levers of the political executives are weakened, i.e. more distance is put between the politicians and the civil-service units, whereby the scope to subvert political control in practice is increased. The agencies are controlled through the formal letter of intent mentioned above and a formal and informal steering dialogue, while the SOEs are overseen by a board and a director.

Horizontal specialization in NPM is based on the principle of "single-purpose organizations", which was first exemplified in reforms implemented in New Zealand (Boston et al. 1996). According to this principle, the various functions and roles – including ownership, administrative, regulatory, policy advisory, services procurement and provision – are to be organized separately (Christensen and Lægreid 2003). The aim is to ensure that control and activities are less ambiguous and that it is easier to achieve goals, produce results and guarantee accountability. However, this approach requires more coordination and creates capacity problems for executive politicians (Dunn 1997).

Post-NPM returns to some of the principles of the old administrative state, albeit in a new context. The main thrust of the post-NPM reform wave is that NPM rendered the government apparatus too fragmented and that increased coordination is needed, requiring more political and administrative resources and increased capacity at the top (Christensen and Lægreid 2007). This means that agencies and SOEs must be subject to stricter control once again and that coordination between sectors and units within sectors must be tightened through formal reorganization and the launch of new networks, programmes and projects, among other things. Moreover, post-NPM is more preoccupied with developing a common collective culture than was its predecessor.

An important driver of the post-NPM counter-wave has been the ever-growing feeling among executive politicians that NPM undermined their ability to carry out the popular mandate of controlling and steering (Christensen and Lægreid 2007). The anti-political sentiment of NPM – which calls for politicians to "steer at a distance" within a system based on devolution – has met with increasing scepticism. There was also the feeling among executive politicians that NPM was unable to deliver on promises of increased efficiency either at the macroeconomic level or in relation to services at the micro level. Moreover, in this context it has been argued, including by scholars, that NPM created significantly more bureaucracy owing to increased reporting, scrutiny and control in the regulatory state.

A third reason for the emergence of post-NPM is the "fear factor". When the world feels like a more insecure place, there is a tendency towards contraction, meaning more control and less autonomy in the government apparatus (Christensen and Lægreid 2007). In recent years, terrorism has led to more or less draconic control measures in countries throughout the world, regardless of whether the ruling regime is right- or left-leaning. A similar development was witnessed during the global economic crisis around 2008, while the threat of the catastrophic impact of global warming has enabled governments to implement stricter environmental measure. Other triggers for the "fear factor" include pandemics and natural disasters such as tsunamis, which make it possible to introduce tighter control and regulatory measures.

Similarities and Diversity in Scandinavia's Reform Profile

In the 1980s, the Nordic countries began to institutionalize government bodies whose remit was to conduct administrative policy, regardless of whether they were new ministries, agencies or other units (Lægreid 2001). In general, this approach allowed questions of administrative reform and change to be dealt with more systematically and expertise on administrative policy to grow. It became easier for officials to learn from their own experience as well as from that of others. Furthermore, the necessary personnel were in place to pursue reform agendas much more aggressively, both as symbols and in practice.

Another important aspect of institutionalization was enshrined in the Scandinavia-wide reform programmes of the 1980s. Studies of political leadership and reform programmes indicate that such programmes serve different purposes (March and Olsen 1983). They can help get across a political statement or political agenda and thus can help bring about real change. But at the same time, they serve a symbolic function. Political leaders seldom miss an opportunity to boost their legitimacy by propagating NPM-related symbols of rationality and modernity. However, they have a tendency to lose interest in reform programmes once they have realized that they are unlikely to win the next election on administrative policy issues (March and Olsen 1983). Thus reform processes tend to run out of steam. But there are many examples of reform programmes that appear to have failed in the short term but end up proving successful in the long term; this is because public opinion warms to the idea of practical reform, i.e. there is some kind of "civic education" at work. At the same time, reforms can run into trouble because of disagreement within the executive, cultural resistance, the lack of rational calculation (meaning that the reforms have not been well prepared) or public debates about the negative impact (Aberbach and Christensen 2014).

From the 1980s onwards, Nordic countries typically opted for less radical approaches (Lægreid 2001), which meant preferring management by objectives and internal management reforms over more radical NPM measures such as downsizing and privatization – both of which were popular among the more daring Anglo-Saxon reform countries (Pollitt and Bouckaert 2011). For this reason, Nordic countries were often characterized as "reluctant reformers" (Olsen and Peters 1996). Since they have been more inclined from the 1990s onwards to adopt more radical measures, they can perhaps be more accurately described today as "modernizers" or "in-betweeners" (Christensen and Lægreid 2012, Greve and Ejersbo 2016). The Nordic profile established in the 1990s persists to this day, albeit with some variation.

Another Nordic idiosyncrasy is the close collaboration with interest groups in programme execution, particularly the civil-service trade unions (Olsen 1983). It goes without saying that the most radical reform elements will tend to be watered down during negotiations with affected parties. Moreover, those talks will highlight pragmatic capacity while increasing the legitimacy of the political executives. But it should also be pointed out that interest groups, such as the trade unions, have adapted to some recent reforms and at times have even supported them.

Even though the reform profiles of the Nordic countries are broadly similar, there are some clear differences. Below we discuss these differences in detail.

Denmark has a reform profile that has been dubbed one of "negotiated strategy" (Lægreid 2001). The Ministry of Finance is the main administrative policy body in Denmark, reflecting the generally more centralized nature of that country's government. It has promoted reforms by insisting that efficiency measures be implemented and that other ministries pursue the same reform implementation strategy while remaining willing to address the concerns of the employees and their unions. Traditionally, the government's negotiation strategy has been to hold talks with the various units of the civil service and to encourage other ministries and agencies to become more committed to reform.

Denmark's first administrative reform programme, launched in 1983, included the decentralization of management responsibility and decision-making, deregulation and the promotion of e-government (Greve and Ejersbo 2016). Every government since then has had its own programme, which has been a new version of the original. While the colour of the party in government at the time has lent some ideological variety to these programmes, there are many similarities to be found, indicating that left-leaning parties have subscribed to much of the NPM-oriented reform rhetoric.

In the early 1980s, administrative reforms tended to serve an ideological purpose, at least as far as leading politicians were concerned. In the 1990s, they became more technical in nature, and more recently they have returned to their ideological roots. Negotiations with the unions proceeded relatively well for a long time; however, dissention and controversy grew in the late 1990s, while the last decade or so has witnessed sharp reactions and a more activist approach. Today, the unions appear to be mainly concerned about preventing more extreme devolution, downsizing and privatization, but they have also been worried about large structural reforms affecting the municipalities and regions as well as primary schools.

Just like Norway, Denmark has witnessed the implementation of large structural reforms over the past 10–15 years (Greve and Ejersbo 2016). These include the local government reform of 2007, which slashed the number of municipalities from 271 to 98, merged 14 counties into five regions and changed the relationship between the centre and the lower administrative levels. In the 2007 reform of the police service, the number of police districts was cut from 54 to 12 – the same amount as in Norway following the two police reforms undertaken by that country. Also in 2007, a reform of the judicial system reallocated responsibilities between courts at the various levels and changed the jury system. There followed a reform of primary education, whose implementation triggered many conflicts with the teachers' unions.

Overall, administrative reforms in Denmark have been more technical and less ideological in nature than those in Norway and Sweden, although over the past decade they have also become more neoliberalist-oriented. Throughout, the Ministry of Finance has played a relatively large role, often negotiating with both internal and external stakeholders.

Finland, for its part, appears rather reluctant to reform its public sector, i.e. the central civil service has remained largely unchanged and stable. Reform processes have involved many different stakeholders and, ultimately, the passage of new legislation, which has slowed the pace of reform. However, those reforms implemented have received the backing of the entire leadership, which is important in a country that often has majority coalition governments. The backbone of the reform processes has been the stable relationship between the ministries and the agencies based on the Swedish model (which Norway, too, has adopted) (Greve and Ejersbo 2016). Since Finland joined the EU in 1995, it has repeatedly debated the issue of improving coordination between ministries, while merging some of those bodies has been on the agenda as well, even if no changes have been made. It is also worth mentioning that the merger of municipalities has often been discussed, but in the end the government has decided to pool resources rather than carry out mergers. Thus, in this respect, Finland is similar to Norway but different from Denmark.

With regard to introducing NPM elements, Finland's approach has tended to be hybrid and complex (Ahonen 2013). The 1990s were an active reform period in which some management reforms were implemented. During this period, strong agencies secured more autonomy while public corporations were either turned into something resembling the British agencies or granted more autonomy and eventually privatized (Tiihonen 1999). The privatization process over time was piecemeal and not particularly ideological in nature.

Finland has also introduced post-NPM elements. Starting as early as the 1980s, the number of ministerial aides was increased. This trend grew initially – not least at the Prime Minster's Office – because of the need for EU coordination and later because of the ownership steering of 30 out of Finland's 50 largest SOEs (Ahonen 2013). In 2005, the position of state secretary was established at nine ministries in order to increase ownership steering capacity (Tiihonen 2007). In 2007 Finland passed a new act on the government ownership and ownership steering of SOEs, which was followed by the establishment of a new ownership steering unit at the Prime Minister's Office (Ahonen 2016). Over the past five years, three different governments have tried to draw up and implement both horizontal and vertical structural coordination measures, including mergers, in order to unify the government. Vertical structural measures are aimed at centralizing power by increasing control over municipalities and horizontal ones at improving coordination with the central government. Currently, it remains unclear just how many of these measures will end up being implemented.

Overall, Finland has on the whole been a somewhat reluctant reformer, its reform processes slow (not least because changes to legislation have frequently been needed) and the number of actors involved large. The reform efforts have been led by the Ministry of Finance and the Ministry of Internal Affairs. Central government structures have remained largely unchanged and hence stable over the past few decades; the traditional minister-agency relationship, based on the Swedish model, has served as the backbone of those structures. Since 1995, when the country joined the EU, coordination issues have been a constant challenge (Greve and Ejersbo 2016). Reducing the number of ministries has been on the agenda for some time, but so far no steps have been taken in that direction.

In 1991, *Iceland* began a process dubbed "Restructuring the Public Sector", which was launched by a right-wing government with a view to modernizing the administrative apparatus. Two years later, the Ministry of Finance introduced an NPM reform initiative and in 1995 follow-up reforms (Matthiasson 2014).[3] Even though NPM elements were introduced throughout the public sector – for examples, performance contracts from 1995 onwards and, more broadly, performance management from 1997 (Ministry of Finance, Iceland 2002) – they were pursued less aggressively when from 1998 onwards Iceland's

3 Some of the information in this section is taken from diverse PPT presentations by Pètur Berg Mathiasson.

economy began performing better. However, NPM initiatives were implemented later as well. The agencies underwent further reforms during the period 1991–2007, including the decentralization of responsibility (from the ministries to the agencies), the introduction of performance contracts (mentioned above), the establishment of public procurement and private-sector providers and the promotion of e-government.

In 2007, a new strategy for improving both governance and performance-oriented government was introduced whereby the focus was on effectiveness and efficiency in the services sector; measures included reforming the structure of government, governance, fiscal management, human resource management and PPP relationships. The Ministry of Finance was unable to implement the strategy in full, not least because of the financial crisis from 2008 onwards. Indeed, that crisis resulted in more post-NPM measures being implemented, as can be seen from a 2010 report focusing on central joined-up government, closer supervision of independent organizations, increased capacity of ministries to formulate policies and the formation of strategic management teams (Kristinsson 2013). Between 2009 and 2012, some agencies were merged; but the current right-wing government, which took office in 2013, has done little to follow up these reform efforts. Finally, an increase in the number of political appointees over the last decade completes the picture (Kristinsson 2016).

Overall, the Icelandic central civil service has been by and large structurally stable over the past few decades. The main reform period in Iceland was the 1990s, which witnessed the implementation of various NPM elements that later had an influence on the administrative system. During the last 10 years, more post-NPM than NPM measures have been introduced, not least in response to the financial crisis.

In *Norway*, the first NPM reform efforts took place in the 1980s. Two reform programmes were launched in 1986 and 1987 by a conservative and a labour government, respectively, both of which used the NPM rhetoric of efficiency and services orientation; however, no major reforms were implemented (Christensen et al. 2014). Under a centre-right government from the mid-1990s onwards, Norway embarked on a slightly more radical reform path (Christensen and Lægreid 2003). The emphasis at this time was on structural devolution to agencies and SOEs; indeed, some of the largest state-owned companies were part-privatized during this period. Regulatory agencies were given more autonomy, and eight to ten of them were relocated out of Oslo. And horizontal specialization in non-overlapping roles was pursued more actively in the case of agencies, especially regulatory ones, with a view to boosting competition and the use of markets. While such efforts did not put Norway among the reform front runners, they did anchor it firmly in the reform mainstream.

The 2000s began with the one-year rule of a Labour-led government (2000–01), after which another centre-right cabinet took office. This was a period of intensive reform – one characterized by various reform principles, most of which advocated post-NPM elements (Christensen and Lægreid 2007). In 2000 there was a major reform of the police system in which many police districts were merged; a follow-up reform was launched in 2015. The immigration reform of 2001 granted the Norwegian immigration agency more autonomy and established an immigration appeals board, which enjoyed a high level of autonomy; during the period that followed, the political executive tried, albeit unsuccessfully, to regain some control over these agencies. In the hospital reform of 2002, the central government assumed ownership of the regional health enterprises but delegated authority to them, i.e. it combined post-NPM and NPM elements (Byrkjeflot, Christensen and Lægreid 2014).

The largest-ever reform undertaken in Norway – the welfare administrative reform of2005–06 – merged the pensions and employment agencies to form a new body that worked together with local social services. The Labour-led coalition that ruled from 2005 to 2013 campaigned on an anti-NPM ticket but delivered few of its campaign promises. When a minority coalition government composed of the Conservative Party and the anti-immigration Progressive Party came to power in 2013, it drew up a typical post-NPM agenda. The current government's main reform is aimed at merging municipalities, but it has been struggling to make headway. Another reform seeks to merge universities and colleges and has enjoyed more success.

Over the past three decades, Norway's reform profile has been characterized by an "incremental sector-based strategy" (Lægreid 2001), whereby the driving force for pragmatic change in a climate of reform reluctance has been the combined efforts of various sectors, ministries, agencies and SOEs rather than the efforts of a single central political or administrative body or a general government plan. Fragmented governments have produced fragmented reforms: ministries and agencies have been more concerned about pushing their reform agendas than about joining forces to pursue a common reform strategy, not least because the lead ministry in charge of administrative policy and reforms in Norway – traditionally, the Ministry of Labour and Government Administration – is one of the weaker government bodies.[4] Early reforms implemented in Norway were mostly NPM-inspired while those adopted more recently have been much more hybrid and, in part, post-NPM oriented. While the Norwegian parties have tended not to disagree significantly about the overall direction of the reforms, there have been conflicts from time to time, albeit of a symbolic nature.

4 Since 2013 Norway's lead ministry for administrative policy and reforms has been the Ministry of Local Government and Modernization, which, however, has limited success in this area judging from the problems it has encountered implementing its current main reform project – the merging of municipalities.

Sweden is the Scandinavian front runner in embracing radical reform. Its reform profile has been described as one of a "dual employers strategy" (Lægreid 2001), whereby duality refers to a system that combines a strong cabinet (as discussed above, Sweden practises collective government responsibility, not the individual ministerial responsibility preferred by its neighbours) and strong, independent agencies that have a long history. Over two decades, reforms have been initiated and supervised by the Swedish government to a far greater extent than has been the case in Norway. Moreover, Sweden has been more focused on rationality, efficiency and productivity than have the other Nordic countries. But at the same time, Swedish reforms are very much influenced and their implementation controlled by the independent agencies, while some of the regulatory agencies have achieved prominence thanks to structural devolution to the SOEs.

Sweden started with NPM-oriented reforms in the early 1990s in response to an economic crisis. The focus at that time was on performance management, and the lead actors were the Ministry of Finance together with the Swedish Agency of Public Management and the National Audit Office (Sundstrøm 2015). The reforms were characterized, above all, by managerialism as well as by decentralization and marketization – a reform orientation supported by the political-administrative leadership (Greve and Ejersbo 2016). Later, reforms became more wide-ranging and more post-NPM oriented: for example, the reform programme launched in 2010 by the then centre-rightist government, called 'Public Administration for Democracy, Participation and Growth', which was aimed at making agencies more innovative and more inclined to collaborate.

Historically, reforms have had a more local focus in Sweden than in Norway. This is partly due to agreements having been reached with interest groups, which seems to have made it easier to implement reforms in regions governed by socialist-driven local authorities, and partly owing to the influence of, and duplication by, local private-sector interests in solutions development and services provision. At the local level, market solutions and greater wage inequality have met with less resistance in Sweden than in Denmark and Norway. In recent years, Swedish local government has shown a growing interest in marketization, consumer choice and voucher systems (Wockelberg and Ahlbäck Öhberg 2016).

Overall, Sweden is the Nordic country that has followed the most radical reform path while eschewing, at least to some extent, the trends in Anglo-Saxon countries. The main factors for this approach are the dynamics of Sweden's dual system, a more overall rationalistic culture, the scare triggered by the economic crisis in the early 1990s and the weakening of corporatist elements.

Table 6.2 below shows the differences between the reform processes in the individual Nordic countries.

TABLE 6.2 DIFFERENCES BETWEEN THE REFORM PROCESSES OF THE NORDIC COUNTRIES

	Denmark	Finland	Iceland	Norway	Sweden
Reform profile	Negotiated strategy	Incremental	Incremental	Incremental and sectorbased	Dual employers strategy
Leading actors	Ministry of Finance	Ministry of Finance	Ministries and agencies	Ministries and sectors	Cabinet and agencies
Long-term stance on reforms	Reluctant turned modernizer	Reluctant modernizer	Reluctant modernizer	Reluctant modernizer	Active, rationality- and efficiencyori-ented
Importance of reform symbols	Moderate- low	Moderate	Moderate	High	Moderate
Current reform situation	Consolidation after more radical reform stance; ideology-driven	Reluctant reformer	Reluctant reformer	More radical reform stance, ideologydriven, structural reform	Consolidation, elaboration, wider democratic perspective

Empirical Relevance of the Perspectives

How can we use the perspectives outlined above to understand the reform processes in the Nordic countries? As previously mentioned, none of the Nordic countries wanted to adopt NPM in its most radical incarnations. During the past three decades, there has been hardly any environmental pressure in any of the Nordic countries, whether of a technical or institutional nature, although the overall picture is obviously somewhat more complicated (Christensen, Lægreid and Wise 2002). Moreover, there is rather limited compatibility between the cultural norms and values of NPM reforms and those traditionally espoused by the Nordic civil services. Nordic countries have long nurtured a strong state tradition that favours centralized government and a large public sector, which fit better with post-NPM. Equality is an important principle, along with high levels of trust between politicians and civil servants and, indeed, between political leaders and the general public. Governments have been willing to work with interest groups to implement reforms, opting for peaceful coexistence and "revolution in slow motion" (Olsen, Roness and Sætren 1982, Premfors 1991). And while the Nordic countries have been structurally homogeneous – a potentially reform-friendly factor – despite the profusion of political parties, they have frequently had minority governments (see chapter 4 for details) that have had to conduct extensive reform negotiations, which is not particularly reform-friendly.

Denmark, Finland, Iceland and Norway have all marched largely to the same tune – i.e. they are all more or less reluctant modernizers – while Sweden has followed its own path. Sweden's dual-structured political executive (a strong cabinet and strong agencies) is good for reform action. At the same time, the country has been more outward-looking and more aware of its place in the international arena than have the other four Nordic states, not least thanks to its closer ties with the main reform-promoting international bodies (such as the OECD) and some Anglo-American countries (Lerdell and sahlin-Andersson 1997). Moreover, Sweden has tended to be more efficiency- and rationality-centred. The economic downturn of 1990 prepared the ground for a more radical reform approach than the other countries were willing to contemplate. And finally, corporatism first began showing signs of decay in Sweden as far back as the 1980s; this trend became more pronounced in the 1990s and may have helped remove reform obstacles (see chapter 7 for the decline of corporatism).

More recently, the reform approaches of three of the Nordic countries – Denmark, Finland and Norway – have converged. All three have rightist governments whose members include entrepreneurs with a penchant for NPM-related reforms and populism. The crucial question is, however, to what extent this will lead to real change. The cultural and structural obstacles to reform that remain in these countries should not be underestimated.

A DISTINCT NORDIC REFORM PROFILE?

Looking at the Nordic reform efforts with the benefit of 30 years' hindsight, we can say that the group of five Nordic countries is composed mainly of reluctant reformers turned modernizers and thus represents a distinctive Nordic model. The main driver behind this model appears to be cultural (Peters 1997). First, the Nordic countries were and remain preoccupied more with democratic values than with efficiency. Second, they are focused on social responsibility and protecting the welfare state from some of the adverse effects of NPM; indeed, they were among the first in Europe to implement post-NPM measures and have been deploying them extensively over the past 10–15 years, in combination with NPM measures. Third, they tend to be more rule-centred and less goal-centred, although increasingly this does not apply to NPM measures. Fourth, they care more about egalitarian and collective values and less about competition, individualism and the market. Fifth, they encourage professional expertise in the public sector and discourage the politicization of the civil service. And sixth, they are more likely to welcome the role of interest groups in the reform process – a reflection of their lengthy corporatist past, which gave non-public sector actors an opportunity to work with government in order to promote collective values alongside their special interests.

During the past decade, these typically Nordic norms and values have come under pressure – both ideological and financial – as a result of which there has been a gradual shift towards a greater post-NPM orientation. That said, NPM reforms are still alive and kicking, albeit modified, slimmed down, revised and redefined in an ongoing process of pragmatic and hybrid adaptation.

CHAPTER 7

SCANDINAVIAN CORPORATISM IN DECLINE[1]

Hilmar Rommetvedt

If asked what characterizes the Nordic countries or the 'Nordic model' with regard to interest intermediation and interest group representation in the policy process, most international political scientists would answer *Corporatism*. In this chapter, I question whether this is (still) an appropriate answer. In the absence of comparable data on Finland and Iceland, I focus on the three Scandinavian countries, Denmark, Norway and Sweden. However, towards the end of the chapter, we will have a look at Finland and Iceland as well.

What, then, is corporatism? In his analysis of Norwegian numerical democracy and corporate pluralism, Rokkan (1966) described two channels of political influence. The numerical-democratic channel is based on territorial representation where the distribution of votes at elections determines who is going to represent the constituency in the Parliament. In the functional-corporatist channel various sectors or functions are represented by organized interests, corporations or interest groups.

The political importance of the two channels may vary. In the 1960s, Rokkan claimed that '[v]otes count in the choice of governing personnel but other resources decide the actual policies pursued by the authorities'. The 'other resources' referred to the resources various interest organizations carry into bargaining processes. The 'crucial decisions on economic policy are rarely taken in the parties or in Parliament'. The 'central arena', or channel of influence, was the corporatist channel or 'the bargaining table where the government authorities meet directly with the trade union leaders, the representatives of the

1 The presentation given in this chapter would not have been possible without a longstanding collaboration with Peter Munk Christiansen and Asbjørn Sonne Nørgaard from Denmark, PerOla Öberg and Torsten Svensson from Sweden, and Gunnar Thesen from Norway (see Christiansen et al. (2010), Öberg et al. (2011), and Rommetvedt et al. (2013)). I thank my colleagues for their invaluable contributions to the understanding of Scandinavian corporatism. I am also grateful to Anne Maria Holli and Stefanía Óskarsdóttir for their advice on Finland and Iceland respectively.

farmers, the smallholders, and the fishermen, and the delegates of the Employers' Association' (Rokkan 1966: 106 ff.).

Rokkan focused primarily on Norway, but his analysis was relevant for the other Scandinavian countries as well. In the 1970s, Schmitter (1979: 18–22) made a distinction between a highly centralized 'state corporatism' (including among others Fascist Italy under Mussolini) and a more open 'societal corporatism'. The latter was 'best exemplified by the cases of Sweden, Switzerland, the Netherlands, Norway and Denmark'. 'Societal corporatism' was characterized by 'noncompetitive, hierarchically ordered, sectorally compartmentalized interest associations exercising representational monopolics' in negotiations with the state on public policy. In other words, in a political system characterized by societal corporatism, a limited number of interest groups are recognized by the state and given an exclusive right to represent specific functions or sectors.

In numerous, more recent comparative studies, the Scandinavian countries are ranked at, or close to, the top of the lists of the most corporatist countries (e.g. Lijphart and Crepaz 1991, Siaroff 1999). If not explicitly, at least implicitly these (and other) studies clearly indicate that corporatism is an important element in Scandinavian politics and policy. In this chapter, we take a closer look at the concept of corporatism and its operationalization and measurement. In the 1970s, Schmitter (1979) raised the question: 'Still the Century of Corporatism?' I extend this question and ask: What has happened to Scandinavian corporatism in the late 20th and early 21st centuries? Furthermore, we will look at possible explanations of recent developments as well as their implications with regard to policy processes and interest group strategies.

VARIETIES OF CORPORATISM AND DEMOCRACY

Corporatism is a contested concept and there are different definitions and attempts to measure the phenomenon. Christiansen et al. (2010: 26 ff.) have made a distinction between a 'political economy school' focusing on 'varieties of capitalism', on the one hand, and an 'interest group school' drawing attention to 'varieties of democracy', on the other. As we have already seen, Rokkan related his analysis of corporatist bargaining primarily to *economic* policy. The political economy school is preoccupied with economic interests, their interaction with the state, and the effects on macro-economic performance. Sometimes, corporatism is simply defined as macro-level policy concertation, which leads to distinct macro-economic outcomes or growth strategies. From the outset, political economy scholars focused on industrial relations, economic policy and labour market policy. They hardly acknowledged corporatism outside these sectors.

The interest group school perceives corporatism as a more widespread phenomenon and a part of liberal democracy rather than capitalism. Corporatism is seen as an element of consensual and negotiation democracy, and it can be found in various sectors. The analysis of corporatism in this chapter is based primarily on the varieties of democracy perspective of the interest group school. As suggested by Christiansen et al. (2010: 27), corporatism is defined as the *institutionalized and privileged integration of organized interest in the preparation and/or implementation of public policies*.

The focus on privileged integration in the definition implies that some interest groups are given access to the institutionalized corporatist channel while others are excluded. Furthermore, a distinction is made between policy formulation and implementation. This opens up for the possibility that the degree of corporatism may vary between the two phases of the policy process. And finally, the definition implies that we should distinguish between the structural and institutional prerequisites or causes of corporatism, corporatism as such (as defined above), and the effects or consequences of corporatism with regard to both process and policy characteristics (see Figure 7.1). These are different independent and dependent variables which are frequently conflated in studies of corporatism.

When we speak of varieties of democracy, we cannot focus only on corporatism; we need to take possible alternatives into consideration. In a book on private interests in national policy-making, Heinz et al. (1993: 395) present a fourfold typology of governmental systems based on two dimensions: concentrations of private and government power respectively. A system combining high concentration of private power with low concentration of government power is labelled 'private government' while low concentration of private power together with high concentration of government power constitutes a 'state-directed' system. In the Heinz et al. typology 'corporatism' is related to high concentrations of both private and government power while the opposite, low concentrations of both private and government power, leads to 'pluralism'.[2]

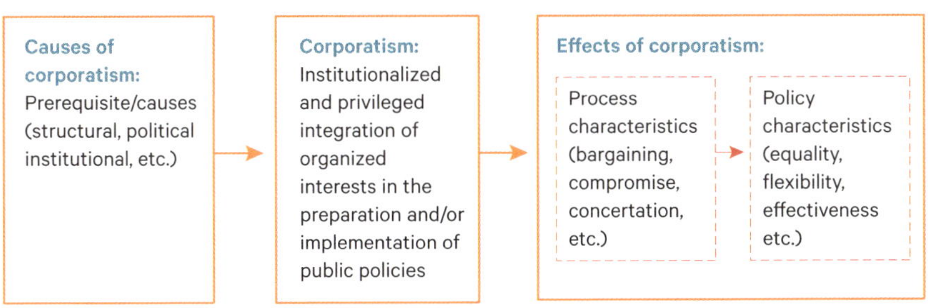

Figure 7.1 Corporatism, causes and effects. (Source: Christiansen et al. 2010: 27)

2 For an elaboration of the typology, separating monolithic and sectorized concentrations of power, and adding the 'segmented state' type of governmental systems, see Rommetvedt (2003: 9; 2005: 742; 2011: 22).

Heinz et al.'s typology is related to policy *making*. Not only pluralism, but also the electoral channel of representation via political parties and the Parliament may be seen as a 'conceptual opposite' to corporatism in the policy formulation process. In the *implementation* phase of public policies, the alternative to corporatism may be the classical bureaucracy of the executive (Christiansen et al. 2010: 27).

The wording of Heinz et al., 'high' and 'low' concentrations of power, indicates that corporatism and pluralism are not categorical variables. Corporatism and pluralism are opposite extremes on a continuous variable, or in other words, matters of degree. Similarly, Schmitter's definition of corporatism can be interpreted as an ideal type in a non-normative Weberian sense. Some empirical cases, such as those of Scandinavia, may show characteristics comparatively close to the ideal type, while others position themselves farther away from corporatism and closer to pluralism. Perceiving corporatism as a continuous variable opens up for more gradual changes over time.

SCANDINAVIAN CORPORATISM IN DECLINE

How then, should we analyze the development with regard to corporatism versus pluralism in the Scandinavian countries? A number of scholars have analyzed the development of corporatism by studying the role of interest organizations at different times, in various sectors and in specific policy-making processes (see for example Blom-Hansen and Daugbjerg 1999 and Christiansen et al. 2004 for Denmark; Nordby 1994, Klausen and Rommetvedt 1997 and Farsund 2004 for Norway; and Rothstein 1992, Hermansson 1993 and Öberg 1994 for Sweden). The studies clearly indicate that interest groups can have an impact on policy-making processes, but success rates can vary over time, and some groups are more influential than others.

The birth of Danish corporatism has been dated to the period immediately before the outbreak of World War I by Christiansen and Nørgaard (2003: ch. 3), while Rothstein (1992: 112) has argued that the 'formative moment' of Swedish corporatism is related to an agreement between the farmers' association and the government minister of agriculture in 1932. However, most scholars would argue that Scandinavian corporatism is not the outcome of a 'grand design' (Christiansen, forthcoming), or a specific decision made at a specific moment in time. The 1930s was an important period in the development of Scandinavian corporatism, but it emerged and developed over several decades, particularly after World War II (Blom-Hansen 2000, Nordby 1994, Öberg 1994).

In this chapter, we will see how Scandinavian corporatism has developed during the last few decades. I follow Christiansen et al. (2010: 28 ff.) and focus on the representation of organized interests in public boards, councils, committees and commissions appointed by central government (hereafter 'committees'). Such committees are highly institutionalized, having room for a limited number of members, and consequently only some privileged organizations can be represented. Some of the public committees are appointed on a temporary basis while others are permanent. Members may include representatives of various interest organizations, civil servants, experts and sometimes politicians. Their mandate is to analyze policy problems and prepare new public policies, or to implement public policies and manage public services in various areas.

Public committees with members representing organized interests are frequently perceived as the core expression of Scandinavian corporatism and thus well suited for the measurement of developments in the degree of corporatism.[3] Figures 7.2 and 7.3 show the development in the number of, respectively, policy preparation committees and policy implementation committees with at least one member representing an interest organization. (The figures are based on Christiansen et al. 2010: Tables 1 and 2.)

Even though there are nuances in the figures, these clearly indicate that Scandinavian corporatism has declined. In the beginning, we see surprisingly large differences between the three countries, particularly Denmark and Sweden. However, differences are significantly reduced towards the end of the timeline, particularly with regard to preparation committees. This is not in line with what one would expect if there were a single Scandinavian model of corporatism, and when the number of public committees in the three countries converged towards the turn of the millennium, they then converged at a relatively low level of corporatism.

The Danish development illustrates the necessity of making a distinction between preparation and implementation corporatism. The number of Danish policy *preparation* committees increased in the 1960s and 1970s. The number of preparation committees peaked around 1980, and since then Denmark has experienced a rather dramatic decrease in their numbers. The development with regard to Danish policy *implementation* shows a somewhat different picture. The number of implementation committees peaked somewhat earlier than that of preparation committees. From 1975 to 1980 we find a significant decrease in the number of implementation committees, but then the number stabilized. From the 1990s onwards we even see a moderate increase in the number of Danish implementation committees. A more recent study of Danish public committees indicates that that the 'dualist' development with decreasing preparation corporatism and increasing implementation corporatism continued. In 2010, Binderkrantz and Christensen (2015: 1029 ff.) found a total of 273 committees with interest group representation. Only three of the committees were assigned to drafting specific policies.

Unfortunately, in the case of Norway we cannot distinguish between preparation and implementation committees prior to 1983. However, the total

3 For a detailed discussion of methodological aspects, see Christiansen et al. 2010: 29f.

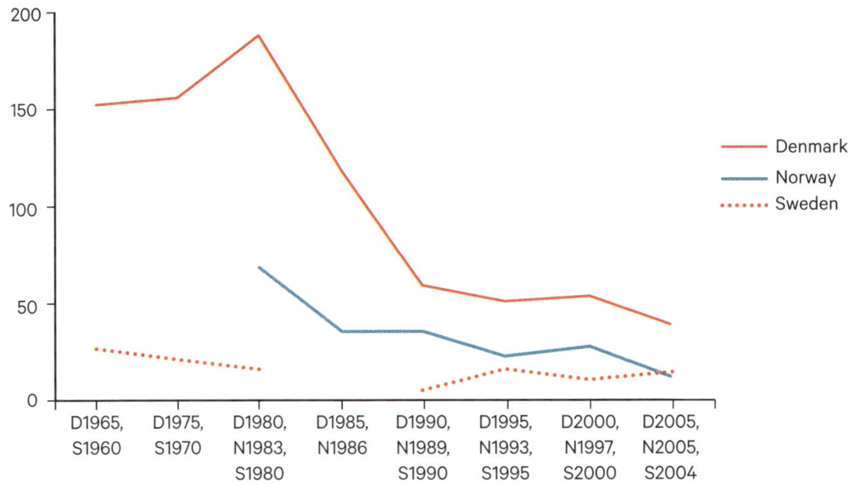

Figure 7.2 Policy preparation committees with interest group representation

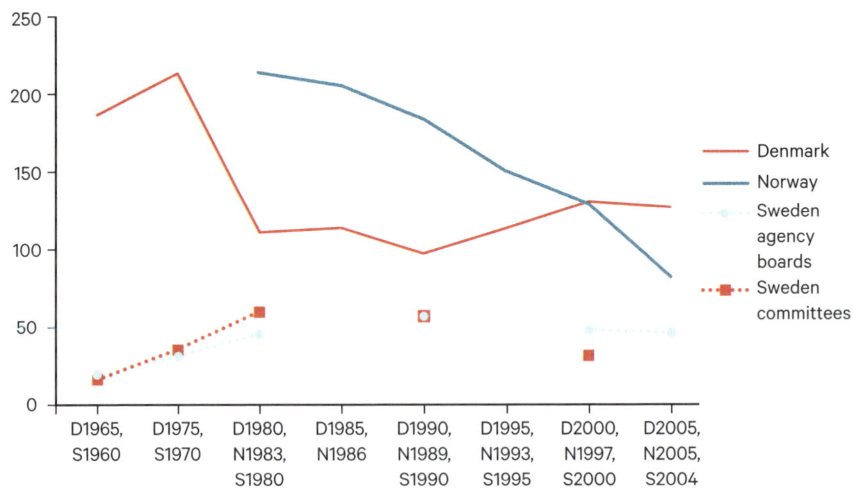

Figure 7.3 Policy implementation committees with interest group representation

number of committees with interest group representatives peaked around 1980. Thereafter, the total number of both public committees and committees with members from interest groups dropped rather dramatically (cf. Rommetvedt 2011: 25). As we can see in Figures 7.2 and 7.3, since the beginning of the 1980s the number of both preparation and implementation committees has decreased significantly in Norway. In other words, since 1980 policy preparation corporatism has declined in both Norway and Denmark. In Norway, policy implementation corporatism has also declined, while Denmark has experienced a moderate revival of implementation corporatism after a significant decline in the late1970s.

The Swedish findings are rather surprising. Sweden is often considered to be one of the most corporatist countries. However, throughout the whole period covered by Figures 7.2 and 7.3, we see that the levels of both preparation corporatism and implementation corporatism have been considerably lower than in Denmark and Norway. The data are somewhat limited, but they clearly demonstrate that the number of Swedish preparation and implementation committees with members from interest groups are the lowest in Scandinavia.

Furthermore, Figure 7.2 shows that the decline in preparation corporatism started earlier in Sweden than in Denmark and Norway. The number of Swedish preparation committees decreased from 1960 to 1980, but thereafter the number of preparation committees stabilized. State agencies that implement policies are more independent of government ministries in Sweden than in Denmark and Norway. Consequently, Christiansen et al. (2010: 30) make a distinction between implementation committees (in the Swedish regulatory administration) and agency boards. From 1960 to 1980, the number of both implementation committees and agency boards increased, thus indicating an increasing level of implementation corporatism (but still at a lower level than in Denmark and Norway). From 1990 to 2000, the number of implementation committees and agency boards decreased. After the turn of the millennium, the number of Swedish agency boards seems to have stabilized while the development with regard to other implementation committees is uncertain due to lack of data.

The findings of Christiansen et al. (2010: 33 ff.) clearly demonstrate that *Scandinavian corporatism has declined* since its heyday in the 1960s and 1970s. Since 1980, the decline of corporatism has been most pronounced in the *preparation* of public policies in Denmark and Norway. In Sweden, the decline of preparation corporatism started earlier. In the period covered by Figure 7.2, preparation corporatism has been more limited in Sweden than in Denmark and Norway, and consequently the decline has not been as strong as in the two neighbouring countries. Developments with regard to corporatism in the phase of policy *implementation* vary among the three countries. Implementation corporatism has declined significantly in Norway since 1980. Danish implementation corporatism declined significantly in the 1970s, but then stabilized before a moderate increase was experienced in the 1990s. Finally, after an increase in the 1970s, Sweden has experienced a certain decline in implementation corporatism. Summarizing the findings, we see that even though there are some variations in the changes and timing, the overall result is convergence towards a significantly lower level of corporatism in the Scandinavian countries.

As indicated above, a distinction should be made between the prerequisites or causes of corporatism, corporatism as such, and the consequences of recent developments in corporatism (cf. Figure 7.1). In the following sections, we will take a closer look at possible causes and consequences of the decline of corporatism in Scandinavia.

CORPORATIST EXCHANGE AND ITS DETERIORATION

Scandinavian interest groups have been invited to participate in all stages of the policy process. Corporatism is frequently associated with Social Democratic parties. When corporatism expanded in the first decades after World War II, Scandinavian politics was dominated by Social Democrat/Labour Party governments. This was particularly the case in Sweden and Norway, and to a lesser degree also in Denmark. However, as pointed out by Öberg (2015: 665), in the case of Sweden ideological and strategic considerations not only of the Social Democrats, but also of important parties on the political right, have paved the way for the participation of interest groups in the formulation and implementation of public policies. No doubt, the same can be said about Norway and Denmark. In his analysis of Norway, Rokkan (1966: 106) noted that the non-socialist parties had been 'losing in the fight for votes', but the interests of the non-socialist opposition could 'still be defended through other channels of influence on government decision-making', namely the corporatist channel.

The decline of corporatism since the 1970s indicates that the prerequisites and causes of corporatism have changed. Changing ideological and strategic considerations may contribute to the explanation of the decline (Öberg 2015: 673). The Power Study that was carried out by Norwegian social scientists in the late 1970s and early 1980s claimed that interest groups and civil servants in closed segments or 'iron triangles' had become more powerful than the elected representatives of the people (Egeberg et al. 1978, Hernes 1983). In 1983, the Conservative government in Norway stated that specialized interests had become too powerful, and that it would reduce the number of corporatist committees. In 1991, the Swedish employers' association decided to withdraw its representatives from the boards of agencies (Rothstein 1992: 349, Öberg 2015: 670). The Norwegian employers' association considered doing the same, but decided not to withdraw from public committees (Nordby 1994: 146 ff.). In other words, a growing scepticism towards corporatism can be observed, at least in Norway and Sweden.

As pointed out by Öberg et al. (2011), corporatism can be understood as an exchange between the state and organized interests. On the one hand, favourable public policies are of great importance to various interest groups. The state can control public expenditures and legislation, and give privileged groups access to policy-making processes. On the other hand, interest groups may possess resources of interest to government authorities. Interest groups can moderate and discipline their members in support of government policies. In other words, corporatist exchange 'presupposes that both actors control resources demanded by the other' (Öberg et al. 2011: 367). The prerequisites for (strong) corporatism can be specified according to mandate, unity, assets and intention, as shown in Table 7.1.

In this perspective, a weakening or decline of corporatism may indicate that the 'basic prerequisite for corporatist exchange has been disrupted' (Öberg et al. 2011: 365). Öberg et al. (2011: 374 ff.) present a variety of information which clearly indicates that both governments and interest groups are weakened, and thus less able to deliver what the other side wants in the corporatist exchange.

On the *government* side, the *mandate* or control over national policies may have been undermined by the transfer of authority to the international/European level. The Scandinavian countries are open economies strongly influenced by international cycles and trends. Denmark became a member of the European Union in 1973, and Sweden in 1995. Norway is not a member of the EU, but as a member of the European Economic Area since 1992, Norway is included in the inner market and increasingly influenced by EU regulations.

For several years after World War II, the Labour Party in Norway and the Social Democrats in Sweden won a majority of the seats in the respective parliaments, and consequently could form strong, single-party governments. The Danish Social Democrats never won a majority, but they were the largest party in the Parliament. However, since the 1970s not only the Danish, but also the Norwegian and Swedish governments have been minority and/or coalition governments (Damgaard 1992, Lane 2016). Governments have been weakened vis-à-vis parliaments, and opposition parties have strengthened their influence. In other words, the *unity* of the government together with parliament has been weakened, and consequently the government has become less capable of

TABLE 7.1 REQUIRED PROPERTIES FOR TRUSTWORTHY PARTNERS IN CORPORATIST EXCHANGE (SOURCE: ÖBERG ET AL. 2011: 370)

Prerequisites	Descriptive definitions	
	Government	**Interest group**
Mandate: (authority to make decisions)	Control over policy at national/central government level	Organizations with authority to bargain with central government
Unity: (ability to act as unitary actor)	Strong government vis-à-vis parliament	Organizational cohesiveness and representational monopoly
Assets: (exchange relevant resources)	Sufficient financial resources, control of allocation of privileges	High membership, membership support (control of votes)
Intention: (corporatism-friendly attitudes)	Positive attitude to corporatist actors/exchanges	Positive attitude to participation in corporatist exchanges

guaranteeing that policies negotiated with interest groups in corporatist bodies will actually be confirmed by a majority of the Parliament.[4]

In addition to sufficient mandate and unity, governments need *assets* or means to supply interest groups with policies that may persuade them to participate in corporatist exchanges. In the 1960s and 1970s, the Scandinavian public sectors grew significantly. After the oil crisis in the 1970s, Scandinavia experienced economic setbacks. Economic growth declined in Denmark and Norway in the 1980s, and Sweden experienced a dramatic downturn at the beginning of the 1990s. While Norway profited from the petroleum industry, Denmark and Sweden experienced retrenchment. Governments became less able to deliver advantageous policies. However, it could also be important for interest groups to become involved in negotiations on deregulation and retrenchment in order to curb the damaging effects.

Finally, *intention* or positive attitudes towards corporatism is an important prerequisite. As mentioned above, there was consensus with regard to the corporatist development among both Social Democrats and non-socialist parties. However, the weakening of Social Democrats may have contributed to the development of more sceptical attitudes towards corporatist integration of organized interests in policy preparation and implementation. The downsizing of the corporatist committee system in Norway, which started under the Conservative government in the 1980s, continued after the Labour Party returned to office. Consequently, as pointed out by Öberg et al. (2011: 382), interest groups have 'good reasons ... to question whether governments in Scandinavia have stable intentions to engage in corporatist exchanges'.

Even though there are certain variations in the picture, the overall impression is that since the 1970s the prerequisites for corporatism have been weakened on the government side of the exchange. Turning to the interest group side of the corporatist exchange, the question is: Do organized interests have the necessary capabilities?

For *interest groups* to participate in public policy-making, they need a *mandate* to speak on behalf of their members. Focusing on the statutory authority of the confederations of labour market organizations over their affiliates, Öberg et al. (2011: 383) argue that the degree of centralization has not changed much in the three Scandinavian countries. As argued earlier, corporatism can be relevant in other areas than the economic sector and labour market policy. However, among the growing number of interest groups in other sectors, such as leisure, health, the environment and other citizen groups, the mandate to speak on behalf of their members is more diffuse.

Growing numbers of interest groups indicate that *unity* among organized interests has diminished. In Denmark, the number of national interest groups

4 See chapter 4 for details regarding the relationship between the governments and parliaments.

increased from approximately 2100 in 1975 to more than 2500 in 2010 (Fisker 2015: 61, Binderkrantz et al. 2016) while Norwegian registrations indicate an increase from nearly 1200 nationwide organizations in 1976 to 2400 in 1992, and nearly 3400 in 2013 (Hallenstvedt and Trollvik 1993:XI, Arnesen et al. 2016: 18). Furthermore, the number of Scandinavian confederations of labour market organizations has increased. With a diminishing working class and growing middle class, the share of union members in the Norwegian Confederation of Trade Unions (*Landsorganisasjonen i Norge* [LO]), the blue-collar confederation that cooperates most closely with the Social Democrat/Labour parties, has decreased and consequently trade union concentration has diminished. In Norway, LO's share of the organized workforce has been reduced from 83 per cent in 1958, via 65 per cent in 1982, to 50 per cent in 2014. Today, LO is challenged by three other Norwegian confederations of white-collar workers and academics (Nergaard 2016: 8 ff., Rommetvedt 2011: 28 ff.).[5]

The primary *asset* of an interest group in the exchange with government is the ability to mobilize support among its members. The members' support may include acceptance of deals struck over public policies, or even more important – the members' votes. Since the 1960s and 1970s, both the number of more or less competing interest groups and electoral volatility, or interparty shifts among voters, have increased. Nordic election studies show that class voting and the proportion of voters who consider themselves supporters of a particular party have declined. Increasing complexity with regard to occupational status, decreasing unionization, increasing levels of education and issue voting, together with working class votes for rightist populist parties, are among the factors that may explain this development (Bengtsson et al. 2014: 71, 150 ff., see also chapter 3). In other words, increasingly, 'Scandinavian governments cannot take for granted that interest groups control an asset that is an essential component in a corporatist exchange' (Öberg et al. 2011: 387).

As we have seen, the *intentions* or attitudes among Scandinavian governments have become less corporatist-friendly than previously. To some degree, this is also the case with regard to interest group attitudes. New organizational types, including ad hoc-based, single-issue organizations, have become more important and numerous. Together with more individualist attitudes among the citizens, this may indicate that the (potential) participants in corporatist exchanges have become less trustworthy.

---

5 It could be added that the level of unionization is lower in Norway than in Denmark and Sweden. In 2013, 54 per cent of the Norwegian labour force were members of a union compared to 67 and 68 per cent in Denmark and Sweden. The lower level in Norway can be ascribed to the absence of a Ghent model of organizing the unemployment administration, with links between the unions and the implementing bodies (Christiansen, forthcoming).

Summarizing their findings, Öberg et al. (2011: 389) note that there 'have indeed been changes in the properties that are required of a trustworthy partner in corporatist exchange'. They find a weakening or decline in the prerequisites for corporatism in the Scandinavian governments' mandate (e.g. Europeanization), their unity (fragmentation), assets (strained public budgets), and intention (less social democracy). Among interest groups, decline is found with regard to union (fragmentation), assets (electoral volatility) and intention (individualism), while changes in mandate may seem more uncertain. Clearly, disruptions in the corporatist exchange contribute to an explanation of the decline we have observed in Scandinavian corporatism. Denmark, Norway and Sweden have become more pluralist societies and polities. In the next section, we consider some of the consequences of the observed decline in Scandinavian corporatism.

STRATEGIC CONSEQUENCES: LOBBYING

In a democratic political system, affected individuals and interests are supposed to be informed and to have a say in the preparation of policies. Furthermore, interest groups may contribute new ideas and solutions to policy problems, and the inclusion of affected actors in the policy-making process may facilitate the implementation of new policies. Corporatism can be one way of integrating affected actors in the preparation and implementation of public policies. Corporatist representation may give privileged interest groups an opportunity to influence public policies. However, as we have seen, since the 1970s the corporatist apparatus in Scandinavia has been downsized, and access to policy-making processes through corporatist bodies has been reduced. What, then, are the consequences of reduced access through the corporatist channel?

As noted by Christiansen et al. (2010: 25), the political economy school is concerned with 'the way economic interests are organized, how they interact with state actors and the effects of these variables on macro-economic performance'. Structural variables such as high union membership, strong peak organizations and centralized wage bargaining, together with process variables such as coordination through bargaining, interest mediation and concertation, are assumed to produce specific macro-economic outcomes such as economic growth, reduced strike activity, less unemployment and a more equal distribution of wages. However, I will not go further into the macro-economic consequences of the declinie of corporatism here. Instead of focusing on consequences related to corporatism as a variety of capitalism, I concentrate on corporatism as a variety of democracy and on consequences related to policy-making processes (cf. Figure 7.1).

In this section, we will see how certain strategies applied by interest groups in order to influence public policies have been affected by the decline of corporatism. Alternative interest group strategies may include communication through the media and mobilization of members and the general opinion (Binderkrantz et al. 2015, Thesen and Rommetvedt 2009). However, here I focus on interest group *lobbying*.

As we have seen, corporatism is a highly institutionalized way of integrating privileged interest groups into policy preparation and implementation processes. Lobbying is a less institutionalized, more informal, ad hoc-based and open way of exerting influence. Originally, lobbying referred to personal meetings with politicians in the lobby of the Parliament, but lobbying may also include direct personal contacts with civil servants. The establishment of a corporatist committee can be initiated by an interest group, but the initiative has to be followed up by the government. Corporatist representation presupposes a willingness of the state to establish corporatist bodies and arrangements, and to include organized interests in these arrangements. Lobbying, on the other hand, is both initiated and executed by the organized interests themselves. Furthermore, lobbying is primarily a one-way communication process where interest groups present their views and demands, and try to influence politicians and civil servants. Corporatism is more of a two-way communication and negotiation process where both parties try to influence each other. Lobbyists do not commit themselves to implementing negotiated agreements in the same way as interest group representatives in corporatist committees and negotiation processes (cf. Christiansen and Rommetvedt 1999, Espeli 1999, Hermansson et al. 1999).

Two factors, push and pull, need to be taken into consideration when organized interests decide how to adapt to changing political circumstances. *Push* factors are 'environmental changes that drive actors away from a strategy, for example, by blocking previous channels of influence', while *pull* factors are 'changes that draw actors in new directions because new promising venues for political influence are opened' (Rommetvedt et al. 2013: 460). In our context, corporatism in decline is an obvious push factor, while the pull factor can be related to changes in executive–legislative relations.

For a long time, Scandinavian parliaments were believed to have lost most of their power to single-party, majority governments and strong bureaucracies. The 'decline of parliaments thesis' was popular among political observers and political scientists in Scandinavia. However, commencing in the late 1970s, the Danish, Norwegian and Swedish parliaments became more active and influential vis-à-vis the governments. A 'reparliamentarization' or 'revitalization' of the Scandinavian parliaments occurred after the Social Democrats lost their dominant position in Scandinavian politics, and government parties have been defeated more frequently in parliamentary voting (Damgaard 1992: 204, Rommetvedt 2011: 95). The government of Denmark in particular, but also those of Norway and Sweden, have increasingly negotiated legislative settlements with one or more opposition parties (Christiansen and Damgaard 2008, Grønlie 2014, Bäck and Bergman 2015).

As a consequence of the combined effect of push and pull – corporatism in decline and the revival of parliaments – one might expect interest groups to increase their lobbying efforts towards public authorities in general, and the parliaments in particular. In the absence of comparable Swedish data, we have to concentrate on Denmark and Norway. In a number of surveys, nationwide Danish and Norwegian interest groups have been asked about their contacts with various public authorities. 'Contacts' is a proxy for lobbying, but it should be added that contacts with the bureaucracy may also include contacts through corporatist committees. Figures 7.4 and 7.5 (based on Rommetvedt et al. 2013: 472) show the percentages of Danish and Norwegian panels of interest groups who answered that they had at least monthly contacts with the respective authorities.

In both Denmark and Norway, we see that the bureaucracy was contacted by the highest number of interest groups. However, interest group contacts with the bureaucracy have not changed much over time. Contacts with the parliaments are less frequent, but we note a significant increase in the percentages of interest groups who reported at least monthly contacts with the parliament, particularly in Norway. A similar trend is found with regard to contacts with governments. In addition, we may add that lobbying targeted exclusively at civil servants in the bureaucracy has become significantly less widespread, while the share of interest groups who lobby both bureaucrats and MPs has increased, particularly in Norway (Rommetvedt et al. 2013: 474).

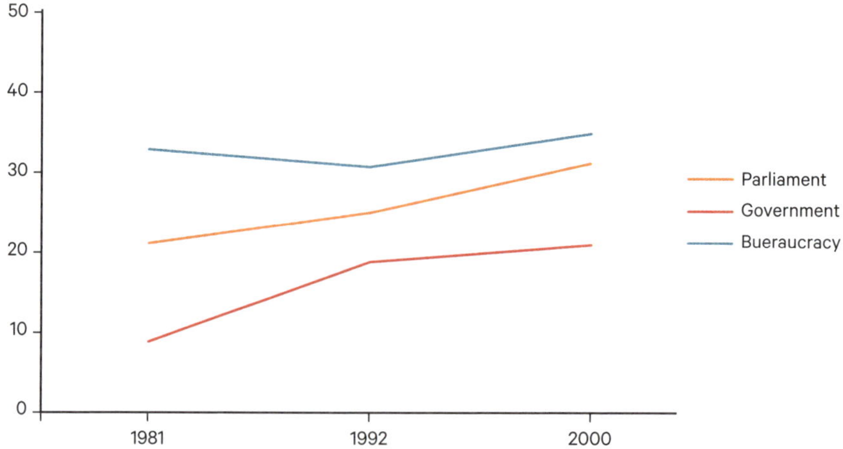

Figure 7.4 Danish interest groups with at least monthly contacts with public authorities

The findings indicate that while being increasingly excluded from a decreasing number of corporatist committees, interest groups have increased their lobbying efforts directed at public authorities. Furthermore, parliaments have become more important targets for the lobbyists. In 2005, 88 per cent of the Norwegian interest groups reported that contact with the Parliament was important, while 85 and 51 per cent respectively said the same about contacts with ministries and the government. From 1982 to 2005, the importance of parliamentary contacts increased by 10 percentage points, while contacts with ministries and the government decreased by 4 and 14 percentage points respectively (Rommetvedt 2011: 107).

Lobbying can serve as a substitute for, or supplement to, corporatist representation. For 'corporatist outsiders', or interest groups that do not have the privilege of been represented in public committees, lobbying may serve as a substitute for corporatist representation. For 'corporatist insiders', or interest groups that are represented in public committees, lobbying may serve as a supplement to corporatist representation. In Norway, Rommetvedt et al. (2013: 474) found significant increases in contacts with parliament and the government among both insiders and – to a lesser degree – outsiders. In Denmark, there was no increase in the contacts with parliament and the government among corporatist outsiders, and only minor increases among insiders. In other words, in Norway lobbying serves as both a substitute for and a supplement to corporatist representation, while in Denmark lobbying seems to serve primarily as a supplement to corporatist representation among corporatist insiders.

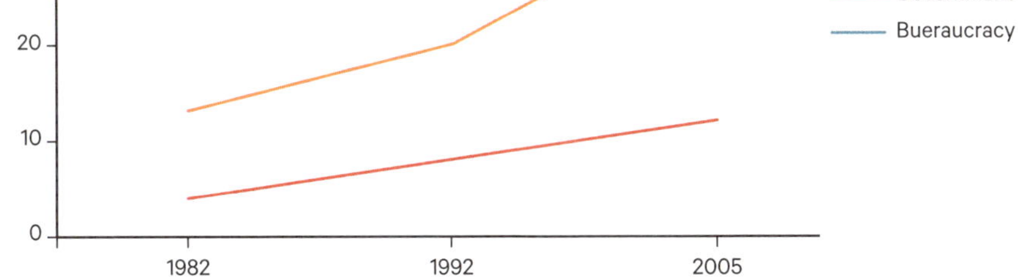

Figure 7.5 Norwegian interest groups with at least monthly contacts with public authorities

POLICY IMPACTS AND DEMOCRATIC CONSEQUENCES OF LOBBYING

The Danish and Norwegian findings clearly indicate that the decline in corporatism has led to increased lobbying. No doubt, organized interests try to influence public policies in new ways, but do they succeed? Do their lobbying efforts have an impact on policy-making? And what are the consequences with regard to representative democracy?

A survey among Norwegian MPs in 1995 indicated that lobbying may in fact have an impact on agenda setting and decision-making processes. The MPs were asked how often lobbying contributed to various actions (see Rommetvedt 2003: 160; 2014: 471). Fifty-nine per cent of the MPs answered very or fairly often when they were asked if the enquiries of the lobbyists were a contributing factor when parliamentary committees or committee members asked a government minister for additional information. Respectively, 33 and 24 per cent said the same about interpellations/question-time questions and private members' bills.

According to 44 per cent of Norwegian MPs, dissenting remarks and proposals in committee recommendations were often related to lobbying. The lobbyists' enquiries were also a contributory factor when amendments were made to government proposals and guidelines. Twenty-eight per cent of the MPs answered very or fairly often with regard to minor amendments. Only 4 per cent said the same with regard to major amendments, but an additional 40 per cent stated that enquiries from lobbyists sometimes contributed to major amendments in government proposals and guidelines.

In a survey carried out in 2005, Norwegian interest groups were asked how often their proposals had 'led to' amendments in government proposals and guidelines (Rommetvedt 2014: 470 ff.). With regard to minor amendments, 9 and 41 per cent respectively said that that this was the case very/fairly often or sometimes. The corresponding figures for major amendments were 3 and 26 per cent. In other words, both MPs and interest groups agree that lobbying can have an impact on policy-making. (When comparing the figures, it should be kept in mind that the assessments of the MPs were based on the sum of contacts with a variety of lobbyists, while the answers from interest groups were related to their own lobbying efforts, that is, only one actor's lobbying.)

A Danish study of administrative consultations and contacts with the Parliament in 2009/10 shows that interest groups may have an impact on legislation. Seventy-two per cent of interest group answers to administrative consultations included substantial objections to the proposed legislation. Eight per cent of the group protests were fully sustained and 29 per cent partially followed by the minister when the proposal was presented to the Danish Parliament. Various interest groups sent 245 letters concerning law proposals to parliamentary committees; 53 of these led to changes (Binderkrantz et al. 2014: 143, 170f).

The definition and operationalization of corporatism applied in this chapter implies that a rather limited number of privileged interest groups are given access to this channel of influence. Furthermore, corporatist representation gives interest groups access primarily to civil servants in the public administration. Lobbying, on the other hand, is more open, and as we have seen, increasingly directed towards the Parliament. Nevertheless, resources are important for interest groups and their activities towards public authorities. A Danish study based on data from 2009/10 shows that high-income groups with a high number of employees hired for political tasks were more active in the legislative process in both the administrative and the parliamentary arenas (Pedersen et al. 2014). Norwegian data from 1982 to 2005 show that business associations and trade unions are more active than other groups (Thesen and Rommetvedt 2009). In other words, in corporatist arrangements, privileged access is highly institutionalized, but in practice lobbying can be biased as well.

In two surveys, Norwegian MPs were asked to assess some of the consequences of lobbying. In 1995, almost all MPs – 93 per cent – agreed that well-organized interest groups may become too influential compared to weakly organized groups; 56 per cent agreed that specialized interests may become too influential compared to more wide-ranging concerns and comprehensive policies. In 2012, the corresponding figures were reduced to 75 and 32 per cent respectively. In both 1995 and 2012, 91 per cent of the members of the Norwegian Parliament agreed that meetings with lobbyists give them better access to alternative information and expertise in relation to the government and the ministries. Furthermore, 81 per cent of MPs in 1995 and 83 per cent in 2012 agreed that the Parliament acquires improved possibilities to control that the government and the public administration follow up parliamentary decisions and intentions. In 1995, 86 per cent of the MPs concluded that lobbying towards the Parliament had mostly positive consequences (Rommetvedt 2014: 474f). The same question was not included in the 2012 survey, but in 2013, 90 per cent of the MPs said that lobbying is generally positive for democracy (Olufsen 2013).

The Norwegian MPs' assessments show that they acknowledge negative consequences of lobbying. However, since the 1990s they have become less concerned about well-organized specialized interests becoming too influential. Furthermore, the negative effects of lobbying are overwhelmingly overshadowed by positive effects regarding access to information and counter expertise in the policy-making process, and parliamentary control of the executive in the implementation process. Increased interest group lobbying is a *consequence* of push and pull, or the decline of corporatism and revival of parliament, but it may in turn also *strengthen the position of the Parliament vis-à-vis the Government.*

THE CASES OF FINLAND AND ICELAND

The Nordic countries include not only Scandinavia, but also Finland and Iceland. The inclusion or exclusion of Finland and Iceland in 'Nordic models' varies. Unfortunately, we do not have access to more recent comparable data of the kind we have applied to the Scandinavian countries. However, the overall impression is that developments in Finland are fairly similar to those in Denmark, Norway and Sweden. Iceland, on the other hand, seems to stand out as an outlier, not only in the geographic sense of the word, but also with regard to corporatism.

In the case of Finland, Helander (1997: 243 ff.) argues that during the 1960s a rather closed governmental decision-making process was opened up to other actors, including various interest groups. The number of public committees increased, reaching a peak in 1972 with a total of 598 temporary and permanent committees. However, in the 1970s the number of temporary committees declined, while the number of permanent committees stabilized. Permanent committees after 1980 are not included in Helander's overview, but the number of temporary committees continued to decrease in the 1980s and the first half of the 1990s.The number of temporary committees declined form 253 in 1970 to 12 in 1995. However, the highly institutionalized temporary committees were gradually replaced by less institutionalized working groups. In 1972, 113 working groups were registered compared to 346 in 1994.

Not all public committees are 'corporatist' committees. Public committees should only be categorized as corporatist if they include members from one or more interest groups. Most likely, the mandate of temporary committees is related to policy preparation, while the tasks of permanent committees are related to the implementation of public policies. Consequently, if they include interest group representatives, temporary and permanent committees can be perceived as expressions of preparation corporatism and implementation corporatism respectively. In the absence of data on interest group representation in permanent Finnish committees, we have to concentrate on temporary committees.

In the beginning of the 1960s, most of the temporary committee members were civil servants and experts. The representation of Finnish interest groups was limited, and in most of the temporary committees, there were no representatives from interest groups at all. During the 1960s, a growing number of interest group representatives were included in the committees. The share of interest group representatives seems to have reached its highest level in the first half of the 1970s. In 1980 and 1993, 27–28 per cent of the members of temporary committees represented various interest groups. However, together with the decrease in the number of committees, the total number of committee seats was reduced from 534 in 1980 to 332 in 1993, and consequently interest group representation was reduced from 146 to 94 members.[6] Furthermore, commencing in the 1990s, policy preparation committees have increasingly been replaced by single person, so-called 'state investigators' (Holli 2016). In other words, in the 1980s and first half of the 1990s, Finnish policy preparation corporatism declined, but we do not know how implementation corporatism developed in this period.

More recent data on Finland have not yet been published. However, an ongoing study by Anne Maria Holli indicates that the consensual Finnish democracy is changing in a more majoritarian direction.[7] Since the 1990s, there has been a clear trend of change from a corporatist organization of state-society relations towards a more pluralist or neo-pluralist organization. The number of policy preparation committees and membership seats has decreased and consequently there are fewer places for interest groups and NGOs in the preparation of public policies. Interest groups increasingly attend parliamentary hearings and lobby the Finnish Parliament.

Data on Iceland are very limited and the picture of corporatist developments is rather blurry. In his corporatist rankings of 24 countries, Siaroff (1999) places Iceland well below the other Nordic countries, even though Iceland has not been 'classified often enough to claim any scholarly agreement'. More recently, Jónsson (2014: 523) has described Iceland as a political system with 'a "pluralist" type of interest organization that is characterized by a low level of corporatism and a high degree of competition between major interest groups'. Thorhallsson (2010) was even more categorical when he claimed that Icelandic corporatism 'fundamentally differs from the social corporatism in Scandinavia', and that social movements have been 'explicitly, and deliberately, side-lined in governmental decision-making processes'. He admitted, however, that 'powerful fisheries and farmers' lobbies have been in ... close contact with the government' (Thorhallsson 2010: 378 ff.).

Icelandic fishermen belong to a variety of unions and associations which, according to Eythórsson (2000), have been 'more or less ... represented in different task forces and committees appointed by the Government to review the fisheries policy'. After a broad consensus in the 1970s, fisheries management became 'the most dividing and conflict-laden issue of Icelandic politics' in the 1990s. Eythórsson claimed that the practice of 'preparing new legislation by task forces with broad representation from different stakeholder groups' was then 'abandoned' (Eythórsson 2000: 484f, 490). However, after the turn of the millennium this turned out not to be the case. New committees with interest group representatives have been set up by Icelandic governments. Changes in the legislation and taxation of the fisheries industry have normally not been

6 Calculated on the basis of Helander 1997: 251, table 5.

7 Source: personal communication with Anne Maria Holli, University of Helsinki.

made without close consultation with interest groups. Furthermore, new legislation on subsidies and regulations of Icelandic agriculture has been adopted by the Parliament on the basis of a negotiated agreement between agricultural producer groups and the state. In other words, corporatist representation in Icelandic fisheries and agricultural policies appears to be relatively strong.[8]

Among scholars belonging to the political economy school, corporatism is characterized by tripartite negotiations on wages and economic policies. In this respect, corporatism is a rather new phenomenon in Iceland. For a long time Icelandic governments relied on unilateral income policies in order to keep inflation and unemployment under control. However, from the late 1960s 'a slow movement towards a more corporatist regime' occurred. Labour unions 'were consulted and occasionally included in different stages of public policy-making', but it was not until the recession of the late 1980s that 'conditions for a closer cooperation between labour, employers and government were created' (Jónsson 2014: 519). In the 1990s, tripartite negotiations between trade unions, employers' associations and the state replaced the former unilateral income policies of the governments (Óskarsdóttir 1999: 92). After the financial crisis in 2008, the director of the federation of employers, Vilhjálmur Egilsson (2012), claimed that 'neo-corporatism gains ground in times of crisis'. In what he labelled 'the Icelandic Neo-corporative Model', the social partners are 'deeply involved in organization and delivery of social services' such as pension funds, education, rehabilitation and services to the unemployed.

In the absence of systematic data, we should be careful not to jump to conclusions. However, it looks as if the general level of corporatism in Iceland remained weak when corporatism in the other Nordic countries was expanding after World War II. Corporatism within the fisheries and agricultural sectors has been relatively strong in Iceland, but corporatism in other sectors developed late. In the other Nordic countries, corporatism had peaked and was in decline before corporatism expanded in Iceland.

CONCLUSION

Most international scholars would probably answer 'corporatism' if they were asked to give a one-word description of the 'Nordic model' of state–interest group relations and interest intermediation. However, on the basis of the data and analysis presented in this chapter it seems appropriate to ask: Is there *really* a 'Nordic corporatist model' of state-interest group relations? The answer depends on how we define corporatism, and the time frame of our analysis.

Sometimes corporatism is loosely defined as close contacts between organized interests and government authorities. In this case, it could be said that all Nordic countries are corporatist. However, one could probably say the same

8 Source: personal communication with Stefanía Óskarsdóttir, University of Iceland.

about most Western democratic countries as well. In this loose sense of corporatism, there is no particular Nordic corporatist model.

In the perspective of the political economy school, corporatism is a matter of tripartite bargaining over economic policy and income, and effects on macroeconomic performance. Within this perspective, we have seen that Iceland is a deviant case. It was not until the 1990s that the unilateral income policies of Icelandic governments were replaced by tripartite negotiations between trade unions, business associations and the state.

In this chapter, I have analyzed corporatism primarily from the perspective of the interest group school. Thus, corporatism has been defined as the institutionalized and privileged integration of organized interests in the preparation and/or implementation of public policies. Furthermore, corporatism has been perceived as a matter of degree, and (potentially) relevant to a variety of public sectors, and not only for economic policy.

In the case of Denmark, Norway and Sweden, corporatism has been measured on the basis of interest group representation in public committees. In this sense, Scandinavian corporatism started early and expanded particularly after World War II. The data indicate that Danish and Norwegian corporatism peaked around 1980, while Swedish corporatism reached its zenith even earlier. Over the last three or four decades, corporatism in Scandinavian has declined. The corporatist committee systems have been significantly downsized.

Unfortunately, we do not have access to comparable Finnish and Icelandic data, but corporatism seems to have declined in Finland as well. In the case of Iceland, data are even more limited, and the development seems rather dualistic. In general, the level of corporatism has been low. For a long time, interest groups have been influential in the development of Icelandic fisheries and agricultural policies, but corporatist income policies developed late in Iceland.

The distinction made here between preparation and implementation committees has revealed important nuances between the Scandinavian countries as well. Preparation corporatism has declined in all three countries. In Norway, implementation corporatism has declined as well, while in Denmark and Sweden the degree of implementation corporatism has stabilized after reaching a much lower level than in the heyday of corporatism. Denmark has even experienced a moderate increase in the number of implementation committees with interest group representation.

This analysis clearly indicates that it is not appropriate to talk about a single 'Nordic model' of corporatism. The label 'Scandinavian model' may have been more appropriate in the 1960s and 1970s, but even then there were substantial differences between Denmark, Norway and Sweden. Towards the turn of the millennium, the three countries moved in a more pluralist direction. The prerequisites for corporatist exchange weakened, and the overall degree of corporatism declined. Interest groups increasingly resort to less institutionalized and less privileged lobbying and media strategies in order to influence public policies. Consequently, to talk about a single 'Scandinavian corporatist model' is less appropriate in the beginning of the 21st century, and it would hide important nuances in Danish, Norwegian and Swedish developments.

CHAPTER 8

LOCAL AND REGIONAL GOVERNMENT IN THE NORDIC COUNTRIES: CO-OPERATIVE DECENTRALIZATION

Harald Baldersheim, Lawrence E. Rose & Siv Sandberg

LOCAL GOVERNMENT IN THE NORDIC STATE TRADITION

In day-to-day operation, the Nordic countries stand out as *decentralized welfare states* (see Sellers & Lidström 2007). It is important in this respect to emphasize *decentralized* because of the prominent roles local and regional governments play in the Nordic political systems.[1] Under a system of *co-operative governance*, many tasks and services that are functions of the state in other countries have been entrusted to local and regional governments in the Nordic countries. Co-operative governance refers not only to the volume of tasks delegated to local and regional decision-makers but above all to the close and trustful relations that typically exist between central and local levels of government.[2]

Co-operative governance the Nordic way must be judged to represent a fairly successful constellation of institutions, but it is not without its problems and tensions. What a well-functioning system of local government entails, moreover, is open to discussion. The criteria against which local government systems are often assessed are those of autonomy, democracy and efficiency (Sharpe 1970). Autonomy is primarily about the relationship existing between

1 Denmark and Finland also have autonomous regions with powers that extend well beyond those of normal institutions of local self-government – namely Greenland, the Faeroe Islands, and the Åland Islands – which are similar in status to, for example, Catalonia and the Basque country in Spain or Sicily and Südtirol in Italy. These regions are not covered in this chapter.

2 Söderström (1998) characterizes the fiscal relations between local and central government in the Nordic countries as "co-operative localism" to highlight the active role of the state in redistributing financial resources between local authorities, while the term "co-operative governance" serves here to denote the more general political interaction between levels of government in the Nordic area, including financial regulations. For a useful discussion of intergovernmental relations in Norway and Sweden, and those found in Europe more generally, see Goldsmith and Page (2010).

local and central governments, whereas the democracy criterion highlights the political involvement and participation of citizens, and efficiency focuses on the local government's ability to satisfy residents who are consumers and taxpayers. To some extent these three criteria are interdependent. For local democracy to be meaningful, for example, some degree of local autonomy is necessary. And as suggested by the Decentralization Theorem attributed to the American economist Wallace Oates (1972), local democracy drives local efficiency by facilitating the adaptation of services to local needs and preferences.

This chapter serves to illuminate how the Nordic systems of local and regional government are organized in relation to these three criteria. Whereas the Nordic model of local and regional government builds upon a common foundation of decentralized co-operative governance, there are contrasts to be found in local government institutions and the way in which they function. These commonalities and differences are spelt out below. In what follows the organization of Nordic local and regional government is first discussed in a broader European context. This provides a backdrop for understanding the special character of the Nordic system of decentralized co-operative governance. The historical development of local self-government is then outlined, after which the current institutional framework of local and regional government is presented. In subsequent sections the functions and finances of sub-national government are briefly summarized, citizen involvement in local self-government is discussed, and finally important aspects relating to various efforts to reform local and regional government are highlighted.

As will be evident, while the Nordic model of local and regional government builds upon a common foundation of decentralized co-operative governance, there are significant contrasts to be found in local government institutions and the way in which they operate. Whether or not a common heritage of highly decentralized government will endure is discussed at the end of the chapter.

NORDIC MUNICIPALITIES AND REGIONS IN A EUROPEAN CONTEXT

There are many similarities across European countries in the organization of territorial governance, but various countries are also marked by different administrative traditions. Based on these traditions, scholars have tried to group European local government into distinct types or "families". A recent work on local government systems in Europe (Loughlin et al. 2011), for instance, identifies five types: Anglo-Saxon, Rhinelandic, Nordic, South European and New (post-communist) Democracies. The Anglo-Saxon type includes Britain and Ireland and is characterized by two-party systems in local politics, weak or absent intermediate levels, and a relatively centralized state tradition in which the relationship between state and local authorities can be antagonistic. The Rhinelandic type encompasses Germany, Netherlands, Belgium, Austria and Switzerland.

This group is characterized by federal traditions, strong intermediate levels and consensus-style decision-making. The South European group includes France, Spain, Italy, Portugal and Greece. In this family a common denominator is the so-called Napoleonic legacy – i.e. a centralized bureaucracy based on Roman law with relatively few tasks allocated to municipalities. A common feature of the Nordic family, on the other hand, is, as already noted, a high degree of decentralization of public tasks (to local "welfare states") within the framework of a unitary state in which the relationship between state and municipality is characterized by "co-operative decentralization". Finally, the New Democracies are marked by legacies of the communist era and the subsequent transition period, often with many small municipalities and few tasks decentralized to the local level together with a highly centralized state bureaucracy. But the authors also emphasize that the parallels in local government reforms across countries are striking, something they attribute to common European norm transmitters such as the Council of Europe and the EU. Learning across country borders is a very active process.

Table 8.1 contains some indicators that allow for more precise comparisons of Nordic local governments with local government in other European

TABLE 8.1 CHARACTERISTICS OF LOCAL GOVERNMENT IN SELECTED EUROPEAN COUNTRIES

Country	Number of municipalities, 2016	Average municipal population, 2016	Level of local autonomy, 2014* (scale: 0–100)
Denmark	**98**	**55,500**	**74**
Finland	**313**	**16,000**	**80**
Iceland	**74**	**4,365**	**75**
Norway	**428**	**11,600**	**72**
Sweden	**289**	**32,000**	**76**
France	36,000	1,700	66
Germany	12,312	6,600	75
Greece	325	33,100	49
Italy	8,101	7,400	68
Netherlands	408	39,000	57
Poland	2,478	15,000	70
Portugal	308	34,380	60
Slovakia	2,891	1,800	46
Switzerland	2,758	2,700	81
United Kingdom	434	142,000	48

* The indicators of local autonomy include the *range* of functions for which municipalities are responsible, their control over those functions, financial powers (taxation and borrowing), organizational and legal autonomy, and access to higher levels of government (see Ladner et al. 2016).

countries. Looking at municipalities, the lowest level of local government, it is apparent from the table that their number and scale vary greatly from one country to another. The largest municipalities are found in the UK, followed by Denmark, the Netherlands, Greece, and Sweden. Norwegian and Finnish municipalities are in the middle of the tree, while Icelandic municipalities are on the smaller side. At present, in other words, there is no common Nordic denominator when it comes to the size of local government at the lowest level of government. But ongoing reforms discussed later in this chapter may possibly change this.

When other characteristics are used for comparison, however, greater similarities among the Nordic countries are to be found. Thus, in an investigation of local autonomy in 39 European countries, the Nordic municipalities were consistently rated among those with the highest level of autonomy (Ladner et al. 2016). On a scale from 0 to 100, the average local autonomy score for the five Nordic countries is 75 points whereas the average for South European countries, for example, is 61 points. The least decentralized countries were Moldova, Malta, Georgia and Turkey. Perhaps somewhat surprisingly, moreover, the United Kingdom and Ireland also fell into the category of low local autonomy. This comparison clearly demonstrates that local governments in the Nordic area, which are responsible for a range of important public functions, have substantial discretion in decisions concerning these functions. Local politicians, in short, are less constrained by central government directives and regulations than are their counterparts in many other countries, and this includes power over their own finances.

THE DEVELOPMENT OF LOCAL AND REGIONAL SELF-GOVERNMENT

The roots of local government in the Nordic countries are deeply planted in the soil of history. The principle of local self-government can be traced back to the time of tribal life and subsequently Viking times. Contemporary democratic local government, however, dates from more recent times – in particular, the years following in the wake of the Enlightenment period and the American and French revolutions. By the beginning of the 19th century local committees had generally been established to administer aid to the poor, and parish councils, in much the same vein, were given responsibility for operating local schools, assisting the poor and maintaining roads. But it was not until 1837, when laws on the local executive (*Formannskapslovene*) were passed in Norway, that the principle of local self-government with popularly elected local councils was formally recognized and given legal status. These laws were largely the result of local groups – primarily farmers and businessmen – seeking greater freedom from representatives of the central bureaucracy and additional rights to make decisions on matters affecting the local community according to local prerogatives.

In Denmark popularly elected local councils were created to advise the ruling magistracy in the same year (1837). But the principle of local government exercising a degree of local autonomy was first given constitutional recognition (rather than recognition by special legislation, as was the case in Norway) in 1849, when a clause explicitly acknowledging "the right of local authorities to manage their own affairs under the control of the state" was included in the constitution adopted at the time. In Sweden, the Local Government Ordinances Act passed in 1862 served as a similar legal watershed, creating 2,500 municipalities and self-governing provincial and city councils. Yet more explicit constitutional recognition of local government did not occur until 1975 when a new Instrument of Government (*Regjeringsform*) was adopted.

In Iceland the right to self-government is also protected under terms of the constitution adopted following dissolution of the union with Denmark in 1944. But in Iceland, as in the other Nordic countries, local authorities are bound to exercise this right in accordance with legislation enacted by parliament. Much the same can be said about local self-government in Finland, which operates under conditions specified in the constitution (most recently revised in 2000) and special legislation passed by parliament.

Denmark, Norway and Sweden have traditionally had a *two-tier* system of local government with municipalities as well as a regional level of government. The latter (known respectively as *amtskommuner*, *fylkeskommuner* and *landsting*) are denoted counties in English. These bodies have been charged with tasks that were deemed too demanding for the (largely small) rural municipalities – building and maintaining hospitals, highways or prisons for example. The counties have historically enjoyed less autonomy than the municipalities, often functioning under the tutelage of state-appointed county governors (prefects). At the outset, county councils were not directly elected but were rather composed of members from or appointed by the respective counties' municipal councils. However, from the 1970s onwards processes of *regionalization* were initiated, manifested in direct, popular elections of county councils and the establishment of separate county council administrations while the tutelage of county governors was toned down. Gradually, during the 1980s and 1990s, county councils gained in self-confidence, demanding more say in regional development policies, and established extensive networks with regional authorities in other countries and a presence in the European "capital" of Brussels in order to stay in contact with decision-making in the EU (Baldersheim et al. 2011).

Finland did not have a similar two-tier system of local government, but a functional equivalent operated through extensive inter-municipal cooperation. Nevertheless, the wave of regionalization also reached Finland and took off in the wake of the accession to the EU 1994, resulting in the establishment of separate boards for regional development composed of representatives of local government in the respective regions. Iceland, on the other hand, has functioned without a second tier of local government.

By now all the Nordic countries have followed up the 1987 recommendation passed by the Council of Europe stating that the principle of democratic local self-government should be incorporated into the constitutional documents of all member countries, although it took until 2015 for this to transpire in Norway. However, the most important stipulations and provisions relating to the nature and operation of local government in all of the Nordic countries are contained in separate legislative acts, not in the constitutions. These acts tend to provide local governments with broad formal authority under terms of what is described as a *negative delimitation* of power. That is, local authorities are granted the right to engage in all activities that are not explicitly denied them or for which responsibility is assigned to other bodies. Such provisions stand in marked contrast to the principle of *ultra vires* which has been followed in the United Kingdom and several other countries – a principle which only permits local authorities to engage in activities specifically permitted or assigned to them. In this connection it is again important to stress that local and regional authorities are not only organs of *self-government*, they have also evolved into *partners* of national governments, a hallmark of the Nordic countries signified by the term *co-operative governance*.

THE INSTITUTIONAL FRAMEWORK OF MUNICIPALITIES AND REGIONS

Municipalities and regions are established according to the principles of representative democracy. This means that popularly elected councils are at the core of local and regional governance. Other elements of the institutional framework are laid out on much the same pattern in all of the Nordic countries: an executive board elected by the council, a mayor likewise elected by the council to chair the council and/or the board meetings, committees appointed by the council to assist in decision-making and overseeing of administrative bodies, and, furthermore, a chief administrative officer appointed to coordinate the council's administrative apparatus. The tasks and roles assigned to these bodies, however, may vary between countries and even within one and the same country at the discretion of individual municipalities and regions.

The principal similarities and contrasts between countries may be highlighted as follows. To begin with, the composition of councils is determined by electoral outcomes in elections which are held according to proportional methods (mostly D'Hondt). The number of council seats varies in relation to the size of the local population, with municipalities and counties generally being allowed to determine the number of seats within a range stipulated by national legislation. For the most part, lists of candidates in local elections are put up by local branches of political parties represented in the national parliaments.

This means that there is an element of policy coordination between national and local levels of government through the political parties. But there may also be purely local lists put up by groups of concerned citizens who wish to promote particular local issues or districts to which the groups feel local councils should pay more attention. The incidence of such local or "independent" lists has been on the increase in later years, although Denmark may be an exception to this trend, as the number of local lists seems to have decreased after the amalgamations that took place in 2007 (cf. Blom-Hansen & Heeager 2011: 230). In any event, elections are still overwhelmingly dominated by the established political parties.

Boards and committees are also composed according to proportional methods, which mean that parties or groups are represented on boards and committees according to their strength on the local council. This gives all parties a hand, or at least a finger, on the steering wheels of the municipality or region, which again makes for consensus-oriented politics typical of the Nordic countries rather than dominance of one party or one coalition. Precisely how many committees are established is usually up to the respective councils to decide as are the responsibilities assigned to the committees. Traditionally the portfolios of the committees have tended to mirror the current tasks and administrative divisions of the municipalities, such as education, health, planning and zoning, and so forth. In later years, however, some councils have tried to move away from this "mirroring" principle in order to give more attention to overarching, long-term strategies. Whatever principle is followed, it would be correct to say that on the whole council committees have a stronger position in local decision-making in Sweden and Finland than in the other countries (cf. Mouritzen & Svara 2002).

Mayors are elected by the council among the members of the council by simple majority. The role of mayors nonetheless varies markedly between countries. In Sweden the mayoral office may be said to be split in two, as there are separate chairs for the municipal councils and the executive committees. The strongest mayor is found in Denmark, where the mayor is not only the leader of the council and the executive committee, but also head of the administration on a day-to-day basis. This is in contrast to the Norwegian mayor, who is basically the speaker of the council, with the main function being to prepare the agenda of council and board meetings, which he/she also chairs. In Norway, a rigorous line of demarcation is maintained between elected members and administrative officers. Leading the administration is strictly the function of the chief administrative officer, who is appointed on a purely meritocratic basis. This practice differs from that of Finland, where the position is seen as being more political and councils often appoint CAOs with a political background. Naturally, the Danish mayor works full time and is paid accordingly. The Norwegian mayor is also paid full-time, and so is the chairperson of the executive committee in Sweden, whereas in Finland and Iceland it is highly unusual to find local politicians similarly salaried.

As the only country in the Nordic area, Norway permitted a series of experiments with directly elected mayors between 1999 and 2007. Nearly fifty municipalities took part in the experiments. In most of these municipalities the status of the mayor was enhanced, and he or she was given more powers, thereby becoming more visible to the population. The motivation of the experiments was to enhance popular interest in municipal affairs and to boost electoral turnout. The latter did not happen, however (Buck et al. 2006). Hence, despite protests from the municipalities involved, the Norwegian parliament voted to terminate the experiments in 2007.

Like other aspects of the institutional framework, the role of the local and regional councils has also developed over the years. In representative democracies elected councils perform basically three functions: representation of electoral opinions, decision-making, and scrutiny of executive-administrative bodies (Lidström et al. 2016). During the 1990s, reforms of council operations were particularly concerned with the decision-making function, seeking to bring the strategic element of decision-making more to the foreground by delegating minor decisions to administrative bodies in order to leave councillors more room to concentrate on larger issues. In later years, reformers have become increasingly concerned with the representativeness of councils, trying to enhance the representation of minorities and groups that may have been neglected, such as immigrants or women. Special regulations have been introduced to ensure a balanced representation of both genders (e.g. in Denmark, Finland and Norway, municipal boards and committees are required to have no less than 40 per cent representation of either gender). As municipal activities have expanded in recent years the task of scrutiny has also become more demanding, resulting in more emphasis being placed on the role of councillors as controllers and stressing awareness of ethical issues relating, for example, to the danger of corruption.

To deliver the range of services for which they are responsible under a decentralized welfare state model, Nordic municipalities and regions operate with a considerable administrative apparatus. In many instances municipalities may be the largest local employers, hiring a wide array of professionals as well as clerical and ancillary staff. How to best organize, run and control this apparatus has become a perennial concern to local authorities, facing as they do the dual problems of "capture" and "responsiveness". *Capture* means that the administrative bodies which are to be controlled by democratically elected politicians instead become so dominant that they in fact become the masters. The problem of *responsiveness*, on the other hand, refers to bureaucratic inertia and self-centeredness that may hit large organizations, especially in the public sector, and the concomitant neglect of the citizen needs that were the raison d'etre of the organization in the first place.

In the 1980s local government claimed that excessive state regulation was the cause of much local maladaptation. In response to the complaints central authorities launched a series of measures, perhaps the most notable being the "free commune experiments" which permitted selected municipalities and regions to try out new ways of organizing local services that were thought to be more in tune with local perceptions of needs. The experiments started in Sweden and spread quickly to Denmark, Finland and Norway, and over time resulted in substantial deregulation of local government (see Baldersheim & Ståhlberg 1994; Rose 1990).

Inspired by the international concept of New Public Management (NPM) (see chapter 6), under which local government sought to emulate managerial practices common in private corporations (such as more attention to performance and results, customer care, and more clear-cut managerial responsibility), a second wave of experimentation occurred in the 1990s. The ideas of NPM have served to modify municipal operations in all of the Nordic countries, but probably with more impact in Sweden than in the other countries (Øgård 2015). Actual privatization of municipal services has not been widespread, but contracting out of municipal activities – i.e. buying service provision from private companies rather than in-house production by own employees – has taken place to some extent. Again, this is more widespread in Sweden, while Danish local authorities have instead established partnerships with voluntary associations, whereas local government in Norway has more than the others stuck to the old ways of in-house production of local services (Sivesind 2016). These differences between countries do not undermine the Nordic model of co-operative governance, however, since local governments continue to be responsible for provision of public goods in accordance with national stipulations, regulations, and oversight.

FUNCTIONS AND FINANCES

Under terms of a *negative delimitation* of power, local governments in the Nordic countries have long had authority to engage in a wide range of discretionary activities. But at present a large portion of local government activity is mandated and/or subject to control by national governments. Indeed, despite long historical roots, local government in the Nordic countries as it functions today is of a more recent vintage, shaped to a large degree by developments since the end of World War II. It is in this period that national governments in all of the Nordic countries adopted a series of policy decisions that created what is commonly referred to as the Scandinavian welfare state, and the results gave rise to what has been termed the *welfare municipality* (Grønlie 1991), or what can perhaps better be called the *local* welfare state, since to a large degree local governments have been used as agents for implementing many national welfare programmes. Not only were local governments to have responsibility for building, maintaining and operating schools and outpatient medical facilities along with other more traditional local infrastructural services (water supply, sewage and refuse disposal, and electric power supply), they were also to be first-line providers of various social security services – care for pre-school children and the elderly, social assistance for the needy and so forth.

It is important in this regard to emphasize that local governments have not merely been passive recipients and implementers of national plans. Historically they have also been active initiators in developing many social welfare practices. Even so, in the period from 1945 to the late 1970s, the primary source of expansion in local government activity came from a concerted push by central authorities to develop a set of welfare programmes, programmes that would provide a safety net and adequate standard of living for all inhabitants (cf. Flora 1986). Particularly important was the idea that the availability and quality of public goods and services provided by local authorities should be virtually the same throughout the country. Given geographic conditions found in these countries – especially in Finland, Norway and Sweden – this has been an ambitious and costly goal, one that enhanced the model of co-operative governance.

Box 8.1 provides an overview of the range of responsibilities currently performed by local governments (either municipal or regional) in the Nordic countries. Looking across the five countries, there are some variations in the allocation of specific tasks and responsibilities from one country to another. Secondary education, for example, is the responsibility of municipalities in Sweden, whereas in Norway counties are responsible, and after the reform of 2007 in Denmark central government took over responsibility for secondary education. Such differences notwithstanding, there is little doubt that local government in the Nordic countries – either primary municipalities or countries (and in the case of Finland joint municipal boards) – in general attend to a broad and largely comparable spectrum of tasks. These range from mandatory

Box 8.1. Typical areas of local government responsibility

- preschool child day-care facilities and child welfare services
- primary, lower secondary and upper secondary schools
- primary and some specialized health care
- care for the elderly and disabled
- financial support for welfare clients
- local roads and transportation services
- technical and infrastructural services (water, waste management, etc.)
- land use planning
- local and regional development

obligations in the fields of education, primary health care, care for the young and elderly, and a number of other social welfare programmes to more discretionary activities such as providing recreational and other leisure time facilities.

This situation is clearly reflected in terms of public finance. In all of the countries local government (including the secondary tier) accounts for roughly one-third or more of all government expenditures. In only a few other European countries does local government hold a comparable fiscal position (see Figure 8.1 below). Denmark stands out in this respect, but this is largely due to a practice of channelling old age pension payments via local government budgets, whereas in the other countries these payments are made through national authorities.

Regardless of national differences, the important point is that the figures shown in Figure 8.1, when placed in a broader cross-national context, serve to place all of the Nordic countries among the top of the list in terms of local government activity and expenditure. It should also mentioned that, as has been observed by others, government expenditures at the local level in the Nordic countries tended to be greater than those in other countries for which comparable evidence is available *even before* local government became a critical instrument for implementing national welfare state policies (see Sellers & Lidström 2007: 623).

A question that arises in this regard is how these expenditures are financed. How are resources generated to cover the costs involved in a broad spectrum of activities? Commenting on the Nordic model of local public finance, Rattsø (2005) draws a comparison to that which is often seen as a classic model found elsewhere. The classic model assumes the importance of local public goods, demographic mobility, and taxation schemes that are linked to the individual benefits received.[3] But as Rattsø notes, conditions in the Nordic countries are not in accord with this model. The public sector in the Nordic countries emphasizes welfare services based on equal access and quality regardless of where people live. The provision of specific local public goods constitutes only a small portion of local spending in this regard. Furthermore, the mobility of the population has traditionally been quite low and the composition of population in most local authorities has been mixed, giving rise to a variety of preferences for welfare services and local public goods. In light of these conditions, public finance has been centralized (despite decentralization of public services), being subject to strong income tax regulation, revenue sharing and redistributive central government grants.

Again variations are to be detected, but there are also some obvious similarities. Taxes on personal income have typically constituted the single most

3 This model is often referred to as the *Musgrave-Oates-Tiebout* model as it is found in the work of Musgrave (1959), Oates (1972) and Tiebout (1956).

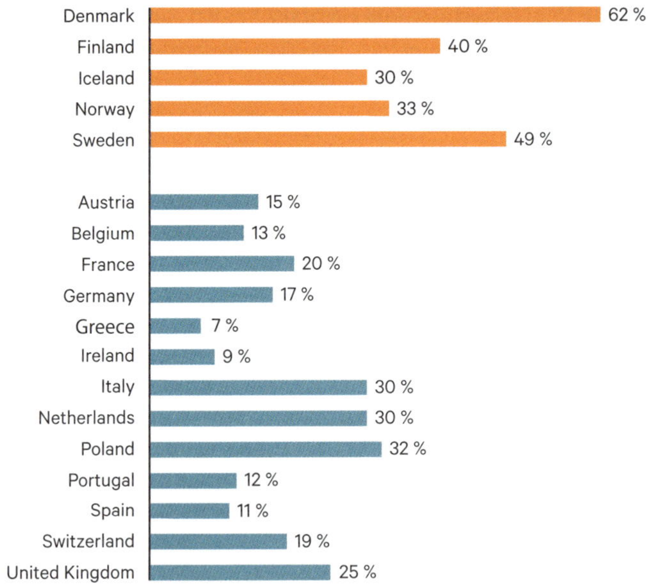

Figure 8.1 Local government expenditures as a share of total government expenditure, 2014

Source: OECD Fiscal Decentralization Database, Table 5, Consolidated government expenditure as % of total general government expenditure. https://www.oecd.org/ctp/federalism/oecdfiscaldecentralisationdatabase.htm#D_9

important source of local revenue in all of the countries (see Table 8.2). This income is supplemented by various local property and business taxes, which in recent years have become a more significant source of income in all countries except Sweden. Intergovernmental transfers in the form of both block grants and earmarked grants are also quite important, especially in Norway, less so in Iceland and Finland. Transfers of this sort have traditionally been important mechanisms in adjusting for differences in local tax revenues and assuring that local authorities have resources necessary to fulfil fundamental policy expectations and responsibilities.

With respect to user fees and charges, on the other hand, a different pattern is to be observed: in recent years these sources of revenue are most significant in Denmark and Finland, least important in Sweden. When placed in a longer time frame, however, it can be noted that user fees and charges have in fact increased in relative importance in both Finland and Norway. In the case of Finland this is explained by the fact that intergovernmental transfers from national to local authorities were substantially reduced in the mid-1990s, largely as a result of economic difficulties faced by the country. For Norway, by comparison, the development is due more to constraints placed on local governments in determining their own revenue.

TABLE 8.2 FINANCING OF THE LOCAL PUBLIC SECTOR. PER CENT.

Revenue source	Denmark	Finland	Iceland	Norway	Sweden
• Taxes	59	48	73	48	53
• Fees	20	20	17	15	8
• General grants	12	16	9	35	22
• Selective grants	9	--	--	--	--
• Other revenues	0	16	1	2	17
Total	100	100	100	100	100

Source: Rattsø (2005) with country figures based on national reports. Data are for the years 2003–04, but the patterns shown have been quite stable in the years since then.

Norway offers a good illustration of how local government finance is a matter of national policy design. Central government plays a critical role in all of the countries since income from taxes is largely a function of two factors – the tax base and the tax rates applied to the tax base (what is taxed and by how much). As a rule, decisions on both counts are made by central governments in all of the Nordic countries. The important difference has to do with the discretion local authorities are granted in setting the tax rates. Local governments in Denmark, Finland and Sweden all have a legal right to set their own tax rates. In Denmark this is subject to negotiations between national and local authorities, and in Sweden there have been a number of temporary caps set on local taxation in recent years due to economic contractions, but in both countries the right of local authorities to set tax rates is in principle guaranteed, as it is in Finland.

In Norway and Iceland, on the other hand, national regulations stipulate a narrow band for minimum and maximum local tax rates, and with only rare exceptions all local authorities have consistently adopted the maximum rate. In essence, in other words, national authorities set the tax rates. Borrowing money to cover operating expenses, moreover, is not allowed, and local governments are prohibited from deficit spending. These conditions place local authorities between a proverbial rock and a hard place; the primary option for local governments in Iceland and Norway to influence their revenue base is through adjustments of local user fees and charges. But in all five countries the combination of mandated service provision, detailed service standards and regulatory stipulations, when combined with requirements for balanced budgets and controls on borrowing, impose a high degree of fiscal discipline on local government.

LOCAL ELECTIONS AND CITIZEN PARTICIPATION

As already noted, local self-government in all five countries builds on a representative model of democracy. Ultimate responsibility for local decision-making is vested in popularly elected municipal and regional councils. Elections to these bodies are currently held at regular four-year intervals. In Sweden these elections now occur on the same day as national parliamentary elections, whereas in the other countries local elections are generally held separately from national elections. Local elections held in Denmark in 2001 were an exception in this respect, occurring as they did at the same time as a parliamentary election which was called on short notice. As is evident in Figure 8.2, this had an obvious impact on turnout for local elections; participation jumped by nearly 15 percentage points compared with local elections held in 1997, from roughly 70 to 85 per cent, and then fell back again in the elections held in 2005.

By comparison with other European countries, election turnout in the Nordic countries has been quite high throughout the post-war period, but not exceptionally so.[4] Equally worthy of note, however, is a long-term tendency of declining electoral participation following the high-water marks found in the 1970s and 1980s. The decline is most evident and dramatic in Iceland, where turnout has declined by over 15 per cent since 1998, dropping by seven percentage points in the most recent local elections alone. A major factor in explaining this sharp drop seems to be consequences of the financial crash in 2008, which were strongly felt by older voters, and a sense among younger voters that they could not be bothered, suggesting both discontent and a lack of efficacy (see Eyþórsson & Kowalczyk 2013; Eyþórsson & Önnudóttir, 2016).

4 For a comparison based on statistics from the period 1994–2001, see Klausen (2005: 363–365).

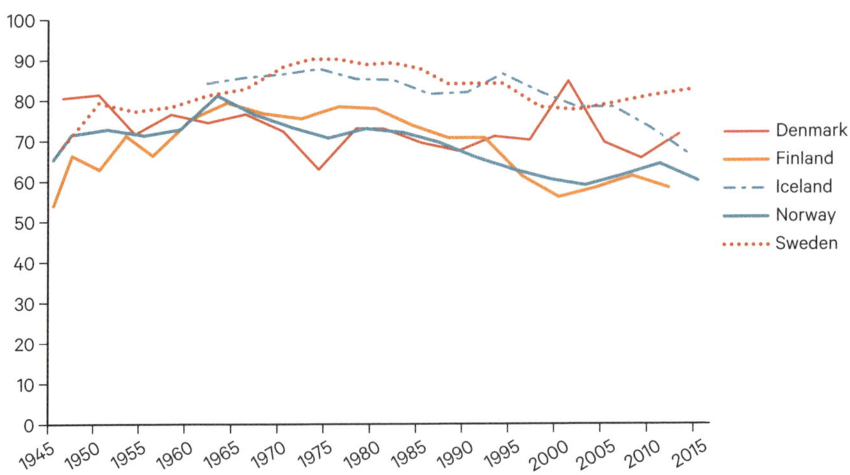

Figure 8.2 Turnout for local elections in five Nordic countries, 1945–2015. Per cent.

The falloff in the other countries has not been quite so precipitous, but Denmark, Finland and Norway have also experienced declines in turnout for local elections, the tendency being most pronounced in Finland, where turnout has dropped by more than 20 percent in the period since the early 1980s. Sweden is an exception in this regard inasmuch as turnout for local elections has stayed at or above 80 per cent throughout the post-war period, soaring to over 90 per cent in the 1970s. But at least some of this mobilization can be accounted for by the fact that all elections – parliamentary, regional and municipal – are held at the same time. When people first decide to vote, they apparently exercise their rights to do so in all election contests even though there is evidence in all of the countries that local and regional elections have what is termed a "second order" status. This means that in the eyes of voters local and regional elections appear to be less important than are national parliamentary elections, and hence that voting is therefore somewhat lower in sub-national elections (see inter alia Dandoy & Schakel 2013; Reif & Schmitt 1980).

Regardless of the circumstances, the decline in turnout for local and regional elections has in the eyes of many commentators been disconcerting, and has led to various efforts to increase electoral participation. Norway, for example, has experimented with the direct election of mayors, the use of internet voting and other techniques designed to mobilize voters, especially young people and immigrants (Bergh et al. 2016; Larsen 2002). These efforts, however, have achieved only mixed results, and, as mentioned above, despite protests among the municipalities that were involved, the experiment with direct election of mayors was terminated after the local elections in 2007.

What underlies the decline in electoral participation is not clear. Presumably there are a variety of factors, but there is no indication of a broader *democratic malaise*. Thus, when asked in public opinion surveys, for instance, citizens in all of the countries typically express a high level of satisfaction with the way in which local democracy works in their country. Equally if not more noteworthy is the fact that the level of trust expressed with respect to local government is generally *higher* than that expressed with respect to national government in the same countries (see Denters 2002; Fitzgerald & Wolak 2016). [5] Satisfaction with local government performance varies a bit depending on the services or facilities in question, but overall various studies find that citizens are quite satisfied with local government services and facilities. Users, moreover, tend to be more satisfied than non-users, which belies the idea that users find local government performance to be inadequate.

5 The exception Fitzgerald and Wolak find in the case of findings relating to Finland from a survey conducted in 2006 should, according to the authors and sources they cite, be seen in light of the circumstances surrounding the collapse of the Soviet Union, which had been a major trading partner for Finland, and the repercussions this caused.

Rather than reflecting a sense of dissatisfaction with local government and a general democratic malaise, the downturn in electoral participation may well reflect a shift in citizen orientations to local government and the political arena which it represents. In the work of Jürgen Habermas, among others, there is a suggestion that the development of the social welfare state carries with it a prospect of facilitating what Habermas (1994: 31) terms "a privatist retreat from citizenship and a particular 'clientelization' of the citizen's role". An extensive if not encompassing set of social rights, in other words, may contribute to citizens emphasizing their roles as recipients and users or consumers of public goods and services more than their roles as voters and politically active members of a local political community. When national legislation stipulates and in many instances sets standards for various forms of local public service provision, the motivation individuals experience to use the ballot box and electoral arena may become less important to them personally than seeking to obtain the benefits prescribed and "due" to them.

There is no comparative evidence to assess whether such a dynamic development and shift in citizen orientations over time has transpired in the Nordic countries and hence may have contributed to lower electoral turnout. What empirical work has been carried out, however, does suggest that in recent years citizens have placed a great deal of weight on their roles as users/consumers of public goods and services provided by local government – indeed, even more weight than on their roles as voters. This has been documented by several studies in Norway (cf. Rose 1999; 2011) and also observed in Denmark.

Without making any explicit assumptions about such developments, local authorities in all of the Nordic countries have sought to strengthen and renew local self-government by adopting and instituting a variety of democratic practices in the non-electoral arena. Among the more prominent mechanisms have been different forms of consultation and dialogue with local residents. These include creation of user boards for selected services, surveys of various service user groups, more general citizen surveys, and open public hearings or meetings as well as hearings using electronic media. In addition, a number of local authorities have experimented with meetings involving invited participants and have instituted procedures allowing for resident initiatives regarding matters to be decided by local councils. Both of these mechanisms are a means of providing residents with greater opportunity to shape the local political agenda, but differ insofar as the former (brainstorming meetings with invited participants) are largely under the control of local authorities, whereas the latter (resident initiatives) are only subject to provisions commonly laid down by national guidelines regarding the procedures to be followed. So far citizen juries, participatory budgeting and deliberative hearings, all of which have enjoyed some favour in other countries, have only to a limited extent been tried in the Nordic countries.

Evidence pertaining to the different practices of "democratic renewal" and how they may affect citizen orientations to local and regional government in the Nordic countries is largely piecemeal. Most studies show that those who choose to engage in the respective activities are not a cross section of the population, but rather dominated by those with special interests. This is a finding which generally holds in many other countries as well. Different mechanisms have different strengths and weaknesses, particularly with respect to the ability to attract participation and the extent to which they involve a more explicit deliberative component (see Geissel 2009; Geissel & Joas 2013; Geissel & Newton 2012). The design of the practices seems to be of critical importance, and at this point public authorities in the Nordic countries, both locally and nationally, seek more evidence in order to "fine tune" their efforts to maintain vibrant and well-anchored local self-government.

REFORM POLITICS AND TERRITORIAL GOVERNANCE IN THE 2000S

This is a concern which raises a number of questions of practical as well as principle importance (cf. Zittel & Fuchs 2006). A point of contention in this regard is what significance, if any, the territorial structure of local government may have for the realization of efficient, effective and democratic local government. Debates on this topic commonly reflect an apparent trade-off and dilemma highlighted by Robert Dahl and Edward Tufte in their discussion of the appropriate size for political authorities (Dahl & Tufte 1973). According to Dahl and Tufte, the size of local authorities has an impact on two critical dimensions of democratic governance, dimensions they term *citizen effectiveness* and *system capacity* respectively. The former concerns the ability of residents to control and influence political decisions, whereas the latter concerns the ability of authorities to deal successfully with the policy challenges they confront. Smaller political units are typically argued to enhance citizen effectiveness, while larger units are argued to provide greater system capacity.

Although not always phrased in precisely these terms, reform initiatives and public debates concerning the structure of local government in all of the Nordic countries mirror these arguments. As decentralized welfare states, an important goal of national governments has been to achieve the highest quality of public service delivery possible for all citizens regardless of where they live. Inasmuch as local governments have been used as first-line service providers in systems of co-operative governance, a foremost concern has therefore been to assure that municipalities and regions have adequate resources and capacity to perform the responsibilities assigned to them. This concern has been evident throughout the post-war period, during which time there has been a series of territorial reform initiatives. In these initiatives national governments have typically been more concerned with the system capacity of local government than with citizen effectiveness (see, for example, Albæk et al. 1996; and relevant chapters in Baldersheim & Rose 2010a). Using catch words such as the need for "robust local governments", by which is meant municipalities and regions able to provide nationally stipulated public services in a satisfactory fashion, national authorities have pressed ahead with amalgamation reforms in all of the countries. At times this has been a rather rocky road, bringing traditional political cleavages to the surface as well as producing some unexpected coalitions along the way. Highlights from reform efforts in each country can be briefly summarized as follows.

Norway[6]

Following a lengthy process of public investigation and parliamentary consideration, a major reform was carried out in Norway in the late 1960's and early 1970's, reducing the number of municipalities from 774 in 1951 to 443 in 1974. By the late 1980's, however, the issue of an appropriate structure of local government emerged anew and the question was subject to further examination, resulting in a public commission report (NOU 1992: 15) and subsequently a parliamentary white paper (St.meld nr. 32 [1994–95]). When the white paper was presented for parliamentary consideration, something unexpected occurred; a member of parliament put forth a proposal stipulating that any further municipal amalgamations should be based on voluntary acceptance by residents of the municipalities affected. This proposal was adopted and established a principle that has constituted standing policy up to the present.

After this aborted top-down reform effort, the national government turned in 2003 to a bottom-up strategy. In a joint initiative undertaken by the Ministry of Local Government and the Norwegian Association of Local and Regional Authorities, municipalities were invited to discuss whether existing structures, and especially the widespread use of inter-municipal agreements, were really adequate for the challenges ahead. The response from the great majority of municipalities was that they were satisfied with the existing situation. There was, in short, no great pressure for increasing the size of municipalities through voluntary mergers. The centre-left coalition government that came into office in 2005 accepted this outcome and shelved any plans for restructuring the system of municipal government, turning its attention instead to a possible reform of regional government. But this alternative also ran aground of opposition from various quarters and was abandoned in 2008.

Only after the elections of 2013, which brought a new right-wing coalition government to office with a pledge to reform the structure of municipal government, was the issue of municipal amalgamation again placed on the national

6 The discussion of Norwegian reforms is largely based on Rose (1996) and Baldersheim and Rose (2010b).

political agenda. A proposal outlining the government's ambitions and various instruments of reform, including financial incentives, was presented and received approval from parliament in 2014. The main arguments outlined in favour of amalgamations were that many existing municipalities, being very small, did not possess the expertise or capacity required to provide services of a satisfactory quality. Many municipalities were also seen as being too small and weak to take on new tasks which the government said it wished to allocate to local government. A transfer of additional functions to the municipalities, it was argued, would be a way of enhancing local democracy.

According to the timetable for the reform, local authorities were expected to enter into discussions with neighbouring authorities about mergers or enhancement of collaboration during the autumn of 2014.[7] Deliberations, including consultations with residents carried out either by referenda or surveys, were to be concluded and final municipal council decisions made by June 2016.[8] By this date 131 municipalities signalled their willingness to merge with others, but 56 of these had not found partners and remained involuntarily "alone". Of the remaining municipalities, 273 had decided not to merge, at least on a voluntary basis, and a few others had not completed their decision processes.

Under the government's reform initiative, the 17 county governors were also put to work as designated facilitators of the local processes. The governors, moreover, were required to submit recommendations for a future municipal structure in their own counties no later than the beginning of October 2016. They did so, in many cases pressing ahead with bold merger proposals that only to a limited extent heeded the outcome of local consultative activities.

When the government's proposal was first put forth a large parliamentary majority expressed support for the overall aims of the reform, but a number of reservations were put in place. For one thing, the governing coalition wanted to abolish the second tier of local authorities (the counties) and transfer their functions to the municipalities. The majority in parliament, however, did not support this view. Instead of abolishing the counties, several parties preferred replacing them with larger regional authorities. In addition, parliament did not want to specify any minimum number of residents for the size of amalgamated authorities, nor did it wish to introduce mandatory amalgamations, although

---

7 A white paper on the transfer of functions from state agencies and county authorities to municipalities was not published until April of 2015. The presentation was fairly open-ended, however, and indicated that further analyses were to be carried out before most of the transfers could be carried out. As a consequence, many local authorities were rather reticent with regard to reform plans, although most did follow the government's injunction to undertake talks with their neighbours about potential merger plans.

8 The results of consultative referenda and opinion polls organized by municipalities on potential mergers demonstrated that citizens on the whole disliked the idea of mergers. Only a few mergers were confirmed by referenda.

some of the speakers in the parliamentary debate as well as government spokespersons preferred to be a bit evasive on the issue of voluntarism.

At this point the outcome of the reform effort is unknown. Mergers among 11 "front runners" that indicated their desires prior to the June 2016 deadline have already been ratified. For all others the government is in the process of considering the results to date and will present a new white paper to parliament with its proposal in the spring of 2017. Any new structures to be adopted are to be in place in time for the next round of local elections in 2019. But in view of the parliamentary elections to be held in the autumn of 2017, much uncertainty around the reform remains.

Sweden[9]

Sweden also carried out a radical amalgamation of municipalities in the 1970s resulting in the creation of some of the largest municipalities in Europe, exceeded only by Great Britain at the time. Hence, there was not much demand for more amalgamations until the 2000s when some unease about the capacities of the smaller rural municipalities began to be aired. However, these ideas were unpopular among citizens in rural areas and were not pursued with vigour by any political party.

The regional level in Sweden, on the other hand, has undergone several rounds of transformation. A major change beginning in 1998 has transformed county councils into regional governments with extended functions for the development of their geographic areas. In 2003 activities were also set in motion that could have led to amalgamation of the existing county councils, but a new conservative government that took office in 2006 was not interested in this type of reform, and the process more or less came to a standstill.

When the Social Democrats regained power in 2014 they restarted the process of regional reform with the aim of augmenting the 21 regions' powers for planning and regional development. To date health care and hospital management have been among the most important functions of the counties. A committee appointed by the Social Democratic government to review the territorial division of the country has recently questioned the capacity of the smaller counties to undertake these obligations in a long-term perspective and has therefore suggested a merger of the counties into six regions (Direktiv 2015: 77; SOU 2016). As yet no political decision has been made on this and the question remains an open issue.

9 Information on Sweden draws in particular on Lidström (2010, 2011) and Strömberg & Engen (1996) along with other material.

Denmark[10]

In 1970, following a decade of planning, the structure of local government in Denmark was also subject to a major reform. This reform consolidated local governments in 275 municipalities and 14 counties and produced a significant decentralization of the public sector.[11] In keeping with a model of co-operative governance, responsibilities for many national programmes were transferred to local authorities and the system of local government finance underwent a change. Although subject to some discussion in the years that followed, there was no serious indication that any far-reaching structural reform was necessary. Other than the Conservative Party questioning the need for county government, there was little public debate, and what public investigations were carried out concluded that the institutions built up around the decentralized welfare state operated in an efficient manner. Even the man who became prime minister after the parliamentary election of 2001 was of this opinion, and the Minister of Interior stated to a parliamentary committee that the new government had no plans for changing the municipal structure.

But within the following year a debate about the efficiency of local government was taken up in the mass media and the government decided to appoint a new commission of inquiry. This commission concluded that a thorough reform was needed. Despite opposition from the Social Democrats, the centre-right coalition government accepted the conclusion and went ahead with a reform initiative. Municipalities were instructed to start talks with neighbours with the aim of finding partners for mergers. The choice of partners was up to the municipalities, but it was made clear that if they did not start merger negotiations they risked being left behind with very little powers and functions. Hence a scramble to find partners ensued. The result was that in 2007 the number of municipalities was reduced from 270 to 98. The reform actually exceeded the stated goal as the average municipal population size rose to 55,000, second largest in Europe, while the government that initiated the reform had hoped for around 30,000.

The reform also had serious consequences for the second tier of local government – the 14 counties. As the reform unfolded it became clear that the cards were stacked against the counties, which predictably tried to oppose this aspect of the reform. Nevertheless, the counties were ultimately merged into five regions that were left with rather limited functions and powers. In a shift in the character of the Danish decentralized welfare state, the new regions continued to exercise what had also been the counties' most important function previously – running the hospitals and managing certain specialized social institutions.

10 This account of Danish reforms is primarily based on Albæk (1996) and Mouritzen (2010).

11 Before 1970, Denmark was divided into 86 boroughs and approx. 1300 parishes within 25 county council districts.

The regions, furthermore, were to be responsible for regional planning and economic development, including responsibilities regarding Denmark's share of the EU's structural funds, but responsibility for secondary schools was transferred from the counties to central government. Severe limitations were also imposed on the regions as political actors since they could not raise taxes, and had to manage their responsibilities in a highly compartmentalized fashion, running each area of responsibility in isolation from other areas. Scholars have subsequently debated as to whether it is conceptually more appropriate to call these entities "regions" in the sense the term is used to describe, for example, Italian, Spanish or Swedish regions.

Finland[12]

Following this reform in Denmark, it is fair to say that reform-minded politicians in other Nordic countries looked to Denmark for inspiration. In Finland, where the territorial structure of local government had long been a matter of political debate, the question received additional impetus.[13] Beginning in 2007 Finland embarked upon a new course of amalgamation reforms that so far has reduced the number of municipalities from 416 to 313 in several rounds. The initial aim was more ambitious but the reform met little enthusiasm among the municipalities that were its main target – the many small municipalities in the periphery that were experiencing population decline, especially the loss of young people. Paradoxically, there were more mergers in central areas in southern Finland than in peripheral areas in the north. As a consequence, Finland has continued its tradition of producing public services that require a larger geographical scale through inter-municipal boards. This applies in particular to secondary education and hospitals, but there has been an effort to restructure and rationalize the board system more generally.

In 1994, motivated primarily by eligibility for EU's structural funds following accession to the EU, Finland established 18 regional councils. The councils are formally statutory joint municipal authorities, and every municipality has been required to be a member of a council. These councils do not have general competence in regional matters. Rather, their two main functions are regional development and regional planning of building and land use according to special legislation. The highest decision-making body of the regional council is the regional assembly. Members of these assemblies are elected indirectly by the executives or other decision-making bodies of the member municipalities as decided by the municipal councils in question.

---

12 Description of the Finnish reforms is based on Sandberg (2010, 2011), Sjöblom (2011) and Ståhlberg (1996) as well as additional material.

13 In a series of policy decisions, the number of municipalities was reduced from 547 in 1950 to 455 in 1993 (Ståhlberg 1996:93).

Beside the regional councils, 20 hospital districts responsible for specialized health care are also important actors on the regional level. Like the regional councils, the hospital districts are joint municipal bodies. Unlike the regional councils, however, the financial importance of the hospital districts is considerable, representing up to 15 per cent of all local government expenditures.

In 2014 the Finnish government launched a plan to restructure the regional councils into five regions having responsibilities for health care and social welfare along with regional development. But due to constitutional constraints this plan was abandoned in early 2015. Hence, in November 2015 the government published a revised reform package on health care, social welfare and autonomous regions. Under this plan the country is to be divided into 18 semi-autonomous regions effective as of 2019. The parliamentary bills to achieve this reform are scheduled to be passed in early 2017 (see Finnish Government 2016). The regions will be governed by directly elected councils, but will not be given powers of taxation. The constitutional status of the new regions will thus bear some resemblance to that of the Danish regions established in 2007, although the task portfolio of the Finnish regions will be more extensive. According to the plan, full responsibilities for health care and social services will be transferred from the municipalities to the regions. Current responsibilities of the regional councils, as well as a number of responsibilities of regional state agencies (transport, employment, etc.) will similarly be incorporated into the portfolio of the regions. If implemented as intended, the reform will result in major changes in the system of local self-government in Finland. Municipalities will lose approximately half of their staff and finances, and will be left with a much smaller portfolio of responsibilities.

Iceland[14]

Inasmuch as the majority of municipalities in Iceland are very small, the national government has for several decades pursued a policy of amalgamations as a prerequisite for further decentralization of public functions. The policy rests on voluntary mergers and has since 1990 brought the number of municipalities down from 204 to 73 in 2016. These changes are the result of two referenda on municipal amalgamations – the first held in 1993, the second in 2005. In the first instance merger proposals met broad resistance; virtually all of the proposals were defeated. Yet the outcome set a ball in motion and in the following years mergers were approved in increasing numbers.

Then in 2003 a reform project was initiated by the Ministry of Social Affairs in cooperation with the Federation of Municipalities, the intent being to strengthen municipal service capacity and allow for decentralization of additional responsibilities. To do so it was seen as important to reduce the number

14 Information on Iceland draws in particular on Eyþórsson (2009, 2015).

of small municipalities. Proposals set forth in referenda held in 2005 met with modest success, being accepted in 25 municipalities while being voted down in 42. The immediate outcome was a reduction of only eight municipalities. This is still not enough in the opinion of some observers, since quite a few of the smaller municipalities are not able to fulfil their obligations on their own and must instead rely on neighbouring municipalities for important services (Council of Europe, Chamber of Local Authorities 2010). Even so, national politicians seem reluctant to contemplate a more top-down, compulsory approach to the structural issue at present, and further developments will continue to depend upon voluntary mergers.

Structural reforms – A summary commentary

The course of reforms outlined here contains a series of lessons about reform politics in the Nordic countries as well as about constraints on change in the Nordic polities. For one thing, as already noted, structural reforms have tended to reflect national government concerns with the system capacity of municipalities more than that of citizen effectiveness. Not surprisingly, these reforms have triggered conflicts and opposition that mirror traditional cleavages as well as new patterns of strife. In Finland and Norway, centre-periphery cleavages have influenced the course of reforms, while in Sweden and Denmark a left-right dimension has been more in the foreground.

A more surprising aspect of the reforms is that in three of the countries – Denmark, Finland and Norway – amalgamation reforms have been championed by centre-right governments, not by social democrats. Traditionally, right-wing parties have been defenders of small-scale local government and have extolled the virtues of heeding local identities and preferences. But in the 2000s these parties have taken the opposite position, seeking large-scale local government to support the production of local welfare services.

The position of the right-wing parties on regional government is more predictable, however. Scepticism towards regional government, which among these parties is seen as superfluous bureaucracy, has coloured their attitudes to the intermediate level of government. Thus, the Norwegian right-wing coalition government that came to power in 2013, for example, was at the outset in favour of abolishing the county councils, whereas the Danish reform of 2007 produced hybrid regions that were more creatures of the state than political authorities in their own right. The centre-right government of Sweden, when in power, deliberately dragged its feet on regional reform, leaving on-going experiments in a void. Nevertheless, with the exception of Iceland, where it did not exist in the first place, it seems likely that regional government in some form will continue to exist in the Nordic countries.

It is also noteworthy that recent reforms in the health care systems of the Nordic countries have further enhanced the *co-operative* character of centre-local relations. The capacity of specialized health care systems is under great pressure from medical developments and an aging population, and all the Nordic countries (like other European countries) are searching for ways of coping with this pressure. The common denominator of responses in Denmark, Finland, Norway and Sweden is to develop co-operative arrangements between hospitals and municipalities to enable speedier and more seamless discharge of patients from hospitals into municipal care (Magnussen et al. 2009; Grimsmo & Magnussen 2015).

CONCLUSION

So where do the systems of decentralized welfare states and co-operative governance in the Nordic Countries stand at present? As indicated in the introduction, the character and quality of local self-government systems may be assessed according to the criteria of autonomy, democracy and efficiency. Seen in a wider European context, Nordic local governments, and especially municipalities, get quite high marks on these criteria. In terms of local autonomy, municipalities have been entrusted with a series of important functions and local politicians enjoy fairly wide powers of decision-making. Regional autonomy has been somewhat eroded over the last decade in Denmark and Norway, and is also rather circumscribed in Finland and Iceland, while Swedish regions may be set on a course of further enhancement of status and powers.

Nordic local governments also measure up fairly well on the criterion of local democracy. Again, this applies mostly to municipalities; regions are more difficult to assess in this regard since citizens have a more distant relationship to this level of government, which in Finland is only indirectly elected. Although turnout in local elections has fallen off somewhat over the last decade or so, it is still quite high in international comparisons. Furthermore, citizens express high levels of trust in local politicians and local institutions, often in astonishing contrast to other European countries. Municipalities are definitely concerned over citizen interest and involvement in local politics and have tried out a series of measures to stimulate citizen interest and participation, including new electronic channels of information and deliberation, direct election of mayors and tentative experiments in participatory budgeting. Yet such initiatives have not yielded spectacular results in terms of citizen engagement, so for the time being Nordic local government remains firmly anchored on the model of representative and party-driven democracy.

Finally, the efficiency of local government may be assessed in terms of both cost-effectiveness and allocative efficiency. In the absence of reliable comparative data, cost-effectiveness – or the price per unit of services provided – is hard to judge in a cross-national perspective. Allocative efficiency or value for money, on the other hand, may be evaluated through data on citizen satisfaction with services provided by local governments. The assumption here is, of course, that citizen satisfaction is a result of the ability of local government to allocate resources between tasks in a way that corresponds to local needs and preferences. Overall, Nordic local governments seem to do a fair job in this regard. There are, to be sure, variations in citizens' satisfaction between local authorities, but satisfaction is, on the whole, quite high in the Nordic countries (see among others Denters et al. 2014: 202).

Structural reforms, which seem to be almost a permanent feature of Nordic local and regional government, do not appear to have had a great impact on any of these three considerations. In many ways the local and regional levels are the most dynamic elements of the Nordic political systems, driven by their proximity to citizens. In the middle of the second decade of the 21st century the regional level of government seems the most unstable of the sub-national levels of government. The management of specialized health care – hospitals – is at the core of the regional conundrum with repercussions for municipalities. If existing regions and municipalities seem too small for ever larger and more demanding hospitals, the quest for appropriate structures will go on. But interestingly, responses to pressures on health services reflect the co-operative approach so typical for central-local relations in the Nordic countries.

Despite turmoil over reforms, in short, the Nordic states are likely to continue as highly decentralized welfare states in the foreseeable future, with important functions allocated to the local level and managed in a spirit of co-operative governance across different levels of government.

CHAPTER 9
THE NORDIC WELFARE STATE MODEL

Axel West Pedersen & Stein Kuhnle

INTRODUCTION: THE CONCEPT OF A 'NORDIC MODEL'

The idea that the Nordic countries make up a special group or 'family' of democratic, welfare- capitalist countries is widely accepted and is reflected in a number of studies. A selection of book titles since the 1930s illustrates some of the distinct characteristics of the Nordic countries. The terms 'Norden' and 'the Nordic countries' were invented in the interwar period, after Finland and Iceland gained independence (see chapter 1), and began to replace the term 'Scandinavia' in referring to the Northern countries of Europe. In 1937, a book with the title *The Northern Countries in World Economy: Denmark, Finland, Iceland, Norway, Sweden* was published (Classen 1937), where it was argued that the five countries, though politically quite independent, had so much in common historically, culturally and economically that they could claim to appear before the world under the name of 'the Northern Countries'. In the previous year, an American journalist had highlighted the political path of Sweden, as a core representative of Scandinavian development, with a book called *Sweden: The Middle Way* (Childs 1936), arguing that Sweden had found a middle way between unregulated, laissez-faire capitalism and the Soviet-style socialist, command economy. Scholars and commentators, within and beyond Scandinavia and Norden, have in the long period after WWII further conveyed the perception of Nordic exceptionalism in that these countries have chosen a *Sonderweg*. This perception is reflected in book titles such as *Freedom and Welfare: Social Patterns in the Northern Countries of Europe* (Nelson, ed., 1953); *The Politics of Compromise* (Rustow 1955); *Scandinavian Democracy* (Lauwerys, ed., 1958); *Nordic Democracy* (Allardt et al., eds., 1981); *Consensual Democracies* (Elder et al. 1982), and for the first time with 'model' in the title: *The Scandinavian Model: Welfare States and Welfare Research* (Erikson et al., eds., 1987), where the type of welfare state that had been established in the northern countries of Europe was seen as representing a prime, distinguishing characteristic of the Scandinavian/Nordic societies. Since then, academic books and articles as well as media commentaries on the topic of the Scandinavian or Nordic model of welfare – often labelled 'social-democratic' – have proliferated (e.g. Christiansen et al., eds., 2006; Hilson 2008; Kautto 2010).

The concept of a 'Nordic or Scandinavian model' or a special 'social democratic welfare regime' (Esping-Andersen 1990) has over the last 25 years successfully entered the international vocabulary with a largely positive connotation. But the Nordic countries have not always been admired for their type of welfare state. The Nordic type of welfare state has, by some, been perceived as too comprehensive, too generous, economically unsustainable, as making people lazy and welfare dependent and as being unfavourable for economic growth (e.g. Lindbeck 1997). Such perceptions, in their general manifestation, can be contested, at least in a long-term, comparative view. But, notwithstanding that view, the positive connotation derives from the relative success, normatively speaking, in terms of policy outcomes, such as egalitarian income distributions, low poverty level, political stability and, in fact, economic development in a long-term perspective, as can be seen from studying comparative national statistics (e.g. OECD statistics). This positive picture has recently been presented by international organisations, e.g. World Economic Forum (2011), and by mass media and Nordic and international scholars commenting on and analysing the Nordic countries (see e.g. references in Kautto 2010). Recently, there have been 'cultural wars' over the model's legacy within the Nordic countries. Nordic social democratic parties, the Swedish social democratic party in particular, has tended to claim that it is *their* model, at the same time as conservatives and liberals have claimed a larger share in it than previously. The Nordic Council has argued that the concept is a valid, common reference across the party spectrum.[1] Without joining the polemic about who can justifiably adopt the concept, the cross-political claim to 'ownership' of the model is in itself interesting, and at least an indicator of the current perception of success of the model. All parties want to be on the winning side. Even the liberal British weekly magazine *The Economist*, traditionally critical of the comprehensive and generous Nordic welfare states, presented the Nordic countries as 'the supermodel', which other countries should look to in the aftermath of the most recent global financial crisis (*The Economist* 2 February 2013).

There is no consensus in the literature on the exact nature or contents of a Nordic model. It can be said to consist of a number of elements which, taken

1. The Swedish Social Democratic Party applied to the Swedish Patent and Registration Office (PRV) in 2012 for the right to register 'the Nordic model' as a trademark. The application was approved. This decision led to debates and comments in Nordic mass media. The Nordic Council decided to challenge the Social Democrats' exclusive right to use the term 'the Nordic model,' and the case is now at the Swedish Supreme Court. (http://www.norden.org/en/news-and-events/news/the-nordic-council-appeals-the-registration-of-the-brand-201cthe-nordic-model201d, downloaded 20 November 2016).

together, make up a 'package' that puts the Nordic welfare states in a distinct category of welfare states. Some of these elements have been relatively stable over a long period of time, such as an active social state with a comprehensive public responsibility for the welfare and well-being of citizens and residents, implying a large public sector and also relatively generous benefits, and fundamentally based on principles of universality and egalitarianism. But, in our view, the model also contains a dynamic element, exemplified by the way in which social policies and reforms are made and implemented. Let us briefly elaborate on major dimensions of what in our view can be understood as the Nordic model.

The state – and local government – have played and continue to play a relatively strong role in the Nordic countries. The peculiar s*tateness* of the Nordic countries, meaning the active, core role of the state and local government, can be considered a positive one. The state has been less of a coercive apparatus of oppression in the hands of the ruling classes than in most countries. Moreover, local governments were historically recognised legal units and run by literate laymen guided more by the clergy than by noblemen or royal prefects. The role of the contemporary local government and central state is seen in extensive public services and public employment and in many taxation-based cash-benefits and benefits-in-kind schemes.

Another key characteristic of the Nordic welfare states is the principle of *universal social rights*, which are extended to the whole population or entire relevant categories of the population (Kildal and Kuhnle 2005). Services and cash benefits are not only targeted towards the have-nots but also cover the middle classes. Social security programmes were initiated at the time of political and economic modernisation and the development of the nation-building project. Historically, the similar life chances of poor farmers and poor workers contributed to the recognition of similar risks and social rights, and the principle of universalism gained ground and was put into practice in the two decades following WWII.

A third important characteristic is the value of *equality*, or put more strongly: 'passion for equality' (Graubart 1986). The historical inheritance of the Nordic countries is that of fairly small class, income, gender and regional differences. The modern industrial bourgeoisies did not acquire a strong political position in the central state, though they gradually, and especially after WWII, became influential through corporatist channels. The Nordic route towards the modern class structure was paved with the strong position of the peasantry, the weakening position of the landlords and the rather easy access of the working class to the parliamentary system and to labour market negotiations. The Nordic experience is one of small income differences and, in a comparative perspective, extraordinarily low levels of poverty (Ringen and Uusitalo 1992; Fritzell and Lundberg 2005). Moreover, the Nordic countries are famous for their small gender differences. A high degree of gender equality has become a major characteristic of the Nordic model (see chapter 5).

The Nordic model is normally identified by reference to the above-mentioned characteristics of welfare state institutions (stateness, universalism) and welfare policy outcomes (equality). But it seems appropriate to add *forms of democratic governance* as another important component. This refers to the way in – or process through – which political decisions are made. In this respect, the 1930s represented a political watershed in all Nordic countries with national class compromises between industrial and agricultural/primary sector interests and between labour and capital through the major trade union federations and employers' associations.[2] These compromises also came to be reflected at the parliamentary and governmental level, with political compromises reaching across party lines and representing various class or economic interests.

But a wider understanding of the concept of the Nordic welfare model must include aspects of the *actual* democratic form of government – or *governance* – in the Nordic countries, the evolution of a specific pattern for conflict resolution and creation of policy legitimacy as the basis for political decision-making. This pattern has developed over a long period of time and is characterised by active involvement and participation in various, often institutionalised, ways of civil society organisations in political processes before decisions are formally made by parliaments and governments. This is most particularly pronounced through triangular relationships between government, trade unions, employers' associations or similar organisations in, for instance, agriculture. This system of governance can be labelled '*consensual governance*'. The Nordic countries are small and unitary, which makes decision-making easier than in big and/or federal states. The existence of electoral systems based on proportional representation, which encourages the development of true multi-party systems, has made coalition governments common, often even minority coalition governments. This has in turn led to close and frequent contact between government and opposition parties at any given time to secure parliamentary majorities for reforms and legislation (see chapter 4).

HISTORICAL ROOTS AND DEVELOPMENT PATHS

The origins of the Western welfare state date back to the last quarter of the nineteenth century. Flora and Alber (1981) describe this period as 'the take-off of the modern welfare state'. Social insurance programmes were introduced,

2. Denmark was in fact the first country in the world, in 1899, to institute a collective agreement between trade unions and employers, an agreement between 'De samvirkende Fagforbund' (today Danish Confederation of Trade Unions) and 'Dansk Arbejdsgiver- og Mesterforening' (today Confederation of Danish Employers). Similar agreements were made in other Nordic countries during the 1930s.

with Germany as the front-runner with a major programme for insurance covering sickness, industrial accidents, old age and disability for workers in the 1880s. As elsewhere in Europe, the beginning of the development of the Nordic welfare states is closely associated with major social, economic and political transformations at the time (Castles et al., eds., 2010), and Nordic social policy initiatives at the time were directly or indirectly influenced by the German example (Kuhnle 1983). However, from the beginning a specific Scandinavian (or Nordic) route to the welfare state could be identified (e.g. Baldwin 1990; Alestalo and Kuhnle 1987; Esping-Andersen and Korpi 1987; Christiansen et al., eds., 2006). Based on Kautto (2010), a number of historical circumstances and factors can be listed which made the Nordic way different from that of the rest of Europe in the first formative phases of welfare state development until WWII: (1) the role of religion and the merging of the Lutheran church and the state as a result of the Reformation, thus giving the state and municipalities – and not the church – responsibility for poor relief; (2) the pattern of land ownership, i.e. the politically relatively strong and autonomous position of the peasant population; (3) the role of the social democratic parties when coming to power in the 1930s in all three Scandinavian countries in alliance with agrarian and/or liberal parties and the compromises between labour and capital; (4) social structures and cultural values that have been conducive to gender equality, exemplified through relatively early women's suffrage[3] and the active role of female reformers in early social policy legislation.

Although the concept of a Nordic model primarily invites thinking about similarities between the Nordic countries, there has, of course, been historical intra-Nordic variation in welfare state construction, both as to the timing and the sequence of introducing various types of social policies and ways of organising these. In general, Denmark led the way in social policy expansion from the late 19th century onwards, followed by Sweden and Norway, and Iceland until WWII. Finland was a relative latecomer.

The 1930s can be regarded as the decade when the phenomenon of a Nordic model (but not the concept) was born. Key social security programmes, such as old age pensions and unemployment insurance, were established or fundamentally reformed. Taking old age pensions as an example, all the Nordic countries had in the 1930s established public pension systems – so-called 'people's pensions' – providing comparatively generous flat-rate benefits to all elderly, subject to a means-test that only excluded a minority of well-off pensioners. In unemployment insurance, however, there were differences, with Norway opting for a national social insurance approach while Sweden, Finland and Denmark remained faithful to the so-called Ghent systems of semi-private

3. Finland was the second country in the world, after New Zealand (1893), to introduce universal female suffrage in 1906.

voluntary insurance in cooperation with trade unions (Rasmussen and Pontusson 2016).

The first post-war decades saw a strong further expansion of Nordic social security and social services, both quantitatively and qualitatively. Disability benefits were introduced and the coverage of sickness benefits schemes became universal and replacement rates increased. Old age pension policy followed a common development path in all countries, with Sweden as the pioneering country (Salminen 1993). The first step on this common path was to abolish the means test and introduce truly universal, flat-rate benefits. The second step was to add an earnings-related second tier in the public pension system on top of the existing flat-rate benefits. This second step was realised in Sweden in 1959 after a fierce political struggle (see Heclo 1974), and Finland and Norway followed suit in the 1960s. Also, in Denmark there were discussions about introducing a second tier of earnings-related pensions on several occasions both in the 1960s and later, but the reform proposals never gained sufficient support (Vesterø-Jensen 1984).

In the 1990s, the concept of 'flexicurity' was introduced by Danish researchers and policy makers to characterise the idea of using generous unemployment insurance and active labour market policies to facilitate economic restructuring and cushion the effects of relatively low employment protection (Madsen 2004).

THE NORDIC MODEL OF THE 'GOLDEN ERA'

The notion of a distinct and particularly successful Nordic welfare model gained especially wide popularity in the 1980s, a period that has been described as the 'Golden Era' of the Nordic welfare states (see e.g. Kautto et al. 1999). While most developed Western economies suffered from a combination of stagnation and inflation in the decades following the first oil crisis in 1973, Sweden, Norway and to a lesser extent Finland managed to maintain full employment and adequate economic growth rates up until the late 1980s. Denmark, however, deviated from the other Nordic countries with significant, chronic unemployment problems from the early 1970s onwards, coupled with government budget deficits and balance of payment problems. Also in Denmark, however, a strong commitment to generous welfare services and social protection was unchallenged in this period, and despite the high unemployment rates, social outcomes appeared to remain comparatively favourable, also after the country managed to get its balance of payment problems under control (Andersen 1997).

In comparative welfare state research of the time, the idea of a unique and successful Nordic version of welfare capitalism was reflected in a number of important contributions by both American and Scandinavian researchers (see Stephens 1979; Myles 1989 [1984]; Esping-Andersen and Korpi 1987; Esping-Andersen 1985; 1990). The dominant theoretical perspective in this literature was the so-called power mobilisation theory emphasising the strength of organised labour and social democracy as the primary explanation for Scandinavian exceptionalism. Even contributions that were profoundly critical of the theory of social democratic power mobilisation did not challenge the notion of a particularly redistributive and solidaristic Nordic welfare state model (Baldwin 1990).

Based on the actual configuration of welfare policies in place in the four (large) Nordic countries, it is possible to draw a rough sketch of the ideal-typical Nordic welfare state of the 1980s. It rests on two pillars: an encompassing and generous social security system and comprehensive welfare services. This welfare state model was in turn assumed to have produced attractive outcomes in terms of low levels of economic inequality and poverty in interaction with egalitarian labour market institutions.

Social security

A core component of the Nordic model is a comprehensive and generous social security system giving protection to the entire population against classic social risks: unemployment, sickness, disability and old age. The ideal-typical Nordic welfare state offers generous income replacement for average wage earners and – at least for disability benefits receivers and old age pensioners – a comparatively high benefit floor that is unrelated to previous earnings. In this way, the Nordic welfare state model can be seen to embody a compromise between two distinct social policy traditions: the Continental European (Bismarckian)[4] tradition with its exclusive emphasis on insurance-based, earnings-related benefits and the 'liberal' Anglo-Saxon tradition with its heavy reliance on flat rate and means-tested benefits.

The distinctive features of the Golden Era Nordic Welfare State are more clearly borne out empirically using institutional data and statistics on replacement rates rather than other conventional indicators of 'welfare stateness', such as total social expenditure as a percentage of GDP. The latter will tend to reflect variation in demographic variables and the scope of social problems (such as unemployment) in different countries rather than variation in the 'quality of social protection' as such (see Esping-Andersen 1990 for a critique of social spending as a welfare state indicator).

Figure 9.1 compares the generosity of social security provided in the four large Nordic countries to the average of 14 OECD countries[5] as of 1985.[6] It shows the net replacement rates offered to single wage earners with an average full-time wage in three social security programmes: unemployment insurance,

4. This term refers to the German Chancellor, who in the late 1880s pioneered the introduction of insurance-based social protection for the German working class.
5. The countries included are: Australia, Austria, Belgium, Canada, France, (West) Germany, Ireland, Italy, Japan, the Netherlands, New Zealand, Switzerland, the UK and the US.
6. The data source we use to describe the generosity of social security programmes does not include Iceland, and therefore we have in the following chosen to leave out Iceland from the discussion.

sickness benefits and old age pensions. In addition, it shows the relative level of the minimum old age pensions provided to people without prior labour market attachment. Unfortunately, the data do not cover disability benefits, but in some countries (such as Norway) disability benefits are calculated in a similar way as old age benefits.

Despite substantial intra-Nordic differences, it is apparent that net replacement rates are higher in the Nordic countries than the OECD average – typically by 10 to 20 percentage points. The only exception is the standard old age pension in Denmark that is slightly less generous than the comparative OECD benchmark. While the public old age pension systems in the three other Nordic countries in the 1950s and 1960s had been designed to provide a combination of flat-rate and earning-related benefits, the Danish public pension system continued to rely primarily on flat-rate and means-tested benefits, and therefore there is only a small difference between the (comparatively generous) minimum pension and the (not so generous) standard pension for the average wage earner (see Pedersen 1999). In other words: the Danish social security system deviated from the Nordic ideal type by being less Bismarckian. Note, however, that the level of minimum protection is higher in Denmark

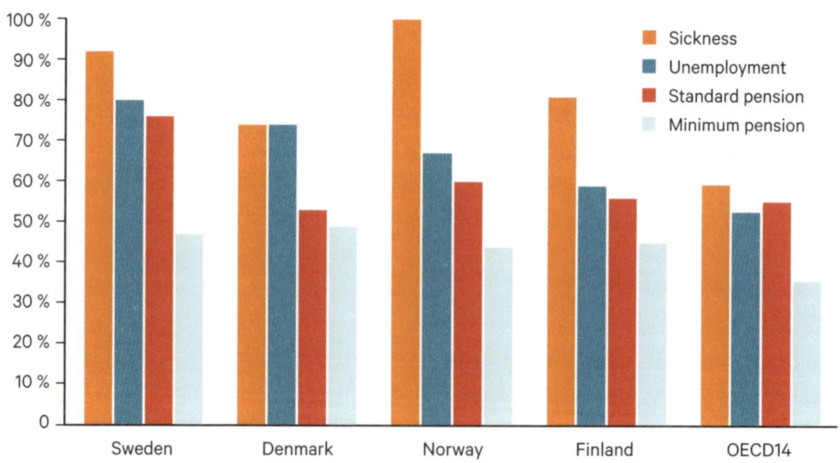

Figure 9.1 Net replacement rates for an average production worker in three social security programmes in the Nordic countries compared with the (unweighted) average of 14 non-Nordic OECD countries, 1985.

Source: Comparative Welfare Entitlements Dataset 2. Version 2014–03 (CWED2)[7]

7. Scruggs, Jahn and Kuitto (2014a), see also Scruggs, Jahn and Kuitto (2014b) for documentation of the data. The figure shown for the minimum pension is not strictly a replacement rate. It is the net minimum benefit provided to old age pensioners as a percentage of the net wage of the average production worker.

than in the other Nordic countries and significantly higher than the OECD average.

A related typical feature of the Nordic social security systems – setting them apart from most counterparts in Continental Europe – is that not only old age pensions but also disability benefits are open to all residents and offer minimum benefits to individuals without prior labour market attachment and prior social security contributions. In Sweden, Finland and (partly) in Denmark, this applies also to unemployment benefits. The tradition of granting social security rights based on residency is particularly favourable to married women without a strong labour market attachment. By contrast, in typical Bismarckian welfare states, married women who devote most of their time to unpaid care work will be dependent on intra-family transfers and deferred social security rights from their husbands (Daly 2000).

The Nordic tradition of granting individual rights to categorical social security benefits also contrasts with the liberal Anglo-Saxon welfare states, where means-tested benefits tend to play a very important role. Means-tested benefits in these countries are typically targeted towards households rather than individuals, and are means-tested against total household income. An unemployed or disabled woman who is married to a full-time working spouse will not be entitled to benefits, and the spouse of a benefit recipient is likely to face serious disincentives to work because of the tapering of benefits against total household income.

It should be recognised, however, that means-tested social assistance and housing allowances do play a role in the Nordic welfare states as a last-resort social safety net. The share of the population who depends on social assistance tends to be low due to the inclusive nature of the categorical and non-means-tested social security programmes. At the same time, however, the residual characteristic of social assistance is particularly pronounced in the Nordic countries with weakly defined rights, a large scope for discretion in the administration of benefits and relatively harsh forms of means testing. A plausible explanation for this paradoxical 'residualism within universalism' is that the most 'deserving' groups have been catered for in the categorical social security systems, and therefore the Nordic social assistance schemes serve a particularly marginal and presumably 'undeserving' group of recipients (see Lødemel 1997).

A further feature that can be added to the ideal-typical Nordic approach to social protection is the tradition – particularly in Sweden – for pursuing Active Labour Market Policies (ALMP) in combination with generous unemployment benefits (Rehn 1988; Calmfors 1995). In its traditional form – which in Sweden goes back at least to the 1950s – Swedish/Nordic ALMP involve offering opportunities for training, temporary jobs and different kinds of support for the unemployed to return to the labour market. The Nordic countries have for decades tended to spend a relatively high share of the total support for the unemployed on these kinds of active measures.[8]

Welfare services and female employment

The second pillar of the Nordic welfare state model consists of a comprehensive service state offering free or heavily subsidised health care, old age care and child care, as well as free education from primary school to higher education, all financed by general taxation.

The Nordic countries all have public health care systems – similar to the National Health Service in the UK – covering all residents and (primarily) financed by general taxation. The British/Nordic model of tax-financed and publicly provided health care deviates from the continental European systems with their stronger emphasis on earmarked, insurance-based financing and a larger role for private and non-profit providers. In practice, however, the difference is not dramatic since the principle of universal coverage through obligatory and subsidised participation has been adopted by all Western democracies, with the US as a unique exception.

Education is free in the Nordic countries and, as a main rule, delivered by public institutions including state-owned universities. In addition to providing free education, the Nordic countries also take responsibility for covering living expenses of students through a combination of student grants and student loans (see chapter 10).

An arguably more unique feature of the Nordic welfare states is the advanced development of universal child care and long-term care for the elderly – publicly provided for free or heavily subsidised. Socialising the responsibility for and financing of day care institutions for children as well as home-based and institutionalised care for the frail elderly has helped facilitate the entry of married women into the labour market. The expansion of publicly provided care and female labour force participation is likely to have been mutually reinforcing. The provision of care facilities has helped improve the work-life balance of the two-earner family and is in essence a precondition for liberating female labour power to engage in formal employment. At the same time, the very strong expansion of tax-financed public services in the Nordic countries since the 1960s has been an important job-creation machine for women (see Kolberg et al. 1992). In other words, two key characteristics of the ideal-typical Nordic welfare model are closely related to the expansion of publicly provided and publicly financed welfare services: high female labour force participation and a large share of public sector employment.

---

8. This is well documented in the historical editions of the annual report 'Social Protection in the Nordic Countries' published by the Nordic Council of Ministers going back to the mid-1990s, http://nowbase.org/da/publications/social-protection-older

The Nordic countries differ in the speed and degree to which they have approached fulfilling this aspect of the ideal-typical Nordic welfare state. Denmark and Sweden were pioneers in expanding both public child care and long-term care for the elderly from the 1960s, and closely related to this, they had for a long period significantly higher rates of female employment than did Finland and Norway. Around 1990, the female labour market participation rate was about 80 % in Sweden and Denmark compared with about 70 % in Norway and Finland (Marklund and Nordlund 1999: 35), with similar differences in the share of public sector employment. In Denmark and Sweden, the share of the workforce in public sector employment had reached about one third in the early 1980s, while Norway and Finland were trailing behind with 25 % and 20 % respectively (Marklund and Nordlund 1999: 36). However, already at the turn of the new millennium, Norway had caught up with the two other Scandinavian countries in terms of the coverage of public care provision, female labour force participation rates and public sector employment.

In order to simultaneously finance a comparatively generous social security system and comprehensive public services, the Nordic welfare states depend on being able to collect high tax revenues. The Nordic countries – and in particular Denmark and Sweden – have since the early 1970s had tax loads noticeably above the OECD average. In addition to high and progressive income taxation, the Nordic countries rely on comparatively high consumer taxes that tend to be regressive.

It should be emphasised, however, that in periods when the Nordic countries have managed to maintain comparatively low unemployment rates, the level of social expenditure has not been dramatically higher than in other OECD countries, and the same can be said about the general level of taxation.

High employment rates, which have been an integrated feature of Nordic societies, help to foster a broad base for income taxation, and a relatively egalitarian income distribution can be argued to do the same for consumption taxation. In addition to female labour force participation, high overall employment rates (and hence a large income tax base) have been facilitated by comparatively high labour force participation among the elderly. Although the Nordic old age pension systems have offered comparatively high replacement rates – as we have seen – old age pension expenditure has not been higher than in most other OECD countries due to a relatively high effective retirement age (Gruber and Wise 1999).

Income inequality and poverty

The appeal of the Nordic model in both academic and political circles rests on the belief that it promises to combine economic competitiveness with beneficial social outcomes in terms of a relatively egalitarian distribution of income, living conditions and life chances.

As already mentioned, Sweden, Norway and Finland featured low levels of unemployment and high growth rates in the 15-year period following the first oil shock in 1973. In the late 1980s, new comparative data sources, such as the so-called Luxembourg Income Study, became available, and they provided solid evidence that the Nordic countries clearly out-performed other OECD countries in terms of low levels of income inequality and financial poverty (see e.g. Smeeding et al., eds., 1990; Ringen and Uusitalo 1992; Atkinson et al. 1995). A number of studies also seemed to indicate that the social security and tax systems of the Nordic countries played an important role in achieving a low level of inequality in the final distribution of income (Ringen 1987; Castles and Mitchell 1991; Korpi and Palme 1998).

It can be argued, however, that the Nordic welfare states (conceived narrowly as tax and transfer systems) operate in a favourable environment with strong trade unions and collective wage bargaining, and egalitarian labour market institutions, resulting in low wage dispersion. The comparatively egalitarian distribution of wages found in all the Nordic countries is in itself likely to contribute significantly to the egalitarian distribution of household income in the Nordic countries (see Barth et al. 2014 and Pedersen 1994).[9]

DEVELOPMENTS SINCE THE 'GOLDEN ERA'

Around 1990, Sweden, Finland and Norway ran into severe economic difficulties, with dramatically increasing unemployment rates, negative growth rates and substantial government budget deficits (see Mjøset 1986).

The crisis was most severe in Finland, which suffered from the sudden disappearance of export markets in connection with the collapse of the Soviet Union; but it was also very deep in Sweden, which experienced comparatively high unemployment rates for the first time since WWII. In Sweden, the crisis led to a rather dramatic change in the political climate. Coinciding with a sudden appearance of huge public sector deficits, the Swedish employers' association announced its withdrawal from the existing system of collective wage bargaining and corporativist policy making, and these developments resulted in widespread doubts about the economic sustainability of the Swedish model in general and the social security system in particular. During the most acute crisis period in the first half of the 1990s, a number of retrenchment measures in the social security system were enacted, including the introduction of waiting days in the sickness benefit system and a reduction of the replacement rate. Even more importantly, the main principles of a structural reform in the

9. Barth et al. (2014) suggest that egalitarian labour market structures and generous social security systems mutually reinforce each other with the important implication that collective wage bargaining and low wage dispersion are key components of the Nordic welfare model.

public old age pension system were decided by a broad parliamentary coalition, promising a radical reduction of public pension expenditure in the long term.

In Norway, the crisis was much less severe, and instead of a dismantling of collective wage bargaining at the national level, three-partite cooperation was reinforced in the early 1990s and used to achieve a significant improvement of Norwegian competitiveness through wage restraint (Dølvik and Stokke 1998).

From the mid-1990s onwards, Norway and Denmark were leading on the path towards full employment while Sweden and Finland were still lagging behind. Rapidly increasing revenues from the production of North Sea oil and gas of course helped to reinforce the Norwegian recovery and to contribute to very high annual growth rates over the entire 20-year period from the mid-1990s to the present.

In the first half of the 2000s, the economic performance of all four Nordic countries was comparatively good and Norway, Sweden and Finland all did relatively well through the initial years of the financial crisis. Denmark was immediately most seriously hit by the financial crisis, and the country has continued to struggle with very low growth rates in the first half of the 2010s. Also, Finland has in recent years experienced very low or even negative growth rates. By contrast the Swedish and Norwegian economies have continued to perform relatively well, and in the Norwegian case, this is despite a dramatic drop in oil prices since the summer of 2014.

All OECD countries have experienced different types and degrees of welfare state retrenchment and restructuring over the last decades (Pierson 1996). In the following section, we will try to document how this has played out in the Nordic countries and discuss what implications it has had for the Nordic welfare states and for the notion of a distinctive Nordic model.

Reduced generosity of social security

Figure 9.2 updates the picture of the generosity of core social security programmes in the four large Nordic countries given in Figure 9.1 until the most recent year for which we have available data, 2010. While the level of replacement rates for a single standard worker has remained fairly stable among the comparison group of 14 OECD countries, large changes have taken place, particularly in Sweden.

In 2010, Norway was the only Nordic country that consistently scored higher than the (non-Nordic) OECD average across all four types of social security benefits. Sweden and Finland still scored higher than the OECD average on sickness benefits and (marginally so) on unemployment benefits, while they scored below average on the two old age pension indicators, including the level of minimum pensions, which is remarkable since a high level of minimum protection has historically been a hallmark of the Scandinavian approach to pension provision.

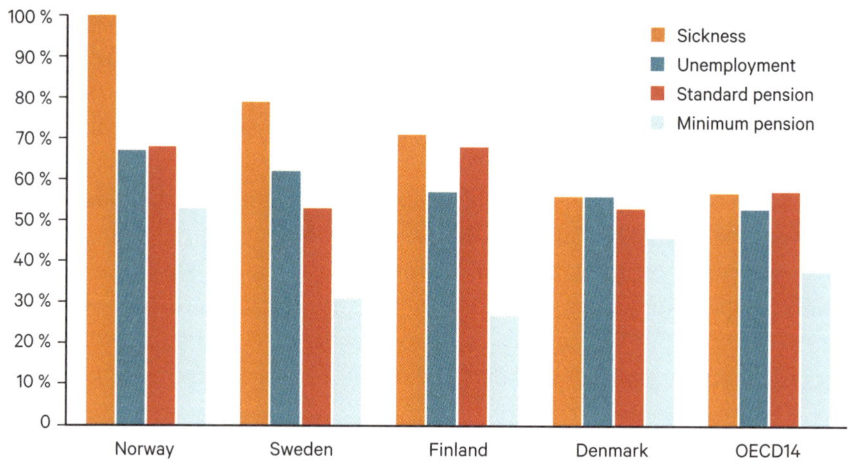

Figure 9.2 Net replacement rates for an average production worker in three social security programmes in the Nordic countries compared with the (unweighted) average of 14 non-Nordic OECD countries. 2010.
Source: CWED2

A more parsimonious picture of the aggregate annual development across the three social security programmes (and the four indicators) is shown in Figure 9.3. With the exception of Norway, it reveals a strong tendency of convergence towards the OECD average. It appears that the average generosity of the Swedish social security system has been reduced by 17 percentage points – from 78 % in 1985 to 61 % in 2010, which is still somewhat above the OECD14 average of 52 %. Also, the Danish and Finnish systems have experienced significant declines in generosity from about 65 % in 1985 to 55 % and 59 % respectively in 2010. Norway is the only Nordic country where net replacement rates for standard workers and minimum pension have remained stable at a level 20 % above the OECD average.

It should be noted that these figures do not adequately show the full effect of the old age pension reforms that have been carried out in the Nordic countries – since the figures refer to the pensions to be received by a worker retiring in the indicated year and not to the level of replacement to be expected by the present generation of workers. In order to adapt their old- age pension systems to the demographics of ageing, all the Nordic countries have enacted pension reforms that promise to improve the long-term financial sustainability of the systems. The Swedish reform is the most radical in this respect – transforming the Swedish pension system from one of the most generous among the OECD countries to one of the most meagre (see European Commission 2015, OECD 2015a and Pedersen and Finseraas 2009).

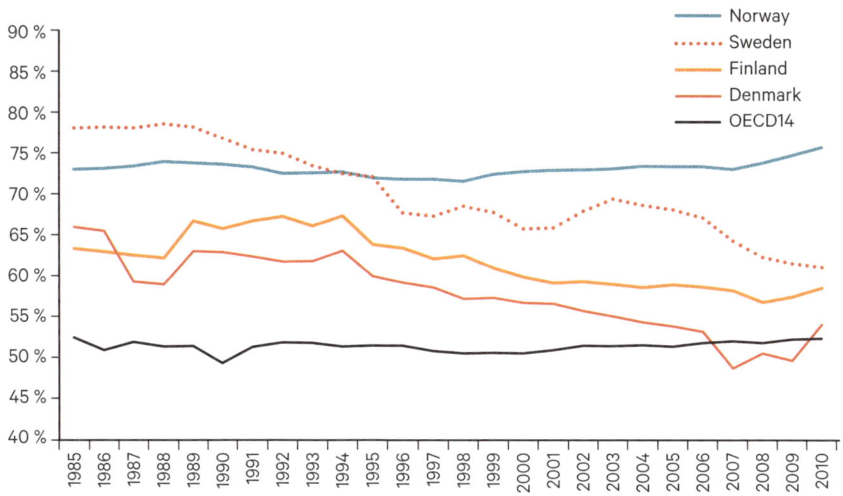

Figure 9.3 Average net replacement rates in three social security programmes from 1985 to 2010. The Nordic countries compared with the (unweighted) average of 14 non-Nordic OECD countries.
Source: Own calculations based on CWED2

Alongside the general tendency for retrenchment, some aspects of Nordic social security have been significantly expanded and strengthened since the mid-1980s. This applies in particular to parental leave schemes, where the Nordic countries, Sweden in particular, have continued to play a pioneering role.[10] The Nordic tradition for adopting policies to help improve the work-life balance of parents and two-earner couples is still very vital through a combination of generous parental leave schemes allowing both mothers and fathers to stay home and care for children during the first year and (virtually) full coverage, with high quality public child care facilities after the expiry of the parental leave scheme, which is around the time the child reaches one year (Bouget et al. 2015, see also chapter 5).

Activation and privatisation

Throughout the OECD area, social policy has taken a turn towards activation in the last two decades. This has also affected the Nordic countries, and one can argue that this policy approach is basically following up on the Nordic/Swedish tradition for Active Labour Market Policies (ALMP) that we have already mentioned. However, contemporary activation policies differ from traditional ALMP in emphasising the conditionality of cash benefits on participation in activation measures that are sometimes more punitive and designed to probe

10. Norway was the first country in the world to introduce a paid 'father's quota' in parental leave schemes in 1993 and was followed by Sweden the following year (see chapter 5 for details).

the recipients' willingness to work rather than a complementary offer to provide work and training. Another important difference is that the target group for activation policies has been expanded; previously focus was placed only on the unemployed, while now receivers of health-related benefits (sickness and disability benefits) and social assistance are also included (see Clasen and Clegg 2006 and Lødemel and Morena 2014 for comparative studies of activation).

Denmark is perhaps the Nordic country with the weakest tradition for ALMP, but from the mid-1990s onwards the country was among the pioneers in the contemporary activation wave. The right to social security benefits in the case of disability was replaced with a right to be exposed to activation measures by the municipal employment/social administration (Kvist and Pedersen 2007).

Arguably one of the characteristic features of the ideal-typical Nordic model is the rather modest role played by private provision – of both cash benefits and social services (see e.g. Esping-Andersen and Korpi 1987 and Korpi and Palme 1998). However, the crowding out of private welfare provision was never fully realised in practice. In Denmark, the expansion of occupational pensions was encouraged by the flat-rate old age pension system, and even in Sweden and Norway, private occupational pensions continued to play a role despite the expansion of an earnings-related second tier and the resulting comparative generosity of the public pension system (Hippe and Pedersen 1996; Pedersen 1999). Partly as a result of the more recent retrenchment in public pension systems, the significance of occupational pension systems has continued to grow, particularly in Sweden (see Pedersen and Finseraas 2009). Supplementary sickness benefits and unemployment benefits anchored in collective wage agreements have also expanded in Sweden and Denmark, compensating core groups of wage earners for the lowered generosity of the public systems (Greve 2016).

In the field of service provision, commercial and non-profit providers have (to a varying degree) been expanding at the expense of traditional public provision, but often within the public system of financing and under public control in terms of the distribution of services. In the secondary school system in Sweden, commercial companies have taken a considerable share of the market (Arreman and Holm 2011), and the same applies to long-term care for the elderly. In Denmark, non-profit enterprises are relatively important in the same sectors, while private commercial companies play an important role in the provision of child care in Norway.

Consolidation of publicly financed welfare services

While the core social programmes in the Nordic countries have become less generous since the Golden Era – or at the very best remained stable – the commitment to provide universal publicly financed services has, if anything, been maintained and sometimes reinforced. An example of the latter is the very substantial expansion of publicly financed child care in Norway from the late

1990s to the late 2000s, resulting in full coverage and an above 90 % take-up of day care/early childhood education among children between two and six years of age.

As shown in Figure 9.4, the Nordic countries all spend a significantly higher fraction of GDP on social services than the OECD average with Sweden, Denmark and Finland among the top four spenders. The fact that the share of GDP spent in Norway is somewhat lower is readily explained by the exceptionally high GDP in Norway, and the fact that Norway continues to put aside the part of its annual production that stems from the extraction of oil and gas, saving it in a provident fund for future generations.

We can conclude that the universal service state is still very much alive as a shared distinctive feature of the contemporary Nordic welfare states. Associated with this, female labour force participation and overall employment rates are high in the Nordic countries, although there has been a significant catch up by most of the Continental and Southern European countries.

Changing outcomes: increasing income inequality and poverty

It is well known that economic inequality has been growing in most of the developed world since the late 1970s, particularly in Anglo-Saxon countries like the US and UK. Up until the beginning of the 1990s, it appeared that the

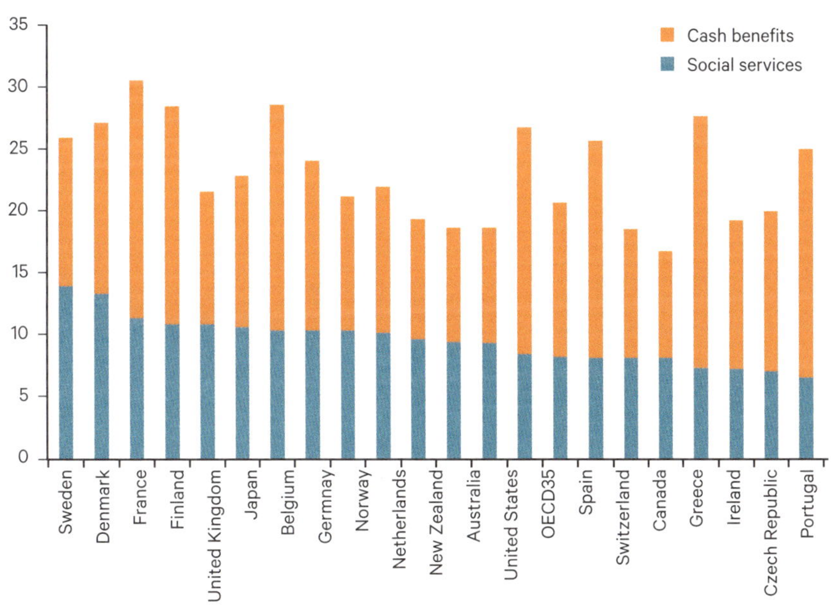

Figure 9.4 Social expenditure on social services and cash benefits in percentage of GDP. 2015

Source: OECD Social Expenditure Database

Nordic countries were an exception to the general trend and that they had been able to maintain low levels of income inequality and financial poverty (see e.g. Atkinson et al. 1995). Over the last two decades, however, the Nordic countries have also been affected by the trend towards increasing economic inequality.

Figure 9.5 shows the level and change in income inequality in selected OECD countries between 1985 and 2013. While Sweden and Finland had the lowest levels of inequality in household incomes in the middle of the 1980s, followed by Denmark and Norway, these two countries experienced the largest absolute increase in income inequality in the period with Sweden reaching a Gini coefficient of 0.28 (compared with 0.20 in 1985). Denmark and Norway have also had an increase in Gini inequality, but it is of much more modest proportions, and the income distribution in these two countries remains among the most egalitarian in the OECD.

A similar pattern appears in the poverty indicator used by the EU, where individuals with household income below 60 % of the national median are classified as being 'at risk of poverty.' As shown in Figure 9.6, the poverty rate in Sweden has risen from 9 % in 2001 to above 15 % in 2014, compared with only 11 % in Norway, where overall poverty rates have been stable since 2001.

Although it is notoriously difficult to prove causal relationships between macro-level variables, there is good reason to believe that the overall trend towards increasing economic inequality in the OECD area is at least partly driven by retrenchment of social security and reduced redistribution through the tax system (OECD 2015b; Atkinson 2015). The fact that economic inequality

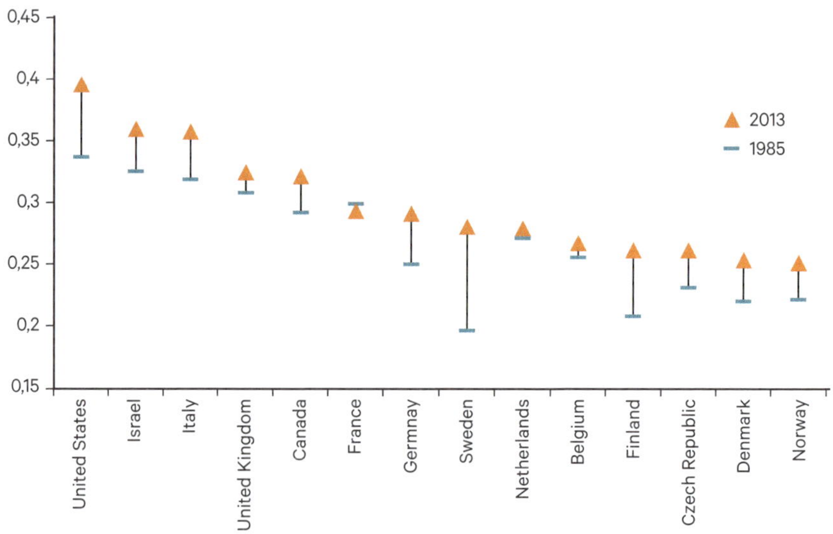

Figure 9.5 Household income inequality in selected OECD countries. Gini coefficient. 1985 and 2013

Source: OECD Income Distribution Database

appears to be increasing quite considerably in Sweden and Finland fits into this diagnosis since these two countries have also had the strongest reduction of social security generosity and the strongest departure from the Golden Era Nordic Welfare State.

THE FUTURE OF THE NORDIC WELFARE STATE MODEL

The Nordic welfare states are constantly being renegotiated and adapted to changing political, economic and social forces of change. Among the contemporary challenges facing the Nordic welfare states, the most pertinent appear to be ageing, globalisation and large-scale immigration.

The demographics of ageing have clearly called the economic sustainability of the Nordic pension systems into question, and as we have mentioned, all the Nordic countries have (to a varying degree) responded by implementing reforms that promise to reduce the future financial burden to the state. Ageing also has a strong effect on public expenditure and the need for manpower in long-term care services for the elderly. The fact that the Nordic countries have taken on a wide-reaching public responsibility to run and finance professional care for the frail elderly appears to make them more vulnerable than countries that rely more heavily on informal care within the family. On the other hand, the real burden of providing care is not dramatically different whether provided by formal or informal care, and while countries that rely primarily on informal care will face severe difficulties in achieving and maintaining high female labour force participation rates if most adult women must care for their frail

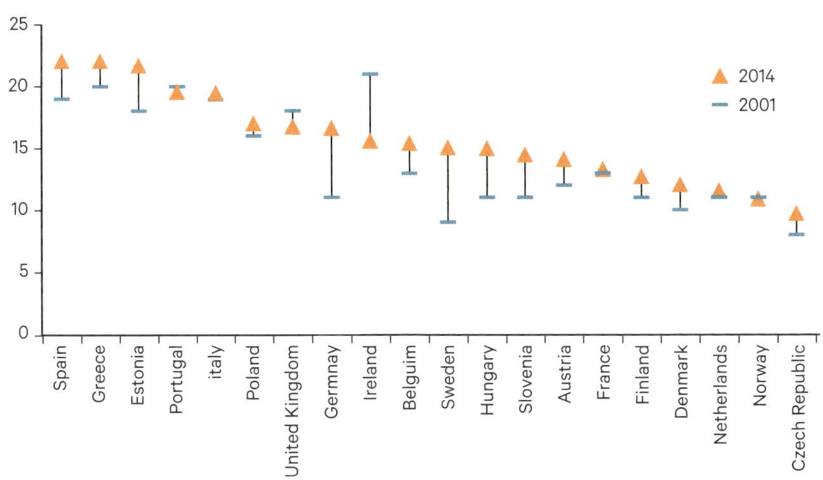

Figure 9.6 'At risk of poverty' rate (household income below 60 % of national median) in selected European countries. Percentage of entire population 2001 and 2014.

Source: Eurostat Social Inclusion Indicators

parents, this does not apply to the same extent in each of the Nordic countries (see Bouget et al. 2016).

Economic globalisation is a permanent challenge to the Nordic welfare states through different mechanisms. The Nordic welfare states depend on their ability to collect comparatively high levels of taxation, and tendencies for increased international tax competition are a source of worry (Ganghof 2006; Plümper et al. 2009). On the other hand, it can be argued that the Nordic welfare states have always been open economies that are exposed to international competition, and that the Nordic welfare states are in fact functional in allowing the Nordic societies to cope with the risks and uncertainties of international market forces (see Katzenstein 1986).

Immigration is arguably a third major challenge to the economic, social and political sustainability of the Nordic welfare states (Brochmann and Hagelund 2011). The Nordic countries have all to a varying degree received large-scale immigration flows over the last decades – partly in the form of asylum-seekers from developing countries and partly in the form of labour migrants from (in particular) Eastern European countries that have gained access to the internal EU labour market since the mid-2000s. In particular, asylum migration involves short-term costs for national governments that might contribute to narrowing the scope of public expenditure for other purposes, including social welfare. If immigrants in the long term do not reach the same high level of labour force participation as the native population and are more dependent on social transfers, there will be a long-term increase in costs that will add to the financial burden of maintaining a generous welfare state. A further mechanism through which immigration is liable to influence welfare policy is increased wage dispersion and higher income inequality and poverty rates. As we have seen, inequality and poverty have risen over the last decades, also in the Nordic countries, and it cannot be ruled out a priori that immigration is one of the driving forces behind this development. Finally, it has been suggested that immigration and increased ethnic heterogeneity of the population will make it more difficult to foster the kind of solidarity necessary to uphold popular support for the Nordic welfare state, and hence the political sustainability of the model might be threatened (see Alesina and Glaeser 2004 for an argument along these lines for the European welfare states in general).

There can be little doubt that these are very serious challenges and that the Nordic welfare states must adapt in order to cope with them. Whether in the process the very core of the Nordic welfare model will be lost or reinvented is still an open question.

CHAPTER 10
KNOWLEDGE REGIMES IN THE NORDIC COUNTRIES

Johan Christensen, Åse Gornitzka & Cathrine Holst

INTRODUCTION

Expert knowledge plays an increasing role in economic, social and political life. The Nordic countries are no exception. Arguably, the Nordic region is at the forefront in the transition to what is often referred to as 'the knowledge society' or 'the knowledge economy' of the post-war era. If we add to this the relatively egalitarian distribution of knowledge and the publicly funded education in this region, and the significant and growing role assigned to expert advice and knowledge-based policy-making in these political systems, we could even talk of the Nordic countries as 'knowledge democracies'.

This distinctive and significant aspect of the Nordic political, economic and social models is less celebrated, and also less well known and publicized in scholarly literature. Illustrative of this is how the Nordic approach to organizing and governing the production and use of knowledge is not modelled into the idea of the Nordic welfare state and a Nordic variety of capitalism (for example Busemeyer & Iversen 2012; Esping-Andersen 2009), despite the centrality of knowledge for how political, social and economic systems work. Knowledge shapes worldviews, organizations, participatory patterns and problem-solving capacity, and having a sound knowledge basis is a prerequisite for ensuring policy quality, the quality of government and political support and legitimacy (Rothstein 2011).

The aim of this chapter is to shed light on the 'knowledge regimes' of the Nordic countries. A knowledge regime can be understood as *the range of organizations and institutions that produce and disseminate policy-relevant knowledge and how these organizations and institutions are governed* (Campbell & Pedersen 2014). The knowledge regime encompasses such elements as how universities operate and are governed, what kind of expertise government bureaucracies possess, and what channels exist for transmitting research to policy-makers. There are of course huge variations across countries in how knowledge is organized and governed. In this chapter, we outline some key dimensions along which knowledge regimes can be categorized: whether knowledge production is dominated by public or private institutions, to what extent policy knowledge is located within government or controlled by government, and to what extent the production and distribution of knowledge is democratized.

The bulk of the chapter is devoted to describing and discussing the main characteristics of knowledge regimes in the Nordic countries: what does the Nordic knowledge landscape look like and how has it contributed to the Nordic political model? We argue that knowledge can be seen as the backbone of the post-war Nordic economic, political and social models, based on features such as free public higher education and very high levels of educational attainment, extensive public funding of research in universities and research institutes, public bureaucracies with strong professional knowledge, and the regular use of *ad hoc* advisory commissions for including expert and stakeholder knowledge in policy-making. Furthermore, we look at whether the Nordic knowledge systems are in transition, and if so, in what way they have developed. In particular, we discuss trends towards greater competition among knowledge providers, a loosening of the ties between government and research and advisory institutions, and new challenges for democracy. Yet, we argue that despite certain revisions to the model, the public, state-centred and relatively inclusive character of the Nordic knowledge regimes remains intact. In the conclusion, we revisit the arguments for seeing knowledge regimes in the Nordic countries as organized according to a common template.

KNOWLEDGE REGIMES – WHAT ARE THEY AND WHY DO THEY MATTER?

Although knowledge has always been an element of politics and policy-making, its role has increased dramatically over the last century. Several forces have driven this development. Most fundamentally, the growing technological and regulatory complexity and level of specialization of modern society have made governments increasingly dependent on expertise (Haas 1992; Kitcher 2011; Majone 1996). An expression of this is the growth in so-called depoliticized expert bodies – courts, agencies, central banks, etc. – inhabited by experts delegated with substantive discretionary powers (Olsen 2010; Vibert 2007). Moreover, the access to information and higher education has increased exponentially in the post-war era. This has expanded the supply of citizens with claims to expert knowledge, leading some to speak of a 'knowledge democracy' (In't Veld 2010). Yet, others see an emerging 'diploma democracy', with an increasing gap between the well-educated and the less well-educated in the access to policy-making arenas and political-administrative elites (Bovens & Wille 2009). In conjunction with these structural changes, the idea that policy-making should be rational and knowledge-based has gained currency (for example Nutley, Davies, & Smith 2000; Thaler & Sunstein 2009). Not only has the global spread of ideas about science and education meant that schooled knowledge and personnel are seen as appropriate for a wide variety of social positions (Drori, Meyer, Ramirez, & Schofer 2003; Schofer & Meyer 2005), but politicians, organizations and interest groups also increasingly need to justify political claims with reference to knowledge and research. Thus political processes and policy-making have taken on an epistemic logic (Fischer 2009).

In the field of political science, much has been written about policy-making regimes (i.e. political institutions) and production regimes (i.e. varieties of capitalism). Knowledge regimes have received much less attention. Yet, explaining the content, shape and legitimacy of public policies is impossible without an analysis of the knowledge that underlies policy solutions and the institutions and mechanisms through which this knowledge is produced and disseminated. "Knowledge regimes", argue Campbell and Pedersen, "are just as important for modern political economies as policymaking and production regimes at least insofar as knowledge regimes produce the ideas that inform what political and economic elites do" (Campbell & Pedersen 2014: 6). A clearer conception of knowledge regimes is therefore necessary to gain a fuller understanding of political systems in general and the Nordic model in particular.

What exactly is a knowledge regime? We rely mainly on two notions. One is Campbell and Pedersen's notion of regimes for the production of policy knowledge. They define knowledge regimes as "the organizational and institutional machinery that generates data, research, policy recommendations, and other ideas that influence public debate and policymaking" (Campbell & Pedersen 2014: 3). The other is the notion of 'policy advisory systems', that is, "the interlocking set of actors and organizations with unique configurations in each sector and jurisdiction that provides recommendations for action to policy-makers" (Craft & Halligan 2016: 2). These two notions place emphasis on slightly different aspects of knowledge utilization in policy-making, that is, on the generation of policy-relevant knowledge vs. the provision of advice to policy-makers. Yet, they both highlight two important points, namely (1) that there exists a broad range of organizations and institutions that produce and spread knowledge to political decision-makers, and (2) that the configuration of organizations and institutions varies across countries or groups of countries and across policy sectors. Identifying the organizations and institutions that produce and process knowledge and understanding how these operate and are governed are thus at the core of the study of knowledge regimes. Significantly, this notion of a knowledge regime fits well with the idea of a 'Nordic model' that is based on common features but also allows for internal variation.

To be sure, defining the exact boundaries of the knowledge regime is not straightforward. We opt for a broad understanding, according to which the knowledge regime stretches all the way from academic research to professional advice offered by ministerial bureaucrats. So defined, the knowledge regime includes institutions such as universities, research institutes, think tanks, party research units, permanent and temporary advisory bodies, consultancy companies, parliamentary analysis units, and government agencies and ministries.

Knowledge regimes and the institutions within them can be classified along some principal dimensions. A first dimension is whether the knowledge regime is dominated by *public or private* institutions. In some knowledge regimes, private actors such as private universities, private research institutes and think-tanks play a major role. A second dimension is the *location* of knowledge production and advice vis-à-vis government: is the provider of knowledge and advice located inside or outside the government apparatus? Think, for instance, about the difference between advice provided by a ministerial bureaucrat and a university professor. A third and related dimension is the degree of *government control*: to what extent does government have the means for controlling the advice provided by different bodies? For example, advisory bodies can be subject to different degrees and kinds of government control, depending on how they are organized? Finally, knowledge production and knowledge distribution can be more or less *democratized*. Advanced knowledge can remain within elites and be disseminated and utilized top-down, or citizens and civil society can be relatively knowledgeable and lay knowledge and perspectives be included in knowledge production.

How does the character of knowledge regimes relate to other features of the political system? We take as a starting point that knowledge regimes cannot be understood in isolation; they are bound to and shaped by the character and dynamics of the wider political order (see Campbell & Pedersen 2014). For instance, we can expect a strong role of the state in the political system to have consequences for how knowledge is produced and utilized. At the same time, knowledge regimes shape politics and policy-making. The specific configuration of institutions for producing and channelling knowledge into politics influences the extent to which knowledge is used in politics, the kind of knowledge used and how knowledge is used by policy-makers. This, in turn, has an impact on the content and quality of political decisions and the overall sustainability of the political system.

KNOWLEDGE REGIMES IN THE NORDIC COUNTRIES

1. The Nordic countries as knowledge economies and knowledge societies

Among the key defining characteristics of the Nordic socio-economic model is public investments in knowledge sectors. In international benchmarking exercises the Nordic region persistently scores high on indicators relating to productivity and quality of education and science systems. With in total around 50 universities, and over 100 other types of higher education institutions, the Nordic countries together constitute a significant knowledge region. Seven universities are in the top 100 in the so-called Shanghai ranking of 'world-class universities'. Relative to the number of people living in these countries, few regions outperform the Nordic universities in this respect. As concerns primary and secondary education, the PISA[1] study showcases in particular Finland as the role model for how to develop high-quality schooling (Simola 2005). Educational attainment and spending per capita is in general high in the Nordic countries (OECD 2016). As we can see from Table 10.1, all the Nordic countries are above the OECD average when it comes to share of the younger population with at least three years of higher education. Norway ranks highest in educational attainment, and this has been the case all through the 2000s. Even when the overall participation rate in tertiary education in this age group reaches 50 per cent or more it continues to grow in this region. Obviously, these countries have successfully mastered the transition to mass – if not universal – higher education (Trow 1972) and the corresponding trend towards professionalization of the labour force. There are still differences in participation rates based on social background. Students from families where parents only have compulsory education are much less likely to pursue higher education than students whose parents have higher education. Widening participation in higher education the last 20 years, has, on the other hand, implied a strong increase in higher education participation also among student from families with low levels of education (Hovdhaugen 2013: 11).

With the exception of Iceland, the Nordic countries are among the big spenders in the OECD area as measured in expenditure per student in primary, secondary and higher education. The Nordic countries are far from the only countries spending considerably on educating its citizens. However, when we

TABLE 10.1 PROPORTION OF POPULATION AGED 25–34 WITH AT LEAST THREE YEARS OF HIGHER EDUCATION 2003–2012

	2003	2007	2012	Change 2003–2012
Denmark	27	32	35	8
Finland	23	32	39	16
Iceland	23	28	36	13
Norway	37	41	44	7
Sweden	24	31	34	10
OECD average	20	26	30	10

Source: Swedish Higher Education Authority, 2015, p. 9

1 PISA stands for Programme for International Student Assessment, which has become a major and influential component of the Organisation for Economic Cooperation and Development's (OECD) educational work. This is a study that measures the comparative performance of national educational systems.

look at where the investments come from, the Nordic region stands out. The Nordic countries are among those where, on the whole, *higher education funding* comes mainly from the public purse, while in other 'big spenders' such as Canada, South Korea, the USA and Australia funding comes largely from private sources.

There are several characteristics that mark the Nordic approach to governing and funding knowledge systems. First of all, national student support system approaches are universalistic, geared towards students and their welfare state entitlements. Student support is not seen as part of parental responsibility or private investment in human capital. Access to higher education and a state regulated and funded school system have been core elements of the Nordic welfare state model. Moreover, in higher education the 'public approach' is evident when it comes to the issue of tuition fees. Higher education systems outside the Nordic region are heavily and increasingly dependent on tuition fees for funding tertiary education. Tuition fees for national students in public Nordic institutions have not been introduced. Despite strained public budgets at times, the issue of tuition fees has been somewhat of a political taboo in these countries (T. Christensen et al. 2014). However, Sweden and Finland have now abandoned the no-fee policy for one group of students, namely foreign students from outside the EU-EEA area. The Nordic knowledge region also stands out when it comes to the public responsibility for funding of knowledge institutions. Danish, Finnish and Norwegian universities and university colleges receive between 60–90 per cent of their funding as a basic appropriation from the state. These characteristics are an indication that education is perceived as a public and not a private good.

2. Governance of universities and research

The Nordic countries share some characteristics in terms of state steering approaches to their knowledge institutions rooted in the idea that they are instruments for achieving national policy goals (Gornitzka & Maassen 2007). As suggested already, knowledge institutions and knowledge policy are part of a Nordic social model (see chapter 9), as is visible in the high level of public funding for higher education, and in the emphasis on equal access opportunities to higher education as a primary value in democratic societies. The latter concern has triggered a steep increase in the number, types and regional spread of higher education institutions at key points in the post-war period. The national regimes have been in part designed specifically to educate the professions necessary for providing public services in an expanding Nordic welfare state. The key knowledge disseminating institutions – primary and secondary schools, and universities and (university) colleges – are in this respect part of what we can call a publicly regulated knowledge regime where public funding and national regulations are intended to ensure equality in access to education and a means to mitigate the reproduction of inequalities that segregated education systems can imply (Aamodt & Kyvik 2005).

As with access to and expansion of higher education in this region, we see the same propensity of the Nordic region to build up a knowledge economy based on investments in research and development (R&D). This set of countries has a comparatively large share of researchers in relation to the total population – with just over 1 per cent Sweden has the largest share of researchers, followed by Finland, Denmark and Norway. With the exception of Norway, these countries also spend a high share of GNP on R&D (Vetenskapsrådet 2016: 14). R&D policies are not only policies on their own right but instruments in sectoral policies, such as technological development in agriculture, fisheries, energy policy and so on. There are, however, some differences in the structure of knowledge regimes as far as R&D is concerned. Sweden and Finland belong to the group of countries where the majority (around 70 per cent) of R&D activities are carried out within the business enterprise sector. In Norway, on the other hand, the business share of R&D is just over half of total R&D expenditure. In the Norwegian knowledge regime a relatively large proportion of R&D (about 12–15 per cent) is undertaken in government research institutes. The differences in the R&D systems in the Nordic countries reflect both differences in historical trajectories and underlying differences in the economy. Predating ideas of transition to a knowledge-based economy, the Nordic countries have used research and development as a state instrument for modernizing industries. We see also communalities in the current emphasis on investing in knowledge for industrial development, innovation, job creation and international competitiveness of Nordic economies. International indicators that try to capture how countries perform as knowledge economies fairly consistently place the Nordic countries among the top-scoring countries. For instance, the World Bank's Knowledge Economy Index lists Sweden, Finland, Denmark and Norway among the top five countries. This index uses key variables as proxies for each Knowledge Economy 'pillar': economic incentive and institutional regime for promoting efficient use of existing and new knowledge and for entrepreneurship; education; innovation; and access to and structure of information and communications technology (ICT) (see Figure 10.1). There is a range of well-argued reasons for being sceptical to what such rankings can actually tell us about country differences (Høyland, Moene, & Willumsen 2012), yet taken together they can serve as a crude indication of a prominent feature of Nordic production and knowledge regimes.

State approaches to governing knowledge in the Nordic countries also include establishing research structures to support public policy, in Sweden and Denmark traditionally referred to as 'sectoral research' (Kyvik & Ødegård 1990). The Nordic countries have approached this in different ways. All Nordic countries have considerable resources channelled to research with an

Figure 10.1 Top 20 countries in the World Bank Knowledge Economy Scoreboard 2012. Weighted by population. Score on a scale from 1 to 10 where 1=lowest and 10=highest.
Source: World Bank https://knoema.com/WBKEI2013/knowledge-economy-index-world-bank-2012

applied orientation, including the social sciences, to feed public policy and state governance of key societal sectors, such as health and social policy, education, environment or foreign policy, with relevant research and expert advice. In Sweden, universities and colleges have been expected to undertake such an instrumental role for the state, whereas in Norway and Denmark specialized applied research institutes have long traditions for establishing an organized link between research and policy. In core areas, for instance labour market policy and social policy, social science institutes have held the niche that in other knowledge regimes has been filled by think-tanks and for-profit consultancy firms. Some of the research institutes with a national reach were established and owned by a 'parent' sector ministry (Gornitzka 2003), and government research institutes were closely linked, both institutionally and culturally, to their user community, as in the case of transport research and the Norwegian Ministry of Transport and Communications (Baklien 1983). In the 1980s the Norwegian system also established regional social science research institutes in order to provide expertise to local and regional government and to boost regional development. This model for organizing social science policy advice was part of the 'social engineering state'. In both Denmark and Norway the formal status changed for most of these institutes (from being part of the state apparatus to becoming independent foundations) or they merged with universities/university colleges. Loosening the formal ties between these institutes and sectoral ministries has changed the knowledge regimes in these countries and implied a stronger emphasis on competitive bids for providing policy-relevant research. At the same time, social science research institutes have been faced with increasing pressure to perform academically, implying especially an increase in the number of articles published in international scientific journals.

The Nordic countries have their own particular history when it comes to reforms and changes in the governance of knowledge institutions. Overall, one could argue that in the Nordic countries the 'rethinking' of the role of the state in public sector governance started in the 1970s and 1980s, amongst other things as a consequence of serious public budget deficits. Yet, before the 1990s none of the Nordic countries initiated major reforms focused especially on governance of knowledge regimes, for instance with respect to institutional autonomy and funding mechanisms in higher education and research. Since then, however, the Nordic countries have been influenced by what can be identified as the 'global script' for modern knowledge governance, reflected in increasing formal institutional and financial autonomy, and in a focus on economic aspects of knowledge systems, as well as the more recent instruments to boost 'world class universities' in the global academic competition (T. Christensen et al. 2014). Overall, the governance of knowledge regimes has undergone changes in the government steering models as part of general public sector reforms (see chapter 6). State governance has moved in the direction of more competition among knowledge providers and educational institutions, loosening the organized ties between government and research institutes, and a shift towards performance management. Government reforms have also included a push towards introducing changes in management *within* knowledge institutions, especially with respect to staff and student participation. Global trends in management reforms and their 'local' versions have challenged the traditional Nordic emphasis on university and college democracy and participatory governance. The design and timing of these reforms have varied across the Nordic countries. The most radical reforms of knowledge regimes in recent decades are probably the market-type reforms that were advanced in the Swedish primary school system, mainly by introducing competition through the support for private schools (Green-Pedersen 2002). In other reform efforts, attempts by governments to introduce change have been hampered or stopped by strong opposition from stakeholder groups in the sector, as was the case, for instance, when the Swedish and Norwegian governments proposed to change the formal status of universities (T. Christensen et al. 2014). In general, we see that the overall state involvement remains a defining characteristic of Nordic knowledge regimes, especially in terms of relatively high commitment to funding knowledge generation and dissemination, while we have seen transformative changes in the way in which state governance takes place in these expanding sectors. In sum, the Nordic model has strong links between government and knowledge institutions although the ways of governing knowledge have changed.

3. Knowledge in government

The Nordic countries are often described as 'strong states', and an important aspect of this is the strength of professional expertise within state bureaucracies. Civil servants in ministries and agencies have traditionally been important providers of information and analysis in the formulation and implementation of public policies (see chapter 6). By contrast, parliaments have had little independent capacity to carry out research and analyses, and thus limited ability to challenge the premises of government policy. The central role of the state in the knowledge regime is one of the defining features of the Nordic systems.

The Nordic countries have long traditions of professional bureaucracy. A permanent civil service busy with administering the affairs of the state existed long before the introduction of parliamentary democracy. In Norway, for instance, the political order of the nineteenth century has been characterized as the 'the civil servant state' (*embedsmannsstaten*), given that a small élite of civil servants effectively governed the country in this period. In this period, administrators were almost exclusively trained in law. In Denmark, law graduates even had a formal monopoly on most civil service positions until 1919. The early formation of an administrative state distinguished the Nordic countries from, say, the United Kingdom and the United States, where political parties and democracy arrived before the construction of a civil service. The consequence was that administrators in the Nordic countries already had a well-established role in policy-making once partics and parliaments entered the scene. Based on "administrative resources of information, analysis, and expertise" (Heclo 1974: 306) – resources that could not be matched elsewhere in the political system – civil servants defined many of the premises for public policy.

The rise of social-democratic parties and new types of experts in the decades before and after World War II further increased the emphasis on professional expertise in the Nordic state bureaucracies. The social-democratic governments in power in Sweden, Norway and (to a lesser extent) Denmark in this period had a strong belief in social engineering, rationalism and planning – that is, that society could be improved by using scientific methods to guide public policies (Lindvall & Rothstein 2006). As mentioned above, in some of the Nordic countries this period saw the establishment of specialized and applied research institutes to match sectoral public policies. This went hand in hand with the influx of new professions in public administration. Most importantly, scores of economists were brought into state bureaucracies to manage the more active economic policies pursued in this period, especially in Sweden and Norway.

Economics thus emerged as an important 'science of government', challenging the previous dominance of legal knowledge (J. Christensen 2017). But also other professional groups such as doctors, educators and engineers were integrated in the bureaucracy and came to play an important role in defining the premises for public policy in the post-war period. From the 1970s onwards, there was also a marked increase in the number of social scientists, especially political scientists, in the government bureaucracy (T. Christensen, Lægreid, & Zuna 2001). The drivers behind the changing constellations of disciplines and professions in Nordic governments have been functional demands and internal professional struggles, but also interest groups and social movements pushing and intervening from the outside. Historical analyses have, for example, emphasized how civil society and 'counter-cultures' from *embedsmannsstaten* and onward have contributed to mobilizing 'counter-expertise' against dominant professions and the hegemonic expertise in state bureaucracy (Skirbekk 2010; Slagstad 1998).

Whereas the bureaucracies of the Nordic states have traditionally possessed extensive technical expertise, parliaments have had limited capacities for carrying out their own research and analysis. This is an important difference compared with the USA, where Congress has its own research and analysis units that provide independent analyses that can match those of the executive (Campbell & Pedersen 2014). In Nordic parliaments, standing committees have played an important role, and members of parliament have often developed issue-specific expertise through this work (Arter 2008a). However, these committees have had limited technical resources at their disposal and therefore have usually not had the opportunity to commission independent research that could counter the analyses produced by the government.

The role of professional knowledge in government has, however, been reshaped in recent decades by changes in the organization of the state. In particular, 'agencification' – that is, the transfer of administrative functions to independent agencies – has introduced a clearer distinction between the political secretariat functions carried out by ministries and the technical functions carried out by agencies. This has implied a more autonomous role for professional knowledge, as technical expertise is increasingly located at arm's length from politicians. A special case of this is the independence given to central banks, which entails that decisions about interest rates have been removed from the political ambit and left to economic experts (Marcussen 2006). At the same time, the analytical capacities of Nordic bureaucracies are under pressure, due not only to limited administrative resources and a growing demand for specialized knowledge to handle complex societal issues but also to a proliferation of competing sources of expertise. Processes of agencification, and of expertization of policy-making in a broader sense (Turner 2003), are also questioned from a democratic point of view (Østerud, Engelstad, & Selle 2003). Whereas some see in these developments an undermining of democracy as we know it and of the Nordic egalitarian political model in particular, others welcome them as part of a breakthrough for the idea of knowledge-based policy-making.

4. Bridging science and government: ad hoc advisory commissions

Just as important as the analytical capacities of government and the knowledge produced in universities and research institutes are the institutions that bridge these two spheres. In the Nordic countries, ad hoc advisory commissions have played an especially important role in this regard. Routinely being called upon to examine major policy issues and provide advice about policy solutions, these commissions have been a core element of the Nordic knowledge regimes and, indeed, of the whole 'Nordic model of government' (Arter 2008b)

In the Nordic context, ad hoc advisory commissions – also known as 'commissions of inquiry' or 'governmental commissions' – are commissions appointed by the government to look into a specific policy problem and propose appropriate solutions based on an in-depth investigation of the issue. This kind of commission has been used extensively in Sweden, Norway and Denmark, while they are less important in Finland and Iceland (Arter 2008a). Commissions usually work for a year or longer, synthesizing existing knowledge and sometimes also carrying out or commissioning new research. Commissions are composed of members from the civil service, political parties, interest groups, academia or the private sector, and are led by a chairman and supported by a secretariat. According to many accounts, these commissions have played a vital role in the formulation of public policy in the Nordic countries (Meijer 1969). Whereas an important strand of literature has emphasized the corporatist character of commissions (Christiansen et al. 2010; Egeberg 1981; Moren 1974; Rommetvedt, Thesen, Christiansen, & Nørgaard 2013), others have seen commissions as mechanisms for rational and consensual policy-making (Anton 1969), for puzzling over policy solutions (Heclo 1974) or for incorporating certain types of academic knowledge in policy-making (Weir & Skocpol 1985).

Several features distinguish Nordic commissions from advisory bodies elsewhere. The first is their *routinized* character: for most major policy issues, appointing an advisory commission has been a necessary and taken-for-granted step in the policy formulation process (Meijer 1969). A reflection of this is the large number of commission reports produced every year. In Sweden, which makes the most extensive use of commissions, between 50 and 200 official commissions reports (Statens offentliga utredningar – SOU) have been published annually over the last 50 years (Petersson 2015). In Norway, an average of 35 Norwegian Official Reports (Norges offentlige utredninger – NOU) were produced annually by advisory commissions in the period 1972–2015. Second, the work of Nordic commissions usually feeds into the *early stages of the decision-making process,* that is, before concrete policies are proposed by the government. This distinguishes them from advisory bodies elsewhere whose role is to provide an opinion on policies put forward by the government, such as in Belgium (Fobé, Brans, Vancoppenolle, & Van Damme 2013). This means that Nordic commissions potentially have considerable influence, since their advice can define a problem and shape what policy solutions are seen as viable. A third defining feature of Nordic commissions is their *close links to the government bureaucracy*. Not only does government appoint commissions, formulate the terms of reference and pick the chairman and members; civil servants also frequently participate as commission members and usually make up the commission secretariat. This gives government considerable control over commissions (Meijer 1969; Nordby 1999). Finally, at least up until recently, Nordic commissions have been so-called 'hybrid' committees, including scientists and civil servants, but also stakeholders and interest group representatives (J. Christensen, n.d.; Krick 2014). This has given these committees certain *democratic* credentials and they could be regarded as a cornerstone in the Nordic approach to the 'democratization' of expertise. Whereas international literature emphasizes how the dominance of expert knowledge has more recently been challenged by more 'pluralist' and 'hybrid' forms (Gibbons 1999; Nowotny, Scott, & Gibbons 2001), this has arguably been a characteristic of the Nordic commission system with a longer tradition.

Advisory commissions in the Nordic countries have, however, undergone significant changes over recent decades. Most importantly, the broad *de-corporatization* of the Nordic political systems has led to a dramatic reduction in the number of advisory commissions and other bodies where interest groups were represented, at least in Norway and Denmark (Christiansen & Nørgaard 2003; Christiansen et al. 2010; see Hermansson, Svensson, & Öberg 1997 for a discussion of the Swedish case; Nordby 1994). In Norway, the number of reports issued by ad hoc commissions per year has dropped from around 60 in the 1970s to between 15 and 20 in the 2010s. In Denmark, too, the number of commissions has declined significantly (Christiansen et al. 2010). In Sweden, the number of official commission reports has remained high, yet an increasing number of the reports are written by single investigators (Petersson 2015). Danish observers also point to an increasing *politicization* of the commission institution in this period, in which the appointment of advisory commissions has gone from being an 'institutional norm' to becoming a 'strategic choice' (J. G. Christensen, Mouritzen, & Nørgaard 2009). At the same time, recent research points to an 'expertization' of ad hoc commissions in Norway, that is, a growing reliance on academics as commission members and chairmen and an increasing use of academic knowledge and forms of argumentation on commissions (J. Christensen & Holst, n.d.; Tellmann 2016). Campbell and Pedersen make a similar argument about Danish commissions, asserting that there has been a shift from tripartite commissions to pure expert groups in economic policy (Campbell & Pedersen 2014: chap. 5). In other words, while ad hoc advisory commissions remain an important institution in the Nordic countries, the character of the commission institution is changing. But whether this implies a weakening or strengthening of commissions as 'bridges' between research and policy-making is very much an open question.

5. Research and advocacy organizations

Another type of knowledge actor is privately funded research and advocacy organizations, commonly known as think tanks. Whereas think tanks are important knowledge actors in some countries, such as in the USA, they are a relatively recent phenomenon in the Nordic countries. Sweden is somewhat of an exception. In Sweden, employers founded a free-market think tank, Timbro, as early as the late 1970s, which exerted considerable influence in debates about economic policy in the 1980s (Blyth 2001). Recent research has also pointed to the large and growing role of 'policy professionals' in the Swedish political system, that is, people working in think tanks, consultancy firms, parties, etc., whose job it is to provide politicians with policy advice (Garsten, Rothstein, & Svallfors 2015). In Denmark and Norway, by contrast, the first think tanks worthy of the name were established only in the 2000s. In Denmark, "a few embryonic advocacy organizations emerged" in this period (Campbell & Pedersen 2014: 173). The most important of these is the market-liberal think tank CEPOS (Center for Political Studies), which is funded by private foundations and corporations and primarily focuses on economic policy. In Norway, the right-of-centre think tank Civita was established in 2003, based on donations from employers and private corporations. Civita has a somewhat different profile, focusing on a wider set of policies and on liberal philosophy and values in a broader sense. Only in the late 2000s and early 2010s were a series of left-leaning think tanks established in Norway to counter the ideational influence of Civita. Funded by trade unions and private donors sympathetic to social-democratic ideals, these organizations focus on issues related to equality and the welfare state. Organizations that have taken on features of think tanks have also played a role in other policy fields, for example environmental organizations such as Zero and Bellona. Yet, think tanks play a relatively modest role in both the Danish and the Norwegian knowledge regimes, something that might have to do with the role that specialized social science research institutes have had as expertise providers and advisors in these countries (see above). However, with the proliferation of organizations offering policy advice, this may be changing.

CONCLUSION

The Nordic countries have strong knowledge systems. They are among the countries in the world with the highest levels of educational attainment in the population and they spend considerably more on primary, secondary and tertiary education than the average OECD country. Even the most careful reading of international comparative indicators leads us to the conclusion that the Nordic region is among the most knowledge-intensive societies and economies in the world. Knowledge systems have been a key instrument for social policy, which is especially evident in policy for educational expansion and for access to higher education, for industrial policy and economic competitiveness of small, open economies in the Nordic region, and for boosting government problem-solving capacity in key sectors of society. Moreover, there is a clear state orientation in the Nordic approach to *governing knowledge*. Education has been perceived as a public rather than a private good. Public funding of education and student support is predominant. There are structural, historical, and policy differences in these countries in how state, society and economy link to knowledge systems. Yet, the Nordic countries converge when it comes to the state approach to funding and regulating national R&D and higher education systems.

There have been shifts in the state steering approach to governing knowledge in the Nordic countries. Some of these are part of general public sector reforms from which knowledge systems have not been exempted. These include the introduction of stronger competition among knowledge producers, performance management of schools and higher education institutions, and a stronger instrumentalization of knowledge and higher education in order for the Nordic countries to enhance their position in global competitive markets. The particular balance in favour of public responsibility over private investment has, however, been a persistent feature in the Nordic countries in the post-war period.

Furthermore, policy-making in the Nordic countries is characterized by *governing through knowledge*. A well-educated civil service able to provide politicians with professional advice in the formulation and implementation of policies is crucial in this regard. This can also be seen as an important ingredient in the success of the Nordic model: as comparative research has shown, the type of meritocratic bureaucracy characteristic of the Nordic countries is strongly correlated with good socio-economic outcomes (Dahlström, Lapuente, & Teorell 2011). The recent trend towards the agencification of the state has, if anything, increased the emphasis on specialized expertise, although it has also moved this expertise further away from political control. Beyond the knowledge capacities of the state itself, the presence of strong institutional mechanisms for examining societal problems and puzzling over policy solutions is characteristic of the Nordic countries. In particular, ad hoc advisory commissions make an important contribution to knowledge-based policy-making by facilitating the interaction of bureaucrats, academics and organized interests. The role and character of commissions have changed over time, with a decline in their corporatist character and a growing presence of academics. Yet, commissions remain an integral element of 'Nordic-style' policy-making.

Ongoing processes of expertization, along with other processes such as marketization and judicialization, no doubt come with significant democratic challenges. Yet, the Nordic polities qualify in several respects as knowledge democracies. Modern societies are characterized by specialization and informational asymmetries, but the robust, publicly funded educational systems embedded in the broader redistributive schemes of the Nordic welfare states provide the average citizen with education and cognitive resources on a comparatively high level. This, together with formal mechanisms for including stakeholders and interest groups in knowledge production and policy-making, and the *longue durée* institutionalization of relatively vibrant civil societies and public spheres where problem definitions and policy solutions 'from above' are questioned and scrutinized by movements 'from below' (see Hernes 1987: for a classical formulation of the Nordic region 'social democratic ideal') , are all central ingredients in what is arguably – still – a distinctive Nordic model of democratic, knowledge-based governance.

CONCLUSIONS: ARE THE NORDIC MODELS STILL VIABLE?

Oddbjørn Knutsen

The point of departure for this book was the idea of Nordic models for central politics and policies areas. The chosen topics are central within political science and are areas where we expected to encounter Nordic models. In this chapter, the first part will review the main approaches and findings from the various chapters. The second part will briefly focus on the various aspects of the use of concept of Nordic models that were addressed in the introduction chapter.

THE MAIN FINDINGS

In his chapter *State- and nation-building*, Berntzen underscored that for most of the early modern period, Denmark and Sweden had fought for domination in the Nordic region. Nordic state- and nation-building before the end of the Napoleonic Wars was equally militaristic and war-like as in the rest of Europe. However, the year 1814 represented a major change in this respect. Nordic state- and nation-building has been exceptionally peaceful during the last 200 years. The sense of the region as a cultural community gradually grew, eventually becoming an important basis for the termination of the pre-Napoleonic image of Scandinavia as an area of natural warriors. There have been no wars between the traditional enemies in the Scandinavian region since 1814. The new geopolitical balance established after the Kiel Treaty laid the foundation not only for the elimination of the idea of war as a natural feature of the region, but also for the absence of violence in conflict resolution.

The two Scandinavian conglomerate states were dismantled and they were split apart: Sweden slid out of the continent, while Denmark was forced away from the Scandinavian Peninsula. The long-term effects of war losses for both countries appear to have been largely beneficial. Instead of leading to revanchism against the former enemy (Russia in the case of Sweden, Prussia for Denmark), the result in both cases was an acceptance of military defeat and territorial loss and an acceptance of being reduced to “small states”.

Berntzen emphasised that the Nordic roads to liberal democracy have been equally smooth and uniquely peaceful. With regard to the democratisation of executive power, constitutional monarchies were transformed into democratic parliamentary monarchies in the three Scandinavian countries by 1917, and democratically elected presidents in semi-presidential regimes appeared in Finland and Iceland in 1919 and 1944 respectively. With regard to the democratisation of legislative power, all five Nordic countries had introduced universal suffrage around 1920. The Nordic roads to liberal democracy were smooth and uniquely peaceful. In addition, they were completed relatively early and quite quickly during a short time span of 20 years, from approximately 1900 to 1920.

In conclusion, Berntzen argued that the "Nordic model" of state- and nation-building is still valid and viable. The state- and nation-building trajectories of the Nordic countries stand out as exceptionally peaceful with the notable, but partial, exception of Finland.

Knutsen's chapter, *Political parties and party systems*, showed several distinctive traits of the party families and party systems. The Nordic five-party system model comprises Agrarian parties that are unique compared with the party system elsewhere in Western Europe.

The policy location of the other party families has shown the following main differences between parties in the same party families elsewhere in Western Europe: The Liberal parties (apart from the Danish Agrarian Liberals) are centre parties positioned between the Conservatives and the Social Democrats. They are not the main rightist parties on economic policy as in many central European countries. The Conservative parties in the Nordic countries are first and foremost located firmly to the right on the economic left–right dimension. On moral and religious issues, they are considerably less restrictive than elsewhere in Western Europe. Compared with the larger Christian parties in Central Europe, the Nordic parties are quite distinct: they are considerably more restrictive regarding moral policy compared with their continental sister parties. They also have a more leftist and green policy, and a less restrictive policy towards immigration.

The two party families in the five-party model that have declined the most are the Social Democrats and the Liberals. For the other party families, long-term support is fairly stable although there are compensating tendencies within the party family. The new party families have gained considerable support among the electorate in the last decade and have challenged the five-party system model. The increase in support for the Radical Right is most pronounced. The five-party system model is thus challenged, but it is far from dead. Whereas 94% of voters on average supported parties in the model in the 1950s, an average of more than 81% of voters still supported parties in this model in the 2000s. So far in the 2010s it is evident that there has been a sharp decline over the previous decade.

The party systems in the Nordic countries have become considerably more fragmented over time. Net electoral volatility increased significantly between the 1960s and the 1970s, and has remained at the same level since. Polarisation in the party systems is measured by the aggregated support for Radical Right, Left Socialists and Communists. First and foremost, due to the increase in support for the Radical Right, polarisation has increased, notably after 2000.

In Chapter 3, on *the impact of social cleavages and political value conflicts on voting choice*, it was documented that a significant number of determinants of party choice are higher in the Nordic countries than elsewhere in Western Europe. This is most pronounced for the impact of economic left-right orientations and the overall impact of all value orientations (Old and New Politics) when controlling for social structure. For these aspects of voting behaviour, the impacts in all the Nordic countries are clearly higher than in other regions in Western Europe.

There are also Nordic models regarding a series of other elements, but these are not as pronounced. These are reflected in:

- the modern gender gap where women support the leftist parties to a larger extent than men, and men support the rightist parties (Conservative and Radical Right) to a larger extent than women,
- various types of new class voting such as total class voting and total or overall left–right class voting,
- the impact of urban–rural residence, sector employment, environmental orientation and immigration orientation, and the overall impact of both social structure and value orientations.

The following elements can be placed in the group where there is no Nordic model: the impact of region, religion (both religious denomination and religious–secular values), traditional class voting, the impact of libertarian–authoritarian values, and finally the total impact of social structural variables.

In sum, new structural cleavages and new types of class voting are more significant than in other regions, and value orientations – controlled for the influence of social structure – have a larger impact on voting choice that elsewhere. Possible explanations for these traits are that the social structure is advanced and that voters are more "cognitively mobilised".

Heidar and Rasch's chapter, *Political representation and parliamentarism*, emphasised that the similarities between the five Nordic countries are possibly more striking than the differences. All countries have proportional electoral systems. All the parliaments today are unicameral, organised in a roughly similar way internally. All the countries, except Finland after 2000, have a negative form of parliamentarism. The negative rule implies that the government simply has to be tolerated by the parliament, but it does not need to achieve active support of any majority in the chamber when it is formed.

Even if all elections are conducted by proportional systems, the countries differ significantly with respect to the candidate choice given to the voters. Finland and Norway are the Nordic extremes with open party lists and closed party lists, respectively. The countries differ with respect to type of government. In Scandinavia, minority governments have over time been far more common than majority governments. Another common trait is the frequent occurrence of one-party governments, which indicates that political parties may be reluctant to enter into formal coalitions. The Scandinavian types of governments are unique in a comparative European setting. Heidar and Rasch emphasise that the prevalence of minority governments is not associated with political malaise, instability and poor performance, which used to be the conventional wisdom associated with governments without majority backing in parliament. Finland and Iceland typically are governed by majority coalition cabinets, which is very similar to patterns found in Continental European countries.

Nordic parliaments can be regarded as "working parliaments", in contrast to the less influential "debating parliaments" that are also found in some Western European countries. They can influence the formulation of policy and legislation in a variety of ways. They have a specialised system of standing committees that broadly correspond to government ministries. Committees are organised to facilitate the dispersal of policy-making influence throughout the assembly, spreading it to opposition groups as well as to members of the government parties. Influential committees have "invested" in expertise and use their specialised knowledge to control and revise, rather than just rubber-stamp, decisions by the government.

Scandinavian parliaments stand out as strong and influential. There are signs of a trend indicating a "decline of governments", and not a "decline of parliaments" over time, as claimed in some of the standard literature. There are indications that parliaments in the Scandinavian countries are stronger than in Finland and Iceland, but empirical findings are not consistent with this.

In the chapter *The Nordic Gender Equality Model*, Teigen and Skjeie utilised the average scores on the EU's Gender Equality Index to examine the Nordic countries in a comparative perspective. They concluded that Nordic EU member countries form a distinct group of high achievers with only the Netherlands in close proximity. When the analysis was concentrated on indicators of economic equity and democratic parity, and average Nordic scores were compared to the average EU scores, it was found that the Nordic scores for democratic parity were more exceptional than those for economic equity. When European countries were clustered according to type of welfare regime, the Nordic social democratic regime countries were still shown to score higher on gender equality than countries within both the liberal and the conservative regimes. On the economic equity dimension, the distance is highest between social democratic and conservative-corporatist countries; on the democratic parity dimension, the conservative welfare states are closest to the scores of the social democratic welfare states.

As to the question of policy models, the authors analysed whether it is possible to identify a distinctive policy profile common to the Nordic countries concerning how to promote economic equity and democratic parity. However, on most of the indicators used to identify levels of economic equity there were few, if any, comprehensive policy reviews and impact analyses available. The only policy cluster that was thoroughly mapped and analysed at present were policies to promote work–family balance. Such policies prevail in all the Nordic countries in the form of extensive public subsidisation of parental leave and childcare arrangements. Work–family balance policies as an infrastructure that promotes economic equity have been gradually expanded in all the Nordic countries. The policies mainly contribute to facilitate women's inclusion within the Nordic labour markets.

Some form of parity policy has been established in all the Nordic countries to promote and regulate the gender composition of decision-making assemblies. Voluntary gender quotas have been adopted by some political parties in most countries, most broadly in Norway. Legal gender quotas for corporate boards exist in Norway, Finland and Iceland; Denmark has a less specified gender balance law while Sweden still relies on voluntary measures. There is thus no discernible common Nordic policy model in policy adoptions to promote democratic parity.

The main conclusions were that in terms of gender equality performance, it still makes sense to talk about a Nordic model. Its core traits have not been eroded although its existence might not be as dependent on a common set of policies as is often assumed.

Bjurstrøm and Christensen's chapter outlined *the main formal structures of the civil services* in the Nordic countries and analysed the main public sector reforms from three perspectives. All countries are large welfare states with a strong tradition of well-established central agencies and a high degree of autonomy. Despite several similarities, there are some important differences between what may be referred to as the West Nordic model (Denmark, Iceland and Norway) and the East Nordic model (Finland and Sweden). The most important differences between the two models are individual ministerial responsibility practised in the West Nordic model, while the East Nordic model favours collective ministerial responsibility and somewhat higher agency autonomy. In recent years, Finland has moved towards the West Nordic model. Hence, rather than talking about an East-West divide, we can say that Sweden stands out more compared to the other Nordic countries.

Commencing in the 1980s, New Public Management (NPM) and post-NPM have been the main reforms in the Nordic countries. NPM focused on cost efficiency, market orientation and structural fragmentation of public organisations. As a consequence of increased fragmentation, executive politicians felt that

NPM undermined their ability to control and manage public organisations. This led to stricter control and coordination – central elements of post-NPM. During the last 10–15 years, the Nordic countries have extensively implemented post-NPM reforms, although in combination with NPM measures.

None of the Nordic countries wanted to implement NPM in its most radical incarnations. The Nordic reform profile represents a distinct Nordic model composed of reluctant reformers (although Sweden took a somewhat more radical approach that tended to be more efficiency- and rationality-centred). The driving force behind this model appears to be cultural. This can be understood from a cultural perspective as the Nordic countries have strong state traditions favouring centralisation and a large public sector, which is a better fit with post-NPM. The Nordic countries are more preoccupied with democratic values, social responsibility, collective values and professional expertise, including interest groups and rule-centred administration. These cultural traditions contrast with NPM's focus on efficiency, individualism and market orientation, and may explain why the Nordic countries were among the first in Europe to implement post-NPM measures.

The Nordic countries have been acknowledged for their *high degree of corporatism*. However, in his chapter on corporatism, primarily in Scandinavia, Rommetvedt showed that important causes or prerequisites for corporatism have been weakened. A growing number of competing interest groups, higher electoral volatility, minority governments and strengthened parliaments are among the factors that have distorted the corporatist exchange. Since the 1960s and 1970s, the corporatist apparatus based on governmental committees with members from interest groups has been significantly down-sized. Danish and Norwegian corporatism peaked around 1980, while the decline of Swedish corporatism commenced even earlier.

In Rommetvedt's chapter, a distinction was made between corporatist representation in policy preparation and policy implementation committees. The distinction revealed interesting nuances between the Scandinavian countries. In Norway, the number of both preparation and implementation committees continued to be reduced in the 1990s and in the early years of the 21st century. However, in Denmark a minor increase in the number of implementation committees has occurred since the 1990s.

Reduced access to government authorities through the corporatist channel can, of course, have an impact on interest group strategies. Rommetvedt's chapter shows that interest groups have increased their lobbying efforts, particularly towards the parliaments. Lobbying is an alternative to corporatist representation for interest groups that are not given access to public committees, and a supplementary strategy for interest groups that are still given privileged access to such committees. Case studies and surveys clearly indicate that lobbying can have an impact on policy-making and the activities of MPs.

Lobbying is frequently perceived as something suspicious and/or negative. Norwegian MPs acknowledge the risk whereby well-organised groups and specialised interests may become too influential. However, lobbying may also give MPs access to information and counter-expertise, and strengthen the parliamentary control of the executive. Thus, the MPs' overall assessment of lobbying is positive.

Clearly, the Scandinavian countries have developed in a less corporatist, more pluralist direction. Comparable data from Finland have not been published yet, but broadly speaking the Finnish experience seems to be fairly similar to that of the Scandinavian countries. Research on corporatism in Iceland is very limited indeed, but corporatism in areas such as economic and income policy developed much later in Iceland than in the other Nordic countries.

In the chapter on *local and regional government*, Baldersheim, Rose and Sandberg emphasised that structural reforms in local and regional governments have tended to reflect national government concerns with the system capacity of municipalities more than that of citizen effectiveness. The reforms have triggered conflicts and opposition that mirror traditional as well as new conflict lines. A surprising aspect of the reform coalitions is that in three of the countries – Denmark, Finland and Norway – amalgamation reforms have been championed by centre-right governments, not by social democrats. Traditionally, right-wing parties have been defenders of small-scale local government and have extolled the virtues of heeding local identities and preferences. But in the 2000s these parties have taken the opposite position, seeking the support of large-scale local government for the provision of local welfare services.

Recent reforms in the health care systems of the Nordic countries have further enhanced the *co-operative* character of centre-local relations. The capacity of specialised health care systems is under great pressure from medical developments and an aging population, and all the Nordic countries (like other European countries) are searching for ways of coping with this pressure. The common denominator of responses has been to develop co-operative structures between hospitals and municipalities to enable speedier and more seamless discharge of patients from hospital into municipal care.

The authors evaluated the character and quality of the local self-government system according to the criteria of autonomy, democracy and efficiency. Seen from a wider European perspective, Nordic local governments, especially municipalities, get high marks on these criteria. In terms of local autonomy, municipalities have been entrusted with a series of important functions, and local politicians enjoy fairly wide powers in decision-making. Nordic local governments also measure up fairly well on the criterion of local democracy and stay firmly anchored on the model of representative and party-driven democracy. The efficiency of local government may be assessed in terms of both cost-effectiveness and allocative efficiency. The authors concluded that

Nordic local governments seem to do a fair job in this regard. There are, to be sure, variations in citizens' satisfaction between local authorities, but on the whole satisfaction is quite high in the Nordic countries. The authors conclude that despite the turmoil over reforms the Nordic states are likely to continue as highly decentralised welfare states in the foreseeable future with important functions allocated to the local level and managed in a spirit of co-operative governance across different levels of government.

In Chapter 9, Pedersen and Kuhnle argued that it may be justifiable to talk about *a Nordic welfare state model*, although the concept is vague and there is hardly any consensus in the literature as to what it includes. In this context, reference was made to a "package" of elements which, taken together, place the Nordic countries in a distinct category of welfare states, characterised by an active social state with a comprehensive public responsibility for the welfare of citizens, implying a large public sector, generous benefits, and programmes based on principles of universality and egalitarianism, and resulting in relatively equal income distributions and limited poverty.

The comparative empirical analysis of the generosity of unemployment insurance, sickness benefits and old-age pensions showed that in 1985 the net replacement rate for an average production worker was generally higher in the four Nordic countries of Denmark, Finland, Norway and Sweden than the average for 14 (non-Nordic) OECD countries, with the partial exception of Denmark. By 2010, the profile of the Nordic countries was less distinct. On the two old-age pension indicators, Finland and Sweden now scored lower than the average for the 14 OECD countries. Generally, with the exception of Norway, aggregate developments in benefit generosity over time revealed a strong tendency of convergence towards the OECD average. The Nordic welfare states have also been affected by welfare state retrenchment.

In other areas, Nordic distinctiveness has largely been maintained, with comprehensive social services offering free or heavily subsidised health care, old-age care and child care as well as free education from primary school to higher education, all financed through general taxation. Thanks to the extensive public services, public employment is higher than in other OECD countries. The level of female employment is also higher. The chapter showed that while the core social programmes, generally speaking, have become less generous since the so-called Golden Era of the early post-WWII decades, the provision of universal publicly financed services has been maintained and even expanded (e.g. child care, activation policies).

The chapter showed that some elements of the Nordic model have become less distinctive compared with other European welfare states over time, while other elements hold ground, such as extensive public responsibility for welfare broadly defined, principles of universalism and equality, and the emphasis on publicly financed and/or provided social services of various kinds. Core dimensions of the Nordic model persist, but in light of current pressures and challenges, the way forward is by no means given.

Christensen, Gornitzka and Holst argued in Chapter 10 that the Nordic countries have strong *knowledge systems*. According to a number of international indicators, the Nordic countries are among the most knowledge-intensive societies and economies in the world. They have some of the highest levels of educational attainment, and spend considerably more per capita on primary, secondary and tertiary education than the average for OECD countries. Education has been perceived as a public rather than a private good. Public authorities have played a prominent role not only in funding education accessible to all, but also in funding research at universities and research institutes.

Moreover, policy-making in the Nordic countries is characterised by *governing through knowledge*. Crucial in this respect is a well-educated civil service able to provide politicians with professional advice in the formulation and implementation of policies. This has been complemented by strong institutional mechanisms for examining societal problems and puzzling over policy solutions. In particular, *ad hoc* advisory commissions have facilitated the interaction of bureaucrats, academics and organised interests in the Nordic countries. The dominant roles of public institutions in the knowledge regime and the high degree of government control over policy advice are features that set the Nordic countries apart from other Western democracies where private actors play a more prominent role and where policy advice is provided by a broad range of competing actors.

There have, of course, been changes to Nordic knowledge regimes over time, including stronger competition among knowledge producers, performance management of schools and higher education institutions, and a stronger instrumentalisation of knowledge and higher education in order for the Nordic countries to enhance their position in globally competitive markets. Yet, the particular balance in favour of public responsibility over private investment has been a persistent feature of the Nordic knowledge regimes. The large and growing role of knowledge and expertise surely also comes with challenges, such as the increasing gap between the "knowledge elite" and those with less education. However, universal access to free public education and egalitarian income distributions make the Nordic countries comparatively well poised to address this challenge.

FINDINGS REGARDING ASPECTS OF THE NORDIC MODELS

In the introduction chapter several aspects of the use of the model concept were addressed. These were: 1) Is there one Nordic model or are there several? 2) What is the evidence of specific Nordic traits in a wider cross-national comparison? 3) Have the patterns in the Nordic countries (or elsewhere) changed such that the Nordic models are less distinctive? 4) Do we have any evidence of the roots of the Nordic models? The main findings regarding these aspects will be briefly examined here.

1. It is evident that there are several Nordic models and that the relationship between all of them is far from clear. The chapter on gender equality emphasised, however, how closely the the gender equality model and the Nordic welfare state model are intertwined. Gender equality is also incorporated into the Nordic welfare state model. The chapter on knowledge regimes underscored that knowledge institutions and knowledge policy are a part of Nordic models, and considered this the backbone of the post-war Nordic political and social models. However, as the authors of this chapter showed, the knowledge dimension is not included in the other relevant models and the authors argued that there are close relationships. The chapters on central political-administrative systems and local and regional governments underscored the close and trustful relationship that exists between the various levels, and pointed out that the relationship is characterised by autonomy.

2. Wider cross-national comparisons, which included comparisons with relevant (regional groups of) countries, were found in nearly all chapters. These comparisons generally documented a distinct Nordic model for central aspects addressed in the various chapters. *Generally, the Nordic models are still viable.*

3. As to the issue of changes over time, the empirical analyses in most of the chapters gave evidence of persistence, and also new forms of distinctiveness as illustrated in the chapter on social cleavages and value conflicts. It should, however, be underscored that not all chapters examined changes over time in a wider comparative setting.

The exceptions to this were first and foremost the following: a) the welfare state model, where the benefit generosity reveals a strong tendency to convergence with the OECD by the Nordic countries. On the other hand, Nordic distinctiveness has largely been maintained regarding comprehensive services; b) the decline of corporatism, which first and foremost implies that a distinctive trait in Nordic politics has evaporated; and c) the large decline in traditional class voting, indicating convergence towards traditional class voting levels in other (regional groups of) countries.

4. Regarding the roots of the Nordic models, the causes and timing were addressed in several chapters. Chapter 2 on the five-party system model underscored that this party system was completed during the 1920s, when the major social groups in Nordic industrial communities had been politically mobilised. The chapters on corporatism and the welfare state focused on the 1930s in particular as being decisive for the development of the distinctiveness of the Nordic models. The first decades after WWII were also indicated as having been decisive.

Other authors have also focused on the red-green class cooperation in the 1930s as decisive for the distinctiveness of some Nordic models. Underlying the institutional arrangements that characterise the Nordic models was a particular class compromise, initially between capital, labour and agrarian interests, and later the white collar salaried strata (Arter 2008b: 172–173).

REFERENCES

Aamodt, Per Olaf and Svein Kyvik (2005). "Access to higher education in the Nordic countries". In: Tapper, Ted and David Palfreyman (eds.). *Understanding Mass Higher Education. Comparative perspectives on access*. London: RoutledgeFalmer.

Aberbach, Joel D. and Tom Christensen (2014). "Why reforms so often fail". *American Review of Public Administration*, 44(1): 3–16.

Ahlbäck Öberg, Shirin and Helena Wockelberg (2016). "Nordic Administrative Heritages and Contemporary Institutional Design". In: Carsten Greve, Per Lægreid and Lise H. Rykkja (eds.). *Nordic Administrative Reforms. Lessons for Public Management*. London: Palgrave Macmillan.

Ahonen, Pertti (2013). "The context of public administration from a neo-institutionalist point of view: an analysis with Finland as the case." In: Christopher Pollitt (ed.). *Context in Public Policy and Management: The Missing Link*? Cheltenham: Edward Elgar.

Ahonen, Pertti (2016). "Holdings of national and local governments in companies in Finland: Persistence and change in the long term". *Annals of Public and Cooperative Economics*, 87(2): 257–74.

Albæk, Erik (1996). "Denmark". In: Albæk et al. *Nordic Local Government: Developmental Trends and Reform Activities in the Postwar Period*. Helsinki: The Association of Finnish Local Authorities.

Albæk, Erik, Lawrence Rose, Lars Strömberg & Krister Ståhlberg (1996). *Nordic Local Government: Developmental Trends and Reform Activities in the Postwar Period*. Helsinki: The Association of Finnish Local Authorities.

Alesina, Alberto and Edward Glaeser (2004). *Fighting Poverty in the US and Europe: A World of Difference*. Oxford: Oxford University Press.

Alestalo, Matti and Stein Kuhnle (1987). "The Scandinavian Route: Economic, Social, and Political Developments in Denmark, Finland, Norway, and Sweden". In: Robert Erikson et al. (eds). *The Scandinavian Model*. Armonk, NY: M.E.Sharpe, Inc.

Allardt, Erik and Pertti Pesonen (1967). "Cleavages in Finnish Politics". In: Seymour Martin Lipset and Stein Rokkan (eds.). *Party systems and voter alignments*. New York: The Free Press.

Allardt, Erik et al. (eds.) (1981). *Nordic Democracy*. Copenhagen: Det Danske Selskab.

Allern, Elin Haugsgjerd, Rune Karlsen and Hanne Marthe Narud (2014). "Stortingets sosiale sammensetning". In Hanne Marthe Narud, Knut Heidar and Tore Grønlie (eds.). *Stortingets historie 1964–2014*. Bergen: Fagbokforlaget.

Andersen, Jørgen Goul (1997). "The Scandinavian welfare model in crisis? Achievements and problems of the Danish welfare state in an age of unemployment and low growth". *Scandinavian Political Studies* 20(1): 1–31.

Andersen, Jørgen Goul and Tor Bjørklund (2000). "Radical right-wing populism in Scandinavia: from tax revolt to neo-liberalism and xenophobia". In: Paul Hainsworth (ed.): *The politics of the extreme right. From the margins to the mainstream*. London and New York: Pinter.

Andersen, Jørgen Goul and Jan Bendix Jensen (2001): "The Danish Venstre: Liberal, Agrarian or Centrist". In: David Arter (ed.). *From farmyard to city square? The electoral adaptation of the Nordic Agrarian parties*. Aldershot: Ashgate.

Anderson, Perry (1974). *Lineages of the Absolutist State* (London: NLB).

Anton, Thomas J. (1969). "Policy-Making and Political Culture in Sweden". *Scandinavian Political Studies*, 4(A4): 88–102.

Armstrong, Jo, & Sylvia Walby (2012). *Gender Quotas in Management Boards*. Note. Directorate-General for Internal Policies, Policy Department, Citizen's Rights and Constitutional Affairs. http://www.europarl.europa.eu/document/activities/cont/201202/20120216ATT38420/20120216ATT38420EN.pdf.

Arnesen, Daniel, Henrik Sivesind and Trygve Gulbrandsen (2016). *Fra medlemsbaserte organisasjoner til koordinert frivillighet? Det norske organisasjonssamfunnet fra 1980 til 2013*. Rapport 2016: 5. Oslo: Senter for forskning på sivilsamfunn og frivillig sektor.

Arreman, Inger Erixon and Ann-Sofie Holm (2011). "Privatisation of public education? The emergence of independent upper secondary schools in Sweden". *Journal of Education Policy*. 26(2).

Arter, David (ed.) (2001a). *From farmyard to city square? The electoral adaptation of the Nordic Agrarian parties*. Aldershot: Ashgate.

Arter, David (2001b). "The Finnish Centre Party: A case of successful transformation?". In: David Arter (ed.). *From farmyard to city square? The electoral adaptation of the Nordic Agrarian parties*. Aldershot: Ashgate.

Arter, David (2002). "'Communists we are no longer, Social Democrats we can never be': The Evolution of the Leftist Parties in Finland and Sweden". *Journal of Communist Studies and Transition Politics, 18*(3), 1–28.

Arter, David (2008a). "From 'parliamentary control' to 'accountable government'? The role of public committee hearings in the Swedish Riksdag". *Parliamentary Affairs, 61*(1), 122–143.

Arter, David (2008b). *Scandinavian Politics Today*. Second edition. Manchester and New York: Manchester University Press.

Arter, David (2010). "The breakthrough of another West European Radical Right party? The case of the True Finns". *Government and Opposition* 54: 484–504.

Arter, David (2012). "'Big Bang" elections and party system change in Scandinavia: Farewell to the 'enduring party system'". *Parliamentary Affairs* 65: 822–844.

Atkinson, Anthony B. (2015). *Inequality. What can be done*? Cambridge, MA:Harvard University Press.

Atkinson, Anthony B., Lee Rainwater, Timothy M. Smeeding (1995). *Income distribution in OECD countries. Evidence from the Luxembourg Income Study*. Paris: OECD.

Aylott, Nicholas (2011). "Parties and Party Systems in the North". In: Torbjörn Bergman and Kaare Strøm. (eds.). *The Madisonian Turn: Political Parties and Parliamentary Democracy in Nordic Europe*, Ann Arbor: The University of Michigan Press.

Bagge, Sverre (2015). "Borgerkrig og statsutvikling". *Historisk Tidsskrift*, 94: 91–110.

Baklien, Bergljot (1983). "The Use of Social Science in a Norwegian Ministry: As a Tool of Policy or Mode of Thinking?". *Acta Sociologica*, 26(1): 33–47.

Baldersheim, Harald & Krister Ståhlberg (eds.) (1994). *Towards the Self-Regulating Municipality: Free Communes and Administrative Modernization in Scandinavia*. Aldershot: Dartmouth.

Baldersheim, Harald & Lawrence E. Rose (eds.) (2010a). *Territorial Choice: The Politics of Boundaries and Borders*. Basingstoke: Palgrave Macmillan.

Baldersheim, Harald & Lawrence E. Rose (2010b). "The Staying Power of the Norwegian Periphery". In Harald Baldersheim & Lawrence E. Rose (eds). *Territorial Choice: The Politics of Boundaries and Borders*. Basingstoke: Palgrave Macmillan.

Baldersheim, Harald, Are Vegard Haug & Morten Øgård (eds.) (2011). *The Rise of the Networking Region: The Challenges of Regional Collaboration in a Globalized World*. Farnham, Surrey: Ashgate.

Baldersheim, Harald & Lawrence E. Rose (2011). "The Decline of Subnational Democracy?" In: John Loughlin, Frank Hendriks & Anders Lidström (eds.). *The Oxford Handbook of Local and Regional Democracy in Europe*. Oxford: Oxford University Press.

Baldwin, Peter (1990). *The politics of solidarity*. Cambridge: Cambridge University Press.

Bart, Erling, Ines Hardoy, Pål Schøṇe & Kjersti Misje Østbakken (2014). "Hva betyr høy yrkesdeltakelse for kjønnssegregering?" In: Reisel, L. & Mari Teigen (eds.). *Kjønnsdeling og etniske skillelinjer på arbeidsmarkedet*. Oslo: Gyldendal Akademisk.

Barth, Erling, Kalle Moene and Fredrik Willumsen (2014). "The Scandinavian model – An interpretation". *Journal of Public Economics* 117: 60–72.

Barton, H. Arnold (2006). "Finland and Norway, 1808–1917". *Scandinavian Journal of History*, 31 (3-4): 221–236).

Bäck, Hanna and Torbjörn Bergman (2015). "The Parties in Government Formation". In: Jon Pierre (ed.). *The Oxford Handbook of Swedish Politics*, Oxford: Oxford University Press.

Bengtsson, Åsa, Kasper M. Hansen, Ólafur Þ. Harðarson, Hanne Marthe Narud and Henrik Oscarsson (2014). *The Nordic Voter. Myths of Exceptionalism*. Colchester: ECPR Press.

Benoit, Kenneth and Michael Laver (2006). *Party policy in modern democracies*. London and New York: Routledge.

Berg, Roald (2014). "Denmark, Norway and Sweden in 1814: a geopolitical and contemporary perspective". *Scandinavian Journal of History*, 39(3): 265–286.

Bergh, Johannes, Dag Arne Christensen & Richard E. Matland (2016). *Getting out the vote: Experiments in voter mobilization among immigrants and natives in Norway*. Report 2016: 12. Oslo: Institute of Social Research.

Berglund, Sten and Ulf Lindström (1978). *The Scandinavian Party system(s)*. Lund: Studentlitteratur.

Bergman, Torbjörn (2004). "Sweden: Democratic Reforms and Partisan Decline in an Emerging Separation-of-Powers System". *Scandinavian Political Studies* 27:203–225.

Bergman, Torbjörn and Kaare Strøm (2011). "Nordic Europe in Comparative Perspective". In: Torbjörn Bergman and Kaare Strøm (eds.) *The Madisonian Turn: Political Parties and Parliamentary Democracy in Nordic Europe*. Ann Arbor: The University of Michigan Press.

Bergqvist, Christina et al. (eds.) (1999). *Equal Democracies: Gender and Politics in the Nordic Countries*. Oslo: Scandinavian University Press.

Bettio, Francesca & Alina Verashchagina (2009). *Frontiers in the economics of gender*. London: Routledge.

Binderkrantz, Anne Skorkjær, Peter Munk Christiansen and Helene Helboe Pedersen (2014). *Organisationer i politik. Danske interesseorganisationer i forvaltning, Folketing og medier*. København: Hans Reitzel.

Binderkrantz, Anne Skorkjær, and Peter Munk Christiansen (2015). "From classic to modern corporatism. Interest group representation in Danish public committees in 1975 and 2010". *Journal of European Public Policy*, 22 (7): 1022–1039.

Binderkrantz, Anne Skorkjær, Peter Munk Christiansen and Helene Helboe Pedersen (2015). "Interest Group Access to the Bureaucracy, Parliament, and the Media". *Governance*, 28 (1), 95–112.

Binderkrantz, Anne Skorkjær, Helene Marie Fisker and Helene Helboe Pedersen (2016). "The Rise of Citizen Groups? The Mobilization and Representation of Danish Interest Groups, 1975–2010". *Scandinavian Political Studies*, 39 (4): 291–311.

Birkelund, Gunn-Elisabeth & Torun Sandnes (2003). "Paradoxes of Welfare States and Equal Opportunities: Gender and Managerial Power in Norway and the USA". *Comparative Social Research*, 21: 203–242.

Blom-Hansen, Jens (2000). "Still Corporatism in Scandinavia? A Survey of Recent Findings". *Scandinavian Political Studies*, 23 (2): 157–181.

Blom-Hansen, Jens, and Carsten Daugbjerg (eds.) (1999). *Magtens organisering: Stat og interesseorganisationer i Danmark*. Herning: Systime.

Blom-Hansen, Jens & Anne Heeager (2011). "Denmark: Between Local Democracy and Implementing Agency of the Welfare State". In: John Loughlin, Frank Hendriks and Anders Lidström (eds.). *The Oxford Handbook of Local and Regional Democracy in Europe*. Oxford: Oxford University Press.

Blyth, M. (2001). "The Transformation of the Swedish Model: Economic Ideas, Distributional Conflict, and Institutional Change". *World Politics, 54*(1): 1–26.

Bolin, Niklas (2016). "Green parties in Finland and Sweden. Successful cases of the north". In: Emilie van Haute (ed.). *Green parties in Europe*. London and New York: Routledge.

Borchorst, Anette (2008): "Woman-friendly policy paradoxes? Childcare policies and gender equality visions in Scandinavia". In: Kari Melby, Anne-Birte Ravn & Christina. C. Wetterberg (eds.). *Gender equality and welfare politics in Scandinavia: The limits of political ambition*, Bristol: Policy Press.

Borchorst, Anette, Lenita Freidenvall, Johanna Kantola, Liza Reisel, & Mari Teigen (2012). "Institutionalizing Intersectionality in the Nordic Countries? Anti-Discrimination and Equality in Denmark, Finland, Norway and Sweden". In: Andrea Krizsan, Hege Skjeie & Judith Squires (eds.). *Institutionalizing Intersectionality? The Changing Nature of European Equality Regimes*. Basingstoke: Palgrave Macmillan

Borchorst, Anette & Mari Teigen 2010. "Political intersectionality: Tackling inequalities in public policies in Scandinavia". *Kvinder, kön og forskning*, 2010(2): 19–28.

Borchorst, Anette & Mari Teigen (2015). "Gleichstellungspolitik in Nordeuropa – Quotenregelungen für Eltern und Führungskräfte". *WSI-Mitteilungen* 1: 35–42.

Bo Smith-utvalget (2015). *Embedsmanden i det modern folkestyre*. Copenhagen: Jurist- og Økonomforbundets Forlag.

Boston, Jonathan, John Martin, June Pallot and Pat Walsh (1996). *Public Management: The New Zealand Model*. Auckland: Oxford University Press.

Bouget, Dennis et al. (2015). *Social Investment in Europe: A study of national policies*. An ESPN synthesis report. Brussels: European Commission.

Bouget, Dennis et al. (2016). *Work-life balance measures for persons of working age with dependent relatives in Europe. A study of national policies*. An ESPN synthesis report. Brussels: European Commission.

Bovens, Mark and Anchrit Wille (2009). *Diploma democracy: On the Tensions between Meritocracy and Democracy*, Utrecht/Leiden: Netherlands Organisation for Scientific Research.

Brochmann, G. and A. Hagelund (2011). "Migrants in the Scandinavian Welfare State. The emergence of a social policy problem". *Nordic Journal of Migration -Research*, 1 (1): 13–24.

Brunsson, Nils (1989). *The Organization of Hypocrisy. Talk, Decisions and Actions in Organizations*. Chichester: Wiley.

Buck, Marcus, Helge O. Larsen & Tord Willumsen (2006). *Når folket får velge. Forsøkene med direkte valg av ordfører som deltakelses- og styringsform*. Oslo: Kommuneforlaget.

Budge, Ian, Hans-Dieter Klingemann, Andrea Volkens, Judith Bara and Erik Tanenbaum (2001). *Mapping Policy Preferences: Estimates for Parties, Electors, and Governments 1945–1998*. Oxford: Oxford University Press.

Busemeyer, Marius R and Torben Iversen (2012). "Collective skill systems, wage bargaining, and labor market stratification". In: Busemeyer, Marius. R. and Christine Trampusch (eds.). *The Political Economy of Collective Skill Formation*. Oxford: Oxford University Press.

Byrkjeflot, Haldor, Tom Christensen and Per Lægreid (2014). "The Many Faces of Accountability: Comparing Reforms in Welfare, Hospitals and Migration". *Scandinavian Political Studies*, 37(2): 171–95.

Calmfors Lars (1995). "Labour market policy and unemployment". *European Economic* Review 39.

Campbell, John L. and Ove K. Pedersen (2014). *The national origins of policy ideas: Knowledge regimes in the United States, France, Germany, and Denmark*, Princeton and Oxford: Princeton University Press.

Caramani, Daniele (2004). *The nationalization of politics: The formation of national electorates and party systems in Western Europe*. Cambridge: Cambridge University Press.

Castles, Francis and Deborah Mitchell (1991). Three worlds of welfare capitalism or four? (Working Paper). Luxembourg: Luxembourg Income Studies.

Chafetz, Jant Saltzman & Jacqueline Hagen (1996). "The gender division of labour and family change in industrial societies". *Journal of Comparative Family Studies*, 27: 187–219.

Childs, Marquis (1936). *Sweden: The Middle Way*. New Haven: Yale University Press.

Christensen, Johan (2017). *The Power of Economists within the State*. Stanford CA: Stanford University Press.

Christensen, Johan (n.d.). "The Growing Reliance on Academic Economic Knowledge in Hybrid Advisory Commissions". *Working Paper*.

Christensen, Johan and Cathrine Holst (n.d.). "Advisory Commissions, Academic Expertise and Democratic Legitimacy: The Case of Norway". *Working paper*.

Christensen, Jørgen Grønnegård, Poul Erik Mouritzen and Asbjørn Sonne Nørgaard (eds.). (2009). *De store kommissioner: Vise mænd, smagsdommere eller nyttige idioter*. Odense: University Press of Southern Denmark.

Christensen, Tom (2003). "Narrative of Norwegian Governance: Elaborating the Strong State". *Public Administration*, 81(1):163–90.

Christensen, Tom, Morten Egeberg, Per Lægreid and Jacob Aars (2014). *Politikk og forvaltning*. Oslo: University Press.

Christensen, Tom, Åse Gornitzka and Peter Maassen (2014). "Global Pressures and National Cultures: A Nordic University Template?". In: *University Adaptation in Difficult Economic Times*: Oxford University Press.

Christensen, Tom and Per Lægreid (2001). *New Public Management. The Transformation of Ideas and Practice*. Aldershot: Ashgate.

Christensen, Tom and Per Lægreid (2003). "Coping with Complex Leadership Roles: The Problematic Redefinition of Government-Owned Enterprises". *Public Administration*, 81(4): 803–31.

Christensen, Tom and Per Lægreid (2007). "The Whole-of-Government Approach to Public Sector Reform". *Public Administration Review*, 67(6): 1057–1064.

Christensen, Tom and Per Lægreid (2012). "Administrative Reforms in Western Countries". In: Brainard Guy Peters and Jon Pierre (eds.). *The SAGE Handbook of Public Administration*. London: Sage.

Christensen, Tom, Per Lægreid, Paul G. Roness and Kjell A. Røvik (2015). *Organization Theory and the Public Sector. Instrument, Culture and Myth*. London and New York: Routledge.

Christensen, Tom, Per Lægreid and Lois R. Wise (2002). "Transforming Administrative Policy. *Public Administration*, 80(1): 153–78.

Christensen, Tom, Per Lægreid and Hans Robert Zuna (2001). *Profesjoner i regjeringsapparatet 1976–1996. Økende heterogenitet – effekter og implikasjoner*. Oslo: Makt- og demokratiutrednings rapportserie, University of Oslo.

Christiansen, Flemming Juul, and Erik Damgaard (2008). "Parliamentary opposition under minority parliamentarism: Scandinavia". *Journal of Legislative Studies*, 14 (1/2): 46–76.

Christiansen, Niels Finn et al. (eds.) (2006). *The Nordic Model of Welfare. A Historical Appraisal*. Copenhagen: Museum Tusculanum Press.

Christiansen, Peter Munk (forthcoming). "The Corporatist Darlings". In: Peter Nedergaard and Anders Wivel (eds.). *Routledge Handbook on Scandinavian Politics*. London and New York: Routledge.

Christiansen, Peter Munk and Hilmar Rommetvedt (1999). "From Corporatism to Lobbyism? Parliaments, Executives, and Organized Interests in Denmark and Norway". *Scandinavian Political Studies*, 22 (3): 195–220.

Christiansen, Peter Munk and Asbjørn Sonne Nørgaard (2003). *Faste forhold – flygtige forbindelser. Stat og interesseorganisationer i Danmark i det 20. århundrede*. Aarhus: Aarhus Universitetsforlag.

Christiansen, Peter Munk, Asbjørn Sonne Nørgaard and Nils Chr. Sidenius (2004). *Hvem skriver lovene? Interesseorganisationer og politiske beslutninger*. Aarhus: Aarhus Universitetsforlag.

Christiansen, Peter Munk, Asbjørn Sonne Nørgaard, Hilmar Rommetvedt, Torsten Svensson, Gunnar Thesen and PerOla Öberg (2010). "Varieties of Democracy: Interest Groups and Corporatist Committees in Scandinavian Policy Making". *VOLUNTAS: International Journal of Voluntary and Nonprofit Organizations*, 21(1): 22–40.

Clasen, Jochen and Daniel Clegg (2006). "Beyond activation: reforming European unemployment protection systems in post-industrial labour markets". *European Societies* 8(4): 527–553.

Classen, Ernest (1937). *The Northern Countries in World Economy: Denmark, Finland, Iceland, Norway, Sweden*. Published by the Delegations for the Promotion of Economic Co-operation between the Northern Countries. Otava.

Council of Europe; Congress of Local and Regional Authorities (2010). *Local Democracy in Iceland*. 18th SESSION CPL(18)3, 2nd March 2010 (Chamber of Local Authorities).

Craft, Jonathan and John Halligan (2016). "Assessing 30 years of Westminster policy advisory system experience". *Policy Sciences* 1–16.

Crombez, Christophe (1996). "Minority Governments, Minimal Winning Coalitions and Surplus Majorities in Parliamentary Systems". *European Journal of Political Research* 29:1–29.

Dahl, Robert A. & Edward R. Tufte (1973). *Size and Democracy*. Stanford: Stanford University Press.

Dahlerup, Drude (2011). "Women in Nordic Politics – A continuing Success Story?" In: Niskanen, K. (ed.). *Gender and Power in the Nordic Countries*. Nordic Gender Institute, NIKK Publications 2011: 1. Oslo.

Dahlström, Carl, Victor Lapuente and Jan Teorell (2011). "The merit of meritocratization: Politics, bureaucracy, and the institutional deterrents of corruption". *Political Research Quarterly*, 65(3): 656–668.

Dalton, Russell J. (2009). "Economics, environmentalism and party alignments". *European Journal of Political Research* 48: 161–175.

Dalton, Russell J., Scott C. Flanagan and Paul Allen Beck (1984). "Political forces and partisan change". In: Russell J. Dalton, Scott C. Flanagan and Paul Allen Beck (eds.). *Electoral Change in Advanced Industrial Democracies*. Princeton, N.J.: Princeton University Press.

Daly, Mary (2000). *The gender division of welfare: The impact of the British and German welfare states*. Cambridge: Cambridge University Press.

Damgaard, Erik (ed.) (1990). *Parlamentarisk forandring i Norden*. Oslo: Universitetsforlaget.

Damgaard, Erik (ed.) (1992). *Parliamentary Change in the Nordic Countries*. Oslo: Scandinavian University Press.

Damgaard, Erik (1994). "The Strong Parliaments of Scandinavia: Continuity and Change of Scandinavian Parliaments". In: Gary W. Copeland and Samuel C. Patterson (eds). *Parliaments in the Modern World: Changing Institutions*. Ann Arbor: The University of Michigan Press.

Damgaard, Erik (2000). "Parliament and Government". In: Peter Esaiasson and Knut Heidar (eds.). *Beyond Westminster and Congress: The Nordic Government*. Columbus: Ohio State University Press.

Damgaard, Erik (2004). "Developments in Danish Parliamentary Democracy: Accountability, Parties and External Constraints". *Scandinavian Political Studies* 27:115–131.

Damgaard, Erik (2008). "Cabinet Termination". In: Kaare Strøm, Wolfgang C. Müller and Torbjörn Bergman (eds.). *Cabinets and Coalition Bargaining: The Democratic Life Cycle in Western Europe*. Oxford: Oxford University Press.

Dandoy, Régis & Arian H. Schakel, eds. (2013). *Regional and National Elections in Western Europe: Territoriality of the Vote in Thirteen Countries*. Basingstoke: Palgrave Macmillan.

Davis, Kathy (2008). "Intersectionalty as 'buzzword'". Feminist Theory, 9(1): 67–85.

Delhey, Jan & Kenneth Newton (2005). "Predicting Cross-National Levels of Social Trust: Global Patterns or Nordic Exceptionalism?" *European Sociological Review* 21(4): 311–327.

Denters, Bas (2002). "Size and Political Trust: Evidence from Denmark, the Netherlands, Norway, and the United Kingdom". *Environment and Planning C: Government and Policy* 20 (6):793–812.

Denters, Bas, Michael Goldsmith, Andreas Ladner, Poul Erik Mouritzen & Lawrence E. Rose (2014). *Size and Local Democracy*. Cheltenham, UK: Edward Elgar.

Direktiv 2015: 77 *Ny indelning av län och landsting*. Stockholm: Swedish Government.

Döring, Herbert (1995). "Time as a Scarce Resource: Government Control of the Agenda". In: Herbert Döring (ed.). *Parliaments and Majority Rule in Western Europe*. Frankfurt/New York: Campus Verlag/St. Martin's Press.

Drori, Gili S., John w. Meyer, Francisco O. Ramirez and Evan Schofer (2003). *Science in the Modern World Polity: Institutionalization and Globalization*. Standford: Stanford University Press.

Dunn, Delmer (1997). *Politics and Administration at the Top: Lessons from Down Under*. Pittsburgh: University of Pittsburgh Press.

Dølvik, Jon Erik and Torgeir A. Stokke (1998). "The revival of centralised concertation". In: A. Ferner & R. Hyman (eds.). *Changing industrial relations in Europe* (2nd ed.). Hoboken, NJ: Wiley.

Egeberg, Morten, Johan P. Olsen and Harald Sætren (1978): "Organisasjonssamfunnet og den segmenterte stat". In: Johan P. Olsen (ed.). *Politisk organisering*. Oslo: Universitetsforlaget

Egeberg, Morten (1981). *Stat og organisasjoner: flertallsstyre, partsstyre og byråkrati i norsk politikk*, Oslo: Universitetsforlaget.

Egeberg, Morten (2012). "How Bureaucratic Structure Matters: An Organizational Perspective". In: Brainard Guy Peters and Jon Pierre (eds.). *The SAGE Handbook of Public Administration*. London: Sage.

Egilsson, Vilhjálmur (2012). *"The Icelandic Neo-corporative Model"*. Power Point presentation. SA – Business Iceland.

Elder, Neil, Alistair H. Thomas and David Arter (1982). *The Consensual Democracies? The Government and Politics of the Scandinavian States*. Oxford: Martin Robertson.

Elklit, Jørgen (1984). "Det klassiske danske partisystem bliver til". In: Jørgen Elklit and Ole Tonsgaard (eds.). *Valg og vælgeradfærd. Studier i dansk politik*. Århus: Politica.

Ellingsæter, Anne-Lise (2014). "Nordic Earner-Carer Models – Why Stability and Instability?". *Journal of Social Policy*, 43(3): 555–574.

Ellingsæter, Anne-Lise & Arnlaug Leira (2006). *Politicising Parenthood in Scandinavia: Gender Relations in Welfare States*. Bristol: The Policy Press.

Engelstad, Fredrik & Anniken Hagelund (2015). *Cooperation and conflict the Nordic way: work, welfare and institutional change in Scandinavia*. Berlin: De Gruyter.

Erikson, Robert and John H. Goldthorpe (1992). *The constant flux. A study of class mobility in industrial societies*. Oxford: Clarendon Press.

Erikson, Robert et al. (eds.) (1987). *The Scandinavian Model. Welfare States and -Welfare Research*. Armonk, New York: M.E. Sharpe, Inc.

Espeli, Harald (1999). *Lobbyvirksomhet på Stortinget*. Oslo: Tano-Aschehoug.

Esping-Andersen, Gøsta (1985). *Politics against markets. The social democratic road to power*. Princeton: Princeton University Press.

Esping-Andersen, Gøsta (1990). *The Three Worlds of Welfare Capitalism*. Cambridge: Polity Press.

Esping-Andersen, Gøsta (1999). *Social Foundation of Postindustrial Economies*. Oxford: Oxford University Press.

Esping-Andersen, Gøsta (2009). *The Incomplete Revolution*. Cambridge: Polity Press.

Esping-Andersen, Gøsta and Walter Korpi (1987). "From poor relief to institutional welfare state: The development of Scandinavian social policy". *The Scandinavian model*, Robert Erikson et al. Armonk, N.Y.: M.E. Sharpe.

European Commission (2015). *The 2015 Pension Adequacy Report: Current and future income adequacy in old age in the EU*. Brussels: European Commission.

Eythórsson, Einar (2000). "A decade of ITQ-management in Icelandic fisheries: consolidation without consensus". *Marine Policy*, 24: 483–492.

Eyþórsson, Grétar Þór (2009). "Municipal Amalgamations in Iceland: Past, Present and Future". In: Godfrey Baldacchino, Rob Greenwood & Lawrence Felt (eds.). *Remote Control: Lessons For and From Small, Insular, and Remote Regions*. St. John's, Nfld: ISER Books.

Eyþórsson, Grétar Þór (2015). "Is tiny really so beautiful? Is small really so ugly? Local democracy in Faroe Islands, Greenland and Iceland". Paper presented at NORKOM 2015, Göteborg, Sweden, 26–28 November 2015. Akureyri: University of Akureyri.

Eyþórsson, Grétar Þór & Marcin Kowalczyk (2013). "Explaining the low voter turnout in Iceland's 2010 local government elections". *Samtíð* 1 (2).

Eyþórsson, Grétar Þór & Eva H. Önnudóttir (2016). Abstainers' reasoning for not voting: The Icelandic Local Government Election 2014. Draft manuscript. Akureyri: University of Akureyri.

Fagan, Colette, Maria C. Gonzalez Menendez & Silvia Gomez Ansón (2012). *Women on Corporate Boards and in Top Management. European Trends and Policy*. London: Palgrave.

Farsund, Arild Aurvåg (2004). *Stabilitet og endring i norsk landbrukspolitikk: En studie av parlamentariske beslutninger og korporative forhandlinger*. RF-rapport 2004/072. Stavanger: Rogalandsforskning.

Field, Bonnie N. (2016). *Why Minority Governments Work: Multilevel Territorial Politics in Spain*. New York: Palgrave Macmillan.

Finnish Government (2016). *Regeringens proposition till riksdagen med förslag till landskapsreform och reform av ordnandet av social- och hälsovården samt till lagar som har samband med dem* 14.9.2016

Fischer, Frank (2009). *Democracy and expertise: Reorienting policy inquiry*. Oxford: Oxford University Press.

Fisker, Helene Marie (2015). *Studies on the Development of Interest Group Populations in Corporative Systems*. PhD Dissertation, Aarhus University. Aarhus: Politica.

Fitzgerald, Jennifer & Jennifer Wolak (2016). "The Roots of Trust in Local Government in Western Europe". *International Political Science Review*, 37 (1): 130–146.

Flanagan, Scott C. (1987). "Value change in industrial societies". *American Political Science Review* 81: 1289–1319.

Flanagan, Scott C. and Aie-Rie Lee (2003). "The new politics, culture wars, and the authoritarian-libertarian value change in advanced industrial democracies". *Comparative Political Studies* 36: 235–270.

Flora, Peter (1996). "Introduction". In: Peter Flora (ed.) *Growth to Limits: The Western European Welfare States Since World War II*, vol. 1. Berlin: Walter de Gruyter.

Flora, Peter and Jens Alber (1981). "Modernization, democratization, and the development of welfare states in Western Europe". In: Peter Flora and Arnold J. Heidenheimer (eds.). *The Development of Welfare States in Europe and America*. New Brunswick, NJ: Transaction Books.

Fobé, Ellen, Marleen Brans, Diederik Vancoppenolle and Jan Van Damme (2013). "Institutionalized advisory systems: An analysis of member satisfaction of advice production and use across 9 strategic advisory councils in Flanders (Belgium)". *Policy and Society*, 32(3): 225–240.

Foss Hansen, Hanne (1999). «Den historiske arven – Danmark». In: Per Lægreid and Ove Kaj Pedersen (eds.). *Fra opbygning til ombygning av staten.Organisationsforandringer i tre nordiske lande*. Copenhagen: Jurist- og Økonomforbundets Forlag.

Franklin, Mark N., Thomas T. Mackie, Henry Valen et al. (1992). *Electoral Change: Responses to Evolving Social and Attitudinal Structures in Western Countries*. Cambridge: Cambridge University Press.

Fraser, Nancy (1997). *Justice Interruptus. Critical Reflections on the "Postcolonial" Condition*. New York & London: Routledge.

Freidenvall, Lenita, Drude Dahlerup & Hege Skjeie (2006). *Women, quotas and politics*. London: Routledge.

Freidenvall, Lenita & H. Hallonsten (2013). "Why not corporate gender quotas in Sweden?". *Representation: Journal of Representative Democracy*. 49(4): 467–485.

Fritzell, Johan and Olle Lundberg (2005). "Fighting Inequalities in Health and Income: One Important Road to Welfare and Social Development". In: Olli Kangas and Joakim Palme (eds.). *Social Policy and Economic Development in the Nordic Countries*. London: Palgrave/Macmillan.

Gabriel, Oscar W. and Silke I. Keil (2014). "Introduction: Society and democracy in Europe". In: Silke I. Keil and Oscar W. Gabriel (eds). *Society and democracy in Europe*. London and New York: Routledge.

Ganghof, Steffen (2006). "Tax mixes and the size of the welfare state: causal mechanisms and policy implications". *Journal of European Social Policy*, 16(4): 360–373.

Garsten, Christina, Bo Rothstein and Stefan Svallfors (2015). *Makt utan mandat: De policyprofessionella i svensk politik*. Stockholm: Dialogos Förlag.

Geissel, Brigitte (2009). "How to Improve the Quality of Democracy? Experiences with Participatory Innovations at the Local Level in Germany". *German Politics and Society*, 27 (4): 51–71.

Geissel, Brigitte & Kenneth Newton eds. (2012). *Evaluating Democratic Innovations: Curing the Democratic Malaise*? Abington: Routledge.

George, Alexander L. and Andrew Bennett (2005). *Case studies and theory development in the social sciences*. Cambridge, Mass: MIT Press.

Gibbons, Michael (1999). "Science' New Social Contract with Society", *Nature* (402): 81–84.

Goldsmith, Michael J. & Edward C. Page (2010). *Changing Government Relations in Europe: From Localism to Intergovernmentalism*. London: Routledge.

Goldthorpe, John H. (1980). *Social mobility and class structure in modern Britain*. Oxford: Clarendon Press.

Gornitzka, Åse (2003). *Science, clients, and the state: a study of scientific knowledge production and use*. Enschede: CHEPS.

Gornitzka, Åse and Peter Maassen (2007). "An instrument for national political agendas: the hierarchical vision". In: in Maassen, Peter and Johan P. Olsen (eds.). *University dynamics and European integration*. Dordrecht: Springer.

Graubart, Stephen Richards (1986), *Norden. The Passion for Equality*. Oslo: Scandinavian University Press.

Green-Pedersen, Christoffer (2002). "New Public Management Reforms of the Danish and Swedish Welfare States: The Role of Different Social Democratic Responses". *Governance, 15*(2): 271–294.

Greve, Bent (2016). "The Politics of Occupational Welfare". In: Jonathan Murray (ed.). *Labor Markets: analysis, regulations and outcomes*. Nova Science Publishers, Incorporated.

Greve, Carsten and Niels Ejersbo (2016). "Reform Context and Status". In: Carsten Greve, Per Lægreid and Lise Hellebø Rykkja (eds.). *Nordic Administrative Reforms. Lessons for Public Management*. London: Palgrave Macmillan.

Greve, Carsten, Per Lægreid and Lise Hellebø Rykkja (eds.) (2016). *Nordic Administrative Reforms. Lessons for Public Management*. London: Palgrave Macmillan.

Grimsmo, Anders & Jon Magnussen (2015). *Norsk samhandlingsreform i et internasjonalt perspektiv*. Oslo: Forskningsrådet.

Gruber, Jonathan and David A. Wise (eds.) (1999). *Social security and retirement around the world*. Chicago: The University of Chicago Press.

Grønlie, Tore (1991). "Velferdskommunen". In: Anne-Hilde Nagel (ed.). *Velferdskommunen: Kommunenes rolle i utvikling av velferdsstaten*. Bergen: Alma Mater Forlag.

Grønlie, Tore (2014). «Til forsvar for folkestyret». In: Hanne Marthe Narud, Knut Heidar and Tore Grønlie (eds.). *Stortingets historie 1964–2014*. Bergen: Fagbokforlaget.

Gulick, Luther (1937). "Notes on the Theory on Organizations. With Special Reference to Government". In: Luther Gulick and Lyndall Urwin (eds.). *Papers on the Science of Administration*. New York: A. M. Kelley.

Haas, Peter M. (1992). "Introduction: Epistemic Communities and International Policy Co-ordination". *International Organization*, 46(1): 1–35.

Habermas, Jürgen (1994). "Citizenship and National Identity". In: Bart van Steenbergen (ed.). *The Condition of Citizenship*. London: Sage Publications.

Hagevi, Magnus (2000). "Nordic light on committee assignments". In: Peter Esaiasson and Knut Heidar (eds.). *Beyond Westminster and Congress: The Nordic Experience*. Columbus: Ohio State University Press.

Hainmueller, Jens and Michael J. Hiscox (2007). "Educated preferences: Explaining attitudes towards immigration in Europe". *International Organisation* 61: 399–442.

Hálfdanarson, Gudmundur (2000). "Iceland: A Peaceful Secession". *Scandinavian Journal of History*, 25(1-2): 87–100.

Hálfdanarson, Gudmundur (2006). "Severing the ties – Iceland's Journey from a Union with Denmark to a Nation-State". *Scandinavian Journal of History*, 31(3-4): 237–254.

Hallenstvedt, Abraham and Jan Trollvik (eds.) (1993). *Norske organisasjoner*. Oslo: Fabritius.

Halman, Loek and Ruud de Moor (1994). "Religion, churches and moral values". In: Peter Ester, Loek Halmann and Ruud de Moor (eds.). *The individualizing society: Value change in Europe and North America*. Tilburg: Tilburg University Press.

Halrynjo, Sigtona & Ragni Hege Kitterød (2016). *Deling av foreldrepermisjon: konsekvenser for arbeid, familietilpasning og velferd i Norge og Norden*. 2016: 07, Oslo: Institute for Social Research.

Hansen, Morten Balle, Per Lægreid, Jon Pierre and Ari Salminen (2012). "Comparing agencification". In: Koen Verhoest, Sandra Van Thiel, Geert Bouckaert and Per Lægreid (eds.). *Government Agencies – Practices and Lessons from 30 Countries*. Basingstoke: Palgrave Macmillan.

Hardarson, Olafur Th. (1995). *Parties & Voters in Iceland. A Study of the 1983 and 1987 Althingi Elections*. Reykjavik: Social Science Research Institute.

Hardarson, Olafur Th. and Gunnar Helgi Kristinsson (1987). "The Icelandic Parliamentary Election of 1987". *Electoral Studies* 6: 219–234.

Hardarson, Olafur Th. and Gunnar Helgi Kristinsson (2001). "The 1999 Parliamentary Election in Iceland". *Electoral Studies* 20: 325–330.

Heclo, Hugh (1974). *Social policy in Britain and Sweden: From Relief to Income Maintenance*, Yale University Press.

Heidar, Knut (2000). "Parliamentary Party Groups". In: Peter Esaiasson and Knut Heidar (eds.) *Beyond Westminster and Congress: The Nordic Experience*. Columbus: Ohio State University Press.

Heidar, Knut (2004a). "Parties and party systems". In: Knut Heidar (ed.). *Nordic Politics. Comparative perspectives*. Oslo: Universitetsforlaget.

Heidar, Knut (ed.) (2004b). *Nordic Politics: Comparative Perspectives*. Oslo: Universitetsforlaget.

Heidar, Knut (2014a). "Partiene – fra aristokratiske diskusjonsklubber til populistiske meningsbyråer?" In: Harald Baldersheim and Øyvind Østerud (eds.) *Det norske demokratiet i det 21. århundre*. Bergen: Fagbokforlaget.

Heidar, Knut (2014b). "Partigruppene: samordnings og maktarena". In: Hanne Marthe Narud, Knut Heidar and Tore Grønlie (eds.). *Stortingets historie 1964–2014*. Bergen: Fagbokforlaget.

Heidenreich, Vibeke (2012). "Why Gender Quotas in Company Boards in Norway – and not in Sweden?" In: Fredrik Engelstad and Mari Teigen (eds.). *Firms, Boards and Gender Quotas: Comparative Perspectives*. Comparative Social Research, Bingley: Emerald.

Helander, Voitto (1997). "Under byråkraternas allsmäktiga beskydd". In: Voitto Helander and Siv Sandberg (eds.). *Festskrift till Krister Ståhlberg*. Åbo: Åbo Akademi University Press.

Herman, Valentine and John Pope (1973). "Minority Governments in Western Democracies". *British Journal of Political Science* 3:191–212.

Hermansson, Jörgen (1993). *Politik som interessekamp. Parlamentariskt beslutsfattande och organiserade intressen i Sverige*. Stockholm: Norstedts.

Hermansson, Jörgen, Anna Lund, Torsten Svensson and PerOla Öberg (1999). *Avkorporativisering och lobbyism*. Demokratiutredningens forskarvolym XIII. SOU 1999: 121.

Hermansson, Jörgen, Torsten Svensson and PerOla Öberg (1997). «Hvor ble det av den svenska korporatismen?', *Politica*, 29(4): 365–384.

Hernes, Gudmund (1983). *Det moderne Norge 5. Makt og styring*. Oslo: Gyldendal.

Hernes, Helga (1987). *Welfare State and Woman Power: Essays in State Feminism*. Oslo: Norwegian University Press.

Hilson, Mary (2008). *The Nordic Model. Scandinavia since 1945*. London: Reaktion Books.

Hippe, Jon M. and Axel West Pedersen (1996). "Labor Movement, Social Policy, and Occupational Welfare in Norway". In: Shalev, Michael (ed.). *The Privatization of Social Policy? Occupational Welfare and the Welfare State in America, Scandinavia and Japan*. London: Macmillan.

Holli, Anne Maria (2016). "Selvityshenkilöt uudella vuosituhannella". *Hallinnon Tutkimus*, 35(1), 5–23.

Holmberg, Sören (2000). "Issue Agreement". In: Peter Esaiasson and Knut Heidar (eds.). *Beyond Westminster and Congress: The Nordic Experience*. Columbus: Ohio State University Press.

Hood, Christopher (1996). "Exploring Variations in Public Management Reform of the 1980s". In: Hans A. G. M. Bekke, James. L. Perry and Theo. A. J. Toonen (eds.). *Civil Service Systems*. Bloomington: Indiana University Press.

Hovdhaugen, Elisabeth (2013). *Widening Participation in Norwegian Higher Education*. Leicester: CFE and HEFCE.

Høyland, Bjørn, Karl Moene and Fredrik Willumsen (2012). "The tyranny of international index rankings". *Journal of Development Economics*, 97(1): 1–14.

Indridason, Indridi H. (2005). "A theory of coalitions and clientelism: Coalition politics in Iceland, 1945–2000". *European Journal of Political Research* 44: 439–464.

Ingimundarson, Valur (2012). "Britain, the United States and the Militarization of Iceland 1945–1951". *Scandinavian Journal of History*, 37(2): 198–220.

Inglehart, Ronald (1977). *The Silent Revolution – Changing Values and Political Styles among Western Publics*. Princeton, N.J.: Princeton University Press.

Inglehart, Ronald (1990). *Cultural Shift in Advanced Industrial Society*. Princeton, N.J.: Princeton University Press.

In't Veld, Roeland Jaap (ed.) (2010). *Knowledge democracy: Consequences for science, politics, and media*, Heidelberg: Springer.

Iversen, Torben and Anna Wren (1998). "Equality, employment, and budgetary restraint: The trilemma of the service economy". *World Politics* 50: 507–546.

Janson, Florence E. (1928). "Minority Governments in Sweden". *American Political Science Review* 22:407–413.

Jensen, Torben K. (2000). "Party Cohesion". In: Peter Esaiasson and Knut Heidar (eds.). *Beyond Westminster and Congress: The Nordic Experience*. Columbus: Ohio State University Press.

Johansen, Jens Chr. V. (2006). "Absolutism and the 'rule of law' in Denmark 1660–c. 1750". *The Journal of Legal History*, 27(2): 153–173.

Jónsson, Guðmundur (2014). "Iceland and the Nordic Model of Consensus Democracy. *Scandinavian Journal of History*, 39 (4), 510–528.

Kantola, Johanna (2010). *Gender and the European Union*. New York: Palgrave Macmillan.

Karvonen, Lauri (1994). "Christian parties in Scandinavia: Victory over the windmills?". In: David Hanley (ed.). *Christian democracy in Europe: A comparative perspective*. London: Pinter.

Karvonen, Lauri (2014). *Parties, governments and voters in Finland: Politics under fundamental societal transformation*. Colchester: ECPR Press.

Karvonen, Lauri & Per Selle (1995). *Women in Nordic Politics: closing the gap*. Aldershot: Dartmouth.

Kaspersen, Lars Bo (2004). "How Denmark Became Democratic: The Impact of Warfare and Military Reforms". *Acta Sociologica*, 47(1): 71–89.

Katz, Richard S., and Peter Mair (2009). "The Cartel Party Thesis: A Restatement." *Perspectives on Politics* 7: 753–66.

Katzenstein, Peter J. (1986). *Small States in World Markets. Industrial Policy in Europe*. Cornell University Press.

Kautto, Mikko (2010). "The Nordic Countries". In: Francis G. Castles, Stephan Leibfried, Jane. Lewis, Herbert Obinger and Christopher Pierson (eds.)., *The Oxford Handbook of the Welfare State*. Oxford: Oxford University Press.

Kautto, Mikko et al. (1999). *Nordic social policy. Changing welfare states*. New York: Routledge.

Kildal, Nanna and Stein Kuhnle (2005). "The Nordic welfare model and the idea of universalism". In: Nanna Kildal and Stein Kuhnle (eds.). *Normative Foundations of the Welfare State: The Nordic Experience*. London: Routledge.

Kitcher, Philip (2011). *Science in a democratic society*, Amherst, N.Y.: Prometheus Books.

Kitschelt, Herbert (1994). *The transformation of European social democracy*. Cambridge: Cambridge University Press.

Kitschelt, Herbert (1995). *The Radical Right in Western Europe – A comparative analysis*. Ann Arbor, Michigan: The University of Michigan Press.

Klausen, Jan Erling (2005). "Kan deltakelsen ved lokalvalg økes?" *Tidsskrift for samfunnsforskning*, 46 (3): 363–379.

Klausen, Jan Erling, and Hilmar Rommetvedt (eds.) (1997). *Miljøpolitikk. Organisasjonene, Stortinget og forvaltningen*. Oslo: Tano-Aschehoug.

Knudsen, Tim and Bo Rothstein (1994). "State-building in Scandinavia". *Comparative Politics*, 26(2): 203–220.

Knutsen, Oddbjørn (1995). "Left-right materialist value orientations". In: Jan W. van Deth and Elinor Scarbrough. *The impact of values*. European Science Foundation: Belief in Government, Volume 4. Oxford: Oxford University Press.

Knutsen, Oddbjørn (2001). "Social class, sector employment and gender as political cleavages in the Scandinavian countries: A comparative longitudinal study, 1970–95". *Scandinavian Political Studies* 24, 2001: 311–350.

Knutsen, Oddbjørn (2005). "The impact of sector employment on party choice: A comparative study from eight West European countries". *European Journal of Political Research* 44: 593–621.

Knutsen, Oddbjørn (2006). *Class Voting in Western Europe – A Comparative Longitudinal Study*. Lanham: Lexington Books.

Knutsen, Oddbjørn (2013)."Structural Determinants of Party Choice: The Changing Impact of Socio-Structure Variables on Party Choice in Comparative Perspective". In: Wolfgang C. Müller and Hanne Marthe Narud (eds.). *Party Governance and Party Democracy*. New York: Springer.

Knutsen, Oddbjørn (forthcoming). *Social structure, value orientations and party choice in Western Europe*. Houndmills: Palgrave MacMilllan.

Kolberg, Jon E. (ed.) (1992). *Between work and social citizenship*. New York: M.E. Sharpe.

Korpi, Walter (1981). "Social policy and distributional conflict in the capitalist democracies. A preliminary comparative framework". *West European Politics* 3(3): 297–316.

Korpi, Walter and Joakim Palme (1998). "The Paradox of Redistribution and Strategies of Equality: Welfare State Institutions, Inequality, and Poverty in the Western Countries". *American Sociological Review* 63 (5): 661–687.

Krasner, Stephen D. (1988). "Sovereignty: An Institutional Perspective". *Comparative Political Studies*, 21(1): 66–94.

Krick, Eva (2014). "Negotiated expertise in policy-making: How governments use hybrid advisory committees." *Science and Public Policy*.

Kristinsson, Gunnar Helgi (2012). "Party Patronage in Iceland: Rewards and Control Appointments". In: Petr Kopecký, Peter Mair and Maria Spirova (eds.). *Party Patronage and Party Government in European Democracies*, Oxford: Oxford University Press.

Kristinsson, Gunnar Helgi (2013). Iceland after the revolution. The impact of crisis on governance. Paper presented at the conference titled "The Impact of Fiscal Crisis on Public Administration", Tallin University of Technology, 3–4 May 2013.

Kristinsson, Gunnar Helgi (2016). "Specialists, spinners and networkers: political appointees in Iceland", *Acta Politica* 51(4): 413–432.

Kristjánsson, Svanur (2004). "Iceland: Searching for Democracy along Three Dimensions of Citizen Control". *Scandinavian Political Studies* 27:153–174.

Krizsan, Andrea, Hege Skjeie, & Judith Squires (2012). *Institutionalizing Intersectionality: The changing nature of European equality regimes*. Basingstoke: Palgrave Macmillan.

Kuhnle, Stein (1983). *Velferdsstatens utvikling: Norge i et komparativt perspektiv*. Oslo: Universitetsforlaget.

Kujala, Antti (2000). "The Breakdown of a Society: Finland in the Great Northern War 1700–1714". *Scandinavian Journal of History*, Vol. 25, No. 1–2, pp. 69–86.

Kvist, Jon and Lisbeth Pedersen (2007). "Danish Labour Market Activation Policies". *National Institute Economic Review*. 202(1): 99–112.

Kyvik, Svein and Einar Ødegård (1990). *Universitetene i Norden foran 1990-tallet: Endringer i styring og finansiering av forskning* (Vol. 11). København: Nordiske forskningspolitiska rådet, Nordiska ministerrådet.

Laakso, Markku and Rein Taagepera (1979). "Effective Number of Parties: A Measurement with Application to West Europe". *Comparative Political Studies* 12:3–27.

Ladner, Andreas, Nicolas Keuffer & Harald Baldersheim (2016). "Measuring Local Autonomy in 39 Countries (1990–2014)". *Regional & Federal Studies*, 26: 321–357.

Lane, Jan Erik (2016). "The Nordic Countries: From the Rokkan Model ('uns') to the Touraine Model ('ich')". *Open Journal of Political Science*, 6: 284–309.

Larsen, Helge O. (2002). "Directly Elected Mayors: Democratic Renewal or Constitutional Confusion?". In: Janice Caulfield & Helge O. Larsen (eds.). *Local Government at the Millennium*. Opladen: Leske + Budrich.

Lauwerys, Joseph Albert (ed.) (1958). *Scandinavian Democracy*. Copenhagen: The Danish Institute.

Laver, Michael and Kenneth Benoit (2015). "The Basic Arithmetic of Legislative Decisions". *American Journal of Political Science* 59: 275–291.

Laver, Michael and Norman Schofield (1990). *Multiparty Government: The Politics of Coalition in Europe*. Oxford: Oxford University Press.

Laver, Michael and Kenneth A. Shepsle (2000). "Ministrables and Government Formation: Munchkins, Players and Big Beasts of the Jungle". *Journal of Theoretical Politics* 12:113–124.

Leira, Arnlaug (2002). *Working Parents and the Welfare State: Family Change and Policy Reform in Scandinavia*. Cambridge: Cambridge University Press.

Leira, Arnlaug (2012). «Omsorgens institusjoner, Omsorgens kjønn». In: Ellingsæter, Anne-Lise & Karin Widerberg (eds.). *Velferdsstatens familier – Nye sosiologiske perspektiver*. Oslo: Gyldendal Akademisk.

Lerdell, David and Kerstin Sahlin-Andersson (1997). *Att lära över gränser: En studie av OECD's förvaltningspolitiska samarbete*. Rapport till Förvaltningspolitiska kommissionen.

Lidström, Anders (2010). "The Swedish Model under Stress: The Waning of the Egalitarian, Unitary State?". In: Harald Baldersheim & Lawrence E. Rose (eds.). *Territorial Choice: The Politics of Boundaries and Borders*. Basingstoke: Palgrave Macmillan.

Lidström, Anders (2011). "Sweden: Party-dominated Subnational Democracy under Challenge?". In: John Loughlin, Frank Hendriks & Anders Lidström (eds.). *The Oxford Handbook of Local and Regional Democracy in Europe*. Oxford: Oxford University Press.

Lidström, Anders, Harald Baldersheim, Colin Copus, Eva Marin Hlynsdottir, Pekka Kettunen & Daniel Klimovsky (2016). "Reforming Local Councils and the Role of Councillors: A Comparative Analysis of Fifteen European Countries". In: Sabin Kuhlmann & Geert Bouckaert (eds.). *Local Public Sector Reform in Times of Crisis*. London: Palgrave Macmillan.

Lijphart, Arend (2012). *Patterns of Democracy*, 2. ed, New Haven: Yale University Press.

Lijphart, Arend, and Markus M. L. Crepaz (1991). "Corporatism and Consensus Democracy in Eighteen Countries: Conceptual and Empirical Linkages." *British Journal of Political Science*, 21: 235–246.

Lindbeck, Assar (1997). *The Swedish Experiment*. Stockholm: SNS Förlag.

Lindblom, Anders (1997). *Ministerstyre i praktiken*. Rapport skriven för Förvaltnings-politiska kommissionen. University of Uppsala. Printed in SOU 1997: 57.

Lindvall, Johannes and Bo Rothstein (2006). "Sweden: The fall of the strong state". *Scandinavian Political Studies*, 29(1): 47–63.

Lipset, Seymour Martin and Stein Rokkan (1967). "Cleavage structure, party systems, and voter alignments: An introduction'". In: Seymour Martin Lipset and Stein Rokkan (eds.). *Party systems and voter alignments*. New York: The Free Press.

Lister, Ruth (2009). "A Nordic Nirvana? Gender, citizenship, and social justice in the Nordic Welfare states". *Social Politics*, 16(2): 242–278.

Loughlin, John, Frank Hendriks & Anders Lidström (eds.) (2011). *The Oxford Handbook of Local and Regional Democracy in Europe*. Oxford: Oxford University Press.

Lundell, Krister (2008). "Electoral Reform and Party System Change: An Analysis of Nordic Elections with Two Different Electoral Systems". *Scandinavian Political Studies*, 31 (4): 363–383.

Lægreid, Per (2001). "Administrative Reforms in Scandinavia – Testing the Cooperative Model". In: Brendan Nolan (ed.). *Public Sector Reform: An International Perspective*. Houndsmill: Palgrave Macmillan

Lødemel, Ivar (1997). *The welfare paradox: income maintenance and personal social services in Norway and Britain 1946–1966*. Oslo: Scandinavian University Press.

Lødemel, Ivar and Amilca Morena (eds.) (2014). *Activation or Workfare? Governance and the Neo-Liberal Convergence*. Oxford: Oxford University Press.

Madeley, John (1982). “Politics and the pulpit: The case of Protestant Europe”. *West European Politics* 5: 149–171.

Madeley, John (2000): “Reading the runes. The religious factor in Scandinavian electoral politics”. In: David Broughton and Hans-Martien ten Napel (eds.). *Religion and Mass Electoral Behaviour in Europe*. London and New York: Routledge/ECPR.

Madeley, John (2004). “Life at the Northern Margin: Christian Democracy in Scandinavia”. In: Steven van Hecke and Emmanuel Gerard (eds.). *Christian Democratic Parties in Europe since the End of the Cold War*. Leuven: Leuven University Press.

Madsen, Per Kongshøj (2004). “The Danish model of ‘flexicurity’: experiences and lessons”. *Transfer: European Review of Labour and Research*. 10 (2): 187–207.

Magnussen, Jon, Karsten Vrangbæk & Richard B. Saltman (2009). *Nordic Health Care Systems: Recent Reforms and Current Policy Challenges*. Maidenhead: McGraw-Hill/Open University Press.

Mahon, Rihanna (2002). “Child Care: Toward What Kind of ‘Social Europe’”? *Social Politics: International Studies in Gender, State & Society*, 9(3): 343–379.

Majone, Giandomenico (1996). *Regulating Europe*, London: Routledge.

Mandel, Hadas & Moshe Semyonov (2006). “A Welfare State Paradox: State Interventions and Women’s Employment Opportunities in 22 Countries”. *American Journal of Sociology*, 111(6): 1910–1949.

March, James G. and Johan P. Olsen (1983). “Organizing Political Life. What Administrative Reorganization Tells Us About Government”. *American Political Science Review*, 77(2): 281– 97.

Marcussen, Martin (2006). “Institutional Transformation? The Scientization of Central Banking as a Case Study”. In: Christensen, Tom and Per Lægreid (eds.). *Autonomy and regulation: coping with agencies in the modern state*. Cheltenham: Edward Elgar.

Marklund, Staffan and Anders Nordlund (1999). “Economic and political development”. In: Kautto, Mikko et al. (eds.). *Nordic social policy. Changing welfare states*. London: Routledge.

Martin, Lanny and Randolph T. Stevenson (2001). “Government Formation in Parliamentary Democracies”. *American Journal of Political Science* 45:33–50.

Martins, M.R. (1995). “Size of municipalities, efficiency, and citizen participation: A Cross-European perspective”. *Environment and Planning C: Government and Policy* 13:441–458.

Matthíasson, Pétur Berg (2014). Icelandic public sector reforms. Manuscript.

Mattila, Mikko and Tapio Raunio (2002). “Government Formation in the Nordic Countries: The Electoral Connection”. *Scandinavian Political Studies* 25: 259–280.

Mattson, Ingvar and Kaare Strøm (1995). “Parliamentary Committees”. In: Herbert Döring (ed.). *Parliaments and Majority Rule in Western Europe*. Frankfurt/New York: Campus Verlag/St. Martin’s Press.

Meijer, Hans (1969). “Bureaucracy and policy formulation in Sweden”. *Scandinavian Political Studies*, 4(A4): 103–116.

Meyer, John W. and Brian Rowan (1977). "Institutionalized Organizations: Formal Structure as Myth and Ceremony". *American Journal of Sociology*, 83 (2): 340–63.

Ministry of Finance, Finland (2016). *Administrative structures* http://vm.fi/en/ administrative- structures [04.10.2016].

Ministry of Finance, Iceland (2002). *Performance Management in Iceland.* Country Report.

Mjøset, Lars (ed.) (1986). *Norden dagen derpå*. Oslo: Universitetsforlaget.

Moore Jr., Barrington (1968). *The Social Origins of Dictatorship and Democracy.* London: Penguin.

Moren, Jorolv (1974). *Den kollegiale forvaltning – råd og utvalg i sentraladministrasjonen. Oslo: Universitetsforlaget.*

Mouritzen, Poul Erik (2010). "The Danish Revolution in Local Government. How and Why?" In: Harald Baldersheim & Lawrence E. Rose (eds.). *Territorial Choice: The Politics of Boundaries and Borders*. Basingstoke: Palgrave Macmillan.

Mouritzen, Poul Erik & James H. Svara (2002). *Leadership at the Apex. Politicians and Administrators in Western Local Government.* Pittsburgh: University of Pittsburgh Press.

Musgrave, Richard A. (1959). *The Theory of Public Finance: A Study in Public -Economy*. New York: McGraw-Hill.

Myles, John (1989). *Old age in the welfare state. The political economy of public pensions*. Lawrence: University Press of Kansas.

Müller, Wolfgang C. and Kaare Strøm (2000). "Conclusion: Coalition Governance in Western Europe". In: Wolfgang C. Müller and Kaare Strøm (eds.). *Coalition Governments in Western Europe*. Oxford: Oxford University Press.)

Narud, Hanne Marthe, and Henry Valen (2000). "Does Background Matter? Social Representation and Political Attitudes". In: Peter Esaiasson and Knut Heidar (eds.). *Beyond Westminster and Congress: The Nordic Experience*. Columbus: Ohio State University Press.

Nelson, George R. (ed.) (1953). *Freedom and Welfare. Social Patterns in the Northern Countries of Europe*. Copenhagen: The Ministry of Social Affairs of Denmark, Finland, Iceland, Norway and Sweden.

Nergaard, Kristine (2016). *Organisasjonsgrader, tariffavtaledekning og arbeidskonflikter 2014*. Fafo-notat 2016: 07. Oslo: Fafo.

Neumann, Iver B. (2000). "State and Nation in the Nineteenth Century: Recent Research on the Norwegian Case". *Scandinavian Journal of Democracy*, 25(3): 239–260.

Nieuwbeerta, Paul (1995). *The democratic class struggle in twenty countries 1945–1990.* Amsterdam: Thesis Publishers

Niskanen, Kirsti (ed.). (2011). *Gender and Power in the Nordic Countries*. Nordic Gender Institute, NIKK Publications. 2011(1). Oslo.

Nordby, Trond (1994). *Korporatisme på norsk 1920–1990*. Oslo: Universitetsforlaget.

Nordby, Trond (1999). "Samvirket mellom organisasjoner og stat: Norge". *Makt-og demokrati-utredningens rapportserie*(4).

Norris, Pippa (1999). "Gender: A gender-generation gap?". In: Geoffrey Evans and Pippa Norris (eds.). *Critical elections. British parties and voters in long-term perspective*. London: Sage.

Norris, Pippa and Ronald Inglehart (2004). *Sacred and secular. Religion and politics worldwide*. Cambridge: Cambridge University Press.

NOU 1992: 15. *Kommune- og fylkesinndelingen i et Norge i forandring*. Oslo: Statens forvaltningstjeneste.

NOU 2012: 15 *Politikk for likestilling*. Oslo: Departementenes servicesenter informasjonsforvaltningen

Nowotny, Helga, Peter Scott and Michael Gibbons (2001). *Re-thinking science: knowledge and the public in an age of uncertainty*, Cambridge: Polity Press.

NSD (Norwegian Center for Research Data) (2016). *Number of public administration units distributed on affiliation*. http://www. nsd. uib.no/polsys/data/en/forvaltning/forvaltningsenhet [04.10.2016].

Nutley, Sandra M, Huw TO Davies and Peter C Smith (2000). *What works?: Evidence-based policy and practice in public services*, Chicago: University of Chicago Press.

Oates, Wallace E. (1972). *Fiscal Federalism*. New York: Harcourt Brace Jovanovich Inc.

Öberg, PerOla (1994). *Särintresse och allmännintresse: Korporatismens ansikten*. Uppsala: Statsvetenskapliga föreningen.

Öberg, PerOla (2015). "Interest Organizations in the Policy Process: Interest Advocacy and Policy Advice". In: Jon Pierre (ed.). *The Oxford Handbook of Swedish Politics*, Oxford: Oxford University Press.

Öberg, PerOla, Torsten Svensson, Peter Munk Christiansen, Asbjørn Sonne Nørgaard, Hilmar Rommetvedt and Gunnar Thesen (2011). "Disrupted Exchange and Declining Corporatism: Government Authority and Interest Group Capability in Scandinavia". *Government and Opposition*, 46 (3): 365–391.

OECD. (2016). *Education at a glance*. Paris: OECD.

OECD (2015a). *Pensions at a Glance 2015 OECD and G20 indicators*. Paris: OECD.

OECD (2015b). *In It Together: Why Less Inequality Benefits All*. Paris: OECD.

Olsen, Johan P. (1983). *Organized Democracy. Political Institutions in a Welfare State – the Case of Norway*. Bergen: Universitetsforlaget.

Olsen, Johan P. (1988). "Administrative Reform and Theories of Organization". In: Colin Campbell and Brainard Guy Peters (eds.). *Organizing Governance: Governing Organizations*. Pittsburgh: University of Pittsburgh Press.

Olsen, Johan P. (2010). *Governing through institution building. Institutional theory and recent European experiments in democratic organization*. Oxford: Oxford University Press.

Olsen, Johan P. and Brainard Guy Peters (eds.) (1996). *Lessons from Experience*. Oslo: Scandinavian University Press.

Olsen, Johan P., Paul G. Roness and Harald Sætren (1982). "Norway: Still Peaceful Coexistence and Revolution in Slow Motion". In: Jeremy J. Richardson (ed.). *Policy Styles in Western Europe*. London: Allen & Unwin.

Olufsen, Øyvind (2013). *"Lobbyundersøkelsen 2013"*. Power Point presentation. Oslo: Geelmuyden.Kiese.

Oscarsson, Henrik and Sören Holmberg (2008). *Regeringsskifte: Väljarna och valet i 2006*. Stockholm: Norsteds Juridik.

Óskarsdóttir, Stefanía (1995). *The Use of Income Policies: Icelandic Incomes Policies, 1969–1995*. W. Lafayette, Indiana: Purdue University.

Óskarsdóttir, Stefanía (1999). «Metamorfosen av industrielle relationer». In: Krister Ståhlberg (ed.). *Den nordiska modellen i en brytningstid*, Nord 1999: 12. København: Nordisk Ministerråd, 81–103.

Oskarson, Maria (1994). *Klassröstning i Sverige: Rationalitet, lojalitet eller bara slentrian*. Stockholm: Nerenius & Santerus.

Oskarson, Maria (1995). "Gender gap in Nordic voting behaviour". In: Lauri Karvonen and Per Selle (eds.). *Women in Nordic Politics: Closing the Gap*. Aldershot: Dartmouth.

Paloheimo, Heikki (2003). "The Rising Power of the Prime Minister in Finland". *Scandinavian Political Studies* 26:219–243.

Pedersen, Axel West (1994). "The welfare state and inequality: Still no answer to the big questions". LIS working paper series no. 109, Walferdange: CEPS/INSTEAD.

Pedersen, Axel West (1999). "The taming of inequality in retirement: A comparative study of pension policy outcomes". Fafo-report no. 317. Oslo: Fafo.

Pedersen, Axel West & Henning Finseraas (2009). "Towards a European convergence in pension policy outputs? Evidence from the OMC on pensions". In: Ervik, Rune et al. (eds.). *The Role of International Organizations in Social Policy: Ideas, Actors and Impact*. Cheltenham, UK: Edward Elgar.

Pedersen, Helene Helboe, Anne Skorkjær Binderkrantz and Peter Munk Christiansen (2014). "Lobbying Across Arenas: Interest Group Involvement in the Legislative Process in Denmark". *Legislative Studies Quarterly*, XXXIX (2): 199–225.

Pesonen, Pertti (1974). "Finland: Party support in a fragmented system". In: Richard Rose (ed.). *Electoral behavior: A Comparative handbook*. New York: The Free Press.

Peters, B. Guy (1997). "Policy transfers between governments: The case of administrative reforms". *Western European Politics*. 20 (4): 71–88.

Petersson, Olof (1994). *The Government and Politics of the Nordic Countries*. Stockholm: Fritzes.

Petersson, Olof (2015). "Rational politics: commissions of inquiry and the referral system in Sweden". In: Jon Pierre (ed.). *The Oxford Handbook of Swedish Politics*. Oxford: Oxford University Press.

Petersson, Olof, Sören Holmberg, Leif Lewin and Hanne Marthe Narud (2002). *Demokrati utan ansvar*. Demokratirådets rapport 2002. Stockholm: SNS Förlag.

Phillips, Anne (1995). *The Politics of Presence*. Oxford: Oxford University Press.

Pierson, Paul (1996). "The new politics of the welfare state". *World Politics* 48 (2): 143–179.

Pitkin, Hanna Fenichel (1967). *The Concept of Representation*. Berkeley: University of California Press.

Plümper, Thomas et al. (2009). "Why Is There No Race to the Bottom in Capital Taxation?" *International Studies Quarterly* 53(3): 761–786.

Poguntke, Thomas, Susan E. Scarrow and Paul Webb (2016). "Party rules, party resources and the politics of parliamentary democracies: How parties organize in the 21st century". *Party Politics*, 22 (6): 661–678.

Poguntke, Thomas and Paul Webb (2005). *The Presidentialization of Politics: A Comparative Study of Modern Democracies*. Oxford: Oxford University Press.

Pollitt, Christopher and Geert Bouckaert (2011). *Public Management Reform: A Comparative Analysis*. Oxford: Oxford University Press (3rd edition).

Powell, G. Bingham (2000). *Elections as Instruments of Democracy. Majoritarian and Proportional Visions*. New Haven: Yale University Press.

Premfors, Rune (1991). "The 'Swedish Model' and Public Sector Reform". *West European Politics*, 14(3): 83–95.

Premfors, Rune (1999). "Organisations förandringar och förvaltningspolitik – Sverige". In: Per Lægreid and Ove Kaj Pedersen (eds.). *Fra opbygning til ombygning i staten*. Copenhagen: Jurist- og Økonomforbundets forlag.

Raaum, Nina (2004). "The Presence of Women in Parliamentary Politics". In: Knut Heidar. *Nordic Politics: Comparative Perspectives*. Oslo: Universitetsforlaget.

Raaum, Nina (2005). "Gender Equality and Political Representation: A Nordic Comparison". *West European Politics*, 28(4): 872–897.

Rasch, Bjørn Erik (2004). *Kampen om regjeringsmakten. Norsk parlamentarisme i europeisk perspektiv*. Bergen: Fagbokforlaget.

Rasch, Bjørn Erik (2014). "Fagkomiteene – politiske verksteder?" In: Hanne Marthe Narud, Knut Heidar and Tore Grønlie (eds.). *Stortingets historie 1964–2014*. Bergen: Fagbokforlaget.

Rasch, Bjørn Erik, Shane Martin and José Antonio Cheibub (eds.) (2015). *Parliaments and Government Formation: Unpacking Investiture Rules*. Oxford: Oxford University Press.

Rasmussen, Magnus Bergli and Jonas Pontusson (2016). "Working-class strength by institutional design? Unionization, partisan politics and unemployment insurance systems, 1870–2010". Paper presented at the APSA conference 2016.

Rattsø, Jørn (2005). "Economic General Report". In: *Yearbook for Nordic Tax Research 2005*. Oslo: Universitetsforlaget.

Raunio, Tapio (2004). "The Changing Finnish Democracy: Stronger Parliamentary Accountability, Coalescing Political Parties and Weaker External Constraints". *Scandinavian Political Studies* 27:133–152.

Rehn, Gösta (1988). *Full sysselsättning utan inflation. Skrifter i urval*. Stockholm: Tidens förlag.

Reif, Karlheinz & Hermann Schmitt (1980). "Nine Second-Order National Elections – A Conceptual Framework for the Analysis of European Election Results". *European Journal of Political Research* 8:3–44.

Reisel, Lisa & Mari Teigen (eds.) (2014). *Kjønnsdeling og etniske skiller på arbeidsmarkedet.* Oslo: Gyldendal Akademisk.

Rentala, Onni (1967). "The political regions of Finland". *Scandinavian Political Studies* 2: 117–140.

Ringen, Stein (1987). *The Possibility of Politics. A Study in the Political Economy of the Welfare State.* Oxford: Oxford University Press.

Ringen, Stein and Hannu Uusitalo (1992). "Income distribution and redistribution in the Nordic welfare states". In: Jon E. Kolberg (ed.). *Between work and social citizenship.* New York: M.E. Sharpe.

Rokkan, Stein (1966). "Norway: Numerical democracy and corporate pluralism". In: Robert A. Dahl (ed.). *Political oppositions in Western democracies.* New Haven and London: Yale University Press.

Rokkan, Stein (1967). "Geography, religion, and social class: Crosscutting cleavages in Norwegian politics". In: Seymour Martin Lipset and Stein Rokkan (eds.). *Party systems and voter alignments.* New York: The Free Press.

Rokkan, Stein (1970). "Nation-building, cleavage formation and the structuring of mass politics". In: Stein Rokkan. *Citizens, Elections, Parties.* Oslo: Universitetsforlaget.

Rokkan, Stein (1987). *Stat, nasjon, klasse.* Oslo: Universitetsforlaget.

Rommetvedt, Hilmar (2003). *The Rise of the Norwegian Parliament.* London: Frank Cass.

Rommetvedt, Hilmar (2005). "Norway: Resources Count, But Votes Decide? From Neo-Corporatist Representation to Neo-Pluralist Parliamentarism". *Scandinavian Political Studies,* 28 (4): 740–763.

Rommetvedt, Hilmar (2011). *Politikkens allmenngjøring og den nypluralistiske parlamentarismen.* 2nd edition. Bergen: Fagbokforlaget.

Rommetvedt, Hilmar (2014). «Lobbyvirksomhet». In: Hanne Marthe Narud, Knut Heidar and Tore Grønlie (eds.). *Stortingets historie 1964–2014.* Bergen: Fagbokforlaget.

Rommetvedt, Hilmar, Gunnar Thesen, Peter Munk Christiansen and Asbjørn Sonne Nørgaard (2013). «Coping With Corporatism in Decline and the Revival of Parliament: Interest Group Lobbyism in Denmark and Norway, 1980–2005". *Comparative Political Studies,* 46 (4): 457–485.

Rose, Lawrence E. (1990). "Nordic Free-Commune Experiments: Increased Local Autonomy or Continued Central Control?". In: Desmond E. King & Jon Pierre (eds.). *Challenges to Local Government.* London: Sage Publications.

Rose, Lawrence E. (1996). "Norway". In: E. Albæk, et al. *Nordic Local Government: Developmental Trends and Reform Activity in the Postwar Period.* Helsinki: The Association of Finnish Local Authorities.

Rose, Lawrence E. (1999). "Citizen (Re)orientations to the Welfare State: From Public to Private Citizens?" In: Jet Bussemaker (ed.). *Citizenship and Welfare State Reform in Europe.* London: Routledge.

Rose, Lawrence E. (2011). "Den krevende borger: Kveles lokaldemokrati?" In: Harald Baldersheim & Eivind Smith (eds.). *Lokalt demokrati uten kommunalt selvstyre*? Oslo: Abstrakt forlag.

Rose, Richard (ed.) (1974). *Electoral behavior: A comparative handbook*. New York: The Free Press.
Rothstein, Bo (1992). *Den korporative staten*. Stockholm: Norstedts.
Rothstein, Bo (2011). *The Quality of Government: Corruption, Social Trust, and Inequality in International Perspective*. Chicago, IL: Chicago University Press.
Rothstein, Bo and Jan Teorell (2015). "Getting to Sweden, Part II: Breaking with Corruption in the Nineteenth Century". *Scandinavian Political Studies*, 38(3): 238–254.
Rustow, Dankwart A. (1955). *The Politics of Compromise*. Princeton, NJ: Princeton University Press.
Rydgren, Jens (2004). "Explaining the emergence of radical right-wing populist parties: The case of Denmark". *West European Politics* 27: 474–502.
Sahlin-Andersson, Kerstin (2001). "National, International and Transnational Construction of New Public Management". In: Tom Christensen and Per Lægreid (eds.). *New Public Management. The Transformation of Ideas and Practice*. Aldershot: Ashgate.
Salminen, Ari (2003). "New Public Management and Finnish Public Sector Organisations: The case of universities". In: Alberto Amaral, V. Lynn Meek and Ingvild M. Larsen (eds.). *The Higher Education Managerial Revolution*? Dordrecht: Kluwer Academic.
Salminen, Ari, Olli-Pella Viinamäki and Johanna Jokisuu (2012). "Finland". In: Koen Verhoest, Sandra Van Thiel, Geert Bouckaert and Per Lægreid (eds.). *Government Agencies – Practices and Lessons from 30 Countries*. Basingstoke: Palgrave Macmillan.
Salminen, Kari (1993). *Pension schemes in the making: A comparative study of the Scandinavian countries*. Helsinki: The Central Pension Security Institute.
Sandberg, Siv (2010). "Finnish Power-Shift: The Defeat of the Periphery?". In: Harald Baldersheim & Lawrence E. Rose (eds.). *Territorial Choice: The Politics of Boundaries and Borders*. Basingstoke: Palgrave Macmillan.
Sandberg, Siv (2011). "The Nordic Regions: Institutional Development and Public Debate 1996–2009". In: Harald Baldersheim, Are Vegard Haug & Morten Øgård (eds.). *The Rise of the Networking Region. The Challenges of Regional Collaboration in a Globalized World*. Farnham, Surrey: Ashgate.
Sannerstedt, Anders (1996). "Negotiations in the Riksdag." In: Lars Göran Stenelo and Magnus Jerneck (eds.). *The Bargaining Democracy*. Lund: Lund University Press.
Savolainen, Raimo (1999). "The Finnish System of Central Government Administration". In: Jorma Selovuori (ed.). *Power and Bureaucracy in Finland: 1809–1998*, Helsinki: Prime Minister's Office and Edita.
Schmitter, Philippe C. (1979). "Still the Century of Corporatism?" In: Philippe C. Schmitter and Gerhard Lehmbruch (eds.). *Trends Towards Corporatist Intermediation*. Beverly Hills/London: Sage.

Schofer, Ewan and John W. Meyer (2005). "The worldwide expansion of higher education in the twentieth century". *American Sociological Review,* 70(6): 898–920.

Schofield, Norman (1993). "Political Competition and Multiparty Coalition Governments". *European Journal of Political Research* 23:1–33.

Scruggs, Lyle, Detlef Jahn and Kati Kuitto (2014a). "Comparative Welfare Entitlements Dataset 2. Version 2014–03". University of Connecticut & University of Greifswald.

Scruggs, Lyle, Detlef Jahn and Kati Kuitto (2014b). "Comparative Welfare Entitlements Dataset 2 Codebook. Version 2014–03". University of Connecticut & University of Greifswald.

Sellers, Jefferey M. & Anders Lidström (2007). "Decentralization, Local Government, and the Welfare State". *Governance* 20 (4):609–632.

Selznick, Peter (1957). *Leadership in Administration.* New York: Harper & Row.

Sharpe, L. J. (1970). "Theories and Values of Local Government". *Political Studies* 18:153–174.

Siaroff, Alan (1999). "Corporatism in 24 industrial democracies: Meaning and measurement". *European Journal of Political Research,* 36: 175–205.

Siim, B. & A. Borchorst (2002). "The women-friendly welfare states revisited". *NORA – Nordic Journal of Feminist and Gender Research,* 19(2): 90–98.

Siim, Birte & Anette Borchorst (2016). "Gendering European welfare states and citizenship – Revisioning Inequalities". To be published in Éléonore Lépinard & Ruth Rubio Marín (forthcoming). *Transforming Gender Equality: The Irresistible Rise of Gender Quotas in Europe.*

Simola, Hannu (2005). "The Finnish miracle of PISA: historical and sociological remarks on teaching and teacher education". *Comparative Education, 41*(4): 455–470.

Sivesind, Karl Henrik (ed.) (2016). *Mot en ny skandinavisk velferdsmodell? Konsekvenser av ideell, kommersiell og offentlig tjenesteyting for aktivt medborgerskap.* Report 2016: 01. Oslo: Institutt for samfunnsforskning.

Sjöblom, Stefan (2011). "Finland: The Limits of the Unitary Decentralized Model". In: John Loughlin, Frank Hendriks & Anders Lidström (eds.). *The Oxford Handbook of Local and Regional Democracy in Europe.* Oxford: Oxford University Press.

Skirbekk, Gunnar (2010). *Norsk og moderne.* Oslo: Res Publica.

Skjeie, Hege, Cathrine Holst & Mari Teigen (2016). Benevolent contestations: Mainstreaming, judicialisation and Europeanisation in the Norwegian gender + equality debate. To be published in Heather McRae & Elaine Weiner (eds.) (forthcoming). *Towards gendering institutionalism.* Rowman & Littlefields.

Skjeie, Hege & Mari Teigen (2005). "Political Constructions of Gender Equality: Travelling Towards ... a Gender Balanced Society?" *NORA – Nordic Journal of Feminist and Gender Research,* 13(3): 187–197.

Skjæveland, Asbjørn (2009). "Modelling Government Formation in Denmark and Beyond". *Party Politics* 15: 715–735.

Slagstad, Rune (1998). *De nasjonale strateger.* Oslo: Pax.

Smeeding, Timothy et al. (eds.) (1990). *Poverty, inequality and income distribution in comparative perspective: The Luxembourg Income Study*. Hertfordshire: Harvester Wheatsheaf.

SOU 2016: 48. *Regional indelning: tre nya län*. Stockholm: Swedish Government.

Steed, Michael and Peter Humphreys (1988). "Identifying liberal parties". In: Emil J. Kirchner (ed.). *Liberal parties in Western Europe*. Cambridge: Cambridge University Press.

Stepan, Alfred, Juan J. Linz, and Juli F. Minoves (2014). "Democratic Parliamentary Monarchies". *Journal of Democracy*, 25 (2, April 2014): 35–51.

Stephens, John (1979). *The transition from capitalism to socialism*. London: Macmillan.

Stjernquist, Nils (1996). *Tvåkammartiden. Sveriges riksdag 1867–1970*. Stockholm: Sveriges Riksdag.

St.meld nr. 32 (1994–95). *Kommune- og fylkesinndelingen*. Oslo: Kommunaldepartementet.

Strøm, Kaare (1984). "Minority Governments in Parliamentary Democracies". *Comparative Political Studies* 17: 199–227.

Strøm, Kaare (1986). "Deferred Gratification and Minority Governments in Scandinavia". *Legislative Studies Quarterly* 11:583–605.

Strøm, Kaare (1990a). "A Behavioral Theory of Competitive Political Parties". *American Journal of Political Science* 34:565–598.

Strøm, Kaare (1990b). *Minority Government and Majority Rule*. Cambridge: Cambridge University Press.

Strömberg, Lars & Tone Engen (1996). "Sweden". In: Albæk et al. *Nordic Local Government: Developmental Trends and Reform Activities in the Postwar Period*. Helsinki: The Association of Finnish Local Authorities.

Ståhlberg, Krister (1996). "Finland". In: Albæk et al., *Nordic Local Government: Developmental Trends and Reform Activities in the Postwar Period*. Helsinki: The Association of Finnish Local Authorities.

Sundberg, Jan (1999). "The enduring Scandinavian party system". *Scandinavian Political Studies* 22: 221–241.

Sundström, Göran (2015). "Administrative Reform". In: Jon Pierre (ed.). *The Oxford Handbook on Swedish Politics*. Oxford: Oxford University Press.

Swedish Agency for Public Management (2015). *Den offentliga sektorn i korthet 2015*. Stockholm: The Swedish Agency for Public Management.

Swedish Higher Education Authority, UKÄ (2015). *Educational attainment and economic investment in the OECD – Tertiary education from an international perspective – a comparison based on Education at a Glance*, Stockholm: Swedish Higher Eudcation Authority.

Söderström, Lars (1998). "Fiscal Federalism: The Nordic Way". In: Jørn Rattsø (ed.). *Fiscal Federalism and State-Local Finance. The Scandinavian Perspective*. Cheltenham, UK: Edward Elgar.

Taagepera, Rein and Matthew Soberg Shugart (1989). *Seats and Votes: The Effects and Determinants of Electoral Systems*. New Haven: Yale University Press.

Teigen, Mari (2012). "Gender Quotas in Corporate Boards – On the diffusion of a distinct national policy reform". In: *Firms, Boards and Gender Quotas: Comparative Perspectives*. Engelstad, Fredrik & Mari Teigen (eds.). Comparative Social Research, Bingley: Emerald.

Tellmann, Silje Maria (2016). *Experts in public policymaking: influential, yet constrained*, Doctoral thesis, Oslo: Oslo and Akershus University College of Applied Sciences.

Teorell, Jan and Bo Rothstein (2015). "Getting to Sweden, Part I: War and Malfeasance, 1720–1850". *Scandinavian Political Studies*, 38(3): 217–237.

Tepe, Markus (2012). "The public/private sector cleavage revisited. The impact of government employment on political attitudes and behavior in West European countries". *Public Administration* 2012: 230–261.

Terjesen, Siri, Ruth Aguilera, & Ruth Lorenz (2015). "Legislating a Woman's Seat on the Board: Institutional Factors Driving Gender Quotas for Boards of Directors". *Journal of Business Ethics* 128(2): 233–251.

Thaler, Richard H. and Cass R. Sunstein (2009). *Nudge*, New York: Penguin Books.

The Economist (2013), 2 February.

Thesen, Gunnar and Hilmar Rommetvedt (2009). "Norske organisasjoners strategier for politisk innflytelse". In Bernard Enjolras and Ragnhild Holmen Waldahl (eds.). *Frivillige organisasjoner og offentlig politikk*. Oslo: Novus Forlag.

Thomas, Alistair H. (1988). "Liberalism in Denmark: Agrarian, radical and still influential". In: Emil J. Kirchner (ed.). *Liberal parties in Western Europe*. Cambridge: Cambridge University Press.

Thorhallsson, Baldur (2010). "The Corporatist Model and its Value in Understanding Small European States in the Neo-Liberal World of the Twenty-First Century: The Case of Iceland". *European Political Science*, 9 (3): 375–386.

Tiebout, Charles M. (1956). "A Pure Theory of Public Expenditures". *Journal of Political Economy* 64 (5):416–424.

Tiihonen, Seppo (1999). From uniform administration to governance and management of diversity. Reforming State functions and public administration in Finland. Paper. OECD.

Tiihonen, Seppo (2007). "Political Leadership in the Finnish Government". In: Hermann Hill (ed.). *Modernizing Government in Europe*, Baden-Baden: NOMOS.

Tilly, Charles (1975). *The Formation of National States in Western Europe*. Princeton: Princeton University Press.

Tilly, Charles (1990). *Coercion, Capital and European States AD 990–1990*. Oxford: Basil Blackwell.

Togeby, Lise Jørgen Goul Andersen, Peter Munk Christiansen, Torben Beck Jørgensen and Signild Vallgårda (2003). *Magt og Demokrati i Danmark – Hovedresultater fra Magtudredningen*. Århus: Aarhus Universitetsforlag.

Trow, Martin (1972). "The expansion and transformation of higher education". *International Review of Higher Education*, 18(1): 61–84.

Turner, Stephen (2003). *Liberal Democracy 3.0*, London: Sage.

Upton, A. F. (1987). "The Riksdag of 1680 and the Establishment of Royal Absolutism in Sweden". *The English Historical Review*, 102(403) April, 1987: 281–308.

Valen, Henry and Stein Rokkan (1974). "Norway: Conflict structure and mass politics in a European periphery". In: Richard Rose (ed.). *Electoral behavior. A Comparative handbook*. New York: The Free Press.

van Biezen, Ingrid, Peter Mair, and Thomas Poguntke (2012). "Going, going, ...gone? The decline of party membership in contemporary Europe". *European Journal of Political Research* 51:24–56.

Van Roozendaal, Peter (1992). "The Effect of Dominant and Central Parties on Cabinet Composition and Durability". *Legislative Studies Quarterly* 17:5–36.

Vesterø-Jensen, Carsten (1984). *Det tvedelte pensionssystem*. Forskningsrapport nr. 1/84. Roskilde: Institut for samfundsøkonomi og planlægning, Roskilde Universitetscenter.

Vetenskapsrådet. (2016). *Research barometer*. Stockholm: Vetenskapsrådet.

Vibert, Frank (2007). *The rise of the unelected: democracy and the new separation of powers*. Cambridge: Cambridge University Press.

Volden, Craig and Clifford J. Carrubba (2004). "The Formation of Oversized Coalitions in Parliamentary Democracies". *American Journal of Political Science* 48:521–537.

Von Sydow, Björn (1991). "Sweden's road to a unicameral parliament". In: Lawrence D. Longley and David M. Olson (eds.). *Two Into One. The Politics and Processes of National Legislative Cameral Change*. Boulder: Westview Press.

Von Sydow, Björn (1997). *Parlamentarismen i Sverige. Utveckling och utforming till 1945*. Stockholm: Gidlunds Förlag.

Walby, Sylvia (2004). "The European Union and Gender Equality: Emergent Varieties of Gender Regimes". *Social Politics: International Studies in Gender, State and Society*, 11(1): 4–29.

Walby, Sylvia (2009). *Globalization and inequalities: Complexity and Contested Modernities*. London: SAGE Publications.

Wägnerud, Lena (2000). "Representing Women". In: Peter Esaiasson and Knut Heidar (eds.). *Beyond Westminster and Congress: The Nordic Experience*. Columbus: Ohio State University Press.

Weir, Margaret and Theda Skocpol (1985). "State structures and the possibilities for'Keynesian'responses to the Great Depression in Sweden, Britain, and the United States". In: Evans, Peter B., Dietrich Rueschemeyer and Theda Skocpol (eds.). *Bringing the state back in*. New York and Cambridge, UK Cambridge University Press.

Winton, Patrik (2012). "The political economy of Swedish absolutism, 1789–1809". *European Review of Economic History*, 16: 430–448.

Wolff, Charlotta (2007). "Aristocratic Republicanism and the Hate of Sovereignty in 18th Century Sweden", *Scandinavian Journal of History*, 32(4): 358–375.

World Economic Forum (2011). Program, Annual Meeting, 26–30 January. Davos.

Wockelberg, Helena and Shirin Ahlbäck Öberg (2016). "Reinventing the Old Reform Agenda: Public Administrative Reform and Performance According to Swedish Top Managers". In: Gerhard Hammerschmid, Steven van de Walle, Rhys Andrews and Philippe Bezes (eds.). *Administration Reforms in Europe: The View from the Top*. Cheltenham: Edgar Elgar.

Ylikangas, Heikki (1999). "The main historical features in the recruitment of senior civil servants". In: Jorma Selovuori (ed.). *Power and Bureaucracy in Finland: 1809–1998*, Helsinki: Prime Minister's Office and Edita.

Zittel, Thomas & Dieter Fuchs, eds. (2006). *Participatory Democracy and Political Participation: Can Participatory Engineering Bring Citizens Back In*? London: Routledge.

Øgård, Morten (2015). "Fra New Public Management til New Public Governance?" In: Harald Baldersheim & Lawrence E. Rose (eds.). *Det kommunale laboratorium. Teoretiske perspektiver på lokal politikk og organisering*. Bergen: Fagbokforlaget, 3rd ed.

Østbakken, Kjersti Misje (2016): *Likestilling og verdiskapning. Om kvinners yrkesdeltakelse og dens betydning for økonomisk vekst*. 2016: 10, Oslo: Institute for Social Research.

Østergård, Uffe (2004). "The Danish Path to Modernity". *Thesis Eleven*, 77: 25–43.

Østergård, Uffe (2008a). "De skandinaviske staters udvikling". *Politica*, 40(4): 442–456.

Østergård, Uffe (2008b). "Færøerne: Nation eller stat?". *Udenrigs*, 1: 54–72.

Østerud, Øyvind, Fredrik Engelstad and Per Selle (2003). *Makten og demokratiet.*, Oslo: Gyldendal Akademisk.

ABOUT THE AUTHORS

Harald Baldersheim
Professor emeritus at the Department of Political Science, University of Oslo
harald.baldersheim@stv.uio.no

Einar Berntzen
Associate Professor at the Department of Comparative Politics,
University of Bergen
einar.berntzen@uib.no

Karl Hagen Bjurstrøm
PhD Candidate at the Department of Political Science, University of Oslo
k.h.bjurstrom@stv.uio.no

Johan Christensen
Assistant professor at the Institute of Public Administration, Leiden University
j.christensen@fgga.leidenuniv.nl

Tom Christensen
Professor at the Department of Political Science, University of Oslo
tom.christensen@stv.uio.no

Åse Gornitzka
Professor at the Department of Political Science, University of Oslo
ase.gornitzka@stv.uio.no

Knut Heidar
Professor at the Department of Political Science, University of Oslo
knut.heidar@stv.uio.no

Cathrine Holst
Associate Professor at the Department of Sociology and Human Geography and
Research Professor at ARENA Centre for European Studies
cathrine.holst@sosgeo.uio.no

Stein Kuhnle
Professor at the Department of Comparative Politics, University of Bergen
stein.kuhnle@uib.no

Axel West Pedersen,
Research Professor at the Institute for Social Research, Oslo
a.w.pedersen@samfunnsforskning.no

Bjørn Erik Rasch
Professor at the Department of Political Science, University of Oslo
b.e.rasch@stv.uio.no

Hilmar Rommetvedt
Head of Research, International Research Institute of Stavanger and Adjunct Professor, University of Stavanger
hilmar.rommetvedt@iris.no

Lawrence E. Rose
Professor emeritus at the Department of Political Science, University of Oslo
l.e.rose@stv.uio.no

Siv Sandberg
Research Fellow and Lecturer at Department of Political Science, Åbo Akademi University
ssandber@abo.fi

Hege Skjeie
Professor at the Department of Political Science, University of Oslo
hege.skjeie@stv.uio.no

Mari Teigen
Research Professor and Director at the Centre for Research on Gender Equality, Institute for Social Research, Oslo
mari.teigen@samfunnsforskning.no

Editor
Oddbjørn Knutsen
Professor at the Department of Political Science, University of Oslo
oddbjorn.knutsen@stv.uio.no